UNITED STATES

100°W 90°W

Monterrey
★ **Nuevo
León** ● Matamoros

*Laguna
Madre*

Gulf of Mexico

★ Ciudad Victoria

Tamaulipas

n Luis
osí

**San Luis
Potosí**

*Laguna de
Tamiahua*

juato

Querétaro
★
Querétaro

Hidalgo ● Pachuca

*Bay of
Campeche*

Mérida
★ **Yucatán**

Cancún ●

*Yucatán
Peninsula*

Campeche ★

**Quintana
Roo**

Mexico
City ★
Toluca ● ★**D.F.** ★**Tlaxcala**
México ★ ● Tlaxcala
Cuernavaca ● ★Puebla

Jalapa
★

● Veracruz

*Laguna de
Términos*

Campeche

Chetumal
★ ●

Morelos

Puebla

Veracruz

Tabasco

Balsas

★ Villahermosa

errero ● Chilpancingo

*Isthmus of
Tehuantepec*

BELIZE

Sierra Madre del Sur
apulco ●

● Oaxaca
★

Oaxaca

Sierra Madre de Chiapas

Tuxtla
Gutiérrez
★

Chiapas

GUATEMALA

*Gulf of
Tehuantepec*

HONDURAS

Oriental

Bravo

Junior Worldmark Encyclopedia of the Mexican States, Second Edition

Junior Worldmark Encyclopedia of the Mexican States,
Second Edition

U·X·L

*An imprint of Thomson Gale,
a part of The Thomson Corporation*

THOMSON
GALE

Detroit • New York • San Francisco
New Haven, Conn. • Waterville, Maine • London

Junior Worldmark Encyclopedia of the Mexican States, Second Edition

Project Editor
Jennifer York Stock

Editorial
Julie Mellors

Rights and Acquisitions
Lisa Person, Kelly A. Quin, Sue Rudolph, Andrew Specht

Imaging and Multimedia
Dean Dauphinais, Lezlie Light

Product Design
Jennifer Wahi

Composition
Evi Seoud

Manufacturing
Rita Wimberly

LIBRARY OF CONGRESS CATALOGING-IN-PUBLICATION DATA

Junior Worldmark encyclopedia of the mexican states / [edited by] Timothy L. Gall and Susan Bevan Gall. --2nd ed.
 p. cm.
 Includes bibliographical references and index.
 ISBN 978-1-4144-1112-5 (hardcover)
 1. Mexican states--Encyclopedias, Juvenile. 2. Mexico--Encyclopedias, Juvenile. I. Gall, Timothy L. II. Gall, Susan B.
 F1204.J86 2007
 972.003--dc22

2007003906

ISBN-13:

978-1-4144-1112-5

ISBN-10:

1-4144-1112-X

This title is also available as an ebook
ISBN 13: 978-1-4144-2957-1, ISBN 10: 1-4144-2966-5
Contact your Thomson Gale representative for ordering information
Printed in the United States of America

10 9 8 7 6 5 4 3 2 1

Table of Contents

Reader's Guide

Junior Worldmark Encyclopedia of the Mexican States, Second Edition, presents profiles of the 31 states and the Distrito Federal (federal district) of Mexico. Entries are arranged alphabetically in one volume. Following the state entries is an article on the country of Mexico itself. The *Worldmark* design organizes facts and data about every state in a common structure. Every profile contains a map showing the state and its location in the nation.

Sources

Due to the broad scope of this encyclopedia many sources were consulted in compiling the information and statistics presented in this volume. However, special recognition is due to the many agencies of the Mexican states, from Aguascalientes to Zacatecas, that contributed data, answered questions, and provided information. Statistical information was gathered with the help of Instituto Nacional de Estadística Geografia e Informatica (INEGI), the agency that oversees publication of statistics on many aspects of Mexico and its citizens. Among the sources consulted during the compilation of this second edition of *Junior Worldmark Encyclopedia of the Mexican States* were INEGI's *Anuario de Estadísticas por Entidad Federativa, Edición 2006* (*Annual Statistics for Federal Entity, 2006 Edition*), *Mexico at a Glance, 2006 edition,* and the *XII Censo General de Población y Vivienda 2000* (*12th General Census of Population 2000*).

The sections on history and government were prepared by Patricio Navia, Ph.D., who is on the faculty of both the Center for Latin American and Caribbean Studies, New York University and the Escuela de Ciencia Politica, Universidad Diego Portales, Santiago, Chile. The editors also acknowledge the assistance provided by staff members of the History and Geography Department, Cleveland Public Library, and Barbara Appel Tenenbaum, Ph.D., Specialist in Mexican Culture, Hispanic Division, Library of Congress, and freelance researcher/writer Gail Rosewater.

Profile Features

This second edition of *Junior Worldmark Encyclopedia of the Mexican States* follows the numbered heading structure, which allows students to compare two or more states in a variety of ways, that is the hallmark of the *Junior Worldmark* series. *Junior Worldmark Encyclopedia of the Mexican States, Second Edition* features 27 numbered headings. Each state entry is accompanied by a map specially prepared for the first edition.

Each state profile begins by presenting basic information about the state, including the pronunciation and origin of the state name, the capital, the date it entered the country, a description of the official coat of arms, and the holidays observed. (The entries also inform the student researcher that the states of Mexico have no official state flags.) The introductory information ends with the standard time given by time zone in relation to Greenwich mean time (GMT). The world is divided into 24 time zones, each one hour apart. The Greenwich meridian, which is 0 degrees, passes through Greenwich, England, a suburb of London. Greenwich is at the center of the initial time zone, known as Greenwich mean time. All times given are converted from noon in this zone. The time reported for each state is the official time zone.

The body of each profile is arranged in 27 numbered headings as follows:

1 Location and Size. Statistics are given on area, with a comparison to a US state. The names of the geographic features that surround the state (other states, bodies of water, or countries) are provided. The number of municipalities identified in each state is included, along

with the name of the capital. An overview of the topography, with principal mountains (and elevations), valley, plains, and islands are listed. The state's major lakes and rivers, along with any other notable geographic features, are described briefly.

2 Climate. Temperature and rainfall are given for the various regions of the state in both English and metric units.

3 Plants and Animals. Described here are the plants and animals native to the state.

4 Environmental Protection. Information on efforts to preserve the environment is provided, along with brief descriptions of the ecological reserves within the state. Unique or protected animal and plant species are listed, along with data on existing forest land and deforestation. Also provided is information on municipal and industrial wastewater treatment facilities.

5 Population, Ethnic Groups, Languages. Statistics on the total population, population by gender, population density, and population of the state capital are provided here. Languages spoken by the majority of state citizens are listed, and prominent indigenous groups are also described.

6 Religions. Statistics from the 2000 census describe the breakdown of the population according to religion and/or denominations. Major religious sites or festivals within the state are mentioned.

7 Transportation. Information on the state's network of roads, railways, and waterways is provided. In addition, the principal airports and seaports serving the state are provided. Statistics on the number of motor vehicles within the state are included.

8 **History.** Includes a concise summary of the state's history from ancient times (where appropriate) through the arrival of European explorers, missionaries, and conquerors, to the present.

9 **State and Local Government.** The election cycle for governor is provided, along with information on the state's legislature. The state's constitution, along with the name of the seat of government, are briefly described. Finally, details of the form of municipal government found in the state are given.

10 **Political Parties.** Describes the significant political parties through history, where appropriate, and the influential parties as of 2006. The current governor is named, and the year of the next scheduled gubernatorial election is provided.

11 **Judicial System.** Structure of the court system and the jurisdiction of courts in each category is provided.

12 **Economy.** This section presents the key elements of the economy. Major industries are summarized.

13 **Industry.** Key industries are listed, and important aspects of industrial development, including the effects of the North American Free Trade Agreement (NAFTA) are described where applicable.

14 **Labor.** An overview of employment, unemployment, wages earned, and labor relations is provided.

15 **Agriculture.** Information on agricultural activity, principal crops, and livestock of the state are given.

16 **Natural Resources.** Information on principal natural resources is provided, including data on mining, forestry, and fishing.

17 **Energy and Power.** Descriptions of the state's power resources, including electricity produced and oil reserves and production, are provided.

18 **Health.** Information on public health facilities, the number of healthcare professionals, and general data on health insurance in the state is provided.

19 **Housing.** Housing statistics and general information on the condition of housing in the state are given here.

20 **Education.** Statistical data on the percentage of students completing primary and secondary school is provided, along with the overall literacy rate. Major public universities in the state are listed.

21 **Arts.** A summary of the major cultural institutions is provided.

22 **Libraries and Museums.** Statistics on the number of branches of the national library in the state are provided. Major museums are listed.

23 **Media.** Major newspapers are listed. Information on radio, television, telephone, and Internet service is also provided.

24 **Tourism, Travel, and Recreation.** Under this heading, the student will find a summary of the important sites of interest to tourists in the state. Major festivals and fairs hosted in the state are also mentioned.

25 **Sports.** The major sports teams and principal stadiums in the state are described.

26 **Famous People.** In this section, some of the best-known citizens of the state through history are listed.

27 **Bibliography.** The bibliographic and web site listings at the end of each profile are provided as a guide for further research.

Because many terms used in this encyclopedia will be new to students, a Words to Know section appears at the back of the volume.

A keyword index completes the volume.

Comments and Suggestions

We welcome your comments on the *Junior Worldmark Encyclopedia of the Mexican States, Second Edition,* as well as your suggestions for features to be included in future editions. Please write: Editors, *Junior Worldmark Encyclopedia of the Mexican States, Second Edition,* U•X•L, 27500 Drake Road, Farmington Hills, MI 48331-3535; or call toll-free: 1-800-877-4253.

Guide to Articles

All information contained within an article is uniformly keyed by means of a number to the left of the subject headings. A heading such as "History," for example, carries the same key numeral (8) in every article. Therefore, to find information about the history of Aguascalientes, consult the table of contents for the page number where the Aguascalientes article begins and look for section 8.

Introductory matter for each province includes:
Pronunciation
Origin of state name
Capital
Entered country
Coat of arms
Holidays
Flag
Time Zone

Sections listed numerically
1   Location and Size
2   Climate
3   Plants and Animals
4   Environmental Protection
5   Population, Ethnic Groups, Languages
6   Religions
7   Transportation
8   History
9   State and Local Government
10   Political Parties
11   Judicial System
12   Economy
13   Industry

14   Labor
15   Agriculture
16   Natural Resources
17   Energy and Power
18   Health
19   Housing
20   Education
21   Arts
22   Libraries and Museums
23   Media
24   Tourism, Travel, and Recreation
25   Sports
26   Famous People
27   Bibliography

Alphabetical listing of sections
Agriculture 15
Arts 21
Bibliography 27
Climate 2
Economy 12
Education 20
Energy and Power 17
Environmental Protection 4
Famous People 26
Health 18
History 8

Housing 19
Industry 13
Judicial System 11
Labor 14
Libraries and Museums 22
Location and Size 1
Media 23
Natural Resources 16
Plants and Animals 3
Political Parties 10
Population, Ethnic Groups, Languages 5
Religions 6
Sports 25
State andLocal Government 9
Tourism, Travel, and Recreation 24
Transportation 7

Explanation of symbols
A fiscal split year is indicated by a stroke (e.g. 2003/04).
The use of a small dash (e.g., 2003–04) normally signifies the full period of calendar years covered (including the end year indicated).

Aguascalientes

PRONUNCIATION: ah-gwas-kah-lee-EHN-tehs.

ORIGIN OF STATE NAME: Spaniards settling in the area in the 1500s discovered the hot springs, or aguas calientes ("hot waters" in Spanish). They named their settlement Villa de Nuestra Señora de la Asunción de las Aguas Calientes (Home of Our Lady of the Assumption of the Hot Springs). This name was eventually shortened to Aguascalientes (which means hot waters).

CAPITAL: Aguascalientes.

ENTERED COUNTRY: 1835.

COAT OF ARMS: The coat of arms of Aguascalientes has a fountain, a caldron, and coals. These represent the hot springs that are a main feature of the state. The image of Our Lady of the Assumption, accompanied by two cherubs, represents the foundation of the city. The gold chain, which is incomplete and surrounded by lips, depicts freedom and the emergence of the independent state. The grapes and dam signify agriculture supported by state irrigation systems. The bee imprisoned within a wheel represents the ordered, constant, and progressive labor of the inhabitants of Aguascalientes.

HOLIDAYS: Año Nuevo (New Year's Day—January 1); Día de la Constitución (Constitution Day—February 5); Benito Juárez's birthday (March 21); Primero de Mayo (Labor Day—May 1); Revolution Day, 1910 (November 20); and Navidad (Christmas—December 25).

FLAG: There is no official state flag.

TIME: 6 AM = noon Greenwich Mean Time (GMT).

1 Location and Size

Aguascalientes, located in the center of the country, has an area of 5,618 square kilometers (2,169 square miles). It ranks at 29th in size among the states and covers about 0.3% of the total land area of Mexico. It is about the same size as the US state of Delaware. It is bordered on the north by the state of Zacatecas and on the south by the state of Jalisco. Aguascalientes is divided into 11 municipalities (similar to US counties). The capital is also named Aguascalientes.

The state has mountains (sierra), valleys, and plains. The mountains in the western part of the state are part of the Sierra Madre Occidental. They include the Sierra Fria, Sierra de las Palomas, and Sierra del Laurel. The highest peak in the state is Cerro el Mirador with an elevation of about 2,700 meters (8,858 feet). The eastern part of the state is called the Mesa Central. There are two main valleys. The Valle de Aguascalientes runs through the center of the state while the Calvillo Valley is found in the southwest. The plains are located in the southeastern part of the state.

The most important rivers are the Aguascalientes (also called the San Pedro) and Calvillo; these form part of the larger Lerma-Santiago River system, which runs into the Pacific Ocean. Tributaries of the Aguascalientes River include the Chicalote and San Francisco Rivers. The largest bodies of water are reservoirs created by river dams. They include Presa Calles and Presa El Niágara.

2 Climate

The climate is dry and warm, with summer rains. Temperatures are fairly constant throughout the year, averaging 19°C (66°F), while its average yearly rain level is 480 millimeters (20 inches). Cooler temperatures can be found in the highest sierra regions.

3 Plants and Animals

There are more than 250 animal species in the state. While there are few forest zones, there are areas of dense shrubbery and small trees. Native trees include scrubby pine, oak, and cedar. Giant cacti and palm trees are found in some regions. There are wildcats, pumas, and wild boars in the mountain regions while coyotes and gray foxes can be found in the valleys. Small mammals such as squirrels, raccoons, and hares are also common. Spotted quail, barn owls, and eagles are among the birds found in the valleys.

4 Environmental Protection

Sierra Fría is an ecological preserve where dwarf pine trees, oak forests, and a variety of animals can be found, including pumas, lynxes, boar, white-tailed deer, wild turkey, and raccoons. Sierra del Laurel is another ecological preserve located west of the capital city of Aguascalientes. In 2003, the state had about 65,447 hectares (161,723 acres) of woodlands. In 2004, about 7 hectares (17 acres) of forest were damaged or destroyed by forest fires. An additional 529 hectares (1,307 acres) of pasture and brush lands were damaged by fires that year.

In 2004, there were a total of 93 municipal sewage treatment plants in operation in the state with a total installed capacity of 2,974 liters per second (785.6 gallons per minute). The volume of treated wastewater was estimated at 2,459 liters per second (649.5 gallons per second). There were an additional 22 industrial wastewater plants in operation statewide. Approximately 98.8% of all residents had access to clean drinking water.

5 Population, Ethnic Groups, Languages

Aguascalientes had an estimated total population of 1,088,400 in 2006, ranking 28th among the states and the Distrito Federal. About 49% of residents were men and 51% were women. About 82% of residents lived in urban areas. The population density was 194.7 people per square kilometer (504 people per square mile). In 2005, the capital, Aguascalientes, had an estimated population of 723,043. The majority of the population speaks Spanish. A small percentage

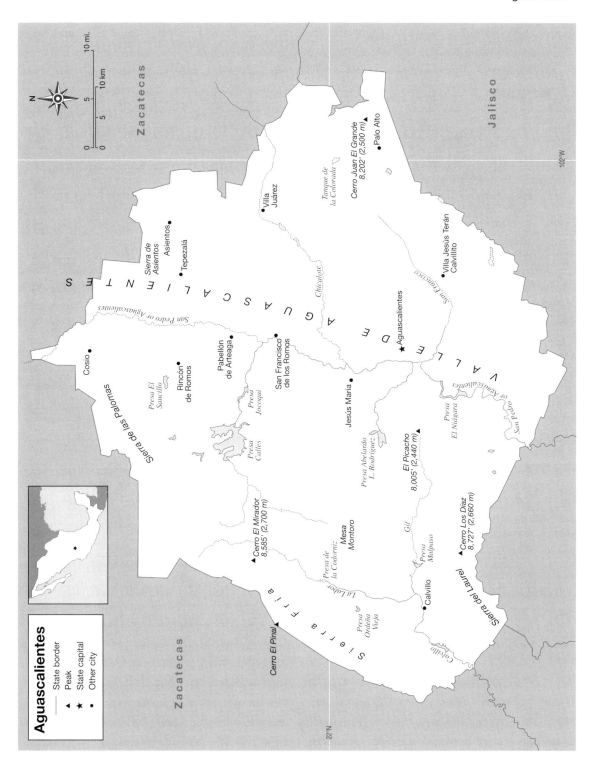

Zacatecas

Jalisco

10 mi.

10 km

5

5

N

Sierra de Asientos

Asientos

Tepezalá

S T N E I L A C S A U G

San Pedro or Aguascalientes

Cosio

Sierra de las Palomas

Presa El Saucillo

Rincón de Romos

Pabellón de Arteaga

Presa Jocoqui

Presa Calles

San Francisco de los Romos

Jesús María

Presa Abelardo L. Rodríguez

Mesa Montoro

Cerro El Mirador 8,585' (2,700 m)

Presa de la Codorniz

La Labor

Presa Ordeña Vieja

Cerro El Pinal

S i e r r a   F r í a

Gil

Presa Malpaso

Calvillo

Calvillo

Sierra del Laurel

Cerro Los Díaz 8,727' (2,660 m)

El Picacho 8,005' (2,440 m)

Presa El Niágara

San Pedro or Aguascalientes

V A L L E   D E   A G U A S C A L I E N T E S

Aguascalientes

★ Aguascalientes

San Francisco

Villa Jesús Terán Calvillito

Chicalote

Tanque de la Colorada

Villa Juárez

Cerro Juan El Grande 8,202' (2,500 m)

Palo Alto

102°W

22°N

Zacatecas

Aguascalientes

—— State border

◀ Peak

★ State capital

• Other city

speaks one of the many indigenous Amerindian languages, including Náhuatl and Mazahua.

6 Religions

According to the 2000 census, 95% of the population, or 785,614 people, were Roman Catholic. Less than 2%, or 15,857 people, were mainline or evangelical Protestants. That year there were also 1,316 Latter-day Saints (Mormons), 4,467 Jehovah's Witnesses, and nearly 12,700 people who reported no religion.

7 Transportation

Aguascalientes has a well-developed system of highways and roads. Until the 1980s, when travel by railroad declined, Aguascalientes was home to the country's largest railroad repair facility. The Aguascalientes Airport serves the state. In 2004, there were 179,103 automobiles registered in the state, along with 1,442 passenger trucks, 104,440 freight trucks, and 10,175 motorcycles.

8 History

The area of Aguascalientes was originally inhabited by different Chichimec (Amerindian) groups. Aguascalientes was first conquered by Spanish soldiers under the command of Cristobal de Oñate around 1530. The conquest was very bloody. The Spaniards indiscriminately killed natives and forcefully took their lands. The native resistance was strong and lasted for centuries.

Spanish settlers founded the city of Nuestra Señora de la Asunción de Aguascalientes in 1575. Twelve colonizers were given land rights. Vineyard agriculture and other fruit products were produced by the new settlers. Soon the area became known for its exports of grapes and other fruits. Some wool production and iron- and wood-crafted products converted Aguascalientes into a small but significant economic regional center.

Mining evolved in the municipality of Asientos de Ibarra, helping boost the local economy. Because of its central geographic location, the city of Aguascalientes became a commercial and transportation center between the Zacatecas and Jalisco regions.

In 1767, the members of the Roman Catholic Jesuit order were expelled from Mexico. This began a period of economic decline. The Jesuits owned a vast amount of land in Aguascalientes, so their departure severely hindered the local economy. In 1785, Aguascalientes was made a section of the Zacatecas Intendancy, a territory with connections to Europe. This caused discontent among the local leaders. They wanted more freedom to conduct their business and make their own decisions. A widespread famine in the late 1780s further hurt the local economy and reduced the population.

A series of public works initiatives and Roman Catholic Church constructions help boost the economy in the years before independence. Several local leaders helped promote independence ideas. Among them, Pedro Parga, Rafael Iriarte, Francisco Primo de Verdad y Ramos, and Valentín Gómez Farías championed the independence cause. On October 9, 1821, a month after the national declaration of independence, Aguascalientes patriots arrested Spanish authorities and joined the movement headed by priest Miguel Hidalgo y Castilla in central

Mexico. Rafael Iriarte formed a 1,500-man battalion that joined the independence army.

After independence was formally declared in 1821, Aguascalientes was made a part of the state of Zacatecas. Independence leader Gómez Farías went on to serve as vice president and president in the 1830s. The political instability that characterized Mexico from the 1830s to the 1860s affected Aguascalientes. It was declared an autonomous state of Mexico several times, only to be periodically incorporated into Zacatecas, depending on the political alliances that controlled the military and political elites in Mexico.

Aguascalientes was occupied by French invaders in the civil war of 1863. The state joined forces with the reform army of Mexican revolutionary and statesman Benito Juárez (1806–1872) to resist the French. During the long government of Porfirio Díaz—who was president from 1877 to 1880, and again from 1884 to 1911—Aguascalientes progressed economically. Railroads were built and electricity was brought to the state in 1890. Telephone lines were installed in 1901.

During the Mexican Revolution (1910–20), different factions fiercely fought for control of Aguascalientes because of its strategic location. Local elites were divided among the different factions. When Álvaro Obregón became president (1920–24) and his faction emerged as winner of the revolution, control of Aguascalientes was easily achieved.

The Institutional Revolutionary Party (PRI) went on to control Aguascalientes from 1934 to 1998, when the conservative National Action Party (PAN) candidate became the first non-PRI governor of the state. In 2004, PAN retained its hold on the state's governorship.

Until the North American Free Trade Agreement (NAFTA) was signed in 1994, the economy of Aguascalientes was primarily tied to farming. Since then, the economy has changed dramatically, becoming based on modern industry. By the first decade of the 21st century, Aguascalientes had become one of Mexico's leading industrial centers even though it ranked 28th among the 31 states and Distrito Federal in population.

9 State and Local Government

Aguascalientes holds gubernatorial elections every six years. The unicameral (one chamber) legislature is comprised of the chamber of deputies. Of the 27 chamber members, 18 are elected from single-member districts and 9 are elected at large, for proportional representation.

The state's constitution dates from 1950. It establishes formal separation of powers, an independent judiciary, and different mechanisms and provisions for government accountability and responsiveness. The state government is located in the municipality of Aguascalientes.

The state is comprised of 11 municipalities, each with its own government. Each elects a municipal president for nonrenewable three-year terms. Former municipal presidents can run again for office after one term out of office. Each municipality also has a city council, whose members are elected for nonrenewable three-year terms.

10 Political Parties

The three main political parties in all of Mexico are the Institutional Revolutionary Party (PRI), the National Action Party (PAN), and the

Party of the Democratic Revolution (PRD). The PRI overwhelmingly controlled politics in Aguascalientes after the end of the Mexican Revolution. Otto Granados Roldán, governor from 1992 to 1998, was a close ally of Carlos Salinas de Gortari, who served as president of Mexico from 1988 to 1994. Otto Granados Roldán was the last PRI politician to win a gubernatorial election in the state. In 1998, Felipe González González from the PAN won the gubernatorial elections. Another PAN candidate, Luis Armando Reynoso Femat, won the governorship in 2004.

11 Judicial System

The Supreme Tribunal of Justice of Aguascalientes is comprised of seven members elected for non-renewable fifteen-year terms. Candidates are elected from a list presented to the state governor by the state court. The president of the Supreme Tribunal is elected by its members for a nonrenewable four-year term.

The state judicial system is independent and autonomous. Its rulings must not challenge the jurisprudence of the Mexican Supreme Court. Other courts in charge of administrative matters are also part of the state judicial system.

12 Economy

In 2004, the economy of Aguascalientes was one of the fastest growing of any Mexican state. From 1997 to 2002, the state's economy grew at almost 7%. This was due in large part to the state's central location, which has made the state a transportation crossroads. Industry, services, and trade account for 85% of the state's gross domestic product (GDP). The state also has one of the highest per person (per capita) GDP rates in all of Mexico. The services sector accounts for the largest portion of the state's workforce at 32%, followed by industry at 24%, commerce at 20%, and agriculture/livestock at 9%.

13 Industry

Most of the state's industrial activity is centered in the region between the capital city of Aguascalientes and the city of Rincon de Romos. There are two industrial parks in the capital and two more in the surrounding area. Main industries are automobiles and auto parts, textiles, and apparel. There is also an electronics sector and an office equipment manufacturing sector. The majority of the capital city's maquiladoras (72%) are geared toward the automotive parts sector, with electronics accounting for 19%. Maquiladoras are assembly plants that are owned by companies headquartered outside Mexico. These plants assemble and export products, using imported parts.

Nissan, Xerox, and Texas Instruments are among the companies that have manufacturing facilities in the state. Textile manufacturing includes women's clothing, tablecloths and handkerchiefs, as well as embroidered textiles and denim clothing.

14 Labor

As of 2005, Aguascalientes had 405,556 eligible workers. Some 384,037 were listed as employed and 21,519 were listed as unemployed. Unemployed workers in rural areas may not be counted, however. The unemployment rate that year was reported to be 5.3%. Of those who were working, services employed 42.5%, followed by manufacturing at 21%, and commerce at 20.4%. Employer-worker relations are generally good. There have been no recent labor strikes.

The US Bureau of Labor Statistics reported that Mexican workers saw their wages increase from $2.49 per hour in 2003 to $2.50 per hour in 2004. (The average US worker earned $15.70 per hour in 2004.) The maximum workweek is set at 48 hours by law. The average worker spends 40 to 45 hours per week on the job. Workers earn twice their regular hourly rate for up to nine hours a week of overtime. When a worker works more than nine hours overtime in a week, he or she earns three times the regular hourly rate.

15 Agriculture

About 35% of the land is devoted to agriculture. The wide plains are well suited to raising cattle and therefore good for the related production of dairy products. Aguascalientes is one of Mexico's leading producers of dairy products. In 2004, the state produced 402.5 million liters of cow's milk (106.3 million gallons), 8,926 tons of eggs, and 305 tons of honey. The state also marketed 43,534 head of beef cattle, 144,471 pigs, 16,599 goats, and 10,159 sheep that year, and produced 133,948 tons of chicken.

Various crops thrive in the moderate climate. Crops include alfalfa, corn, wheat, and chilies. Peaches and grapes for wine are also grown. Major farm products include tomatoes, garlic, guava, and animal feed. In 2005, a total of 49,059 tons of corn was produced, along with 10,793 tons of green chilies, and 15,343 tons of red tomatoes.

16 Natural Resources

The most notable natural resources are the hot springs that flow under about one-third of the state's land area. The forest industry is not significant. Encino (a type of oak) is the most commonly harvested wood. In 2003, sales in forest wood totaled about $251,945. The fish catch in 2003 amounted to only about 507 tons.

17 Energy and Power

Aguascalientes does not produce any electrical power, relying instead on imported power from other states. In 2005, there were 324,093 users of electricity in the state. Residential customers made up 278,219 of all users. Sales of electricity that same year totaled 2,042,864 megawatt hours, of which the largest users were medium-sized industrial firms at 829,869 megawatt hours. Electricity is provided and distributed by the Federal Electricity Commission and Central Light and Power. Both utilities are run by the Mexican government.

18 Health

In 2003, the state had 11 hospitals in the national system and 106 outpatient centers. In 2004, there were about 2,785 nurses, 1,435 doctors, and 67 dentists working in these health centers. There were an additional 18 independent health centers in the state.

Most of the Mexican population is covered under a government health plan. The IMSS (Instituto Mexicano de Seguro Social) covers the general population. The ISSSTE (Instituto de Seguridad y Servicios Sociales de Trabajadores del Estado) covers state workers.

The costumes worn by these members of Ballet Folklorico de Mexico are typical of traditional Aguascalientes. Women's dresses combine traditional embroidery and European influences. PETER LANGER.

19 Housing

Housing in Aguascalientes is some of the best available anywhere in Mexico. Most homes are made of permanent materials such as concrete, brick, and stone. In 2000, about 75% of all homes were owner-occupied. In 2005, there were an estimated 245,625 residential housing units in the state. About 91% of these units were single-family detached homes. The average household was estimated at 4.2 people.

20 Education

Public education in Mexico is free for students ages 6 to 16 and most students in the state attend public schools. However, in 2002/03 about 30% of high school students attended private schools. In 2004/05, it was estimated that 94% of age-eligible students completed primary school, which includes six years of study. About 77% of eligible students completed secondary school, which includes three years of study after primary school. Only 58.8% of eligible students completed the *bachillerato*, which is similar to a high school diploma. The national average for completion of the *bachillerato* was 60.1% that year.

There are at least four major institutions of higher education in the state, including Universidad Autónoma de Aguascalientes (Autonomous University of Aguascalientes) and the Instituto Tecnológico de Aguascalientes (Technical Institute of Aguascalientes). In 2005, there were about 34,939 students age 20 or older who were enrolled in some type of higher education program. The overall literacy rate was estimated at 94.6% in 2005.

21 Arts

Aguascalientes sponsors the Ballet Folklórico Ehécatl. In 2004, there were at least five performing arts auditoriums in the state. There were also about 60 registered film theaters, including multiscreen theaters and single screen galleries. There is also a cultural institute (Casa de Artesenias). There are three theatres: the Teatro de Aguascalientes, an example of modern architecture, seats 1,650; the Teatro Morelos, originally a parish house; and the Teatro del Parque Victor Sandoval, used for theatrical, musical, and film presentations.

The Aguascalientes Symphony Orchestra and Aguascalientes Opera have gained international recognition. The San Marcos Fair is an annual three-week long festival held in the capital city to celebrate both arts and culture. The Festival de las Calaveras (Skulls) takes place during the first week of November and features a traditional parade of skeletons.

22 Libraries and Museums

In 2003, there were 186 libraries in the state with a combined book stock of 1,386,678 volumes.

As of 2003, there were 13 museums. The Aguascalientes Museum (Museo de Aguascalientes), the main museum of fine arts, was built in 1903. Other museums in the state include the Museum of Contemporary Art (Museo del Arte Contemporáneo); the Interactive Museum of Science and Technology, which houses an IMAX theater; a museum ded-

icated to the works of José Guadalupe Posada, a revolutionary artist; and the Museum of Regional History. Specialized museums include La Cristiada, which commemorates the Roman Catholic Church's struggle against the government; the Museo Taurino, which showcases bullfighting; and the Museo Ferrocarril, a museum of the railroad.

23 Media

In 2005, the capital city, Aguascalientes, had two daily newspapers: *El Sol del Centro* (*The Central Sun*) and *El Heraldo* (*The Herald*).

In 2004, there were 15 television stations and 20 radio stations (13 AM and 7 FM). In 2005, there were about 45,100 subscribers to cable and satellite television stations. In 1991, the government-owned phone company, Teléfonos de Mexico, was sold to private investors. Since then service has improved but rates have risen. Teléfonos de Mexico provides 95% of telephone service in Mexico. In 2005, there were about 161,726 residential phone lines, with about 19.6 mainline phones in use for every 100 people.

24 Tourism, Travel, and Recreation

Aguascalientes is famous for the therapeutic hot springs for which the state was named. There are many parks and recreation centers for camping, mountain biking, rock climbing, and fishing. El Tunel de Poterillo offers a beautiful canyon with waterfalls and native flora and fauna. The park at El Ocote has prehistoric wall paintings of humans and animals. The Sierra de Laurel has a wildlife park and places to go mountain biking. The Cerro de Muerte offers rock climbing and rappelling. The San Marcos National Fair, held in late April or early May each year, is the main state tourist event and features art exhibits, rodeos, bullfights, a gambling casino, pageants, and music. There are also grape and guava fairs.

25 Sports

The Aguascalientes Panteras (Panthers) play as part of the southern division of the National Professional Basketball League (LNBP). The Rayos (Rays) de Nexaca play as a first division team of the Mexican Football Association (soccer); their home stadium in Aguascalientes at the 20,000-seat Estadio Victoria (Victoria Stadium). The Rieleros (Railroad Men) de Aguascalientes play in the Mexican League of AAA minor league baseball. In 2004, the state had three bullfighting rings, including the 16,000-seat Plaza Monumental and the smaller 5,000-seat Plaza San Marcos.

26 Famous People

Early leaders in the movement for independence were Pedro Parga (1792–1873), Rafael Iriarte, Francisco Primo de Verdad y Ramos (b.Jalisco, 1760–1808), and Valentín Gómez Farías (b.Jalisco, 1781–1858). Sculptor Jesús Contreras (1866–1902) created 18 statues of famous Mexicans that line the Paseo de la Reforma (Avenida Reforma) in Mexico City. Other notable citizens include composers Alfonso Esparza Oteo (1894–1950) and Manuel M. Ponce (b.Zacatecas, 1882–1948).

27 Bibliography

BOOKS

Carew-Miller, Anna. *Famous People of Mexico.* Philadelphia: Mason Crest Publishers, 2003.

Day-MacLeod, Deirdre. *The States of Central Mexico.* Philadelphia, PA: Mason Crest Publishers, 2003.M/bib>

DeAngelis, Gina. *Mexico.* Mankato, MN: Blue Earth Books, 2003.

Gruber, Beth. *Mexico.* Washington, DC: National Geographic, 2006.

WEB SITES

Government of Mexico. *Mexico for Kids.* www.elbalero.gob.mx/index_kids.html (accessed on March 30, 2007).

Government of the State of Aguascalientes. www.aguascalientes.gob.mx/idiomas/ingles/ (accessed on March 30, 2007).

Baja California

PRONUNCIATION: BAH-hah kah-lee-FOHR-nee-ah.

ORIGIN OF STATE NAME: The name "California" comes from a 16th-century Spanish novel. California was an island close to paradise. Baja comes from the Spanish word for lower. (The US state of California was once known as Alta California, with Alta meaning higher.)

CAPITAL: Mexicali.

ENTERED COUNTRY: 1952.

COAT OF ARMS: The emblem represents the past, the present, and the future of the state. The upper part depicts the Sun, symbol of light, the main element of nature and an inexhaustible source of energy, heat, and life. On each side, two human figures, with hands joined in the middle, project a beam of light, symbol of energy. The man is holding a book, representing culture. The woman is holding items representing intellectual activities and science. The central silhouette represents the missionaries who came to the region during the conquest and evangelized the indigenous population. The planted field in the upper left corner represents the agriculture of the present. On the horizon, a mountain range suggests the possibilities of mining. The silhouette of a factory and a cog (gear tooth) represent industry and the future. In the middle is the desert, and on the bottom is the Colorado River, which flows to the sea. Two waves on either side symbolize the western and eastern coasts.

HOLIDAYS: Año Nuevo (New Year's Day—January 1); Día de la Constitución (Constitution Day—February 5); Benito Juárez's birthday (March 21); Primero de Mayo (Labor Day—May 1); Anniversary of the Battle of Puebla (1862), May 5; Revolution Day, 1910 (November 20); and Navidad (Christmas—December 25).

FLAG: There is no official state flag.

TIME: 4 AM = Greenwich Mean Time (GMT).

1 Location and Size

Baja California lies on the Baja California peninsula, a long finger of land in western Mexico extending south from the US state of California. The state of Baja California covers the northern part of the peninsula and has an area of 71,446 square kilometers (27,585 square miles). It ranks at 12th in size among the states and covers about 3.6% of the total land area of Mexico. It is slightly larger in area than the US state of West Virginia. Its north-south length is similar to the state of Florida. Baja California is bordered on the north by California, on the west by the Pacific Ocean, on the east by the Golfo de California (sometimes called the Sea of Cortés) and the Colorado River, and on the south by Baja California Sur. Baja California is divided into five municipalities (similar to US counties). The capital, Mexicali, is located in the north on the border with California.

The peninsula is covered with mountain ranges (sierra), with broad valleys lying between the mountain peaks. Some of the highest elevations are in the Sierra San Pedro Mártir, which run north-south in the middle of the state. The highest peak in the state is the Picacho del Diablo at about 3,096 meters (10,157 feet). The larger cities and towns, including Mexicali, Las Palmas, Tijuana, Guadalupe, and Real de Castillo, lie in valleys.

The Pacific coastline extends for 880 kilometers (546 miles) and the Golfo de California coastline runs 675 kilometers (419 miles). Water runs down the slopes of the mountain ranges into the Pacific Ocean to the west and into the Golfo de California to the east. Due to its geological formation and to long-lasting droughts, the state of Baja California has no large rivers.

There are 35 islands, most of them lying in the Golfo de California. A few islands lie close to the west coast. Guadalupe Island lies 94 kilometers (150 miles) west of Baja California in the Pacific Ocean.

2 Climate

The climate is primarily dry, with desert-like conditions in some regions. Annual rainfall averages 30 to 60 centimeters (12 to 24 inches). Fog and winter rains are typical in the coastal area around Tijuana near the border with the United States.

In the northeast and the south, the climate has wide temperature differences between the hot days and the very cold nights. The center of the state is cooler, with cold winters (when most of the rain falls) and cool summers.

In Mexicali, the capital, the average annual temperature ranges from about 5°C (42°F) in January to 25°C (77°F) in July. The average annual precipitation in the capital city is 7 centimeters (2.9 inches) per year.

3 Plants and Animals

Tourists enjoy watching gray whales give birth in the protected waters along the coast. Many species of ducks and other marine birds find habitat in the coastal areas. In the mountains, there are coyotes, white-tailed deer, puma, lynx, wild sheep, and many species of snakes. Species of eagles and red-tailed hawk soar above the mountain peaks.

Plants of the state may be categorized by their environments: salt marshes, coastal dunes, chaparral scrub, and forest, which is found in the mountains. Jojoba and palmilla (also called soaptree yucca) are both widespread because they tolerate dry growing conditions. Jojoba seeds have many commercial uses, such as in lubricants, cosmetics, and medicines. The mountainous regions have alpine plants and pine forests. Coastal areas have various low-growing shrubs and cactus.

4 Environmental Protection

The government is concerned about improving air and water quality. Management of hazardous waste is also a concern. Water quality is a particular concern in the Colorado River basin, where untreated sewage and power plant waste pol-

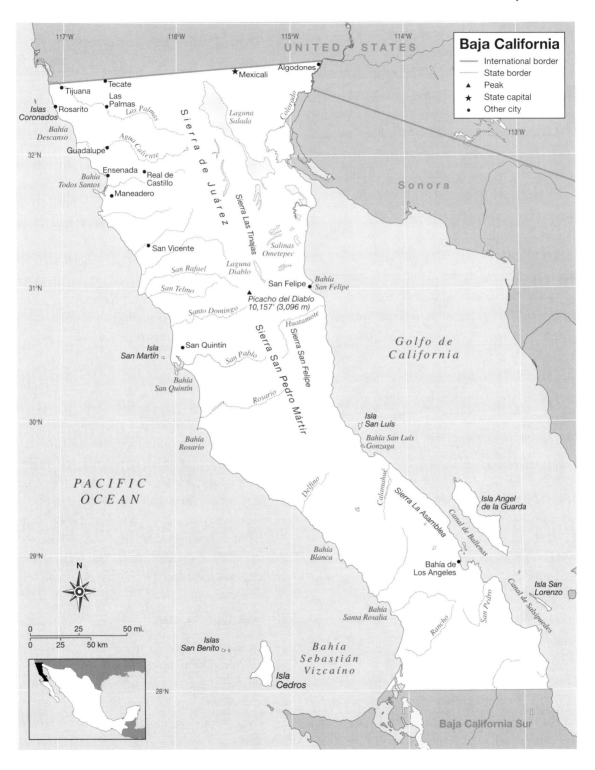

Baja California

- ——— International border
- ——— State border
- ▲ Peak
- ★ State capital
- ● Other city

UNITED STATES

117°W · 116°W · 115°W · 114°W · 113°W

Algodones
★ Mexicali
Tecate
Tijuana
Las Palmas
Islas Coronados
Rosarito
Las Palmas
Bahía Descanso
Sierra de Juárez
Laguna Salada
Colorado
Sonora
32°N
Guadalupe
Agua Caliente
Ensenada
Real de Castillo
Bahía Todos Santos
Maneadero
Sierra Las Tinajas
San Vicente
Salinas Ometepec
San Rafael
Laguna Diablo
San Telmo
31°N
San Felipe
Bahía San Felipe
▲ Picacho del Diablo 10,157' (3,096 m)
Santo Domingo
Huatamote
Isla San Martín
San Quintín
San Pablo
Sierra San Pedro Mártir
Sierra San Felipe
Golfo de California
Bahía San Quintín
Rosario
30°N
Isla San Luís
Bahía Rosario
Bahía San Luís Gonzaga
PACIFIC OCEAN
Delfino
Calamuhué
Sierra La Asamblea
Isla Angel de la Guarda
Canal de Ballenas
29°N
N
Bahía Blanca
Bahía de Los Angeles
Isla San Lorenzo
Canal de Salsipuedes
San Pedro
Rancho
0 25 50 mi.
0 25 50 km
Bahía Santa Rosalía
Islas San Benito
Bahía Sebastián Vizcaíno
Isla Cedros
28°N
Baja California Sur

lute the waters. In 2004, there were 25 municipal sewage treatment plants in operation in the state with a combined installed capacity of 5,626 liters per second (1,486 gallons per second). The volume of treated wastewater was estimated at 4,060 liters per second (1,072 gallons per second). There were an additional 179 industrial wastewater treatment plants in operation the same year. An estimated 97.2% of residents had access to safe drinking water as of 2004.

In 2003, the state had about 204,977 hectares (506,509 acres) of woodland, including about 37,823 hectares (93,462 acres) designated as rain forest. In 2004, fires damaged about 315 hectares (778 acres) of woodlands and about 6,465 hectares (15,975 acres) of pasture and brush lands.

The state has several protected areas. The Isla de Guadalupe biosphere reserve was designated as a protected area in 2005. The terrain of this volcanic island is threatened by the goat population and by the large number of tourists to the island. The Upper Golfo de California and the Colorado River Delta has been protected by the state since 1993 as the last remaining wetlands of the Colorado River. The region was designated as a Ramsar Wetland of International Importance in 1996. The islands of the Golfo de California were designated as a UNESCO World Heritage site in 2005. Estero de Punta Banda was designated as a Ramsar wetland in 2006. As of 2006, there were two other Ramsar sites in the state: Corredor Costero La Asamblea–San Francisquito and Isla Rasa. There are three national parks in the state, including the Archipélago de San Lorenzo, which was designated as such in 2005.

5 Population, Ethnic Groups, Languages

Baja California had a total population of 2,908,100 in 2006, ranking 14th among the states and the Distrito Federal. About 52% of the population were men and 48% were women. About 87% of the population lived in urban areas. The population density was 41.5 people per square kilometer (107 people per square mile). In 2005, the capital of Mexicali had about 855,962 residents.

Almost all residents speak Spanish as their first language; less than 2% of the citizens of Baja California speak one of the Amerindian languages, such as Náhuatl, Triqui, and many languages of the Zapotec and Mixtec ethnic groups.

6 Religions

According to the 2000 census, 81.4% of the population, or over 1.6 million people, were Roman Catholic; 7.9%, or 158,874 people, were mainline or evangelical Protestants. About 2.7% were listed as other Christian faiths, including 6,653 Seventh-day Adventists, 6,334 Latter-day Saints (Mormons), and 41,472 Jehovah's Witnesses. About 6.2% of the population claimed to have no religious affiliation.

7 Transportation

Baja California has about 11,000 kilometers (7,000 miles) of roadways. Four-lane highways connecting the four main cities make up just over 500 kilometers (200 miles).

Four international airports—Tijuana, Mexicali, San Felipe, and Ensenada—provide

Carnival occurs the week before the Christian holiday Ash Wednesday in Ensenada. © ROBERT FRERCK/WOODFIN CAMP.

commercial air service. In 2004, there were 768,078 automobiles registered in the state, along with 9,675 passenger trucks, 278,924 freight trucks, and 4,692 motorcycles.

8 History

Before the first Spaniards reached the region in 1533, different groups of hunters and gatherers occupied Baja California. The Yumano and Cucapás civilizations reached a considerable level of religious and artistic development prior to 1533.

Spaniard Hernán Cortés (1485–1547) led two expeditions to Baja California in 1535 and 1536. He wanted to conquer what he believed was an island. In 1602, Sebastián Vizcaíno (c.

1550–1616) led an expedition that renamed the old Santa Cruz port with its modern name, La Paz. Although there were some efforts to establish a Spanish colony in the 1600s, the first permanent European settlement was a Jesuit (an order of the Roman Catholic Church) mission created in 1697.

Jesuit priests introduced new crops and helped the natives with agricultural techniques. The Spaniards enslaved the native people and brought diseases from home. These two factors combined to greatly reduce the native population throughout the 1700s.

The Jesuits were expelled from Mexico in 1767 by a decree issued by the Spanish crown. This allowed Franciscan monks (from another order of the Roman Catholic Church) the freedom to move in to populate Baja California. Together with Alta California (now the US state of California), Baja California was made a Spanish province in the mid-1700s. It then officially merged with Alta California to create a territory of the Spanish viceroyalty (territory ruled by Spain) of Mexico.

In 1804, Baja and Alta California were divided again into two separate provinces. Because of their physical isolation, the people living in Baja California did not join in the drive for independence in 1810. Governor Fernando de la Toba declared Baja California's independence in 1822. A constitution was created in 1824. Baja California and Alta California were once again merged into a Mexican province, with San Diego as its capital and José María de Echandía as governor.

In 1829, the provincial capital was moved to La Paz, which is the modern-day capital of the state of Baja California Sur.

During the Mexican-American War (1846–48), Baja California was disputed territory. Mexican patriots fought against US soldiers. In the Treaty of Guadalupe Hidalgo in 1848, Mexico ceded Alta California to the United States, and it became the state of California. Mexico kept Baja California. Conflicts over control of Baja California persisted. American pirate William Walker attacked Baja California in 1853 and occupied La Paz and Cabo San Lucas. He declared independence and claimed to be president of the new republic. He was later expelled and deported to the United States.

From 1876 to 1910, Baja California witnessed widespread persecution of native indigenous groups. Lands of the native people were taken by the government for agricultural use in the name of Mexican progress and development. The International Company of Mexico, a Connecticut-based corporation, was granted almost half of the territory for different economic initiatives starting in 1886.

The Mexican Revolution took place from 1910 to 1920. Revolution sympathizers attacked Mexicali in 1911. Political instability in the rest of Mexico led many on both sides of the California border to push for the annexation of Baja California to the United States. Some activists in the United States promoted a movement for Baja California to secede (break away) from Mexico. Opposition from Mexican patriots who wanted to keep Baja California as part of Mexico prevented this from happening.

After the Mexican Revolution, a new constitution established the country of Mexico, but the government was not stable. The new Mexican government took control of Baja California and discouraged the idea that Baja California join the United States. Baja California was a territory of Mexico for the next 35 years.

Baja California was restructured into the Baja California Norte (North) and Baja California Sur (South) territories in 1952. The central Mexican government appointed governors in Baja California Norte and Baja California Sur, solidifying the division of the peninsula into two different provinces.

In 1952, Baja California became Mexico's 29th state, while Baja California Sur remained a territory. Braulio Maldonado Sandez, a member of the Institutional Revolutionary Party (PRI), became the first state governor under the new constitution.

In 1989, the PRI's hold on the state's governorship would be broken, when voters in Baja California elected the state's first non-PRI governor, Ernesto Ruffo Appel of the National Action Party (PAN). In 1995 and in 2001, PAN would again win the state's governorship. Other changes were also taking place in the state.

Beginning in the last half of the 20th century, important changes in the state's economy had begun. Tourism and manufacturing were growing. By the early 21st century, Baja California had become a major tourist and manufacturing center, employing thousands of local workers. However, the state's common border with the United States also fostered problems. Baja California had become a center for the smuggling of illegal immigrants and narcotics into the United States, leading to increased crime and corruption among government officials.

9 State and Local Government

Baja California became Mexico's 29th state officially on December 31, 1952. Its constitution was accepted in 1953. A unicameral (single chamber) legislature is comprised of a 25-member chamber of deputies. The deputies are elected for a nonrenewable three-year term. Sixteen of the deputies are elected from single-member districts and nine are elected at large. The state governor is elected for non-renewable six-year terms.

The governments of Baja California's five municipalities enjoy limited autonomy (self-government). The municipal president is elected to a nonrenewable three-year term. The president governs with a local municipal council. The state legislature has the power to intervene in municipal government under certain circum-

Traffic goes by a fence along the U.S.-Mexico border in Tijuana. Illegal immigration to the United States is an important issue in both countries. AP IMAGES.

stances. By controlling budget allocation, the state government exerts immense influence over local authorities.

10 Political Parties

The three main political parties in all of Mexico are the Institutional Revolutionary Party (PRI), the National Action Party (PAN), and the Party of the Democratic Revolution (PRD). As in the rest of Mexico, the PRI was the most powerful and influential party in Baja California until the late 1980s, controlling the state and most municipal governments. In 1989, PAN leader

Modern building in Tijuana. © MIREILLE VAUTIER/
WOODFIN CAMP.

Ernesto Ruffo became the first non-PRI state governor. In 1995, Hector Terán won the state for the PAN again. In 2001, Eugenio Elorduy Walther of the National Action Party (PAN) won the election to become the 12th governor.

11 Judicial System

The Supreme Tribunal of Justice is comprised of 13 justices elected for nonrenewable six-year terms. The Supreme Tribunal president is elected by the 13 justices for a nonrenewable two-year term. Justices are appointed by a two-thirds majority in the legislature from among a list of nominees presented by the Supreme Tribunal. Only qualified lawyers can be appointed to the Supreme Tribunal. In addition, there is a tribunal of electoral justice comprised of three members elected for three-year terms. Local tribunals complete the state judicial system.

12 Economy

Agriculture, maquiladora (assembly plants), tourism, and mining are important parts of the economy. Some 50 million tourists visit Baja California each year. As of 2003, the state's services sector (which included tourism) accounted for more than 23% of its gross domestic product (GDP), followed by the maquiladora sector, which accounted for 16% of GDP. The state's economy is also heavily affected by its proximity to the United States, through its sharing of a common border with the state of California. Baja California has six highway border crossings into the United States. The busiest border crossing is between Tijuana and San Ysidro, California. About 50,000 cars cross the border there each day, with 25,000 people crossing on foot. The state has approximately 860 miles (1,384 kilometers) of coastline on the Pacific Ocean and along the Golfo de California, but there is only one major port, Ensenada, on the Pacific side. The state's long coastlines are important to fishing and tourist industries.

13 Industry

As of 2003, Baja California's manufacturing sector was centered on its maquiladoras (assembly plants). There were more than 1,000 such plants in the state employing some 221,000 workers. Most were concentrated in and around

Tijuana (460), Tecate (123), and Mexicali (120). However, the state's maquiladora sector declined, from 1,450 plants in late 2000 to 1,025 in January 2003. About 67,000 jobs were eliminated when the plants closed. The majority of the state's maquiladora plants manufacture electronic products. Some 68% of the parts used were imported from the United States. Most of the state's finished maquiladora products are exported to the United States.

Another important industry is the extraction of salt from seawater, which is centered in the town of Guerrero Negro, just across the border in Baja California Sur. Hundreds of shallow tanks are filled with seawater, which are allowed to evaporate in the sun, leaving the salt, which is then purified and processed for either human or industrial consumption. Industrial uses for the salt include insecticides and fertilizers, the manufacture of soap and detergents, and for use in smelting and refining.

Handicraft items made from various types of shells are also produced.

14 Labor

As of 2005, Baja California had 1,270,900 eligible workers. Some 1,255,201 were listed as employed and 15,699 were listed as unemployed. The number of unemployed workers may be higher, however, because workers in rural areas may not be counted. The unemployment rate was reported to be 1.2%. Of those working, services employed 35.5%, followed by manufacturing at 22.4%, and commerce at 18%.

The US Bureau of Labor Statistics reported that Mexican workers saw their wages increase from $2.49 per hour in 2003 to $2.50 per hour in 2004. (The average US worker earned $15.70 per hour in 2004.) The maximum work week is set at 48 hours by law. The average worker spends 40 to 45 hours per week on the job. Workers earn twice their regular hourly rate for up to nine hours a week of overtime. When a worker works more than nine hours overtime in a week, he or she earns three times the regular hourly rate.

After one year, workers are entitled by law to six days paid vacation.

Amerindian migrant agricultural workers, primarily of Mixtec and Zapotec descent, have been discriminated against throughout the state's history. As of 2004, migrant workers were attempting to organize, through the Independent Confederation of Farm Workers and Peasants (CIOAC), to demand better treatment by their employers and the government. In the capital city of Mexicali, only 3% of the workforce were members of a union, but in the city of Tijuana, 75% of the workforce were members of a union.

15 Agriculture

Agriculture is the main economic activity in the state. Most agriculture is done in the region around Mexicali. The main products are wheat, tomatoes, broccoli, alfalfa, cotton, sorghum, and garlic. Other crops include grapes, dates, carob, lemons, and oranges. Agricultural crops grown for export to the United States, Canada, Europe, and Asia are chives, radishes, asparagus, melons, celery, lettuce, onions, and watermelon. In 2004, the state produced 426,653 tons of wheat and 294,076 tons of red tomatoes. That same year it also produced 210 million liters (55 million gallons) of cow's milk and 62,502 tons of beef.

Baja California is also a center for poultry breeding. In 2004, the state produced 9,651 tons of eggs and 1,185 tons of poultry.

16 Natural Resources

Fishing in the coastal waters off Baja California is an important economic activity. Principal fish caught include sole, tuna, sardines, mackerel, lobster, and shark. The coastline of Baja California accounts for about 12% of all seafood caught in Mexico. In 2003, the fish catch amounted to about 118,503 tons, the fourth-largest in the country. Sport fishing is enjoyed by tourists year round.

17 Energy and Power

Electricity is generated by ten power plants. Four plants were geothermal (using heat from the earth's interior) and three were gas-turbine facilities. Baja California generates enough electricity to satisfy its needs and to export energy to neighboring Sonora and to the United States. In 2005, there were 917,692 users of electricity in the state. Of that total, the largest number included residential customers at 818,465. Sales of electricity that same year totaled 2,586,251 megawatt hours, of which the largest users were medium-sized industrial firms at 3,369,213 megawatt hours. Electricity is provided and distributed by the Federal Electricity Commission, and Central Light and Power. Both utilities are run by the Mexican government.

Mexicali has natural gas resources; as of 2004 a pipeline between Mexicali and Tijuana with the capacity to carry 14 million cubic meters (500 million cubic feet) of natural gas per day was under construction.

18 Health

In 2003, the national health system operated 28 hospitals and 212 outpatient centers in the state. In 2004, there were about 2,350 doctors, 4,863 nurses, and 169 dentists working in these centers. There were an additional 129 independent health centers.

Most of the Mexican population is covered under a government health plan. The IMSS (Instituto Mexicano de Seguro Social) covers the general population. The ISSSTE (Instituto de Seguridad y Servicios Sociales de Trabajadores del Estado) covers state workers.

19 Housing

Most of the homes in the state have brick, concrete, or stone walls. However, there are a large number of homes made of wood. The most popular roofing material is *tejamanil*, a wooden shingle also known as a shake roof. In 2000, about 72% of all homes were owner-occupied. In 2005, there were an estimated 738,338 residential housing units in the state. About 73% of these housing units were single-family detached homes. The average household was estimated at 3.8 people.

20 Education

Public education in Mexico is free for students ages 6 to 16 and most of the students in the state attend public schools. However, in 2002/03 about 22.7% of high school students attended private schools. In 2004/05, it was estimated that 93% of age-eligible students completed primary school, which includes six years of study. About 81% of eligible students completed secondary school, which includes three years of study after primary school. About 59% of eligible students completed the *bachillerato*, which is similar to a high school diploma. The national average for completion of the *bachillerato* was 60.1% that year.

There are at least seven major institutions of higher education in the state, including Universidad Autónoma de Baja California (Autonomous University of Baja California) and Instituto Tecnológico de Tijuana (Tijuana Technical Institute). In 2005, there were about 91,382 students age 20 or older who were enrolled in some type of higher education program. The overall literacy rate was estimated at 94.6% in 2005.

21 Arts

The state of Baja California sponsors many dance groups including the Balleto Folklórico de Ticuan, a jazz ensemble (Dat'Z Jazz), Groupo Almalafa, and Groupo Mal Paso. The Baja California Orchestra is a chamber orchestra that performs internationally. The city of Ensenada is home to the Galería de Perez Meillon, which showcases native crafts such as the traditional willow baskets of the Pai-Pai Indians. The annual Vineyards Flowering Festival is also held in Ensenada each spring to mark the beginning of the year's grape harvest and wine production.

In 2004, there were three major auditoriums for the performing arts. There were also about 76 registered film theaters, including multiscreen theaters and single screen galleries.

22 Libraries and Museums

In 2003, there were 281 libraries in the state with a combined book stock of 1,780,861.

As of 2003, there were 13 active museums registered in Baja California that had permanent exhibits, including several history museums in Ensenada and a wax museum and a pre-Columbian museum in Tijuana. In Mexicali, the Sol del Nino is an interactive museum focusing on science, technology, and the environment.

23 Media

In 2005, the capital city, Mexicali, had three daily newspapers: *La Crónica* (*The Chronicle*), *El Centinela* (*The Sentinel*), and *La Voz de la Frontera* (*The Voice of the Frontier*). Tijuana had four daily papers: *El Sol de Tijuana* (*Tijuana Sun*), *El Heraldo de Baja California, El Mexicano*, and *Segunda Edicion* (*Second Edition*).

In 2004, there were 33 television stations and 68 radio stations (34 AM and 34 FM). In 2005, there were about 117,958 subscribers to cable and satellite television stations. Also in 2005, there were about 554,229 residential phone lines, with about 24.4 mainline phones in use for every 100 people.

24 Tourism, Travel, and Recreation

Outdoor water sports such as deep sea fishing, scuba diving, and snorkeling provide vacationers with reasons to visit Baja California. Rosarito Beach, Ensenada, and Mexicali are easy access points from San Diego, California. There is tourist shopping in the border town of Tijuana.

The state capital of Mexicali offers many tourist attractions. The Plaza Calafia offers tour-

The cultural center in Tijuana. AP IMAGES.

ists a look at real bullfighting. The city park has a zoo and local marketplace. In October, Mexicali hosts its annual fair, the Fiesta del Sol. There are beautiful beaches at San Felipe on the Golfo de California. The islands of the Golfo de California were designated as UNESCO World Heritage sites in 2005.

There are more than 400 hotels catering to tourists in Baja California, of which 75% are located in the Tijuana-Ensenada corridor, which attract 60% of all tourists to the state. Of those, 82% stay in Tijuana and Rosarito, with the remainder going to Ensenada.

25 Sports

The Mexicali Águilas (Eagles) of the Mexican Pacific League (a winter league in professional baseball) play in the Estadio Casas GEO Stadium (also called El Nido–the Nest), seating 10,000 people. The Águilas won the Caribbean World Series in 1986. The Potros (Colts) de Tijuana play in the Mexican League of AAA minor league baseball.

Major bullfighting venues include the Plaza de Toros in Tijuana, with seating for 21,621. It is part of the large complex, Playas Tijuana, which also has a racetrack. Mexicali's bullfighting ring, Plaza Calafia, seats 10,000.

Tijuana's First Division "A" soccer team, Gallos Caliente, plays in the Unidad Deportiva Crea, where there is seating for 6,000. The Tecate Astros (Stars), Ensenada Cimarrones (Rams), Tijuana Galgos (Greyhounds), and Mexicali Soles (Suns) are all Northern Division teams of the National Professional Basketball League (LNBP).

An annual International Yacht Race has been held for over 50 years. The race begins in Newport Beach, California, and ends in Ensenada, where a festival is held to complete the event. Downtown Ensenada is also the finish line for the annual Tecate SCORE Baja 500 Race. Over 250 cars, trucks, motorcycles, and ATVs compete in this race that covers 450 miles through forest, desert, and mountain roads.

26 Famous People

Fernando de la Toba declared independence in Baja California. Braulio Maldonado Sandez (1903–1990), a member of the PRI (Institutional Revolutionary Party), became the first state governor. Missionary Father Eusebio Kino (b.Italy, 1645–1711) attempted to establish a mission program in Baja California in the 1670s. Ernesto Ruffo Appel (b.United States, 1952), a member of the PAN (National Action Party), became the first non-PRI governor of the state in 1989. Lupita Jones (b.1968) became the first Mexican woman to win the title of Miss Universe in 1991. In 1994 she founded Nuestra Belleza México, the official beauty pageant of Mexico.

27 Bibliography

BOOKS

Burt, Janet. *The Pacific North States of Mexico.* Philadelphia: Mason Crest Publishers, 2003.

Clampet, Jason. *The Rough Guide to Baja California.* London: Rough Guides, 2006.

Foerster, Leland. *The Californios: Photographs and Stories About the Descendents of the Mission Era in Baja California, Mexico.* Oceanside, CA: Golden Raintree Press, 2003.

Gruber, Beth. *Mexico.* Washington, DC: National Geographic, 2006.

Williams, Jack, *The Magnificent Peninsula: The Comprehensive Guidebook to Mexico's Baja California.* Redding, CA: H. J. Williams, 2001.

WEB SITES

Government of Baja California. www.bajacalifornia.gob.mx/english/index.jsp (accessed on March 30, 2007).

Government of Mexico. *Mexico for Kids.* www.elbalero.gob.mx/index_kids.html (accessed on March 30, 2007).

Baja California Sur

PRONUNCIATION: bah-hah kah-lee-FOHR-nee-ah SOOR.

ORIGIN OF STATE NAME: The name "California" comes from a 16th-century Spanish novel. California was an island close to paradise. Baja comes from the Spanish word for lower. Sur is Spanish for south.

CAPITAL: La Paz.

ENTERED COUNTRY: 1974.

COAT OF ARMS: The navy blue represents justice, truth, and loyalty. The fish represents the resources of the ocean. The center section is divided in half: the red and gold represent unity, wealth, and courage. The shell symbolizes the battle that citizens have fought to defend their borders.

HOLIDAYS: Año Nuevo (New Year's Day—January 1); Día de la Constitución (Constitution Day—February 5); Benito Juárez's birthday (March 21); Primero de Mayo (Labor Day—May 1); Anniversary of the Battle of Puebla (1862), May 5; Revolution Day, 1910 (November 20); and Navidad (Christmas—December 25).

FLAG: There is no official flag.

TIME: 4 AM = Greenwich Mean Time (GMT).

1 Location and Size

Baja California Sur, a very narrow state in western Mexico, covers the southern half of the Baja California peninsula. The peninsula is a long finger of land extending south from the border with the US state of California. Baja California Sur is bordered on the north by the state of Baja California. Baja California Sur's total area is 73,922 square kilometers (28,541 square miles), slightly smaller than the state of South Carolina. It ranks as ninth in size among the states and covers about 3.8% of the total land area of Mexico. Baja California Sur is divided into five municipalities (similar to US counties). The capital, La Paz, is located in the southeast.

There are many islands in Baja California Sur, including Isla Natividad, Isla Magdalena, and Isla Santa Margarita in the Pacific Ocean and Isla San Marcos, Isla Carmen, Isla Monserrat, Isla Santa Catalina, Isla Santa Cruz, Isla San José, Isla San Francisco, Isla la Partida, Isla Espíritu Santo and Cerralvo in the Golfo de California (sometimes called the Sea of Cortés).

Baja California Sur, with a coastline of more than 2,000 kilometers (1,250 miles), has the lon-

Many species of cactii, including the cardón cactus, thrive in Baja California Sur. The cardón cactus may reach 21 meters (70 feet) in height. HENK SIERDSEMA/SAXIFRAGA/EPD PHOTOS.

gest coastline of any Mexican state. It is bordered to the east and south by the Golfo de California. This gulf separates the peninsula from the mainland Mexican states of Sinaloa and Sonora. To the west is the Pacific Ocean. Baja California Sur's largest rivers are the San Ignacio and the San Raymundo, both in the northern portion of the state. The Laguna Ojo de Liebre opens to the Bahía Sabastián Vizcaíno at the northwest border and Laguna San Ignacio connects the San Ignacio River to the Pacific Ocean along the western border.

Mountains form a chain that follows the eastern coastline, ending at the southern tip of the peninsula near Cabo San Lucas. The primary mountain chains are the Sierra de Santa Lucia in the north, the Sierra de la Gigante in the east-central region, and the Sierra de la Laguna in the south. The highest elevations are in the Sierra de la Laguna, including the highest peak in the state, Picacho de la Laguna, at an elevation of about 2,163 meters (7,096 feet).

2 Climate

The climate is mild, with temperatures averaging 24°C (75°F) during the day and 13°C (55°F) at night in January. In July, temperatures average 32°C (90°F) during the day and 27°C (80°F) at night. The climate is generally dry, with annual rainfall averaging 30 to 60 centimeters (12 to 24 inches) per year. In La Paz, the capital city, the

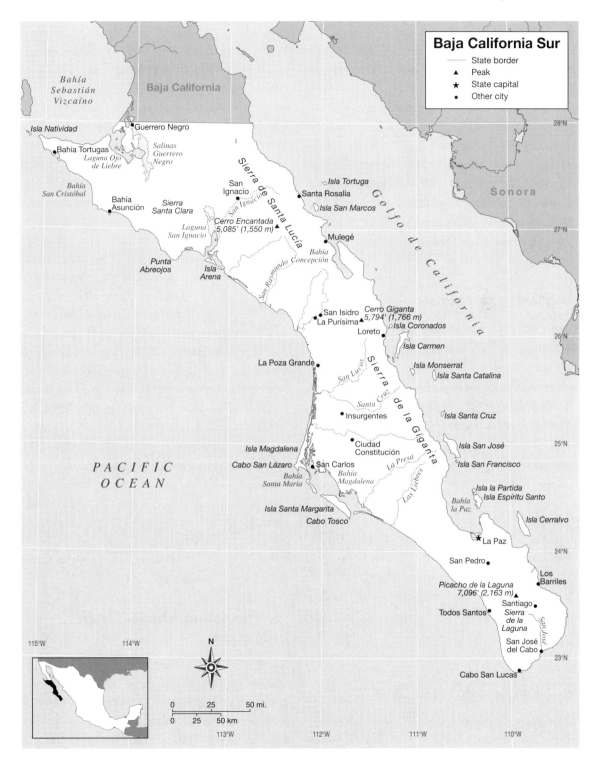

Baja California Sur

- State border
- ▲ Peak
- ★ State capital
- • Other city

Bahía Sebastián Vizcaíno

Baja California

Sonora

28°N

Isla Natividad

•Guerrero Negro

Salinas Guerrero Negro

•Bahía Tortugas

Laguna Ojo de Liebre

Bahía San Cristóbal

San Ignacio

Isla Tortuga

Santa Rosalía•

Golfo de California

•Bahía Asunción

Sierra Santa Clara

Sierra de Santa Lucía

San Ignacio

Isla San Marcos

Cerro Encantada 5,085' (1,550 m) ▲

Laguna San Ignacio

Mulegé•

27°N

Bahía Concepción

Punta Abreojos

San Raymundo

Isla Arena

San Isidro•
La Purísima•

Cerro Giganta 5,794' (1,766 m)▲

Isla Coronados

Loreto•

26°N

Isla Carmen

La Poza Grande•

San Lucas

Sierra de la Giganta

Isla Monserrat

Isla Santa Catalina

Santa Cruz

Isla Santa Cruz

•Insurgentes

Isla San José

25°N

Ciudad Constitución•

La Presa

Isla San Francisco

PACIFIC OCEAN

Isla Magdalena

Cabo San Lázaro•

San Carlos•

Bahía Santa María

Bahía Magdalena

Las Libres

Isla la Partida
Isla Espíritu Santo

Bahía la Paz

Isla Cerralvo

Isla Santa Margarita

Cabo Tosco

★La Paz

24°N

San Pedro•

Los Barriles•

Picacho de la Laguna 7,096' (2,163 m)▲

Santiago•

Sierra de la Laguna

San José

Todos Santos•

San José del Cabo•

23°N

Cabo San Lucas•

N

115°W   114°W

113°W   112°W   111°W   110°W

0   25   50 mi.
0   25   50 km

annual average temperature ranges from 17°C (64°F) to 30°C (86°F). The average annual precipitation in the capital is about 17 centimeters (6.7 inches).

The region has experienced hurricanes on a fairly regular basis. Since 1995, at least one hurricane has hit the state each year. In 2004, Hurricane Javier made landfall at Punta Aberjos as a category four storm with wind speeds of 240 kilometers per hour (149 miles per hour). In 2003, Hurricane Marty landed at San José del Cabo and Hurricane Ignacio landed at Ciudad Constitución.

3 Plants and Animals

Baja California Sur is host to many sea animals along its two coasts. These include iguanas, snakes, turtles, several species of sea birds, swallows, and pelicans. There are many migrating whales and sport fish in the waters along the coast. The desert has mesquite trees; cactus; and small, shrubby pines. The higher elevations are home to deer and mountain lions, rabbits, squirrels, and big-horned sheep.

The cardón cactus, the world's largest cactus, thrives on the Baja California peninsula. It grows slowly and may reach heights of 21 meters (70 feet).

The landscape in the mountainous areas of Baja California Sur is tropical dry forest. The dry forest has a long dry season and a short rainy season, opposite the climate where the rain forest thrives.

4 Environmental Protection

The fish populations in the Golfo de California to the east of Baja California Sur have been depleted by overfishing. Fishing also endangers turtles and other marine animals that get caught accidentally by fishing equipment (hooks or nets).

In 2004, there were 16 municipal sewage treatment plants in operation with a combined installed capacity of 1,105 liters per second (291.9 gallons per minute). The volume of treated wastewater was estimated at 781 liters per second (206.3 gallons per second) that year. There were an additional seven industrial wastewater treatment plants in operation the same year. As of 2004, 97.3% of the population had access to safe drinking water.

In 2003, the state had about 505,611 hectares (1.2 million acres) of woodlands, including 472,914 hectares (1.1 million acres) designated as rain forest. About 26 hectares (64 acres) of woodland were damaged by forest fires in 2004. About 168 hectares (415 acres) of pasture and brush land were also affected by fires. There are several protected areas in the state, El Vizcaíno, the largest biosphere reserve in Mexico. The whale sanctuaries of El Vizcaíno, which include Laguna Ojo de Liebre and Laguna San Ignacio, were designated as UNESCO Natural World Heritage Sites in 1993 and were listed as Ramsar Wetlands of International Importance in 2004. Bahía de Loredo (also a Ramsar site) and Cabo Pulmo are national parks.

5 Population, Ethnic Groups, Languages

Baja California Sur had an estimated total population of 523,800 in 2006, ranking at 32nd among the states and the Distrito Federal. About 52% of the people were men and 48% were women. About 70% of the population lived in

South of Loreto, the Sierra de la Giganta. © ROBERT FRERCK/WOODFIN CAMP.

urban areas. The population density was 7 people per square kilometer (18 people per square mile). In 2005, the capital, La Paz, had an estimated population of 219,596. Almost all residents speak Spanish. There is a small percentage of people who speak one of the Amerindian languages, such as Náhuatl and Mazateco.

6 Religions

According to the 2000 census, 89% of the population, or 333,156 people, were Roman Catholic; 4%, or 15,083 people, were mainline or evangelical Protestant. About 1.9% of the people were counted as other Christian faiths, including 665 Seventh-day Adventists, 995 Latter-day Saints (Mormons), 5,611 and Jehovah's Witnesses. About 3.6% of the population claimed to have no religious affiliation.

7 Transportation

There are highways stretching the length of the Baja California peninsula, but there are relatively few gas stations. Drivers must plan carefully to avoid running out of fuel. La Paz-Manuel de Leon Airport provides international flights to and from Baja California Sur. Los Cabos International Airport at San Jose del Cabo is an international airport serving Cabo San Lucas. There is shipping across the Golfo de California to the mainland states of Sonora and Sinaloa.

In 2004, there were 188,355 automobiles registered in the state, along with 2,925 pas-

Mexican boats patrol off the coast of Cabo San Lucas. AP IMAGES.

senger trucks, 96,629 freight trucks, and 2,981 motorcycles.

8 History

In addition to different groups of hunters and gatherers, there were Yumano and Cucapás civilizations in the area before the arrival of the Spaniards in Baja California. The first Spaniards reached the region in 1533. Spaniard Hernán Cortés (1485–1547) led two expeditions in 1535 and 1536 to conquer what he believed was an island. In 1602, Sebastián Vizcaíno (c. 1550–1616) led an expedition that renamed the old Santa Cruz port with its modern name, La Paz. Although there were some colonization efforts in the 1600s, the first permanent non-indigenous settlement was a Jesuit (an order of the Roman Catholic Church) mission created in 1697. Jesuit priests introduced new crops and helped the natives with new agricultural techniques. Diseases brought by the Spaniards and the enslavement of the indigenous population helped decimate the native population throughout the 1700s.

The expulsion of the Jesuits in 1767 by decree of the Spanish crown gave way to a centralized effort to populate Baja California with Franciscan monks (from the Franciscan order of the Roman Catholic Church) and military garrisons. Together with Alta California (now the US state of California), Baja California was made a Spanish province in the mid-1700s. It then officially merged with Alta California to create a territory of the Spanish viceroyalty (territory ruled by Spain) of Mexico. In 1804, Baja and Alta

California were divided again into two separate provinces.

The drive for independence in 1810 took hold in many Mexican states, but not in Baja California because of its physical isolation. Governor Fernando de la Toba finally declared Baja California's independence from Spain in 1822. A constitution was ratified (approved) in 1824 and Baja and Alta California were once again merged into a Mexican province with San Diego as its capital and José María de Echandía as governor. In 1829, the provincial capital was moved to La Paz.

During the Mexican-American War (1846–48), Baja California was disputed territory. Mexican patriots fought against US soldiers. In the Treaty of Guadalupe Hidalgo of 1848, Mexico ceded (gave up) Alta California but kept Baja California. Conflicts over control of Baja California persisted. American pirate William Walker attacked Baja California in 1853 and occupied La Paz and Cabo San Lucas, declaring independence and claiming to be president of the new republic. He was later expelled and deported to the United States.

From 1876 to 1910, Baja California witnessed widespread persecution of native indigenous groups. Native lands were forcibly taken for agricultural use in the name of Mexican progress and development. The International Company of Mexico, a Connecticut-based corporation, was granted almost half of the territory for different economic initiatives starting in 1886. When the Mexican Revolution (1910–20) toppled the regime of Porfirio Díaz (1830–1915), Baja California was comprised of the Norte (North) and Sur (South) provinces.

After the revolution, the new Mexican government took control of Baja California and suppressed the move towards annexation by the United States. The central government appointed governors in Baja California Norte and Baja California Sur, consolidating the division of the peninsula into two different provinces. From 1916 to 1974, 10 governors were appointed for Baja California Sur. During this period, much progress was made, including the construction of roads, a water system, a system for electricity, and an education system. A shipping route was established with the mainland states. Baja California Sur became a federal state in 1974 under the presidency of Luis Echeverría, with three municipalities: La Paz, Comondú, and Mulegé. Félix Agramont Cota, the appointed governor, convened a constitutional assembly. The new constitution was ratified (approved) on January 9, 1975. The first constitutional governor was Ángel César Mendoza Aramburu. As the population grew, the state further divided its territory, adding the municipality of Los Cabos in 1981 and Loreto in 1992.

In 1999, the Institutional Revolutionary Party's (PRI) hold on the state's governorship was broken for the first time, when Leonel Cota Montaño of the Party of the Democratic Revolution (PRD) was elected governor. He was succeeded by Narciso Agúndez Montaño, also of the PRD, in 2005.

The state's tourism industry was born in the 1950s when wealthy Southern Californians began to vacation in the state, usually arriving by yachts or private aircraft. Around 1948 the first resort hotel was built. Others would follow in the oncoming years. By the first decade of the 21st century, the state's tourism industry was thriving, creating thousands of construction and service jobs in the state.

9 State and Local Government

The state governor is elected for a nonrenewable six-year term. The legislature is comprised of a unicameral (single chamber) state assembly. Fifteen of its 21 members are elected in single-member districts and 6 by proportional representation, all for nonrenewable three-year terms. Legislators can seek election again after sitting out one term of the assembly. Power is highly centralized in the office of the governor, but re-election restrictions and the small size of the state have made the Baja California Sur governor relatively weak when compared to other Mexican states.

Comprised of five municipalities, Baja California Sur has a highly centralized government. Municipal presidents are elected for nonrenewable three-year terms. Each municipality also elects a local council, whose size varies according to the municipal population. Municipal council members are also elected for nonrenewable three-year terms.

10 Political Parties

The three main political parties in all of Mexico are the Institutional Revolutionary Party (PRI), the National Action Party (PAN), and the Party of the Democratic Revolution (PRD). As in the rest of Mexico, candidates of these three parties compete for most elected offices. The PRI exercised dominance over the political system after state was officially separated from Baja California. Until 1999, all state governors belonged to the PRI. In 1999, Leonel Cota Montaño of the PRD was elected governor. He was followed by Narciso Agúndez Montaño, also of the PRD, who won the election in 2005.

11 Judicial System

A superior tribunal of justice is the highest judicial authority in the state. Its seven members are appointed by the legislature from a three-person list presented by the state governor. Justices must be qualified lawyers and they cannot be immediately reappointed after their six-year terms expire. In addition there is a state electoral tribunal and local courts in each municipality. The state electoral tribunal is comprised of three members elected by a two-thirds majority in the legislature for nonrenewable six-year terms.

12 Economy

The economy of Baja California Sur is primarily based on the services sector, of which tourism is the significant portion, followed by construction, manufacturing, agriculture, and fishing. Most of the state's economic activity is centered around the state capital of La Paz (fishing, agriculture, and tourism); Los Cabos, which has an 18 mile (29 kilometer) corridor of high-end resorts, makes up most of the state's hotels and marinas; and salt mining (in the northern part of the state) around Guerrero Negro. A small commercial cotton growing operation exists in the state.

13 Industry

There is little industry, except for tourism-related activities, in the state. Salt, plaster, and phosphorite are also produced, as well as leather handicrafts, baskets made from palm fibers and torote, and decorative objects made from sea shells.

The extraction of salt from seawater is centered in the town of Guerrero Negro. Hundreds of shallow tanks are filled with seawater, which is allowed to evaporate in the sun. The salt that remains is then purified and processed for either human or industrial consumption. Industrial uses for the salt include insecticides and fertilizers, soap and detergents, and in smelting and refining.

14 Labor

As of 2005, Baja California Sur had 210,470 eligible workers. Some 205,629 were listed as employed and 4,841 were listed as unemployed. Unemployed workers in rural areas may not be counted, however. The unemployment rate that year was reported to be 2.3%. Of those who were working, services employed 48%, followed by commerce at 20.7%, and agriculture at 13%.

The US Bureau of Labor Statistics reported that Mexican workers saw their wages increase from $2.49 per hour in 2003 to $2.50 per hour in 2004. (The average US worker earned $15.70 per hour in 2004.) The maximum work week is set at 48 hours by law. The average worker spends 40 to 45 hours per week on the job. Workers earn twice their regular hourly rate for up to nine hours a week of overtime. When a worker works more than nine hours overtime in a week, he or she earns three times the regular hourly rate. After one year, workers are entitled by law to six days of paid vacation.

15 Agriculture

Agriculture is an important economic activity. Principal crops are wheat, corn, green chilies, tomatoes, alfalfa, sorghum, and chickpeas (garbanzo beans). In 2004, Baja California Sur produced 38,301 tons of corn, 30,131 tons of wheat, 68,195 tons of green chilies, and 113,450 tons of red tomatoes. Other crops include oranges, avocados, mangoes, and dates. Honey is also produced.

Ranchers in Baja California Sur raise relatively modest numbers of beef cattle, goats, pigs, and chickens for both meat and eggs.

16 Natural Resources

Fishing in the coastal waters yields abalone, tuna, clams, lobster, and shrimp, among other species. Fishing is an important economic activity, with fish processing facilities located at Santa Rosalía on the east coast, and San Carlos on the west coast. In 2003, the fish catch totaled about 184,679 tons, the third-highest catch in the country after Sonora and Sinaloa. While the forest industry is not as significant to the state, there are harvests and sales of tropical woods.

The state produces salt, plaster, and phosphorite, mostly for export. Small amounts of gold and silver, from 2 to 4 kilograms (4 to 8 pounds), are also produced each year.

17 Energy and Power

Geothermal power (from the heat of Earth's interior) has potential in the state. The only geothermal plant in the state is located near Tres Vírgenes (Three Virgins), a series of three volcanoes near the Golfo de California. Most of the state's electric power comes from diesel generators and gas-turbines. There is also a wind-driven power station in Mulegé and a thermal (non-coal) power station in La Paz. In rural areas, residents formerly paid a flat fee for electricity, with no meter to measure how much electricity was being used. By the late 1990s, most homes had metered electricity.

In 2005, there were 183,870 users of electricity in the state. Of that total, 158,967 were residential customers. Sales of electricity that same year totaled 1,318,421 megawatt hours, of which the largest users were medium-sized industrial firms at 445,427 megawatt hours. Electricity is provided by the Federal Electricity Commission, and Central Light and Power. Both utilities are run by the Mexican government.

18 Health

In 2003, the state had 17 hospitals and 115 outpatient centers that were part of the national health system. In 2004, there were 752 doctors, 1,438 nurses, and 57 dentists working in these centers. There were an additional 14 independent health centers in the state in 2004. AmeriMed (American hospitals) also has a medical center in Cabo San Lucas.

Most of the Mexican population is covered under a government health plan. The IMSS (Instituto Mexicano de Seguro Social) covers the general population. The ISSSTE (Instituto de Seguridad y Servicios Sociales de Trabajadores del Estado) covers state workers.

19 Housing

There is a slight housing shortage in Baja California Sur. Most homes are made of permanent materials such as concrete, stone, and brick. Most of the housing is in good condition, with less that 10% requiring significant upgrading. In 2000, about 75% of all homes were owner-occupied. In 2005, there were an estimated 135,912 residential housing units in the state. About 83% of these were single-family, detached homes. The average household was estimated at 3.7 people.

20 Education

Public education is free for students ages 6 to 16 and most of the students in the state attend public schools. In 2004/05, it was estimated that 95% of age-eligible students completed primary school, which includes six years of study. About 85% of eligible students completed secondary school, which includes three years of study after primary school. Only 55.7% of eligible students completed the *bachillerato*, which is similar to a high school diploma. The national average for completion of the *bachillerato* was 60.1% that year.

The Universidad Autónoma de Baja California Sur (Autonomous University of Baja California Sur) is located in the capital. The Northwest Center for Biological Research is also in La Paz. In 2005, there were about 16,032 students age 20 or older who were enrolled in some type of higher education program. The overall literacy rate was estimated at 94.5% in 2005.

21 Arts

There are over eight theaters, including the Teatro Juárez in La Paz. The city of La Paz also has an open-air theater. The city of Todos Santos is an artists' community that often hosts various art fairs. The Galería de Todos Santos is a fine arts gallery showcasing the works of many famous Mexican artists. There is also El Boleo Centro Cultural in the city of Mulegé, and the French cultural society Alianza Francesa has a chapter. There are also about 13 registered movie

The inland area north of the resort San José del Cabo is sparsely populated. HENK SIERDSEMA/SAXIFRAGA/EPD PHOTOS.

theaters, including multiscreen theaters and single-screen galleries.

22 Libraries and Museums

In 2003, there were 85 libraries in the state with a combined book stock of 527,931 volumes. There were three national museums registered in the state in 2003. The Museum of Anthropology and History of Baja California Sur is in the city of La Paz. The San Ignacio Museum of Rupestrian Painting displays photos of rock art from San Francisco de la Sierra. There is a Jesuit museum in the city of Loreto.

23 Media

In 2005, the capital city, La Paz, had six daily newspapers, the largest of which was *Sudcaliforniano* (*Southern California*). Others included *La Extra*, *Diario Peninsular*, and *Avante*. In 2004, there were 30 television stations and 23 radio stations (13 AM and 10 FM). In 2005, there were about 17,959 subscribers to cable and satellite television stations. Also in 2005, there were about 78,386 residential phone lines, with about 22.4 mainline phones in use for every 100 people.

24 Tourism, Travel, and Recreation

The two main cities of Cabo San Lucas and San Juan del Cabo offer many hotels and recreational facilities. Whale watching (from January through March), deep sea fishing, golf and tennis, motorcycling, scuba diving, and snorkeling are all area attractions. The "Corridor," is a main highway between the two towns. Medano Beach has windsurfing and at the tip of Baja California Sur is a rock formation known as Los Arcos, famous to all photographers. The town of Mulegé offers sport fishing and diving along with tours of prehistoric caves and their paintings. The whale sanctuary at El Vizcaíno was designated as a UNESCO World Heritage site in 1993.

Almost 500,000 tourists visit the state each year to enjoy the state's sun and beaches. Other favorite tourist resorts are Loreto and La Paz.

25 Sports

There are no major sports teams in the state, but people in Baja California Sur enjoy the sporting venues of Baja California to the north. Amateur sports such as deep sea fishing, scuba diving, bicycling, and windsurfing are popular.

26 Famous People

Juan María de Salvatierra (b.Italy, 1648–1717), a Catholic missionary, established the Misión de Nuestra Señora de Loreto Conchó, the first permanent mission in the state. Ángel César Mendoza Aramburu was the first governor; Juan Antonio Flores Ojeda was the governor as of 2004.

27 Bibliography

BOOKS

Burt, Janet. *The Pacific North States of Mexico.* Philadelphia: Mason Crest Publishers, 2003.

Clampet, Jason. *The Rough Guide to Baja California.* London: Rough Guides, 2006.

Sobol, Richard. *Adelina's Whales.* New York: Dutton, 2003.

Williams, Jack. *The Magnificent Peninsula: The Comprehensive Guidebook to Mexico's Baja California.* Redding, CA: H. J. Williams, 2001.

Zronik, John. *Hernando Cortes: Spanish Invader of Mexico.* New York: Crabtree Publishing Co, 2006.

WEB SITES

Mexico for Kids. www.elbalero.gob.mx/index_kids. html (accessed on March 30, 2007).

Campeche

PRONUNCIATION: kahm-PEH-cheh.

ORIGIN OF STATE NAME: The name Campeche is of Mayan origin and has three possible meanings: It may be derived from the words *can* (snake) and *pech* (tick)—the place of snakes and ticks. Some speculate that Can Pech means "the place where the snake is worshipped," because snakes appear on many ancient structures.

CAPITAL: Campeche.

ENTERED COUNTRY: 1862.

COAT OF ARMS: The red background of the upper left and lower right quarters represents the bravery of Campecheans and contrasts with the silver towers. This silver color is the reflection of solidness and honor of its inhabitants, and the towers signify the strength of Campecheans in the defense of their land. The other two quarters bear a sailing ship with a raised anchor, which reminds viewers of the importance of Campeche as a maritime port. The four quarters rest upon a blue background that represents the loyalty and noble sentiments of Campecheans. Finally, above the coat of arms there is a crown decorated with precious stones symbolizing the nobility and grandeur of the state.

HOLIDAYS: Año Nuevo (New Year's Day—January 1); Día de la Constitución (Constitution Day—February 5); Benito Juárez's birthday (March 21); Primero de Mayo (Labor Day—May 1); Revolution Day, 1910 (November 20); and Navidad (Christmas—December 25).

FLAG: There is no official flag.

TIME: 6 AM = noon Greenwich Mean Time (GMT).

1 Location and Size

Campeche, in eastern Mexico on the Yucatán Peninsula, covers an area of 57,925 square kilometers (22,364 square miles). It ranks as 17th in size among the states and covers about 3% of the total land area of Mexico. Campeche is about the same size as the US state of Iowa. Campeche is bordered by the state of Quintana Roo on the east, by the state of Tabasco and the Gulf of Mexico on the west, by the state of Yucatán on the north, and by the Central American nation of Guatemala on the south. It is divided into 11 municipalities. The capital city is also called Campeche.

Campeche has 523 kilometers (324 miles) of coastline and includes the Isla del Carmen, Isla Jaina, Islas Triángulo, and Cayos Arcos.

The state is primarily flat with low-lying mountains situated in the northern and eastern parts of the state. The highest elevation is at Cerro Champerico, which rises to about 390 meters (1,279 feet). The Meseta de Zohlaguna is a large plateau that stretches into Quintana Roo to the east. A great flat plain stretches to the south. The region also includes *cenotes,* natural pools that formed when water seeped through the limestone of underground caves.

There are small lakes throughout Campeche and the coastline is dotted with lagoons. The main rivers are the Candelaria and the Champotón. The Usumacinta forms the border with Tabasco. The Laguna de Términos lies on the southern part of the coastline with the Gulf of Mexico and is fed by several rivers, including the Candelaria.

2 Climate

The warm waters of the Gulf of Mexico contribute to the climate, which is generally warm and humid. The average temperature is 24°C to 28°C (76°F to 82°F). Annual rainfall averages 38 inches (96.5 centimeters). The highest monthly average rainfall occurs in August and September.

In the capital city of Campeche on the northwest coast, temperatures range from an average low of about 22°C (73°F) to an average high of 28°C (83°F). The annual average precipitation in the capital city is 88 centimeters (35 inches). Average temperatures in Ciudad del Carmen, along the southwest coast of the state, are similar to those in the capital; however, average rainfall is higher, at about 137 centimeters (54 inches) per year.

3 Plants and Animals

The jaguar population, most of which may be found in the Calakmul Biosphere Reserve, is estimated at four hundred. It is one the largest jaguar populations anywhere in the world. Alligators and manatees populate the coastal regions, while deer, rabbits, armadillos, and *tepezcuintles* (a type of small dog) can be found inland. Monkeys, pumas, parrots, and peacocks can be found in rain forest areas.

Orchids and other plants of the rain forest are native to the state. Cedar and mahogany stands can be found as well. In coastal regions there are mangroves and many types of palm trees.

4 Environmental Protection

The Calakmul Biosphere Reserve, on the southern border with Guatemala, is the largest tropical protected area in Mexico. The reserve, located 320 kilometers (200 miles) from the capital city, was created in 1989. The archeological zone of the reserve, known as the Ancient Maya City of Calakmul, was designated as a UNESCO World Heritage Site in 2002. Laguna de Términos, Playa Tortuguera Chenkán, and the Los Petenes biosphere are Ramsar Wetlands of International Importance.

Much of the forest areas in Campeche have been cut down and the wood used for housing materials and for cooking and heating. Forests were also cleared to make way for livestock. The government has instituted preservation programs to stop further environmental destruction. In 2003, there were over 3.2 million hectares (8.1 million acres) of rain forest in the state. In 2004, about 2,128 hectares (5,258 acres) of woodlands were damaged or destroyed by forest

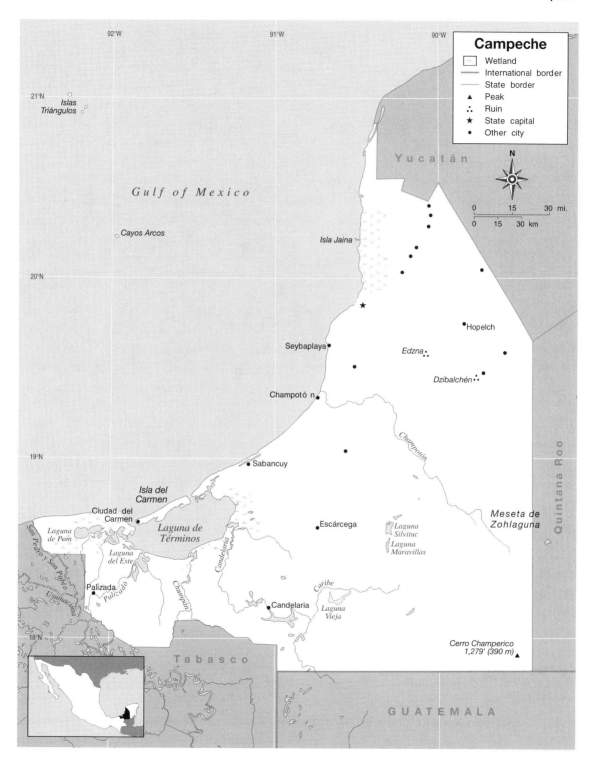

Campeche

- ☐ Wetland
- ⸺ International border
- ⸺ State border
- ▲ Peak
- ∴ Ruin
- ★ State capital
- ● Other city

N

0 15 30 mi.
0 15 30 km

Gulf of Mexico

92°W   91°W   90°W

21°N

Islas Triángulos

○ *Cayos Arcos*

Isla Jaina

20°N

Yucatán

★

●Hopelch

Seybaplaya●

Edzna ∴

Dzibalchén ∴

Champotón●

19°N

Champotón

Quintana Roo

●Sabancuy

Isla del Carmen

Ciudad del Carmen●

Laguna de Términos

Laguna de Pom

Laguna del Este

●Escárcega

Laguna Silvituc

Laguna Maravillas

Meseta de Zohlaguna

San Pedro y San Pablo

Candelaria

Champán

Palizada●

Palizada

Usumacinta

Caribe

Candelaria●

Laguna Vieja

18°N

Cerro Champerico 1,279' (390 m) ▲

T a b a s c o

G U A T E M A L A

Small cargo sailboat on the waters of the Bahía de Campeche (Bay of Campeche). © KAL MULLER/WOODFIN CAMP.

fires. An additional 455 hectares (1,124 acres) of pasture were also affected by fires that year.

In 2004, there were nine municipal sewage treatment plants in operation with a combined installed capacity of 97 liters per second (25.6 gallons per second). The volume of treated wastewater was about 37 liters per second (9.7 gallons per second). There were an additional 27 industrial wastewater treatment plants in operation that same year. As of 2004, about 87.1% of the population had access to safe drinking water.

5 Population, Ethnic Groups, Languages

Campeche had an estimated total population of 768,500 in 2006, ranking 30th among the states

and the Distrito Federal. About 49% of the population were men and 51% were women. About 55% of the population lived in urban areas. The population density was 14.8 people per square kilometer (38 people per square mile). In 2005, the capital, Campeche, had an estimated population of 238,850.

Most citizens speak Spanish as their first language. Campeche has a fairly large population of indigenous (native) people, primarily Mayan. About 12% of citizens speak some indigenous language. Of these, about 9% speak one of the Mayan languages.

6 Religions

According to the 2000 census, 71.3% of the population, or 432,457 people, were Roman

Catholic; 13.2%, or 79,994 people, were mainline or evangelical Protestants. About 4.7% were counted as other Biblical faiths, including 11,558 Seventh-day Adventists, 2,264 Latter-day Saints (Mormons), and 14,585 Jehovah's Witnesses. About 9.9% of the population claimed to have no religious affiliation.

7 Transportation

Campeche International Airport and Ciudad del Carmen Airport provide international flights to and from Campeche.

There are approximately 2,942 kilometers (1,839 miles) of paved roads and about 400 kilometers (250 miles) of railroad track, mostly serving tourists wishing to visit Mayan ruins. A highway, known historically as the royal highway, connects the two important cities on the Yucatán Peninsula—Campeche and Mérida. Other highways link the capital, Campeche, with Villahermosa, the capital of Tabasco. In 2004, there were 77,259 automobiles registered in the state, along with 1,073 passenger trucks, 38,881 freight trucks, and 14,126 motorcycles.

Cayo Arcas is one of Mexico's principal ports for exports. Laguna Azul is the port at Ciudad del Carmen.

8 History

The history of Campeche, which lies on the Yucatán Peninsula, begins in the era from 300 to 900 AD. The Maya built several cities in the Yucatán. The Toltec culture arrived in 987 AD, led by its leader Quetzalcóatl. Toltec became the dominate culture in the region before the arrival of the Spanish.

The first Spaniards to visit the region were the survivors of a shipwreck. Two survivors, Jerónimo de Aguilar and Gonzalo Guerrero, became incorporated into Mayan civilization. Guerrero married the daughter of the Chetumal tribal chief, and their son was the first officially recorded Mestizo (mixed Indian and Spanish) in Mexico. Jerónimo de Aguilar was later rescued by Spanish explorer Hernán Cortés's (1485–1547) expedition.

Spanish explorer Francisco de Montejo initiated the conquest of Yucatán in 1527. The Amerindian resistance was so strong that he fled. He returned three years later with his son, Francisco de Montejo y León, but was again unsuccessful in his effort to overpower the native Indians. A third attempt in 1537 proved successful. De Montejo founded the cities of Campeche in 1540 and Mérida in 1542. Franciscan priests (from an order of the Roman Catholic Church) built more than thirty convents in an effort to convert the indigenous people to the Catholic faith. Indigenous revolts during the colonial period consolidated Yucatán's reputation as a region whose fierce Indians would not easily surrender to Spanish rule. The Spanish built a wall around the city of Campeche to protect it from other European invaders and from indigenous warriors.

Yucatán did not participate in the independence movement of 1810. The Spanish authorities controlled the region and prevented any insurgencies. In 1821, with the Plan of Iguala, Yucatán was made a part of independent Mexico. After the Independence of Mexico, Campeche became one of the five important seats of government that formed Yucatán. Yucatán was formally made a state in 1823 and a new constitution became law in 1825. On August 7, 1857,

Xpuhil Tower on Structure I, part of the ancient ruins preserved in the Calakmul Biosphere Reserve. PETER LANGER.

civil war divided Campeche from Yucatán. A new region was created that was given the name Campeche, with the city of Campeche as the capital.

The constitution was written in 1861, and the Mexican Congress voted in favor of accepting Campeche as a state in 1862, during the presidency of Benito Juárez (1806–1872).

Under the long presidency of Porfirio Díaz (1830–1915), Campeche lost the Quintana Roo territory. Díaz made Quintana Roo a separate territory in 1902. Quintana Roo was returned to Campeche during the short Ortiz Rubio presidency (1930–32). Finally, President Lázaro Cárdenas, who held office from 1934 to 1940, separated Campeche and Quintana Roo permanently by making Quintana Roo an independent

entity, but not a state. Quintana Roo would not became a federal state until 1974.

Also in the mid-19th century, Campeche segregationists sought to force the central government to create a new province independent of Yucatán. Tomás Aznar, Pedro and Perfecto de Baranda, Francisco and Rafael Carvajal, Leando and Miguel Domínguez, and Irineo Lavalle were among the leaders of Campechean separation. Segregationist Campeche leaders occupied Mérida, the Yucatán capital, in the early 1860s.

The invasion of French troops into Mexico in the mid-1860s forced Campeche leaders to decide whether to join the occupying forces, as Yucatán had done, or to resist the foreign invaders. The city of Campeche was attacked and eventually overpowered by the French invading forces. Carlota, the French emperor's wife, visited Campeche during their short tenure as Mexican monarchs. Pro-republican forces occupied Campeche to fight against French emperor Maximilian (1832–1867) and the French invaders. The end of the war and the consolidation of power under Díaz did not bring peace to Campeche, however. From 1876 to 1910, twenty-five different governors ruled Campeche.

The discovery of oil fields off the coast turned Campeche into an extremely important area for the rest of Mexico. Military and political control of the state became central to any government that sought to exercise control over the rest of Mexico. Despite the local instability, the central government has continuously exercised direct control over the area where the oil fields are located.

During the Mexican Revolution (1910–20) Campeche witnessed confrontations by different factions. A new government assumed control of the state shortly before the Mexican Constitution was approved in 1917. Since then, the party that eventually became the Institutional Revolutionary Party (PRI) has exercised political control over Campeche.

When President Cárdenas permanently separated Quintana Roo from the old state of Campeche, opposition from some Campechean leaders to the move was countered by promises of industrial and economic incentives. The presence of the most important oil fields off the coast of Campeche has made the state into one of the most strategically important units of the Mexican federation.

Some efforts at forming guerrilla movements in the region were undertaken in the mid-1960s. The strategic economic importance of the state led the central government to heavily intervene in state politics and to exercise an unusual level of centralized control over the Campechean state affairs.

Following the passage of the North American Free Trade Agreement (NAFTA) in 1992, a trade agreement between Mexico, the United States, and Canada, Campeche became home to many new manufacturing enterprises. However the state remained heavily tied to the oil and natural gas industry.

In the first decade of the 21st century, this dependency began to lessen, as a new growth industry, tourism, began to flourish. Based on the state's ancient historical sites and ecological diversity, new hotels and support-related construction took place, which in turn, acted to broaden the state's economy. Mexico's largest political party, the Institutional Revolutionary Party (PRI), continued to retain control of the state's governorship.

9 State and Local Government

The state government is highly centralized and most powers reside with the governor, who is elected by popular vote for a six-year nonrenewable term. The state congress is comprised of 35 legislators elected in 21 single member districts and 14 multimember districts to promote the representation of minority parties. Legislators are elected for nonrenewable three-year terms. Although there is a formal, well-established separation of power with provisions for checks and balances, state governors have historically exercised strong influence over the legislative branch of government.

Comprised of 11 municipalities, local governments are restricted in their powers and attributions. In spite of this, the wave of democratization that swept Mexican politics since the early 1990s has also brought increased democratization to local governments in Campeche. Municipal presidents are elected for nonrenewable three-year terms as are municipal council members. The size of municipal councils varies according to the population of each municipality.

10 Political Parties

The three main political parties in all of Mexico are the Institutional Revolutionary Party (PRI), the National Action Party (PAN), and the Party of the Democratic Revolution (PRD). As in the rest of Mexico, the PRI heavily controlled politics in Campeche during most of the 20th century. Campeche's strategic importance as an oil producing region made the PRI political control of the state more evident than in most other states. The last two governors, Antonio González (1997–2003) and Jorge Carlos Hurtado Valdez (2003–09), both belonged to the PRI.

11 Judicial System

Comprised of a Superior Tribunal of Justice, an electoral tribunal, and local courts, the judicial system is autonomous and independent. Superior Tribunal justices are appointed by the governor with the legislature's approval. Appointees must be qualified lawyers with previous judicial experience. Appointments are made for six-year terms. After a term expires, if the justice is confirmed, he or she will continue in office for life or until a mandatory retirement age of 65.

12 Economy

Oil, natural gas, and tourism have replaced the state's more traditional economic activities, which were fishing, agriculture, cattle, and timber. The state's oil industry provides Mexico's state-owned oil company, Petroleos Mexicanos (PEMEX), with over 51% of its oil, and over 26% of its natural gas. A more recent development to the state's economy has been the development of tourism, specifically archeological and ecotourism. As of 2003, six hotels had been built and two more were under construction.

13 Industry

Campeche's industrial sector is dominated by the oil and natural gas industries, although the state does have a relatively small manufacturing sector, with its *maquiladoras* (assembly plants) largely involved with textiles. Other manufacturing activities involve leather products, and the extraction of non-metallic, and metallic minerals. There is also an agricultural product processing base, and a major bottling operation. The state's fishing industry is supported by shipyards, freezers, refrigerated warehouses, docks, and landing spaces for small vessels.

The state's handicraft industries produce wood furniture, pottery, cotton, embroidered textiles, silk and cotton threads for use in making hammocks and fishing nets, and tortoiseshell and coral handicrafts.

14 Labor

As of 2005, Campeche had 327,597 eligible workers. Some 318,972 were listed as employed and 8,625 were listed as unemployed. Unemployed workers in rural areas may not be counted, however. The unemployment rate that year was reported to be 2.6%. Of those who worked, services employed 38.6%, followed by agriculture at 23.4%, and commerce at 16.5%.

The US Bureau of Labor Statistics reported that Mexican workers saw their wages increase from $2.49 per hour in 2003 to $2.50 per hour in 2004. (The average US worker earned $15.70 per hour in 2004.) The maximum work week is set at 48 hours by law. The average worker spends 40 to 45 hours per week on the job. Workers earn twice their regular hourly rate for up to nine hours a week of overtime. When a worker works more than nine hours overtime in a week, he or she earns three times the regular hourly rate. After one year, workers are entitled by law to six days paid vacation. The capital city of Campeche has a reputation for friendly labor relations.

15 Agriculture

Agriculture and livestock are an important part of the economy in the northeast, where there is less rainfall. Fruit orchards produce mangoes, citrus fruits, watermelon, and papaya. Other crops grown in the state include corn, rice, sorghum, almonds, sugar cane, and cotton. Campeche was Mexico's leading producer of rice in 2004, producing 81,522 tons. The state also produced 272,186 tons of corn and 31,401 tons of sugar. Campeche is also a leading producer of honey, producing 5,323 tons of honey in 2004.

Livestock raising is relatively modest. In 2004, a total of 18,884 head of beef cattle were marketed, while 84,719 pigs, and 303 sheep were also marketed that year. Meat production was similarly modest at 21,785 tons of beef, 5,949 tons of pork, 404 tons of lamb, and 9,071 tons of poultry.

16 Natural Resources

The oil fields off the Campeche coast are the state's most important mineral resource.

Fishing is an important and growing activity, with facilities for shipping already in existence. There are refrigerated warehouses in the port areas, as well as training centers for fishermen. Fishery products include shrimp, sierra, sea bass, and shark. Large quantities of shrimp are exported to the United States. In 2003, the total fish catch was about 56,888 tons. Forestry is fairly substantial. In 2003, forest wood production was valued at an estimated $6.8 million.

17 Energy and Power

In 2005, there were 201,218 users of electricity in the state of Campeche. Of that total, the largest number were residential customers at 180,339. Sales of electricity that same year totaled 889,303 megawatt hours, of which the largest users were residential at 361,021 megawatt hours, followed by medium-sized industrial firms at 355,357 megawatt hours. All electric power generating plants in the state were gas-turbine facilities. Electricity is provided and distributed by the Federal Electricity Commission, and Central Light and Power. Both utilities are run by the Mexican government.

18 Health

In 2003, the state had 21 hospitals and 192 outpatient centers that were part of the national health system. In 2004, there were 1,040 doctors, 1,764 nurses, and 62 dentists working in these centers. There were an additional eight independent health centers in the state in 2004.

Most of the Mexican population is covered under a government health plan. The IMSS (Instituto Mexicano de Seguro Social) covers the general population. The ISSSTE (Instituto de Seguridad y Servicios Sociales de Trabajadores del Estado) covers state workers.

19 Housing

Most of the homes in the state are made of permanent materials such as stone, concrete, and brick. About 20% of all homes have wooden walls with some type of sheet metal as roofing material. In 2000, about 83.3% of all homes were owner-occupied. In 2005, there were an estimated 184,090 residential housing units in the state. About 88% of these units were single-family detached homes. The average household was estimated at 4.1 people.

20 Education

Public education is free for all students from ages 6 to 16 and most of the students in the state attend public schools. In 2004/05, it was estimated that 88.9% of age-eligible students completed primary school, which includes six years of study. About 74.5% of eligible students completed secondary school, which includes three years of study after primary school. About 56% of eligible students completed the *bachillerato*, which is similar to a high school diploma. The national average for completion of the *bachillerato* was 60.1% that year.

A university was established under Governor Alberto Trueba Urbina's administration (1955–61). It became known as the Universidad Autónoma de Campeche (Independent University of Campeche) in 1989. In 2005, there

were about 26,291 students age 20 or older who were enrolled in some type of higher education program. The overall literacy rate was estimated at 88% in 2005.

21 Arts

Campeche has about 15 auditoriums for the performing arts. There are about six cultural centers, two of which are located in the city of Carmen. The *jarana,* the traditional dance of Campeche, is performed at many of the cultural centers. Many local markets sell crafts made by local artisans. There are also about 22 registered movie theaters, including multiscreen theaters and single-screen galleries.

22 Libraries and Museums

In 2003, there were 102 libraries in the state with a combined book stock of 610,830 volumes. The same year, there were 13 museums registered in Campeche that had permanent exhibits. Museo de la Cultura Maya is housed inside of the Fort of San Miguel. Museo de la Ciudad focuses on the history of the city of Campeche.

23 Media

In 2005, the capital city, Campeche, had three daily newspapers: *Cronica, Novedades de Campeche*, and *Tribuna de Campeche*. The *Tribuna del Carmen* is published in Ciudad del Carmen. In 2004, there were 13 television stations and 16 radio stations (14 AM and 2 FM). In 2005, there were about 46,484 subscribers to cable and satellite television stations. Internet service is not widely available, but several companies had begun offering access as of 2003. In 2005, there were about 63,601 residential phone lines, with about 10.5 mainline phones in use for every 100 people.

24 Tourism, Travel, and Recreation

The city of Campeche is an old fortified colonial city surrounded by walls that were meant to protect it from pirate attacks. The historic city center was designated as a UNESCO World Heritage site in 1999. Tourists can visit the many citadels (fortresses) and thick-walled fortifications (called *baluartes*). There are also many Mayan ruins as a result of Spain's attempt to convert the natives to Christianity. The museum at San Miguel Fort has a collection of pre-Columbian artifacts. There are also Mayan ruins in the town of Edzna, where visitors can see the Temple of Five Stories. The ruins at Calakmul is one of the largest known ancient Mayan city sites. Calakmul was established as a World Heritage site in 2002.

25 Sports

The Piratas (Pirates) of Campeche play in the Mexican League of AAA minor league baseball. The Campeche Bucaneros (Buccaneers) play in the Southern Division of the National Professional Basketball League (LNBP). In 2004, there were about 50 sports centers in the state.

26 Famous People

Notable citizens born in Campeche include lawyer and politician Pablo García Montilla (1824–1895), who was involved in the establishment of the state's government and judicial system; lawyer and journalist Justo Sierra (1848–1912), one of the founders of the University of Mexico; Impressionist painter Joaquin Clausell (1866–1935); writer and folk historian Juan de la Cabada Vera (1899–1986); and musician and historian Francisco Alvares Suarez (1838–1916).

27 Bibliography

BOOKS

Gassos, Dolores. *The Mayas*. Philadelphia, PA: Chelsea House Publishers, 2005.

Green, Jen. *Caribbean Sea and Gulf of Mexico*. Milwaukee, WI: World Almanac Library, 2006.

Gruber, Beth. *Mexico*. Washington, DC: National Geographic, 2006.

Treto Cisneros, Pedro. *The Mexican League: Comprehensive Player Statistics, 1937–2001*, bilingual edition. Jefferson, NC: McFarland, 2002.

WEB SITES

Government of Mexico. *Mexico for Kids*. www.elbalero.gob.mx/index_kids.html (accessed on March 30, 2007).

Mexican Tourism Board. *Visit Mexico: Campeche*. www.visitmexico.com/wb/Visitmexico/Visi_Campeche (accessed on March 30, 2007).

Chiapas

PRONUNCIATION: chee-AH-pahs.

ORIGIN OF STATE NAME: The name of Chiapas is taken from the ancient city of Chiapan, which in Náhuatl means the place where the chia (a kind of sage) grows.

CAPITAL: Tuxtla Gutiérrez.

ENTERED COUNTRY: 1841.

COAT OF ARMS: The coat of arms was initially the emblem of Ciudad Real, now known as San Cristóbal de las Casas, a colonial city located one and one-half hours away from the capital of Tuxlta Gutiérrez. It was founded in 1535 by the Spaniards. The lions, castle, and crown represent the power and authority held by King Carlos V (1500–1558) of Spain.

HOLIDAYS: Año Nuevo (New Year's Day—January 1); Día de la Constitución (Constitution Day—February 5); Benito Juárez's birthday (March 21); Primero de Mayo (Labor Day—May 1); Anniversary of the Battle of Puebla (1862), May 5; Revolution Day, 1910 (November 20); and Navidad (Christmas—December 25).

FLAG: There is no official flag.

TIME: 6 AM = noon Greenwich Mean Time (GMT).

1 Location and Size

Chiapas is situated in southern Mexico. It has an area of 73,289 square kilometers (28,297 square miles). It ranks as 10th in size among the states and covers about 3.7% of the total land area of Mexico. It is slightly smaller than the US state of South Carolina. Chiapas is bordered on the north by the state of Tabasco, on the south by the Pacific Ocean, on the east by the Central American nation of Guatemala, and on the west by the states of Oaxaca and Veracruz. Chiapas is divided into 118 municipalities. Its capital, Tuxtla Gutiérrez, lies near the center of the state.

Chiapas has a coastal plain (*llanura costera*) along the Pacific Ocean to the south. The coastline extends for 256 kilometers (159 miles). In the north, the coastal plain of the Gulf of Mexico begins in Tabasco and extends into Chiapas. The Sierra Madre de Chiapas is a chain of high volcanic mountains that run through the southwestern portion of the state along the coastline. The highest peak is the Volcán Tacaná (4,080 meters/13,385 feet in elevation), which lies on

The spectacular Cañon del Sumidero (Sumidero Canyon) was formed by the Grijalva River. HENK SIERDSEMA/ SAXIFRAGA/EPD PHOTOS.

the border with Guatemala. Tacaná is also the 10th highest peak in the country. The Montañas del Norte de Chiapas run through the northeastern portion of the state. Between the two chains lies the Depresión Central de Chiapas. The Grijalva River flows northwest through this region and passes through the state of Tabasco to empty into the Bahía de Campeche. There are a few major dams (*presas*) along the Grijalva that have formed major lakes, including Presa la Angostura (also known as the Dr. Belasario Domínguez) and Presa Netzahualcóyotl (or Malpaso). These are the two largest dams in the country. The spectacular Cañon del Sumidero (Sumidero Canyon) was formed by the Grijalva River. La Selva Lacandona is a rain forest located on the east-central border with Guatemala.

2 Climate

Temperatures are fairly constant year round, with variation depending on elevation. The north is dry with little rainfall, but the southern part of the state is more humid. The average temperature is 20°C (68°F), but temperatures may reach as high as 40°C (104°F) and as low as 0°C (32°F).

3 Plants and Animals

Orchids and bromeliads (plants of the pineapple family) are native to the tropical areas of the state. Mangrove trees are also native. The rain forest area has jaguars, flying squirrels, monkeys, white-tailed deer, tapirs, toucans, and parrots. At higher elevations there are hardwood trees such as mahogany and cedar. Crocodiles and hundreds of species of birds live along the Pacific coast.

4 Environmental Protection

In 2003, the state contained about 3.9 million hectares (8.1 million acres) of woodland, including over 2.1 million hectares (5.3 million acres) of rain forest. In 2004, about 610 hectares (1,507 acres) of woodland were damaged by forest fires. About 11,600 hectares (28,664 acres) of pasture and brush lands were damaged or destroyed by fires the same year.

Protecting the diverse plant and wildlife of the state has been an important issue. In the

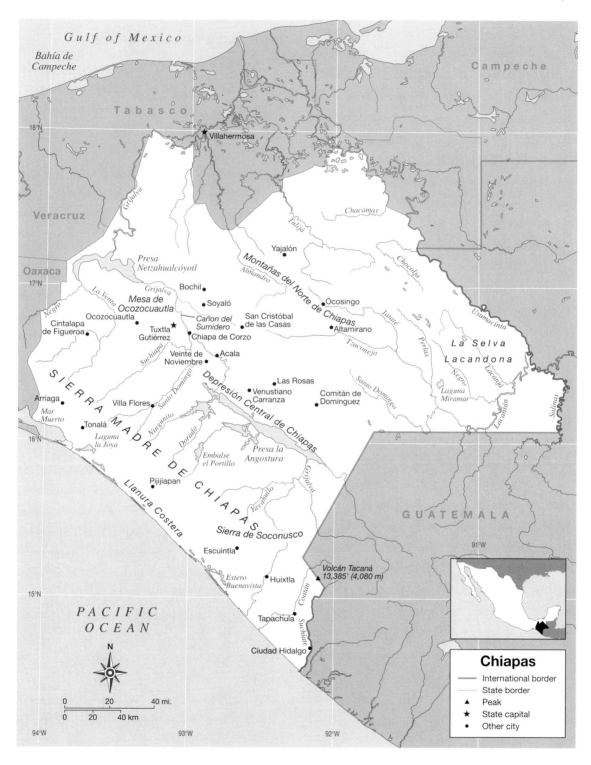

Gulf of Mexico

Bahía de Campeche

Campeche

Tabasco

18°N ★ Villahermosa

Veracruz

Grijalva

Oaxaca

17°N

Presa Netzahualcóyotl

Chacamax

Tulijá

Yajalón

Montañas del Norte de Chiapas

Almandro

Grijalva

Bochil

La Venta

Mesa de Ocozocuautla

Soyaló

Ocosingo

Chocolja

Negro

Ocozocuautla

Cañon del Sumidero

San Cristóbal de las Casas

Jataté

Usumacinta

Cintalapa de Figueroa

Tuxtla Gutiérrez ★

Chiapa de Corzo

Altamirano

La Selva Lacandona

Veinte de Noviembre

Acala

Tsaconejo

Perlas

Negro

Suchiapa

Santo Domingo

Lacantún

Las Rosas

Laguna Miramar

Arriaga

Villa Flores

Venustiano Carranza

Comitán de Dominguez

S I E R R A   M A D R E   D E   C H I A P A S

Ningunito

Santo Domingo

Salinas

Mar Muerto

Tonalá

Laguna la Joya

Dorado

Depresión Central de Chiapas

16°N

Embalse el Portillo

Presa la Angostura

Pijijiapan

Grijalva

GUATEMALA

Yayahuita

91°W

L l a n u r a   C o s t e r a

Sierra de Soconusco

Escuintla

Estero Buenavista

Volcán Tacaná 13,385' (4,080 m)

15°N

Huixtla

Coatán

PACIFIC OCEAN

N

Tapachula

Suchiate

Ciudad Hidalgo

Chiapas

— International border
  State border
▲ Peak
★ State capital
● Other city

0   20   40 mi.
0   20   40 km

94°W   93°W   92°W

1990s, Chiapas began to protect and preserve its cloud forests (forest at high elevations) and coastal areas. The El Triunfo Biosphere Reserve is located in the south in the Sierra Madres. It ranks as one of the most important cloud forests in the Americas and encompasses approximately 119,177 hectares (294,492) acres. La Encrucijada Biosphere Reserve is located in the Pacific coastal area of Chiapas and covers 144,868 hectares (283,845) acres. This reserve offers the tallest mangroves on the Pacific coast and healthy numbers of crocodiles, jaguars, raccoons, and iguanas. It was designated as a Ramsar Wetland of International Importance in 1996. As of 2006, there were three other Ramsar sites in the state, including Lagunas de Montebello and the Cañón del Sumidero. The most recent additions to the list of protected areas in the state include the Selva de Ocote (2000), a rain forest reserve along the Grijalva River basin, and the biosphere reserve surrounding Volcán Tacána (2003), a volcanic peak along the border with Guatemala. La Selva Lacandona along the east-central border is known for its biodiversity.

In 2004, there were nine municipal sewage treatment plants in operation with a combined installed capacity of 1,109 liters per second (292.9 gallons per second). The volume of treated wastewater was about 851 liters per second (224.8 gallons per second). There were an additional 11 industrial wastewater treatment plants in operation in the state the same year. As of 2004, about 78.4% of the population had access to safe drinking water.

5 Population, Ethnic Groups, Languages

Chiapas had an estimated total population of 4,362,500 in 2006, ranking seventh among the states and the Distrito Federal. About 49% of the population were men and 51% were women. Only about 34% of the population lived in urban areas. The population density was 59 people per square kilometer (152 people per square mile). In 2005, the capital, Tuxtla Gutiérrez, had a population of 503,320.

As of 2006, about 23% of the population spoke an indigenous (native) language. Chiapas had the third-largest population of indigenous language speakers in the country (after the Mexican states of Oaxaca and Yucatán). The most common indigenous languages were Tzeltal, Tzotzil, and Chol.

6 Religions

According to the 2000 census, 63.8% of the population, or nearly 2.1 million people, were Roman Catholic. The state had the highest percentage of mainline and evangelical Protestants in the country at 13.9%, or 457,736 people. About 8% were counted as other Biblical faiths, including 173,772 Seventh-day Adventists, 5,316 Latter-day Saints (Mormons), and 82,646 Jehovah's Witnesses. Chiapas also had the highest percentage of people who claimed to have no religious affiliation, with about 13.1%.

A temple of the Church of Jesus Christ of Latter-day Saints was dedicated in Tuxtla Gutiérrez in 2000.

7 Transportation

Most of the state's 7,000 kilometers (4,375 miles) of highways are paved. Many rural areas are accessible only by rough dirt roads. In 2004, there were 148,178 automobiles registered in the state, along with 4,371 passenger trucks, 122,977 freight trucks, and 9,681 motorcycles.

Tuxtla Gutiérrez–Llano San Juan Airport provides international flights to and from Chiapas.

8 History

Human presence in Chiapas dates as far back as 600 AD. Located in the heart of the region of Mayan influence, Chiapas was home to some of the most important Mayan ceremonial centers, like Palenque, Bonampak, Yaxchilán, and Lacanjá. Chiapa Indians eventually conquered the territory. By the 15th century, Aztecs dominated the area, but they were not able to rule over the Chiapa.

When the Spaniards arrived, the Chiapa and a number of other indigenous groups inhabited different parts of the Chiapas region. After several years of fierce fighting between the Spanish and the indigenous peoples (1522–1528), the Spanish conquistadores (conquerors) dominated enough land to found a city, Villa Real, known today as San Cristóbal. As part of Guatemala in the 17th century, the indigenous people in Chiapas continued to stage revolts against Spanish occupation. In 1712, several groups waged a bloody war on the Spanish colonizers, fighting against slavery and other forms of oppression.

Chiapas was highly identified with Spanish colonial rule and connected to its south-ern neighbor, Guatemala. So Chiapas did not immediately join the drive for Mexico's independence. Catholic priest Matías Antonio de Córdoba declared independence from Spanish rule in 1821. A plebiscite (vote) in 1824 ratified Chiapas's union with Mexico. A new state constitution was created in 1826. Despite Guatemala's protest, Chiapas was fully incorporated into Mexico in 1841.

Conflicts between the colonial landowners and the indigenous people continued throughout the 19th century. The Mexican Revolution, which started in 1910, barely extended to Chiapas. Nevertheless, large landowners in Chiapas actively participated in the debates that surrounded the conflicts. Many revolutionary leaders demanded reform of the way farm land was distributed and used. Indigenous groups did not join the revolution in favor of land reform demands.

When the revolution came to an end, the Institutional Revolutionary Party (PRI) emerged as the only important political party. An alliance between PRI leaders and large Chiapas landowners prevented the land reforms from reaching Chiapas and benefiting the indigenous communities. Chiapas remained one of the poorest states, with one of the largest indigenous populations. In Chiapas, unlike other states, the indigenous population remained autonomous and experienced little interaction with the local government, controlled primarily by the landed state elite.

An indigenous revolt triggered by the enactment of the North American Free Trade Agreement (NAFTA), a trade agreement between Mexico, the United States, and Canada, caused worldwide controversy in 1994. The indigenous armed revolt, initiated on January 1, 1994, com-

Chiapas was home to important Mayan ceremonial centers, like this one at Palenque. HENK SIERDSEMA/SAXIFRAGA/EPD PHOTOS.

bined opposition to globalization, rejection of free trade, and indigenous demands for land, respect, and political and cultural autonomy. The Zapatista Army of National Liberation (EZLN) was led by a popular revolutionary leader known as Marcos and by several indigenous leaders. Although the movement successfully brought indigenous demands and concerns over their values and cultural traditions to the forefront of the international debate, the movements' ambitious goals of evolving into a new national revolutionary force that could topple the PRI government eventually failed when the rest of Mexico experienced a process of democratic consolidation starting in the mid 1990s and ending with the PRI defeat in the 2000 presidential elections.

In January 2003, about 20,000 masked militants from the EZLN moved into San Cristóbal. They carried machetes and sticks and lit bonfires in the center of the city to protest government actions. The EZLN protests government treatment of indigenous people.

Well into the first decade of the 21st century, Chiapas remained a state in turmoil, as federal troops continued to maintain a presence in the state. Reports of atrocities against the state's Amerindian population continued to surface, and there were warnings that violent revolution could take place if the state's problems with poverty were not addressed by the federal government. Fueling the turmoil was Chiapas's position as the poorest state in Mexico. In addition, its porous border with Guatemala allowed many

Central Americans to illegally cross into Mexico, creating opportunities for smugglers.

9 State and Local Government

The state governor is the most influential and powerful political figure. Elected for a nonrenewable six-year term, the governor is the chief executive. A ministerial cabinet is appointed by and accountable to the governor. Formal separation of power and check-and-balance provisions also provide for a unicameral (one chamber) legislature. The state congress is comprised of 40 deputies. Twenty-four are elected in single-member districts and 16 are elected at large for proportional representation. All deputies serve for nonrenewable three-year terms.

Comprised of 118 municipalities, Chiapas is one of the most ethnically diverse states in Mexico. Local governments have strong power to determine their own rules, especially in the independent indigenous communities. Political conflicts resulting from the opposition of federal authorities to increased power by indigenous communities regularly force courts to assess the limits of local authorities in exercising power.

10 Political Parties

The three main political parties in all of Mexico are the Institutional Revolutionary Party (PRI), the National Action Party (PAN), and the Party of the Democratic Revolution (PRD). The PRI, in association with large traditional land-owning families, exercised political control of the state throughout most of the 20th century. The 1994 indigenous revolt propelled the Zapatista Army of National Liberation (EZLN) to the forefront of national and state politics. The EZLN rejects electoral politics as a legitimate means of reaching power. This helped the two national opposition parties, the conservative PAN and the leftist PRD, to gain ground and capitalize on discontent against the PRI. Former PRI leader, Pablo Salazar, won the 2000 gubernatorial election with support from the PAN and PRD.

11 Judicial System

The Supreme Tribunal of Justice is the highest court in Chiapas. Its members are appointed by a two-thirds majority in the legislature from a three-person list presented by the governor. Supreme Tribunal justices serve nonrenewable seven-year terms. In addition, the Chiapas judicial system includes an electoral tribunal, a civil service tribunal, and local and indigenous courts. There are additional complexities resulting from Chiapas's strong indigenous presence. The indigenous communities use alternative courts and legal systems.

12 Economy

The economy of the state of Chiapas is primarily agricultural and resource based. Although there is some crude oil production, manufacturing, and small-scale handicrafts, agriculture is the main activity engaged in by the state's residents, much of it intended to meet local needs. Coffee is the main export. The state is considered the poorest of all the Mexican states.

13 Industry

In 2002, the state's first maquiladora (assembly plant) opened in San Cristóbal to manufacture sweaters and T-shirts for sale in the United States. Overall, however, there is little industry in Chiapas. The existing industries involve the manufacture of furniture, canned shrimp, flour, cheese, sugar and honey, wooden toys, leather bags, pottery, embroidered textiles, metal handicrafts, and household goods.

14 Labor

Many workers in Chiapas live in homes with no electricity or running water. They are among the lowest paid workers in Mexico.

As of 2005, Chiapas had 1,619,927 eligible workers. Some 1,586,076 were listed as employed and 33,851 were listed as unemployed. Unemployed workers in rural areas may not be counted, however. The unemployment rate that year was reported to be 2%. Of those who were working, agriculture employed 42%, followed by services at 28.3% and commerce at 16.1%.

The US Bureau of Labor Statistics reported that Mexican workers saw their wages increase from $2.49 per hour in 2003 to $2.50 per hour in 2004. (The average US worker earned $15.70 per hour in 2004.) The maximum work week is set at 48 hours by law. The average worker spends 40 to 45 hours per week on the job. Workers earn twice their regular hourly rate for up to nine hours a week of overtime. When a worker works more than nine hours overtime in a week, he or she earns three times the regular hourly rate. After one year, workers are entitled by law to six days paid vacation.

15 Agriculture

Coffee is Chiapas's most valuable agricultural product. The state produces most of Mexico's coffee and is a leading producer of cacao, the product used to make chocolate.

Other crops grown in Chiapas include sugarcane, cotton, bananas, and other fruits. These are grown especially in the lowland regions near the Pacific coast. Some land is also devoted to pasture for livestock, where cows, pigs, and poultry are raised. In the Depresión Central region, corn, beans, sugarcane, and mangos are grown. There is also livestock breeding. In the northern mountains, coffee, corn, cacao, bananas, meat, and cheese are produced, while in the eastern mountains, honey from bees, pears, apples, peaches, vegetables, and flowers are raised. In the northern Gulf of Mexico coastal plain, avocados, beans, cacao, bananas, and corn are grown, and cattle are bred.

Chiapas was Mexico's largest producer of bananas in 2004, with 830,520 tons produced. In that same year it was a leading producer of corn at, 1,353,159 tons, and of sugar, at 243,106 tons. Livestock production is also important to the state. In 2004, a total of 98,235 head of beef cattle and 18,199 pigs were marketed. Milk from dairy cows totaled 324 million liters (85 million gallons). Honey production totaled 3,377 tons in 2004.

16 Natural Resources

Chiapas has rich natural resources, including tropical rain forests, oil, gas, uranium, iron, aluminum, copper, and amber. One-third of Mexico's crude oil is produced by Chiapas.

Lumber production more than doubled in the 1990s. In 2003, the total value of forest wood was about $3.7 million. Almost 90% of the lumber produced is pine. Fishing for shrimp, mullet, and sea bass is carried out in the coastal Pacific Ocean waters. In 2003, the total fish catch was about 30,500 tons.

17 Energy and Power

All electricity produced in the state is generated by seven hydroelectric plants. In 2005, there were 1,012,229 users of electricity in the state. Of that total, the largest number were residential customers at 928,505. Sales of electricity that same year totaled 2,037,629 megawatt hours, of which the largest users were residential at 1,059,053 megawatt hours. Electricity is provided by the Federal Electricity Commission and Central Light and Power. Both utilities are run by the Mexican government.

A 210-megawatt hydroelectric plant was scheduled to begin operation at Copainalá in 2008. Mexico's existing natural gas reserves are located primarily in the southwestern states of Tabasco and Chiapas.

18 Health

In 2003, the state had 42 hospitals and 1,612 outpatient centers that were part of the national health system. In 2004, there were 2,295 doctors, 5,115 nurses, and 283 dentists working in these centers. There were an additional 66 independent health centers in the state in 2004.

Most of the Mexican population is covered under a government health plan. The IMSS (Instituto Mexicano de Seguro Social) covers the general population. The ISSSTE (Instituto de Seguridad y Servicios Sociales de Trabajadores del Estado) covers state workers.

Government health care services are not always available in zones where there is conflict between the government and rebels.

19 Housing

Most homes in the state have concrete, brick, or stones walls, with sheet metal being the most popular roofing material. Flat roofs of stone, concrete, or tile constructions are also popular. Between 30% to 40% of homes do not have piped water or adequate sanitary drainage systems. In 2000, about 83% of all homes were owner-occupied. In 2005, there were an estimated 916,302 residential housing units in the state. About 93% of these units were single-family detached homes. The average household was estimated at 4.7 people.

20 Education

Public education in Mexico is free for students from ages 6 to 16 and most of the students in the state attend public schools. In 2004/05, it was estimated that 82% of age-eligible students completed primary school, which includes six years of study. About 78% of eligible students completed secondary school, which includes three years of study after primary school. About 67.3% of eligible students completed the *bachillerato*, which is similar to a high school diploma. The national average for completion of the *bachillerato* was 60.1% that year.

Children in the small Mayan communities in rural areas may attend local schools specifically structured to preserve Mayan language and culture.

There are at least six major institutions of higher education in the state, including the Autonomous University of Chiapas and the Chiapas State University of Arts and Sciences. In 2005, there were about 92,797 students age 20 or older who were enrolled in some type of higher education program. The overall literacy rate was estimated at 78.6% in 2005, the lowest rate in the country that year.

21 Arts

The state of Chiapas hosts at least three major theaters for the performing arts including El Teatro de Bellas Artes and Teatro de la Ciudad Emilio Rabasa. The Cultural Center of Chiapas Jaime Sabines, named for the well-known poet, hosts art exhibits and performances of all types. There is also a chapter of the French cultural society, Alianza Francesa, in the capital city of Tuxtla Gutiérrez. The Coro de Cámara Canto Nuevo (Choir of New Song) was founded in 2002. There are over 60 registered movie theaters, including multiscreen theaters and single-screen galleries.

An International Marimba Festival is held in the capital each year. The Festival of San Cristóbal de las Casas is a two-week event featuring marimba music and events highlighting the Tzotzil and Tzetzal cultures.

22 Libraries and Museums

In 2003, there were 246 libraries in the state with a combined stock of 2,037,689 volumes. In 2003, there were six museums registered in the state that had permanent exhibits. The Amber Museum displays objects created by local craftsman and artists. The Chiapas Regional Museum and the Eliseo Palacios Aguilera Paleontology Museum are located in Tuxtla Gutiérrez. There is a museum in Palenque that features items found in the nearby archeological zone.

23 Media

In 2005, the capital, Tuxtla Gutiérrez, had five daily newspapers: *La República en Chiapas*, *Novedades de Chiapas*, *El Sol de Chiapas*, *La Tribuna*, and *La Voz del Sureste*. Tapachula had two daily newspapers: *Sur de Mexico* and *Noticias de Chiapas*. Other papers in the state included the *Ecos del Valle* in Cintalapa.

Television networks Televisa, TV Azteca, and Polytechnic broadcast in the state. There is limited cable service in the cities. In 2004, there were 77 television stations and 50 radio stations (36 AM, 13 FM, and 1 shortwave). In 2005, there were about 49,968 subscribers to cable and satellite television stations. Also in 2005, there were about 187,347 residential phone lines, with about 5.4 mainline phones in use for every 100 people. This was the lowest number of phones per population in the nation for that year.

24 Tourism, Travel, and Recreation

Tuxtla Gutiérrez is the home of the 17th-century Cathedral of San Marcos. The church tower has marching statues of the twelve apostles, which move to mark every hour, accompanied by 48 church bells. One of the best zoos in the country, the Miguel Alvarez del Toro Zoo in Tuxtla Gutiérrez, has an interesting collection of native animals. Nearby, the town of Chiapa de Corzo features the archeological site of an ancient Mayan ceremonial ground. The prehistoric city found in the National Park of Palenque is a UNESCO World Heritage Site.

25 Sports

The Jaguares from Tuxtla Gutiérrez play in the First Division of the Mexican Football (soccer) Association (commonly known as Femexfut). The Jaguares play in the Victor Manuel Reyna stadium, which holds 25,000 people. The Ocelotes of the Autonomous University of Chiapas are a Second Division soccer team of Femexfut.

26 Famous People

Emilio Rabasa (1856–1930), from Ocozocoautla, who became governor and ambassador to the United States, was a prominent legal scholar. Poet Jaime Sabines (1926–1999) was born in Tuxtla Gutiérrez. The rebels of the Zapatista Army of National Liberation (EZLN) take their name from Emiliano Zapata (1879–1919), born in Morelos, who was the leader of a revolution in the early 20th century. Miguel Alvarez del Toro (1917–1996) was a prominent naturalist; the zoo in Tuxtla Gutiérrez is named in his honor.

Belisario Domínguez (1863–1913) was a Mexican physician and senator. He was assassinated a few days after circulating a letter condemning the actions of the dictator Victoriano Huerta. In 1953, President Adolfo Ruiz Cortines established the Belisario Domínguez Medal of Honor. It is the highest award that is given by the Mexican government.

27 Bibliography

BOOKS

Carew-Miller, Anna. *Famous People of Mexico.* Philadelphia: Mason Crest Publishers, 2003.

Gruber, Beth. *Mexico.* Washington, DC: National Geographic, 2006.

Jacobson, Marcey. *The Burden of Time: Photographs from the Highlands of Chiapas.* Stanford, CA: Stanford University Press, 2001.

Moon Handbooks: Yucatán Peninsula. Emeryville, CA: Avalon Travel Pub, 2002.

Nantus, Sheryl. *The Pacific South States of Mexico.* Stockton, NJ: Mason Crest Publishers, 2003.

WEB SITES

Government of Mexico. *Mexico for Kids.* www.elbalero.gob.mx/index_kids.html (accessed on March 30, 2007).

Mexican Tourism Board. *Visit Mexico: Chiapas.* www.visitmexico.com/wb/Visitmexico/Visi_Chiapas (accessed on March 30, 2007).

Chihuahua

PRONUNCIATION: chee-WAH-wah.

ORIGIN OF STATE NAME: Uncertain. May come from the Nahuatl word for "dry, sandy place."

CAPITAL: Chihuahua.

ENTERED COUNTRY: 1824.

COAT OF ARMS: The coat of arms is shield-shaped, with a red border. Across the top is a depiction of the old aqueduct of Chihuahua. In the center section a head of a Spaniard (left) and an Amerindian (right) represents the mestizo, or blending of two peoples; the lower third depicts Chihuahua Cathedral.

HOLIDAYS: Año Nuevo (New Year's Day—January 1); Día de la Constitución (Constitution Day—February 5); Benito Juárez's birthday (March 21); Primero de Mayo (Labor Day—May 1); Anniversary of the Battle of Puebla (1862), May 5; Revolution Day, 1910 (November 20); and Navidad (Christmas—December 25).

FLAG: There is no official flag.

TIME: 5 AM = noon Greenwich Mean Time (GMT).

1 Location and Size

Chihuahua, the largest state, lies in northern Mexico. It has an area of 247,514 square kilometers (95,565 square miles), about one-third the size of the US state of Texas. It covers about 12.6% of the total land area of Mexico. Chihuahua is bordered on the north by the US states of New Mexico and Texas, on the south by the Mexican state of Durango, on the east by the Mexican state of Coahuila, on the west by the Mexican state of Sonora, and on the southwest by the Mexican state of Sinaloa. Chihuahua has 67 municipalities. Its capital is also called Chihuahua.

The natural regions of Chihuahua are plateau and mountains (sierras). The Sierra Madre Occidental runs north and south through the western portion of the state. The highest peak, Cerro Mohinora (3,300 meters/10,826 feet) is located in the southwest corner of the state. The Sierra El Huseo and the Sierra Grande run north and south along the northeastern portion of the state. At the east-central border lies the Llano (plains) de los Caballos Mestenós. A desert area known as the Bolsón de Mapimí, is located in the southeastern corner of the state. Most of the rest of the state is made up of high plateau.

Copper Canyon. PETER LANGER.

Rivers run generally west from the mountains and reach the Golfo de California. These rivers include the Papigochic, Urique, Batopilas, and Bassasseachi. The Conchos River joins the Río Bravo (known as the Rio Grande in the United States) along the Texas border. The Río Bravo flows east to the Gulf of Mexico. Laguna El Barreal is one of the largest lakes.

2 Climate

The climate is dry to semi-arid although there is regular rainfall. The average annual temperature is 20°C (68°F). Annual rainfall ranges from 221 millimeters (8.7 inches) to 1,023 millimeters (40.3 inches). In the capital city of Chihuahua, the average annual temperature ranges from a low of 13°C (56°F) to a high of 25°C (78°F).

3 Plants and Animals

In the high plateau region and on the plains, native plants include lechuguilla (an evergreen), mesquite (a common desert shrub), guayule (a rubber producing plant), and ocotillo (a succulent plant with red flowers). Native animal life includes lizards, rattlesnakes, and small birds and animals such as quail, shrews, rabbits, squirrels, skunks, wild boars, and porcupines.

In the mountains, native plants include pine and fir trees, poplars, and white cedar trees. Native animals include bats, moles, rats, bears, white-tailed deer, wolves, gray foxes, raccoons,

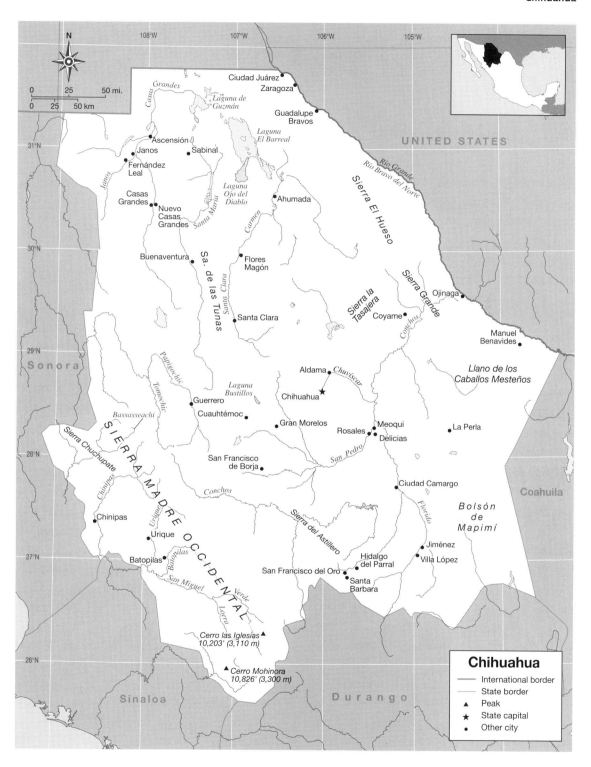

Chihuahua

— International border
---- State border
▲ Peak
★ State capital
● Other city

and squirrels. There are nearly 300 species of migratory and native birds, including spotted owls and blue-throated hummingbirds, along with over eighty species of reptiles.

4 Environmental Protection

Chihuahua has air quality problems in certain areas where there is heavy traffic. Many roads are not paved and trucks create dusty conditions. In the border area around El Paso, Texas, and Ciudad Juárez, Chihuahua, safety of the water supply is sometimes threatened. The Conchos River, which eventually joins the Río Grande, is polluted by wastewater. In 2004, there were 73 municipal wastewater treatment plants in operation with a combined installed capacity of 5,206 liters per second (1,375 gallons per second). The volume of treated wastewater was about 3,954 liters per second (1,044 gallons per second). There were an additional 21 industrial wastewater treatment plants in operation the same year, handling a volume of about 287 liters per second (75.8 gallons per second). As of 2004, about 95.4% of the population had access to safe drinking water.

In 2003, the state had over 7.5 million hectares of woodland (18.7 million acres), including 505,251 hectares (1.24 million acres) of rain forest. In 2004, about 182 hectares (449 acres) of woodland were damaged or destroyed by forest fires. Over 3,900 hectares (over 9,600 acres) of pasture and brush lands were affected by fires that year as well.

Protected areas include two national parks, Cascada de Bassasseachi and Cumbres de Majalca, and four nature reserves, Cañón de Santa Elena, Papigochic, Campo Verde, and Tutuaca.

After the North American Free Trade Agreement (NAFTA) was passed in 1992, the Border Environmental Cooperation Commission (BECC) was created to protect the environment in the border areas where development was rapid.

5 Population, Ethnic Groups, Languages

Chihuahua had an estimated total population of 3,392,400 in 2006, ranking 11th among the states and the Distrito Federal. About 51% of the population were men and 49% were women. About 79% of the population lived in urban areas. The population density was 13 people per square kilometer (34 people per square mile). In 2005, the capital, Chihuahua, had an estimated population of 758,791. Most people in Chihuahua speak Spanish, but a small percentage (3.2%) speak indigenous languages. About 85% of the indigenous language-speakers are Tarahumara.

6 Religions

According to the 2000 census, 84.6% of the population, or over 2.2 million people, were Roman Catholic; about 7.1%, or 185,665 people, were mainline or evangelical Protestants. About 2% were counted as other Biblical faiths, including 5,817 Seventh-day Adventists, 12,016 Latter-day Saints (Mormons), and 34,006 Jehovah's Witnesses. About 5% of the population claimed to have no religious affiliation. The Catedral Metropolitana in the capital city is the seat of a Roman Catholic archdiocese. Mormon temples were dedicated in Colonia Juárez in 1999 and in Ciudad Juárez in 2000.

The Roman Catholic cathedral in the capital, Chihuahua, is built of pink stone. It took almost 100 years to build. PETER LANGER.

7 Transportation

The network of highways and roads is over 16,985 kilometers (10,615 miles) and connects all parts of the state. Over 2,200 kilometers (1,375 miles) of railroad serves the state, especially the tourists areas. By the end of 1910 there were three rail lines in operation. In 1961, the completion of the Chihuahua-Pacifico, known as ChP or Chepe, changed life in Chihuahua. Now remote areas could be reached and both mining and tourism expanded. In 1998, Ferromex, a private company, took over control of the railroad from the government.

In 2004, there were 581,940 automobiles registered in the state, along with 5,332 passenger trucks, 342,933 freight trucks, and 4,318 motorcycles.

There is an international airport in the city of Chihuahua.

8 History

When the Spaniards first arrived, Chihuahua was inhabited by more than 100 different indigenous groups. Among them were the Taraumara, Apache, Comanche, and Guarojío. The first Spaniard to visit was Alvar Nuñez Cabeza de Vaca, whose expedition covered territory from the US state of Florida to the Mexican state of Sinaloa.

The Chihuahua Pacifico Railway. PETER LANGER.

The first Spanish settlements date back to the 16th century, when haciendas (country estates) and mining centers were first established. Some Franciscan (Roman Catholic) missions and the Carapoa villages (which are now a single town) were also founded in the mid 1500s. In 1598, the military garrisons known as El Paso and Ciudad Juárez were first built. Yet, the Spanish colonizers only loosely controlled the region during most of the 16th century.

The growth of the mining industry in the 17th century generated more economic activity but also provoked more indigenous uprisings. Tensions developed between the miners and the hacienda owners, who were interested in forcing indigenous groups to work as slaves. The interest Roman Catholic priests had in converting the indigenous people motivated several interventions by the Spanish crown to reduce tensions in the region.

The Independence War provoked Chihuahua hacienda owners and miners to side with the royalist forces against the independence movement. Yet, by 1821 the inevitable Mexican independence led leaders in Chihuahua to join the new country. The Plan of Iguala of 1821 established the framework that consolidated the new republic. Later, the region of Durango was separated from Chihuahua to create a new province. Chihuahua officially became a state of Mexico in 1824. The first state constitution was ratified in 1825.

An ethnic war that sought to exterminate Apache and Comanche indigenous people in 1830 caused much bloodshed. It almost entirely achieved its goal, nearly wiping out the indigenous population. After Texas achieved independence, Chihuahua resisted an effort to annex the state to the United States. Yet, the Treaty of Guadalupe Hidalgo in 1848 gave the United States a significant part of a territory previously considered part of Chihuahua. With the help of Chihuahua's governor Luis Terrazas, liberal national leader Benito Juárez (1806–1872) resisted the French occupation in Chihuahua in the mid-1860s.

Chihuahua was a central battleground during the Mexican Revolution (1910–20). There was discontent against the Díaz regime, but the historic tensions with neighboring Coahuila, Madero's home state, were strong as well. This tension prevented the discontent against the central government from becoming a fueling force for the revolution in Chihuahua. Yet, even the United States sent troops to the state and occupied it for almost a year. Peasant revolutionary leader Francisco Villa (1878–1923), known as Pancho Villa, extensively fought in Chihuahua. He demanded land distribution and recognition of the peasants as legitimate actors in Mexican politics. Villa's famous military Northern Division was first assembled in Chihuahua.

After the revolution, Chihuahua remained a center of Institutional Revolutionary Party (PRI) influence. Its location close to the United States made it a strategic state for Mexico. It also allowed for the development and eventual consolidation of the oldest and most important opposition party during PRI rule, the National Action Party (PAN). Chihuahua leader Luis H. Álvarez became the PAN presidential candidate in 1958, after an unsuccessful run for the state governorship. This showed Chihuahua's emergence as a center of active political opposition against the ruling PRI. Economic development was strong in the cities and along the Texas border during the 1960s through the 1990s, but people in rural areas continued to live in poverty.

In 1992, Chihuahua was one of the first states to elect a governor who was not a member of the PRI. However, in 2004 the PRI regained the governorship when José Reyes Baeza Terrazas was elected governor. The North American Free Trade Treaty (NAFTA), a trade agreement between Mexico, the United States, and Canada, was signed in 1992 and took effect in 1994. Because Chihuahua shares a border with the United States, much economic development occurred in the state after NAFTA was signed. However, small farmers found it difficult to compete in the North American competitive market.

In the first decade of the 21st century, Chihuahua continued to reap both the benefits and problems that came with the growth of industry, spurred-on by NAFTA. Pollution and economic inequalities continued to trouble the state, particularly for those living along the state's border with the United States. In addition, violent crime linked to drug smuggling also became a problem.

9 State and Local Government

The governor's office is powerful. The governor is democratically elected every six years for a nonrenewable term. In addition, a 33-member state congress is comprised of members elected for nonrenewable three-year terms. Twenty-two of the members are elected in single member districts and 11 in proportional representation. Separation of power provisions have strengthened and consolidated since the election of a non-PRI governor in 1992. Politics in Chihuahua are among the most democratic among the Mexican states, since there are two strong parties.

Chihuahua is comprised of 67 municipalities that vary in range and population. Elections for municipal presidents and council members are held every three years and immediate re-election is not allowed. The competitive nature of politics at the state level has allowed the development of strong municipal governments.

10 Political Parties

The three main political parties in all of Mexico are the Institutional Revolutionary Party (PRI), the National Action Party (PAN), and the Party of the Democratic Revolution (PRD). Chihuahua was the second state in Mexico to elect a non-PRI governor in the post-revolution period. After a contested election in 1986 where the PRI candidate emerged as winner, PAN's Francisco Barrio won the 1992 gubernatorial election. In 1998, Patricio Martínez García, a PRI militant, was elected governor, demonstrating the consolidation of a two party system in the state. José Reyes Baeza Terrazas of the PRI was elected as governor in 2004.

11 Judicial System

The Superior Tribunal of Justice is the highest court in the state. By law it must be made up of at least nine members. They are appointed by the legislature from a three-person list submitted by the executive in consultation with the legislature. Once ratified after their first three-year

period, justices cannot be removed until a mandatory retirement age of 65. In addition, there is an electoral tribunal. Local courts complete the state judicial system.

12 Economy

The state of Chihuahua's economy is one of the most industrialized and fastest growing in all of Mexico, due in part to its proximity to the United States. The economy benefits from its 582 mile-long (936.6 kilometers) border with the US states of Texas and New Mexico. Traditionally, timber production and raising livestock were the main components of the economy, but as of 2003, they represented less than 10% of the state's economic activity. *Maquiladoras* (assembly plants) that produce electronic components, automobile parts, and textile goods are now the primary economic activities. There are also a number of large breweries in the state. Tourism has also become an important and growing segment of the economy ever since railroad travel to the Copper Canyon area was upgraded following privatization of the railroad in 1998. As of 2003, the gross domestic product (GDP) for the state of Chihuahua was put at around $6.2 billion.

However, people living along the border often find barely enough water for drinking and cooking. There is much poverty in rural areas.

13 Industry

Manufacturing in the state of Chihuahua is centered largely in the cities of Ciudad Juárez and the capital city of Chihuahua. The state is home to over 1,000 manufacturers, of which there are 550 *maquiladoras* (assembly plants) that produce electronics, automobile parts, and wood products. As of 2003, there were 298 *maquiladoras* in Ciudad Juárez alone, employing 208,077 people.

The state's handicrafts industry produces woolen textiles, leather products, basketwork, wooden products, toys, and musical instruments.

14 Labor

As of 2005, Chihuahua had 1,351,070 eligible workers. Some 1,322,624 were listed as employed and 28,446 were listed as unemployed. Unemployed workers in rural areas may not be counted, however. The unemployment rate that year was reported to be 2%. Of those who were working, services employed 36.7%, followed by manufacturing at 23.1%, and commerce at 18.3%.

The US Bureau of Labor Statistics reported that Mexican workers saw their wages increase from $2.49 per hour in 2003 to $2.50 per hour in 2004. (The average US worker earned $15.70 per hour in 2004.) The maximum work week is set at 48 hours by law. The average worker spends 40 to 45 hours per week on the job. Workers earn twice their regular hourly rate for up to nine hours a week of overtime. When a worker works more than nine hours overtime in a week, he or she earns three times the regular hourly rate. After one year, workers are entitled by law to six days paid vacation.

After the North American Free Trade Agreement (NAFTA) was signed in 1992, relations between management and labor have been strained in the state. Statewide, about 40% of the state's *maquiladoras* are unionized. However, in the capital city of Chihuahua, less than 10%

of the plants are unionized. In Ciudad Juárez, the city's workforce was largely non-union, and only 5% of the workforce belonged to the Mexican Workers Union (CMT).

15 Agriculture

Despite its arid (dry) climate, agriculture is still an important segment of the economy. Chihuahua farmers in the semi-arid coastal areas to the west produce sugarcane, oats, potatoes, wheat, cotton, corn, sorghum, peanuts, soy, alfalfa, and green chilies. In the valleys of eastern Chihuahua, farmers raise peaches, melons, nuts, and apples. More than 30 species of apples are grown in the state. In 2004, Chihuahua was Mexico's top producer of green chilies at 450,016 tons, second in potatoes at 213,242 tons, and a leading producer of corn at 745,696 tons.

Ranchers raise both beef and dairy cattle, as well as pigs, goats, and sheep on a smaller scale. Chihuahua is also an important producer of milk and cheese. In 2004, a total of 803 million liters (212 million gallons) of milk was produced from dairy cows, while egg production totaled 7,597 tons, and honey output came to 1,164 tons. Livestock brought to market in 2004 totaled 100,029 head of beef cattle, 39,834 pigs, and 839 sheep. In that same year, the state produced 71,779 tons of beef, 7,843 tons of pork, and 7,445 tons of poultry.

16 Natural Resources

Forestry is an important economic activity in Chihuahua. In 2003, the value of forest wood production was over $138 million, the second-highest value in the country (after Durango). Pine accounts for almost 96% of the wood harvest. The fishing industry is fairly small, with a catch of only about 681 tons in 2003.

Chihuahua is known for its gold and silver mines. It is the country's second-largest silver producer after Zacatecas. Silver, lead, and zinc are produced at the Naica mine. Grupo Mexico operates two lead zinc mines, which both produce silver as a byproduct.

Petroleos Mexicanos (Pemex), the state oil company, is the world's fifth-largest oil company and the single most important entity in the Mexican economy. Pemex's natural gas pipeline connects to the US natural gas pipeline at nine locations, crossing the border into California, Arizona, and Texas (at the Chihuahua border at Ciudad Juárez, among other locations).

17 Energy and Power

In 2005, there were 1,018,183 users of electricity in the state Chihuahua. There were 904,832 residential customers. Sales of electricity that same year totaled 8,773,872 megawatt hours, of which the largest users were medium-sized firms at 3,859,452 megawatt hours. There were nine operating electric power generating plants in Chihuahua, of which the Samalayuca II plant was the largest with an effective installed capacity of 522 megawatts. Electricity is provided and distributed by the Federal Electricity Commission, and Central Light and Power. Both utilities are run by the Mexican government.

18 Health

In 2003, the state had 48 hospitals and 501 outpatient centers that were part of the national health system. In 2004, there were about 2,541 doctors, 5,741 nurses, and 154 dentists working in these centers. There were an additional 54 independent health centers in the state in 2004.

Most of the Mexican population is covered under a government health plan. The IMSS (Instituto Mexicano de Seguro Social) covers the general population. The ISSSTE (Instituto de Seguridad y Servicios Sociales de Trabajadores del Estado) covers state workers.

19 Housing

Most homes are made of concrete, brick, and stone walls and floors, with flat roofs of similar materials. However, there are a large number of homes with adobe walls and sheet metal roofs. A type of wooden-shingled roof construction known as *tejamanil*, or a shake roof, is also used. In 2000, about 78% of all homes were owner-occupied. In 2005, there were an estimated 852,596 residential housing units in the state. About 88% of these units were single-family detached homes. The average household was estimated at 3.8 people.

20 Education

Public education in Mexico is free for students ages 6 to 16 and most students in the state attend public schools. In 2004/05, it was estimated that 85.3% of age-eligible students completed primary school, which includes six years of study. About 76.6% of eligible students completed secondary school, which includes three years of study after primary school. About 51.9% of eligible students completed the *bachillerato*, which is similar to a high school diploma. The national average for completion of the *bachillerato* was 60.1%.

There are at least seven major institutions of higher education in the state. The Universidad Autónoma de Chihuahua celebrated its 50th anniversary in 2004. In 2005, there were about 109,927 students ages 20 and older who were enrolled in some type of higher education program. The overall literacy rate was estimated at 94% in 2005.

21 Arts

In 2004, there were at least five major theaters for the performing arts in the state. Popular theaters include el Teatro de Camara del Instituto de Bellas Artes, which is an open-air theater, and el Teatro de Héroes, an older theater of Victorian design that hosts operas, plays, music, and various types of theatrical presentations. There are over 133 registered movie theaters, including multiscreen theaters and single-screen galleries.

22 Libraries and Museums

In 2003, there were 367 libraries in the state with a combined stock of 2,189,952 volumes. The same year, there were 10 museums registered in Chihuahua that had permanent exhibits, including the Museum of the Mexican Revolution and the Museum of Sacred Art. There is also the Museum of Northern Culture, which is located near the archeological site of Paquimé.

23 Media

In 2005, the capital city, Chihuahua, had three daily newspapers: *Diario de Chihuahua* (*Chihuahua Daily*), *El Heraldo de Chihuahua* (*Chihuahua Herald*), and *El Heraldo de la Tarde* (*Afternoon Herald*). Ciudad Juárez published *El Mexicano*, Delicias published *Diario de Delicias*,

and Ciudad Cuauhtemoc published *El Heraldo*. In 2004, there were 106 television stations and 83 radio stations (54 AM and 29 FM). In 2005, there were about 103,788 subscribers to cable and satellite television stations. Also in 2005, there were about 533,544 residential phone lines, with about 19.5 mainline phones in use for every 100 people.

24 Tourism, Travel, and Recreation

The city of Creel is the entryway to the western Sierra Madre mountain range known as Copper Canyon (Barranca del Cobre or Sierra Tarahumara). There are many tours of this region, which has six massive gorges that form a canyon system that is four times as large as the Grand Canyon of the United States. Four of the six canyons are deeper than the Grand Canyon. Copper Canyon takes its name from the copper-colored lichen (a type of mossy plant) that grows on the canyon walls. The culture of the indigenous Tarahumara people also attracts tourists to the area. The Paquimé archeological zone in Casas Grandes is a UNESCO World Heritage site.

25 Sports

The Indios (Indians) of Ciudad Juárez play in the First Division "A" of the Mexican Football (soccer) Association (commonly known as Femexfut). Their home field is at Benito Juárez Stadium, which seats 20,000. There is also a 7,500-seat bullfighting ring. Ciudad Juárez has a baseball team (Los Gallos de Pelea) and a 15,000-seat bullfighting ring in the Plaza Monumental.

26 Famous People

Francisco "Pancho" Villa (1878–1923) was not born in Chihuahua but earned his reputation as a revolutionary leader in Chihuahua and Durango. Actor Anthony Rudolph Oaxaca Quinn (1915–2001) was born in Chihuahua but moved at age four to Los Angeles, California. His films included *Zorba the Greek* and *Lawrence of Arabia.* David Alfaro Siqueiros (1896–1974), a well-known muralist, has works at the National Preparatory School, Mexico City, and the Plaza Art Center in Los Angeles, California. Eduardo Nájera (1976) is a forward for the NBA Denver Nuggets.

27 Bibliography

BOOKS

Day-MacLeod, Deirdre. *The States of Northern Mexico.* Philadelphia, PA: Mason Crest Publishers, 2003.

Fisher, Richard D., et al. *The Copper Canyon, Chihuahua, Mexico.* Tucson, AZ: Sunracer, 2003.

Green, Carl R. *The Mission Trails in American History.* Berkeley Heights, NJ: Enslow Publishers, 2001.

Gruber, Beth. *Mexico.* Washington, DC: National Geographic, 2006.

Marcovitz, Hal. *Pancho Villa.* Philadelphia, PA: Chelsea House Publishers, 2003.

McNeese, Tim. *The Rio Grande.* Philadelphia, PA: Chelsea House, 2005.

WEB SITES

Government of Mexico. *Mexico for Kids.* www. elbalero.gob.mx/index_kids.html (accessed on March 30, 2007).

Mexican Tourism Board. *Visit Mexico: Chihuahua.* www.visitmexico.com/wb/Visitmexico/Visi_ Chihuahua (accessed on March 30, 2007).

Coahuila

PRONUNCIATION: koh-ah-WEE-lah.

ORIGIN OF STATE NAME: The natives living in the territory were the Coahuilas. The Spaniards named them Coahuiltecos and called the territory New Extremadura. They later renamed it Coahuila.

CAPITAL: Saltillo.

ENTERED COUNTRY: 1917.

COAT OF ARMS: The lower section depicts walnut trees growing near the Monclova River, seen at sunrise to depict the state rising up after the Mexican Revolution. The Spanish town known as San Francisco de Coahuila (later renamed Monclova) was founded on the banks of the river; it was the capital of Coahuila for many years. In the left panel an oak tree and two wolves represent Biscay, the home province of many of the Spanish settlers. The right panel features a lion and a column, with a banner bearing the words Plus Ultra (Higher).

HOLIDAYS: Año Nuevo (New Year's Day—January 1); Día de la Constitución (Constitution Day—February 5); Benito Juárez's birthday (March 21); Primero de Mayo (Labor Day—May 1); Anniversary of the Battle of Puebla (1862), May 5; Revolution Day, 1910 (November 20); and Navidad (Christmas—December 25).

FLAG: There is no official flag.

TIME: 6 AM = noon Greenwich Mean Time (GMT).

1 Location and Size

Coahuila, in northern Mexico, has an area of 151,563 square kilometers (58,518 square miles), about the same size as the US state of Michigan. It ranks as third in size among the states and covers about 7.7% of the total land area of Mexico. Coahuila is bordered on the north by the US state of Texas; on the east by the Mexican state of Nuevo León; on the south by the Mexican states of Zacatecas, Durango, and San Luis Potosí; and on the west by the Mexican state of Chihuahua. Coahuila has 38 municipalities. Its capital is Saltillo.

The state is crossed from north to south by the Sierra Madre Oriental, a mountain range that cuts through most of Mexico. Individual ranges within the state include the Sierra del Carmen, the Sierra El Pino, Sierra del Cristo, Sierra de la Gloria, and the Sierra de la Gavia. A series of

Bilbao dunes. © ROBERT FRERCK/WOODFIN CAMP.

lesser mountain chains run to the west of these and a region of plains are found to the east.

Coahuila also has desert plains with sand dunes. The Bolsón de Mapimí desert is an enormous desert region shared with Chihuahua to the west. The fertile Comarca Lagunera region, which extends into the neighboring state of Durango, lies in the southwest. Around the city of Viseca in the southwest are the Bilbao sand dunes, which were created by the erosion of the surrounding mountains of Sierra de Parras and Sierra Jimulco.

The most important rivers are the Rio Bravo (known as the Rio Grande in the United States) along the Texas border, Sabinas, San Rodrigo, San Diego, Castaños, and Patos Rivers. Presa de la Amistad is an artificial lake created by a river dam along the Rio Bravo.

2 Climate

Temperatures average 12°C (53°F) in January and 23°C (73°F) in June and July. Annual rainfall averages 610 millimeters (24 inches), much of which falls during September and October. In the capital city of Saltillo, the average annual temperature is 17°C (62°F) and the average rate of precipitation is 37.3 centimeters (14.6 inches) per year.

3 Plants and Animals

Pine and oak trees are found in the more temperate climate areas of the state. Palm groves are

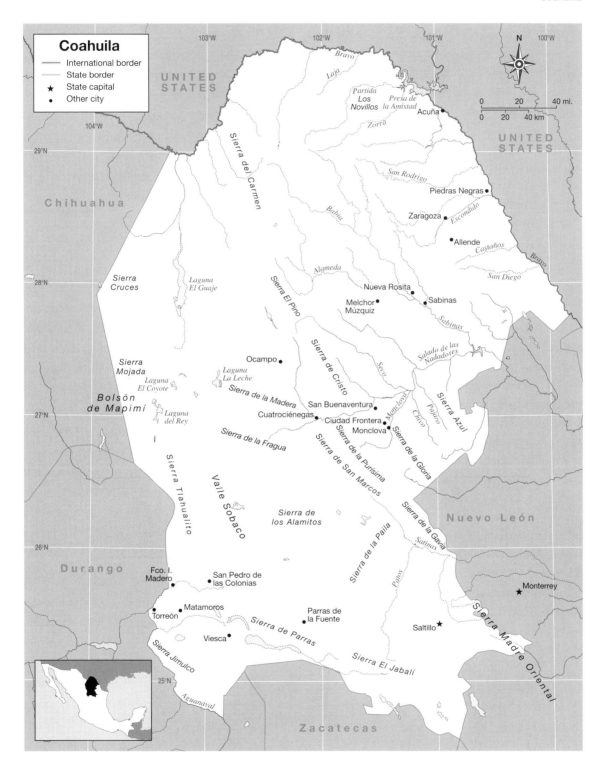

Coahuila

- International border
- State border
- ★ State capital
- • Other city

UNITED STATES

UNITED STATES

Bravo

Laja

Partida Los Novillos

Presa de la Amistad

Zorra

Acuña

29°N

104°W

103°W

102°W

101°W

100°W

N

0   20   40 mi.
0   20   40 km

Chihuahua

Sierra del Carmen

San Rodrigo

Piedras Negras

Zaragoza

Escondido

Allende

Castaños

Bravo

Bahía

Alameda

San Diego

28°N

Sierra Cruces

Laguna El Guaje

Sierra El Pino

Nueva Rosita

Melchor Múzquiz

Sabinas

Sabinas

Salado de las Nadadores

Sierra Mojada

Laguna El Coyote

Laguna La Leche

Ocampo

Sierra de la Madera

Sierra de Cristo

Sexo

Sierra Azul

Bolsón de Mapimí

Laguna del Rey

San Buenaventura

Cuatrociénegas

Ciudad Frontera

Monclova

Monclova

Chivo

Pájaro

Sierra de la Gloria

27°N

Sierra de la Fragua

Sierra de San Marcos

Sierra de la Purísima

Sierra de la Gavia

Sierra Tlahualilo

Valle Sobaco

Sierra de los Alamitos

Sierra de la Palla

Salinas

Nuevo León

26°N

Durango

Fco. I. Madero

San Pedro de las Colonias

Pájaros

Monterrey

Matamoros

Torreón

Parras de la Fuente

Sierra de la Gavia

Saltillo

Sierra Madre Oriental

Viesca

Sierra de Parras

Sierra Jimulco

25°N

Sierra El Jabalí

Aguanaval

Zacatecas

found in more tropical regions. The fibers of the ixtle plant (a type of cactus) are used for handicrafts. In the eastern region, pecan trees and cypress can be found along the rivers. There are many types of low shrubs.

Tortoises nest in the coastal areas and the waters are filled with all kinds of marine life. Animal life ranges from bears to prairie dogs, wild boars, wolves, raccoons, deer, and *berrendos* (which resemble deer). Bird species include dwarf parrots, heron, a variety of geese and ducks, roadrunners, and eagles. The hot, dry desert supports rattlesnakes as well.

4 Environmental Protection

As one of the states that borders the United States, Coahuila participates in the Border Environmental Cooperation Commission (BECC). Environmental issues include safety of the water supply and management of hazardous waste. Air pollution is generated by the burning of sugarcane fields.

In 2004, there were seven municipal wastewater treatment plants in operation in the state with a combined installed capacity of 3,160 liters per second (834 gallons per second). The volume of treated wastewater was about 2,435 liters per second (643 gallons per second). There were an additional 72 industrial wastewater treatment plants in operation that year with a volume of about 623 liters per second (164 gallons per second). As of 2004, about 99.2% of the population had access to safe drinking water.

In 2003, the state had about 444,121 hectares (1 million acres) of woodland, including 2,650 hectares (6,548 acres) of rain forest. In 2004, about 358 hectares (884 acres) of woodland and pasture were damaged or destroyed by fires. The largest protected area in the state is the Maderas del Carmen, a nature reserve covering about 208,381 hectares (514,920 acres) and containing a mixture of woodlands and pasture. The nature reserve at Cuatrociénegas is listed as a Ramsar Wetland of International Importance. Balneario Los Novillos is a small national park (42 hectares/103 acres) protecting an area of walnut trees, willows, and poplars.

5 Population, Ethnic Groups, Languages

Coahuila had an estimated total population of 2,545,100 in 2006, ranking 16th among the states and the Distrito Federal. The population was divided almost evenly between men and women. About 90% of the population lived in urban areas. The population density was 16.8 people per square kilometer (43.5 people per square mile). In 2005, the capital, Saltillo, had a population of 648,929. Almost all residents speak Spanish. A small percentage of people speak one of the Amerindian languages, such as Náhuatl and Mazahua.

6 Religions

According to the 2000 census, 86.4% of the population, or over 1.7 million people, were Roman Catholic; 6.8%, or 137,388 people, were mainline or evangelical Protestants. About 1.8% were counted as other Biblical faiths, including 1,862 Seventh-day Adventists, 8,108 Latter-day Saints (Mormons), and 25,370 Jehovah's Witnesses. About 3.8% of the population claimed to have no religious affiliation.

7 Transportation

Three major highways connect the cities within Coahuila and connect Coahuila to its neighboring states. The capital, Saltillo, is linked by railroad to other major cities in the state, as well as to Monterrey in Nuevo León, Nuevo Laredo in Tamaulipas, and Mexico City. In 2004, there were 381,762 automobiles registered in the state, along with 33,631 passenger trucks, 201,232 freight trucks, and 4,275 motorcycles.

There are two airports. Ramos Arizpe airport is 15 minutes away from Saltillo. Plan de Guadalupe International Airport, also near Saltillo, provides air service to Mexico City and to the Texas cities of Dallas, Forth Worth, and Houston.

8 History

When the Spaniards arrived in the mid-1500s, Coahuila was mostly inhabited by groups of hunters and gatherers. In the Lagunera Comarca region, indigenous people had constructed villages. They practiced rudimentary agriculture and fishing.

The Spaniards settled in the region in the late 16th century, when the city of Santiago del Saltillo del Ojo del Agua was founded. The Spaniards brought native people from neighboring Zacatecas to promote settlements, since the natives of Coahuila tended to migrate while hunting animals and gathering food. The conquest of territories by the Spaniards progressed slowly throughout the 17th century. In 1675, Saltillo mayor Antonio Balcárcel Rivadeneyra led an expedition that took control of the Río Bravo and ventured into what is now Texas.

When independence was declared in central Mexico in 1810, Coahuila mostly ignored the conflict between royalists (people loyal to Spain) and patriots (people interested in independence for Mexico). Landowners were more concerned with fighting indigenous revolts and transforming the precarious economy into a productive agricultural region. In 1811, Mariano Jiménez led troops in a movement to promote and consolidate independence in northern Mexico (including Texas). The failure of this effort caused Coahuila to remain under royalist control until 1821. That year the Plan of Iguala allowed for the consolidation of an independent Mexico.

When it declared independence in 1835, Texas was a territory under the jurisdiction of Coahuila. When the Mexican-American War (1846–48) broke out after Texas was annexed to the United States, leading the Mexicans was general and politician Antonio López de Santa Anna (1794–1876). Santa Anna abandoned the patriots of Saltillo, Coahuila, and they were left alone to resist US occupying forces. US troops occupied Saltillo until the war was over and the Guadalupe Hidalgo treaty was signed in 1848. In the treaty, Coahuila ceded all its territories north of the Río Bravo. Although some leaders in Coahuila had expressed their intent to join Texas as part of the United States, most preferred to remain a part of Mexico.

Coahuila leader Francisco Madero (1873–1913) published *Presidential Succession,* a book that eventually launched his presidential candidacy in 1910. Some people believed that Porfirio Díaz (1830–1915), who had been leading the country as a dictator since 1876, should be replaced. Madero, angry about Díaz's rule, called for a revolution on November 20, 1910. Madero was elected president in 1911 but was assassinated two years later. His ally, Venustiano Carranza (1859–1920), successfully took control of Mexico and declared victory in the revolution. After a new constitution took effect in 1917, Carranza's national reputation grew. He became the first elected president of Mexico after the revolution.

Since it was the home state of two of the most important leaders of the Mexican Revolution (Madero and Carranza), Coahuila occupied an important role in Mexican history. It was also one of the key states where the dominant political party in Mexican politics, the Institutional Revolutionary Party (PRI), developed and grew. In the first decade of the 21st century, Coahuila remained a political stronghold for the PRI.

Since 1994 when the North American Free Trade Agreement (NAFTA) went into effect, Coahuila greatly benefited from the trade pact, becoming one of Mexico's leading industrial states. However, NAFTA has also made the state heavily dependent upon the market in the United States for its products.

Social issues also took center stage in Coahuila. In January 2007, the state legislature passed a bill that made Coahuila the first state to legalize same-sex civil unions. The bishop, speaking on behalf of the Roman Catholic Church in Coahuila, denounced the bill.

9 State and Local Government

The constitution dates from 1818, but reforms were adopted in 1951. Since then, the executive power has been vested in a governor, elected democratically every six years for a nonrenewable term. The legislature is comprised of a 35-member chamber of deputies. Twenty of the deputies are elected in single member districts and the remaining fifteen by proportional representation. Deputies are elected for nonrenewable three-year terms.

There are 38 municipalities. Municipal governments are relatively weak, as the state government exercises enormous influence over local authorities. Municipal presidents and councilors are elected for three-year terms and immediate reelection is not allowed.

10 Political Parties

The three main political parties in all of Mexico are the Institutional Revolutionary Party (PRI), the National Action Party (PAN), and Party of the Democratic Revolution (PRD).

The PRI has exercised absolute control in Coahuila. The 26 governors who have occupied the office since revolutionary leader Venustiano Carranza abandoned the governorship to become president of Mexico have all belonged to the PRI. PRI candidate Humberto Moreira Valdés was elected in 2005.

11 Judicial System

The judiciary is independent in theory. Historically the judicial system has been under the control of the state governor. The Superior Tribunal of Justice is comprised of seven members appointed for nonrenewable six-year terms by the governor, with legislature approval. Only qualified attorneys can be appointed. The tribunal president is elected for a three-year term and can be reelected once. There is also an electoral tribunal. Local courts complete the state's judicial system.

12 Economy

The mining, agriculture, and manufacturing sectors are all important to the state's economy. Coahuila is a leading steel producer, serving automotive manufacturers. Coahuila also has many assembly plants, known as *maquiladoras*. In addition, the state's agricultural and livestock sectors have benefited from the state's irrigation system. The state also has a well developed highway and rail systems, as well as access to several international airports.

13 Industry

Manufacturing of automobiles developed as an important industry in the state after 1992 when the North American Free Trade Agreement (NAFTA) was signed. There are stamping plants, engine production plants, and vehicle assembly plants. Over 30% of the cars and trucks produced in Mexico come from Coahuila. The state also produces over one-third of Mexico's steel, which supplies manufacturing facilities operated by US automakers General Motors and DaimlerChrylser. There were about 200 *maquiladoras* (assembly plants) employing about 100,000 workers in 2003.

Much of the state's manufacturing is centered in the cities of Torreon (motor vehicles, steel, aluminum, and ceramic products), Saltillo (mining, smelting, cotton mills, and textile plants), Monclova (steel and aluminum products), Ramos Arizpe (automotive, steel, and iron works), and Acuna (electronics and mining).

The state's handicraft industries produce woolen textiles, household goods, and products made from ixtle fiber. The production of wine and liquor is centered in Parras and Cuatrocienagas

14 Labor

As of 2005, Coahuila had 981,213 eligible workers. Some 935,120 were listed as employed and 46,093 were listed as unemployed. Unemployed workers in rural areas may not be counted, however. The unemployment rate was reported to be 4.9%. Of those who were working, services employed 38.5%, followed by manufacturing at 25.1%, and commerce at 19.7%.

The US Bureau of Labor Statistics reported that Mexican workers saw their wages increase from $2.49 per hour in 2003 to $2.50 per hour in 2004. (The average US worker earned $15.70 per hour in 2004.) The maximum work week is set at 48 hours by law. The average worker spends 40 to 45 hours per week on the job. Workers earn twice their regular hourly rate for up to nine hours a week of overtime. When a worker works more than nine hours overtime in a week, he or she earns three times the regular hourly rate. After one year, workers are entitled by law to six days paid vacation.

In the southeast region of the state, two labor unions were active: the Mexican Workers Confederation (CTM) with 37,000 members, and the Revolutionary Workers and Peasants Confederation (CROC), with 6,000 members.

15 Agriculture

Agriculture remains a leading economic activity in the state. Cotton, potatoes, grapes, watermelons, apples, alfalfa, wheat, oats, corn, sorghum, and nuts are among the state's agricultural crops. Several dams have been built to create reservoirs that can be used for irrigation. In 2004, the state of Coahuila produced 50,849 tons of corn,

22,999 tons of red tomatoes, and 14,857 tons of sorghum.

Dairy cattle are raised to supply the state's three large milk-processing plants. Cattle and goats are raised in the state's desert region. In 2004, the state was Mexico's second leading producer of milk from dairy cows at 1 billion liters (264 million gallons). Goat's milk production reached 52 million liters (13 million gallons) that year. Coahuila produced 52,184 tons of eggs. Beef cattle brought to market numbered 133,372 and pigs numbered 41,051.

16 Natural Resources

Mining is an important part of the economy of Coahuila. Although coal accounts for only 4% of Mexico's total energy requirements, the majority of the country's coal reserves are located in Coahuila. Other minerals mined in Coahuila include iron, titanium, feldspar, barium oxide, lead, fluorite, and dolomite.

Fishing is a fairly small industry, with only about 1,624 tons of fish caught in 2003. All of the catch was for human consumption. Forest wood production in 2003 was valued at about $814,000.

17 Energy and Power

In 2005, there were 764,050 users of electricity in the state of Coahuila. There were 682,851 residential customers. Sales of electricity totaled 8,372,547 megawatt hours, of which the largest users were large industrial firms at 3,107,321 megawatt hours. There are a total of six operating electric power generating plants in Coahuila. Electricity is provided and distributed by the Federal Electricity Commission (CFE) and

Central Light and Power. Both utilities are run by the Mexican government.

Coahuila has Mexico's only two operating coal-fired power plants, which have a combined capacity of 2,600 megawatts. Coal-fired plants supply a relatively small percentage of the country's electricity, but the CFE approves the use of coal to fuel power plants near the Coahuila mines. Coal is being replaced by natural gas in most power plants, since burning Mexican coal produces a high amount of ash and causes air pollution.

18 Health

In 2003, the state had 36 hospitals and 331 outpatient centers that were part of the national health system. In 2004, there were 2,492 doctors, 6,084 nurses, and 156 dentists working in these centers. There were an additional 34 independent health centers in the state in 2004.

Most of the Mexican population is covered under a government health plan. The IMSS (Instituto Mexicano de Seguro Social) covers the general population. The ISSSTE (Instituto de Seguridad y Servicios Sociales de Trabajadores del Estado) covers state workers.

19 Housing

Most homes are made of permanent materials such as concrete, brick, and stone. About 20% of homes are made of adobe walls with either brick or concrete roofing structures, or a type of wooden-shingled roof known as *tejamanil*, or a shake roof. In 2000, about 78% of all homes were owner-occupied. In 2005, there were an estimated 625,231 residential housing units in the state. About 95% of these units were single-family detached homes. The average household was estimated at four people.

20 Education

Public education in Mexico is free for students from ages 6 to 16. Most students in the state attend public school for primary and secondary education. In 2002/03, about 34% of students attended a private high school. In 2004/05, it was estimated that 94.9% of age-eligible students completed primary school, which includes six years of study. About 83.1% of eligible students completed secondary school, which includes three years of study after primary school. About 62.1% of eligible students completed the bachillerato, which is similar to a high school diploma. The national average for completion of the bachillerato was 60.1%.

The Universidad Autónoma de Coahuila (Autonomous University of Coahuila) is a public school in Saltillo. In 2005, there were about 67,290 students ages 20 and older who were enrolled in some type of higher education program. The overall literacy rate was estimated at 95.3% in 2005.

21 Arts

Coahuila has a dance group, DanzArte. The state is also famous for the serape (wool cape). Many artisans open their studios for people to watch the making of serapes and to purchase serapes. Coahuila is also noted for works made from wrought iron. In 2004, there were eight major theaters for the performing arts. There were also about 113 registered movie theaters, including multiscreen theaters and single-screen galleries.

22 Libraries and Museums

In 2003, the state had 460 libraries with a combined book stock of 2,183,319 volumes. The same year, there were 24 museums that had permanent exhibits registered in the state. The capital, Saltillo, has the Desert Museum, the Museum of Natural History, and the Bird Museum of Mexico. Torreón has the Railroad Museum, La Casa del Cerro (a history museum), and the Museum of the Revolution.

23 Media

In 2005, the capital city, Saltillo, had four daily newspapers: *El Diario de Coahuila* (*Coahuila Daily*), *El Heraldo de Saltillo* (*The Saltillo Herald*), *El Sol de Norte* (*The North Sun*), and *Vanguardia* (*Vanguard*). The city of Piedras Negras has *Zócalo,* and the city of Torreón had three daily papers: *El Siglo de Torreón* (*The Torreón Century*), *La Opinión,* and *Noticias del Sol de La Laguna* (*Laguna Sun News*). *El Tiempo* (*The Times*) is the largest newspaper in Monclova. Other daily papers include *Zócalo* and *El Diario* in Piedras Negras.

In 2004, there were 69 television stations and 81 radio stations (39 AM and 42 FM). In 2005, there were about 107,564 subscribers to cable and satellite television stations.

There is both conventional and wireless telephone service available in the area around the capital, Saltillo. In 2005, there were about 404,885 residential phone lines, with about 20 mainline phones in use for every 100 people.

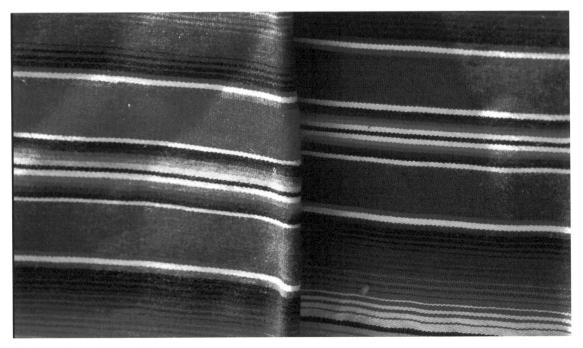

Traditional striped fabric of the serape. PETER LANGER.

24 Tourism, Travel, and Recreation

Saltillo is a popular tourist destination. The city is sometimes called "Athens of Mexico" because of its rich culture. It is also the "city of the serape" (the famous draping scarf worn by Mexican men and women).

Many buildings in Saltillo are constructed of pink quarry and limestone. Zaragoza Park is a large park in the city. The state fair is held in late July and early August each year in Saltillo. Monclova has the Devil's Cave, which has ancient cave paintings. Also in Monclava, an industrial city, the Feria de Acero (Steel Industry Fair) is held the second week of July each year. There is an archeological site at Rincon Colorado.

25 Sports

Los Algodoneros (Cotton Growers) de la Comarca Torreón, a Northern Division team of the National Professional Basketball League (LNBP), play in the Municipal Stadium, which seats 2,500. The Lobos (Wolves) of the Universidad Autónoma de Coahuila, are also part of the LNBP. The Acereros (Steelers) of Monclova, the Saraperos (Serape Makers) de Saltillo, and the Vaqueros (Cowboys) Laguna are teams in the Mexican League of AAA minor league baseball.

The Torreón Santos (Saints) play as a First Division team in the Mexican Football League (soccer). They play in Corona stadium, which holds 20,000 people. Torreón also has a Plaza de Toros (bullfighting ring) that seats 10,000 people. In 2004, there were six sports arenas in the state.

The LALA International Marathon in Torreón is held in March each year. An annual International Motorcycle festival was established in Saltillo in 2002.

26 Famous People

Francisco Indalécio Madero (1873–1913) was called the Father of the Revolution for working to overthrow the dictator Porfirio Díaz. Madero (October 30, 1873) was born in Parras and served as president of Mexico from 1911 to 1913.

Revolutionary leader Venustiano Carranza (1859–1920) was born in Ciénegas. He was elected president of Mexico in 1917, but was assassinated in 1920 while still in office.

27 Bibliography

BOOKS

Carew-Miller, Anna. *Famous People of Mexico.* Philadelphia: Mason Crest Publishers, 2003.

Day-MacLeod, Deirdre. *The States of Northern Mexico*. Philadelphia, PA: Mason Crest Publishers, 2003.

Gruber, Beth. *Mexico.* Washington, DC: National Geographic, 2006.

McNeese, Tim. *The Rio Grande*. Philadelphia, PA: Chelsea House, 2005.

Pastor, Suzanne B. *The Spirit of Hidalgo: The Mexican Revolution in Coahuila.* East Lansing, MI: Michigan State University Press, 2002.

WEB SITES

Government of Mexico. *Mexico for Kids.* www.elbalero.gob.mx/index_kids.html (accessed on March 30, 2007).

Mexican Tourism Board. *Visit Mexico: Coahuila.* www.visitmexico.com/wb/Visitmexico/Visi_Coahuila (accessed on March 30, 2007).

Colima

PRONUNCIATION: koh-LEE-mah.

ORIGIN OF STATE NAME: From the Náhuatl (Amerindian) word *collimaitl. Colli* means either ancestors or volcano, and *maitl* means domain of.

CAPITAL: Colima.

ENTERED COUNTRY: 1857.

COAT OF ARMS: The coat of arms bears a hieroglyph (a picture with special meaning) in the form of an arm. For the state's early inhabitants (Náhuatl), the arm represented the power of one person over all others. This authority essentially fell to the elders, who were greatly respected and obeyed. The coat of arms therefore symbolizes the strength of the people of Colima to improve their living conditions.

HOLIDAYS: Año Nuevo (New Year's Day—January 1); Día de la Constitución (Constitution Day—February 5); Benito Juárez's birthday (March 21); Primero de Mayo (Labor Day—May 1); Anniversary of the Battle of Puebla (1862), May 5; Revolution Day, 1910 (November 20); and Navidad (Christmas—December 25).

FLAG: There is no official flag.

TIME: 6 AM = noon Greenwich Mean Time (GMT).

1 Location and Size

Colima lies in western Mexico. It is bordered on the north, east, and west by the state of Jalisco, on the southeast by the state of Michoacán, and on the south by the Pacific Ocean. Its capital city is Colima. The state has an area of 5,625 square kilometers (2,171 square miles), which is about the same size as the US state of Delaware. It ranks as 28th in size among the states and covers about 0.3% of the total land area of Mexico. Colima is divided into 10 municipalities.

Colima's landscape consists of mountains, hills, valleys, plains, and deep ravines. A branch of the Sierra Madre mountain range runs across the north of the state. The highest peak in the state, the Volcán de Colima at 3,820 meters (12,532 feet), is located in this region. It is the country's most active volcano. It lies on the border with Jalisco and has erupted over 40 times since the 1500s. Damaging earthquakes, the most recent in 2003, are relatively frequent.

Colima's rivers flow from north to south into the Pacific Ocean. Major rivers include the Marabasco River on the northwest border and the Coahuayana (or the Naranjo) River on the southeast border. The Armería River, the largest of all, originates in Jalisco and crosses the central part of the state to the Pacific Ocean. The main fresh water lakes are the Laguna Alcuzahue and the Laguna de Amela in the municipality of Tecomán.

Colima has 160 kilometers (100 miles) of coastline. The Laguna Cuyutlán is a large saltwater lagoon on the Pacific coast. It is used for salt production. The Manzanillo and Santiago Bays are both on the Pacific coastline.

The state includes the Revillagigedo Islands (sometimes referred to as the Revillagigedo Archipelago) in the Pacific. It also includes Isla Roca Partida, Isla San Benedicto, Isla Clarión, and Isla Socorro.

2 Climate

Temperatures are fairly constant year round, with variation depending on elevation. In the winter, temperatures range from 20°C to 28°C (68°F to 76°F). Summers are hotter, with temperatures ranging from 28°C to 34°C (82°F to 93°F). The rainy season falls from June through October, when much of the average annual rain falls. Rainfall during those months averages 1,010 millimeters (40 inches).

In the capital city of Colima, the average temperature is 24°C (75°F) and the average rate of precipitation is 95.7 centimeters (37.6 inches) per year. In the northern city of Miniatitlán, average temperatures are about the same as the capital; however, the annual rainfall averages at about 258 centimeters (101.9 inches).

3 Plants and Animals

The mountain regions feature stands of pine, oak, and myrtle. Mangrove swamps are found along the coastal regions. Fruit trees of mango, papaya, tamarind, and coconut palms can be found in the state. Some common mammals include rabbits, squirrels, foxes, white tail deer, and coyotes. There are also *tlacuaches* (Mexican possums), ocelots, and wild boar. Sharks can be found in coastal waters.

4 Environmental Protection

In 2003, the state had about 242,663 hectares of woodland, including 212,008 hectares of rain forest. In 2004, only about 4 hectares of woodlands (9.8 acres) were damaged by forest fires, but about 671 hectares (1,658 acres) of pasture and brush lands were damaged or destroyed by fire.

Protected areas include the Sierra de Manantlan Biosphere Reserve, which straddles the border with Jalisco. Over 2,700 species of plants, 40% of which are native to Mexico, are protected there. About one-fourth of Mexico's species of mammals and one-third of its bird species find habitat in the reserve. Volcán de Colima, located along the border with Jalisco, is the most active volcano in Mexico. The volcano frequently emits ash plumes and clouds that drift to local areas, affecting both the air and soil. The Revillagigedo Islands consists of a set of volcanic islands that are mostly uninhabited. Located off the coast of Manzanillo, they have been sometimes been called the "little Galapagos" of Mexico because of their unique ecology.

In 2004, there were 41 municipal wastewater treatment plants in operation in the state

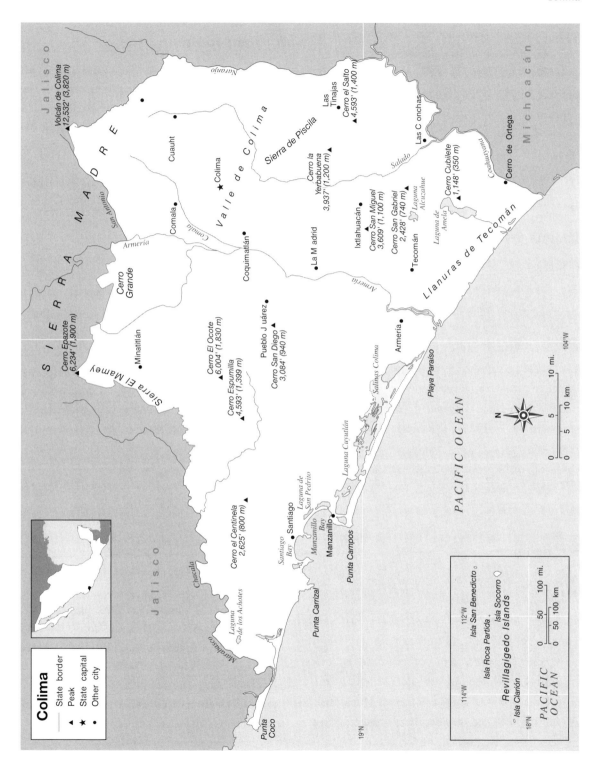

Colima

State border
Peak
State capital
Other city

Jalisco

Volcán de Colima
12,532' (3,820 m)

SIERRA MADRE

Naranjo

Las Tinajas

Cerro el Salto
4,593' (1,400 m)

Las C onchas

Michoacán

Cerro de Ortega

Cuauht

Sierra de Piscila

Valle de Colima

★ Colima

Cerro la Yerbabuena
3,937' (1,200 m)

Comala

Armería

Conalia

Coquimatlán

La M adrid

Ixtlahuacán

Cerro San Miguel
3,609' (1,100 m)

Cerro San Gabriel
2,428' (740 m)

Tecomán

Laguna Alcuzahue

Laguna de Amela

Cerro Cubilete
1,148' (350 m)

Coahuayana

Salado

Llanuras de Tecomán

San Antonio

Cerro Grande

Cerro Epazote
6,234' (1,900 m)

Sierra El Mamey

Minatitlán

Cerro El Ocote
6,004' (1,830 m)

Cerro Espumilla
4,593' (1,399 m)

Pueblo J uárez

Cerro San Diego
3,084' (940 m)

Armería

Armería

Playa Paraíso

104°W

PACIFIC OCEAN

N

10 mi.
10 km
5
5

Cerro el Centinela
2,625' (800 m)

Chacala

Jalisco

Santiago Bay
Santiago

Laguna de San Pedrito

Manzanillo Bay

Manzanillo

Punta Carrizal

Punta Campos

Laguna Cuyutlán

Salinas Colima

19°N

Laguna de los Achotes

Marabasco

Punta Coco

114°W
112°W

Isla San Benedicto

Isla Roca Partida

Isla Socorro

Revillagigedo Islands

Isla Clarión

18°N

PACIFIC OCEAN

0   50   100 mi.
0 50 100 km

with a combined installed capacity of 634 liters per second (167 gallons per second). The volume of treated wastewater was about 374 liters per second (98 gallons per second) that year. An additional 10 industrial wastewater treatment plants were also in operation. As of 2004, about 98% of the population had access to safe drinking water.

5 Population, Ethnic Groups, Languages

Colima had an estimated total population of 577,900 in 2006, ranking 31st among the states and the Distrito Federal. (Only Baja California Sur had fewer people). The population was divided almost evenly between men and women. About 82% of the population lived in urban areas. The population density was 105 people per square kilometer (274 people per square mile). In 2005, the capital, Colima, had a population of 132,273. Almost all the residents speak Spanish, with less than 1% speaking one of the Amerindian languages, such as Náhuatl and Purépecha.

6 Religions

According to the 2000 census, 93% of the population, or 425,954 people, were Roman Catholic; about 2.9%, or 13,214 people, were mainline or evangelical Protestants. About 1.4% were counted as practicing other faiths, including 580 Seventh-day Adventists, 5,185 Jehovah's Witnesses, and 780 Latter-day Saints (Mormons). About 1.8% of the population claimed to have no religious affiliation.

7 Transportation

There are 1,960 kilometers (1,225 miles) of highway connecting the state's ten cities. Eight of the 10 municipalities have four-lane highways. In 2004, there were 69,980 automobiles registered in the state, along with 827 passenger trucks, 65,207 freight trucks, and 10,923 motorcycles.

The Playa del Oro International Airport serves Manzanillo and the Miguel de la Madrid Airport is near the capital, Colima. Both provide domestic and international air service.

Manzanillo on the Pacific Ocean is Mexico's main deep-sea port. The port is equipped to unload large containers from ships and move them around on 13.5 kilometers (8.4 miles) of railway track. Agricultural grains and cement are among the many products shipped through Manzanillo's port. Manzanillo provides Mexico with shipping routes to the nations of Asia (Japan, South Korea, China, Indonesia, Australia, and New Zealand). It also provides shipping to other nations in the Americas, including Canada, the United States, Guatemala, Costa Rica, Colombia, and Peru.

There is no passenger train service in Colima, but 235 kilometers (147 miles) of railroad track transports cargo from the port and other Colima cities to other locations in Mexico.

8 History

The first human settlements date back to 300 AD. Early civilizations, such as the Toltec (around 900) and the Chichimec (around 1100), were the first to build cities and introduce productive agriculture to the region. Colimán, an indigenous leader who ruled in the 15th century, converted Colima into a political, cultural, and military center before the arrival on Europeans.

The Spanish tried three times in the early 1500s to colonize Colima but met with fierce resistance from the native population. Finally, Spaniard Gonzalo de Sandoval conquered the region and built a Spanish settlement, San Sebastián de Colima, in 1523. Later, Viceroy Antonio de Mendoza (c. 1490–1552) visited the city and ordered the construction of a royal road between Mexico City and Colima. (A viceroy is a governor who rules as the representative of a king or queen, in this case of Spain.) By 1575, Colima was already a municipality. It evolved into an important economic, strategic, and cultural center during the colonial period.

When the independence movement broke out in 1810, Colima priest José Antonio Díaz led independence fighters who wanted to follow Miguel Hidalgo and his drive for Mexican independence from Spain. Hidalgo had previously lived and worked as a priest in Colima. Spanish royalists (followers of the king) successfully prevented the independence fighters from gaining control of Colima. The independence struggle continued throughout the decade. Finally in 1821, the royalist forces accepted independence and signed the Plan of Iguala agreement that secured Mexico's independence from Spain.

In 1823, Colima was incorporated into the state of Jalisco. After a short period as a federal territory and as a territory of Michoacán, Colima was declared a state of the Mexican federation in 1857. For a brief period of three months, Colima was the federal capital, under the presidency of Benito Juárez (1806–1872). In November 1864, French troops occupied Colima and incorporated it into the lands effectively ruled by Mexican emperor Maximilian (1832–1867). After Maximilian's defeat, Juárez and, more importantly, Mexican general and politician

Porfirio Díaz (1830–1915) received the support of the leaders in Colima. During Porfirio Díaz's presidency (from 1877 to 1880 and again from 1884 to 1911), economic development favored Colima. A new railroad and important infrastructure investments helped expand agriculture and other economic activities.

In 1910 the Mexican Revolution began. It reached Colima in 1911, when the governor surrendered to the revolutionary forces. After the passage of the Mexican Constitution in 1917, Colima passed its own constitution later that year. The new governor, loyal to the revolutionary victors, assumed power shortly after. However, some political instability remained. Factions loyal to former revolutionary and anti-revolutionary leaders continued to operate in Colima. Eventually, in 1943, stability was finally achieved and governors were able to complete their six-year terms without much opposition. The consolidation of Institutional Revolutionary Party (PRI, the most powerful political party in Mexico) rule also reached Colima. PRI candidates successfully won the gubernatorial races without much opposition from the conservative National Action Party (PAN) in the 1950s, 1960s, and 1970s, or the leftist Party of the Democratic Revolution (PRD) starting in the late 1980s.

In January 2003 the state of Colima was hit by a major earthquake that killed at least 25 people and damaged about 10,000 homes in the capital city of Colima.

The PRI candidate Gustavo Alberto Vázquez Montes was elected governor in 2003. He defeated the candidate of the joint PAN-PRD opposition. However, in February 2005 Governor Montes was killed in a plane crash in the neighboring state of Michoacán. In April 2005, Jesus Silverio

The city of Manzanillo lies on the Pacific coast. © ROBERT FRERCK/WOODFIN CAMP.

Cavazos Ceballo of the PRI was elected to complete Montes's remaining term.

9 State and Local Government

With formal separation of powers and checks-and-balances provisions, the state of Colima has a unicameral (one chamber) state congress and a strong executive power. The congress is elected every three years for nonrenewable terms. Sixteen of its 25 members are elected in single member districts; nine are elected by proportional representation.

There are 10 municipalities, each with a local government. These local governments have limited authority over administrative decisions. Tight control of budgets by the state government reduces the local authorities' leverage and influ-

ence. Municipal president and council members are elected for nonrenewable three-year terms.

10 Political Parties

The three main political parties in all of Mexico are the Institutional Revolutionary Party (PRI), the National Action Party (PAN), and Party of the Democratic Revolution (PRD).

The PRI has dominated Colima politics since the end of the Mexican Revolution (1910–20). All Colima governors have belonged to that party. Because the PRI has exercised control of the powerful governor's office since the end of the revolution, the legislature has not been able to act independently. If politics become more competitive in Colima, the legislature would be more likely to act independently of the governor.

Despite more guarantees for opposition parties and free and fair elections since the early 1990s, the PRI continues to dominate politics in the state. A joint PAN-PRD effort to win the gubernatorial race in 2003 failed. Gustavo Alberto Vázquez Montes of the PRI became governor in 2004. Vázquez Montes died in a plan crash in February 2005. In a new 2005 election, Jesús Silverio Cavazos Ceballos of the PRI was elected governor.

11 Judicial System

The highest court in Colima is the Superior Tribunal of Justice. Its members are appointed for nonrenewable six-year terms by the governor with congressional approval. Only qualified attorneys can be appointed to those posts. In addition, an electoral tribunal and several different local courts make up the judiciary in Colima. Yet, as is the case with the other state-level powers, the dominance enjoyed by the PRI has made it difficult for any branch of government to function independently.

12 Economy

As of 2003, Colima's economy was dominated by the services sector, which accounted for 33% of the state's employment, followed by commerce at 19%, agriculture at 14%, and industry at 13%. A growing sector has been tourism. Hotels are being built to accommodate the increasing demand. The port city of Manzanillo is the busiest Pacific port in Latin America and a key trade link to the countries of the Pacific Rim, as well as the United States, and Central and South America.

13 Industry

Colima's manufacturing sector is based largely upon the production of lemon by-products, coconut-copra, sugar, and seafood processing. Other important industries include the manufacture of beverages (including dairy products), soap, and candies for regional consumption. Family-owned enterprises, such as bakeries and sandal-making shops, form key elements of the state's industrial sector.

14 Labor

As of 2005, Colima had 283,241 eligible workers. Some 276,127 were listed as employed and 7,114 were listed as unemployed. Unemployed workers in rural areas may not be counted, however. The unemployment rate that year was reported to be 2.5%. Of those who were working, services employed 45.9%, followed by commerce at 18.4%, and agriculture at 15.5%.

The US Bureau of Labor Statistics reported that Mexican workers saw their wages increase from $2.49 per hour in 2003 to $2.50 per hour in 2004. (The average US worker earned $15.70 per hour in 2004.) The maximum work week is set at 48 hours by law. The average worker spends 40 to 45 hours per week on the job. Workers earn twice their regular hourly rate for up to nine hours a week of overtime. When a worker works more than nine hours overtime in a week, he or she earns three times the regular hourly rate. After one year, workers are entitled by law to six days paid vacation.

The Cuyutlán Lagoon is a large saltwater lagoon on the Pacific coast. It is used for salt production. © ROBERT FRERCK/ WOODFIN CAMP.

15 Agriculture

Colima is Mexico's largest producer of lemons, providing 60% of the domestic market, as well as a leading producer of bananas and coconuts. In 2004, Colima was Mexico's fourth-largest producer of bananas at 162,117 tons. Other crops grown in Colima are corn, beans, rice, *jicama* (a legume known as yam bean or Mexican turnip), sweet potatoes, coffee, mangos, guava, watermelons, and avocados. The state produced 35,963 tons of corn, and 97,167 tons of sugar in 2004.

The climate is favorable to cattle breeding. There are also pig and poultry farms. In 2004, beef cattle brought to market totaled 37,177 head, and pigs brought to market totaled 120,355 head. Beef output that same year totaled 11,904 tons, pork output stood at 3,626 tons, and poultry at 14,304 tons.

Palms are also cultivated for use in landscaping and for palm fibers to weave hats, placemats, floor mats, and other items.

16 Natural Resources

The Pacific Ocean waters are rich with marine life. There is commercial fishing for tuna, giant squid, and shark, with processing plants located near the port of Manzanillo. Fresh water fishing takes place in the state's rivers and lagoons. Aquaculture (fish farms) are growing in impor-

The Colima volcano. AP IMAGES.

tance. Sport fishing is also popular. In 2003, the total fish catch was about 38,392 tons.

Forest wood production in 2003 was valued at about $600,336. Pine and encino (a type of oak) were the primary woods harvested.

17 Energy and Power

In 2005, there were 210,080 users of electricity in the state of Colima. Of that total, the largest number were residential customers at 182,228. Sales of electricity that same year totaled 1,339,859 megawatt hours, of which the largest users were large industrial firms at 492,333 megawatt hours. Electricity is provided and distributed by the Federal Electricity Commission and Central Light and Power. Both utilities are run by the Mexican government.

Electricity in the state is produced by two steam-turbine generating plants in Manzanillo. The two plants have a combined capacity of 1,900 megawatts. Surplus power is sold to other Mexican states and to other countries in the region.

18 Health

In 2003, the state had 10 hospitals and 143 outpatient centers that were part of the national health system. In 2004, there were 736 doctors, 1,501 nurses, and 54 dentists working in these centers. There were an additional 12 independent health centers in the state in 2004.

Most of the Mexican population is covered under a government health plan. The IMSS (Instituto Mexicano de Seguro Social) covers the general population. The ISSSTE (Instituto de Seguridad y Servicios Sociales de Trabajadores del Estado) covers state workers.

19 Housing

Most homes have concrete, brick, or stone walls with similar materials used for roof construction. Sheet metal is also a popular roofing material. In 2000, about 71% of all homes were owner-occupied. In 2005, there were an estimated 149,189 residential housing units in the state. About 91% of these units were single-family detached homes. The average household was estimated at 3.8 people.

20 Education

Public education is free for all students from ages 6 to 16 and most students in the state attend public school. In 2004/05, it was estimated that 87.6% of age-eligible students completed primary school, which includes six years of study. About 77.5% of eligible students completed secondary school, which includes three years of study after primary school. About 64% of eligible students completed the *bachillerato*, which is similar to a high school diploma. The national average for completion of the *bachillerato* was 60.1%.

The Universidad de Colima (University of Colima) and the Technological Institute of Colima are both public schools located in the capital. In 2005, there were about 20,452 students ages 20 and older who were enrolled in some type of higher education program. The overall literacy rate was estimated at 92.6% in 2005.

21 Arts

The state of Colima has many open-air style theaters. In 2004, there were two officially registered auditoriums for the performing arts. One of the best known is the Teatro Hidalgo. Most major cities sponsor exhibitions and cultural fairs. There are also about five registered movie theaters, including multiscreen theaters and single-screen galleries.

22 Libraries and Museums

In 2003, the state had 80 libraries with a combined stock of 577,236 volumes. The library of the University of Colima serves as a depository library for the United Nations. In 2003, there were seven museums that had permanent exhibits registered in the state. In the capital, Colima, are the Museo Regional de Historia (Museum of Regional History), the Museo de Artes Populares (Folk Art Museum), and the Museo de las Culturas de Occidente (Museum of Western Culture). An annual Salsa and Merengue International Festival is held in Manzanillo to promote the popular music and dance.

23 Media

In 2005, the capital city of Colima had five daily newspapers, with the two largest being *Ecos de la Costa* (*Echoes of the Coast*) and *El Mundo Desde Colima* (*The World From Colima*). In 2004, there were 28 television stations and 17 radio stations (11 AM and 6 FM). Internet service and cable television are available in Manzanillo and the city of Colima. In 2005, there were about

22,138 subscribers to cable and satellite television stations. Also in 2005, there were about 97,600 residential phone lines, with about 21.1 mainline phones in use for every 100 people.

24 Tourism, Travel, and Recreation

The Museo Regional de Historia (Museum of Regional History) houses displays of pre-Hispanic civilizations. The nearby village of Suchitlán is famous for its mask makers. Manzanillo is known for its beautiful beaches and it has also been called the Sailfish Capital of the World. Every February, Manzanillo hosts the International Sailfish Tournament.

Beaches line the nearly 160-kilometer (100-mile) Pacific coast. Some beaches are covered with pebbles, while others have powdery white or black volcanic sand.

A favorite souvenir is the Colima dog, a replica of a ceramic dog figurine dating from the 1500s when Amerindian cultures flourished in the region.

25 Sports

Colima Tuberos have played as part of the National Professional Basketball League (LNBP). The Tuberos are named for a popular local drink known as tuba, which is made from coconut palm flowers. The Pegaso Real De Colima play in the First Division "A" of the Mexican Football (soccer) Association (commonly known as Femexfut).

26 Famous People

José Antonio Díaz led the drive for independence starting in 1810. Vázquez Montes (b.1962) was elected governor in 2003.

27 Bibliography

BOOKS

DeAngelis, Gina. *Mexico.* Mankato, MN: Blue Earth Books, 2003.

De Varona, Frank. *Miguel Hidalgo y Costilla: Father of Mexican Independence.* Brookfield, CT: Millbrook Press, 1993.

Gruber, Beth. *Mexico.* Washington, DC: National Geographic, 2006.

Nantus, Sheryl. *The Pacific South States of Mexico.* Stockton, NJ: Mason Crest Publishers, 2003.

WEB SITES

Government of Mexico. *Mexico for Kids.* www.elbalero.gob.mx/index_kids.html (accessed on March 30, 2007).

Mexican Tourism Board. *Visit Mexico: Colima.* www.visitmexico.com/wb/Visitmexico/Visi_Colima (accessed on March 30, 2007).

Distrito Federal

PRONUNCIATION: dees-TREE-toh feh-deh-RAHL.

ORIGIN OF STATE NAME: Describes the location of the federal government of Mexico.

CAPITAL: Ciudad de México (Mexico City). Established: 1824.

ENTERED COUNTRY: n.a.

COAT OF ARMS: The coat of arms contains a picture of a golden castle that is surrounded by three stone bridges. There are two lions supporting the castle tower. Around the border of the shield are ten thorny cactus leaves.

HOLIDAYS: Año Nuevo (New Year's Day—January 1); Día de la Constitución (Constitution Day—February 5); Benito Juárez's birthday (March 21); Primero de Mayo (Labor Day—May 1); Anniversary of the Battle of Puebla (1862), May 5; Revolution Day, 1910 (November 20); and Navidad (Christmas—December 25).

FLAG: There is no official flag.

TIME: 6 AM = noon Greenwich Mean Time (GMT).

1 Location and Size

The Distrito Federal (Federal District) is the capital of Mexico. Most of its territory is occupied by Ciudad de México (Mexico City). It has an area of 1,486 square kilometers (573.75 square miles) and covers about 0.1% of the total land area of Mexico. It is about 10 times the size of the District of Columbia, the US capital. Although there are no municipalities in Mexico's Distrito Federal, there are 16 political districts.

The Distrito Federal is located in the center of the country. It is bordered on the north and west by the State of México and on the south by the state of Morelos.

The Distrito Federal lies on a high valley of Mexico that is surrounded by the Sierra Volcánica Transversal (also known as the Cordillera Neovolcánica). This same high valley also encompasses parts of the Mexican states of Hidalgo, Puebla, Tlaxcala, and México. The Sierra las Cruces lie on the western border of the Distrito. The Sierra de Chichinautzin are to the south and the Sierra de Guadalupe are in the north.

There are several volcanoes found in the southern part of the Distrito. The highest point in the Distrito is Cerro del Ajusco at an elevation of about 3,937 meters (12,917 feet). Volcán

Tláloc is the second highest peak at 3,690 meters (12,106 feet).

One of the best-known waterways in the Distrito Federal is the Xochimilco canals. The canals surround a network of low lying artificial islands that were made during precolonial times on the surface of a shallow lake. Tourists come to see "floating gardens" that have sprung upon these reclaimed lands.

2 Climate

The climate is generally dry, with the greatest rainfall occurring during the summer months of June, July, and August. Average annual rainfall is 107 centimeters (42 inches). Average overall temperature is 14°C (58°F). In May, the warmest month, the average daily high temperature is 26°C (79°F). In January, the coldest month, the average daily high is 19°C (66°F). In Mexico City (Ciudad de México), the average annual temperature is 17°C (63°F) and average precipitation is 63 centimeters (25 inches) per year.

3 Plants and Animals

Although the area was once home to dense forests, deforestation and heavy development has reduced much of the habitat of the native animals. Pines and cedar are native to the area. In the south, plants such as orchids and ferns can be found. Some of the small mammals common to the area are shrews, weasels, and hares. During the winter months, migrating butterfly species may be viewed around the district. Falcons, doves, woodpeckers, and sparrows are common birds.

4 Environmental Protection

Mexico City has some of the worst air pollution of any city in the world. In 1988, the government passed a law aimed at improving air quality. Regulations aimed at reducing exhaust emissions from the four million cars registered in the Distrito have resulted in improved air quality. In 2004, the Distrito had 30 municipal wastewater treatment plants in operation with a combined installed capacity of 6,809 liters per second (1,798 gallons per second). The volume of treated wastewater that year was estimated at about 3,790 liters per second (1,001 gallons per second). There were three additional industrial wastewater treatment plants in operation that year. As of 2004, about 99.5% of the population had access to safe drinking water.

Mexico's first national park, Desierto de los Leones (Desert of the Lions), was established in the Distrito in 1917. The name "desert" came from its remote location in 1917, although it is a rich forest area. There are six additional national parks located in the Distrito. The government has also created special reserves for protection of native plants and animals. The Chichinautzin Ecological Reserve, established in the late 1980s, has volcanic craters that sprout unique vegetation. Ajusco National Park has pine and oak forests. The freshwater lakes known collectively as the lake system of Xochililco and San Gregario Atlapulco were designated as a Ramsar Wetlands of International Importance in 2004.

In 2003, the Distrito had about 53,719 hectares (132,743 acres) of woodland, including 2,123 hectares (5,246 acres) of rain forest. In 2004, about 228 hectares (563 acres) of woodland were damaged or destroyed by fire. An additional 1, 422 hectares (3,513 acres) of pas-

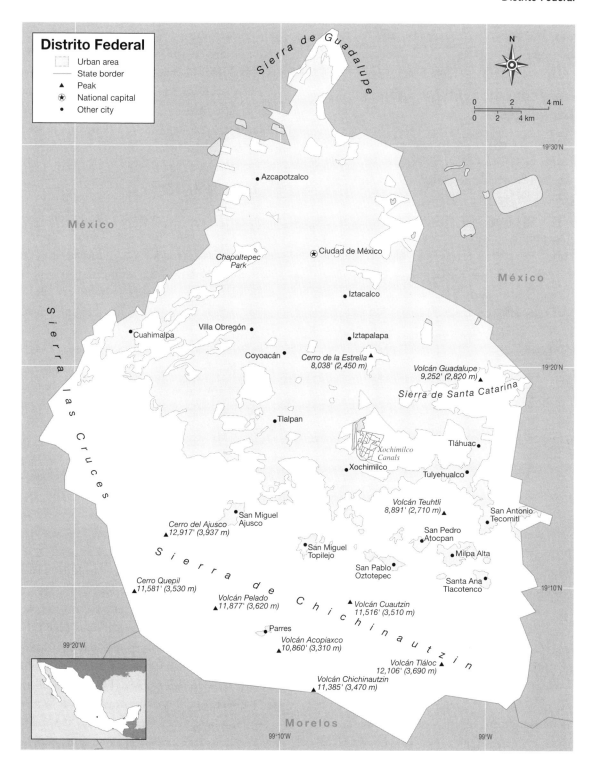

Distrito Federal

- Urban area
- State border
- ▲ Peak
- ⊛ National capital
- • Other city

Sierra de Guadalupe

N

| 0 | 2 | 4 mi. |
| 0 | 2 | 4 km |

19°30'N

México

• Azcapotzalco

⊛ Ciudad de México

México

Chapultepec Park

• Iztacalco

Villa Obregón •

• Iztapalapa

• Cuahimalpa

Coyoacán •

Cerro de la Estrella 8,038' (2,450 m) ▲

Volcán Guadalupe 9,252' (2,820 m) ▲

19°20'N

Sierra de Santa Catarina

S i e r r a   l a s   C r u c e s

• Tlalpan

Xochimilco Canals

• Tláhuac

• Xochimilco

• Tulyehualco

Volcán Teuhtli 8,891' (2,710 m) ▲

San Antonio
Tecomitl •

Cerro del Ajusco 12,917' (3,937 m) ▲

• San Miguel
Ajusco

San Pedro
Atocpan •

• Milpa Alta

S i e r r a   d e   C h i c h i n a u t z i n

• San Miguel
Topilejo

San Pablo
Oztotepec •

Santa Ana
Tlacotenco •

Cerro Quepil 11,581' (3,530 m) ▲

Volcán Pelado 11,877' (3,620 m) ▲

▲ *Volcán Cuautzin 11,516' (3,510 m)*

• Parres

Volcán Acopiaxco 10,860' (3,310 m) ▲

Volcán Tláloc 12,106' (3,690 m) ▲

Volcán Chichinautzin 11,385' (3,470 m)

19°10'N

99°20'W

Morelos

99°10'W

99°W

ture and brush lands were also affected by fires that year.

5 Population, Ethnic Groups, Languages

Distrito Federal had an estimated total population of 8,817,300 in 2006, the second largest population in the nation. About 48% of the population were men and 52% were women. The entire district is considered an urban area. The population density was the highest in the nation at 5,882 people per square kilometer (15,234 people per square mile). Almost all residents speak Spanish, but about 1.4% of the population speaks one of the indigenous languages, such as Náhuatl, Otomi, and many languages of the Mixtecas and Zapotecas ethnic groups.

6 Religions

According to the 2000 census, 90.5% of the population, or nearly 7 million people, were Roman Catholic; about 3.6%, or 277,400 people, were mainline or evangelical Protestants. About 1.3% were counted as other Biblical faiths, including 7,852 Seventh-day Adventists, 21,893 Latter-day Saints (Mormons), and 74,140 Jehovah's Witnesses. The Distrito had the largest Jewish population in the country with about 18,380 Jews. About 2.9% of the population claimed to have no religious affiliation.

Religion plays an important role in the everyday lives of many residents. The Basilica of Our Lady of Guadalupe, who is the patron saint of Mexico, is a national Roman Catholic shrine visited by thousands of pilgrims, some of whom climb the steps of the shrine on their knees. Mexico City's downtown area has a beautiful baroque cathedral called the Catedral Metropolitana that is the largest cathedral in the Western Hemisphere. This cathedral serves as the seat of the Roman Catholic archdiocese of Mexico. A temple of the Church of Jesus Christ of Latter-day Saints (Mormons) was dedicated in Mexico City in 1983.

7 Transportation

Mexico-Benito Juárez Airport provides international flights to and from the Distrito Federal. Mexico City has been served by the Sistema de Transporte Colectivo Metro, an extensive metro system (over 200 kilometers/125 miles), since the 1960s. More than four million people travel on it each day.

In 2004, there were 2,384,533 automobiles registered in the state, along with 25,862 passenger trucks, and 62,087 freight trucks.

8 History

Mexico City is one of the oldest cities continuously inhabited in Latin America. Remains found at Tlatilco point to 1500 BC as the first time when a permanent settlement was built in Mexico City. Between 100 and 900 AD. the center of human activity in the central valley of Mexico moved to Teotihuacán, an area north of modern day Mexico City. There, impressive pyramids were built as sites of worship for the Sun and the Moon. The valley where the city of Mexico is located was populated by Toltec Indians who began to grow and expand from southern Mexico and reached Teotihuacán after the Teotihuacán culture had begun its decline.

During the 13th century, Mexica Amerindians, also known as Aztecs, arrived in the region. According to the historical myth, they left a northern (probably mythical) city of Aztlán. They were led by their god, Huitzilopochtli, represented by a warrior-like figure. The myth says that when they arrived in the lake-filled region, the Aztecs witnessed the vision of an eagle devouring a snake while perched on a cactus. They believed that this was a message that their god wanted them to stay there. Tenochtitlán-Mexico was founded on June 8, 1325.

Under the leadership of monarchs Izcoatl, Montezuma I (Moctezuma I, d. 1469), Axayacatl (15th century), Tizoc, Ahuizotl (d. 1503), and Montezuma II (Moctezuma II, 1466–1520), the Aztecs emerged as the most important civilization in the central valley of Mexico. The highly disciplined warriors, who took the eagle and jaguar as their symbols, rapidly expanded the areas under Aztec domination. Yet, the Aztecs also absorbed and incorporated religious beliefs and cultural values of the groups they entered into contact with and dominated.

One of the most impressive constructions in Mexico City was the Templo Mayor, a double pyramid dedicated to the gods Tlaloc (god of water and rain) and Huitzilopochtli (god of war). They believed that Templo Mayor was the center of a universe, and human sacrifices were required to sustain it as such. In addition, there were other temples dedicated to Quetzalcóatl (father of civilization), Tezcatlipoca (god who creates and changes all things), and Ehecatl (god of wind). Together with the temples, the city rapidly grew as a commercial and military center of a vast Aztec empire. Located in the middle of a number of small lakes, the city gave way to the construction of a number of canals that surrounded plots of lands, called *chinampas.*

When the Spaniards arrived in the 1500s, Mexico-Tenochtitlán was probably one of the most populated cities in the world. Its structures and buildings must have deeply impressed the Spanish conquistadores (conquerors). Because of a religious myth, Aztecs expected the return of Quetzalcóatl. Believing Spanish explorer Hernán Cortés (1485–1547) was the returning god, Emperor Montezuma II met Cortés at the entrance of the city to welcome him. Cortés imprisoned Montezuma and moved on to kill many of the Aztec nobility. Despite the resistance of the Aztecs led by Cuahtémoc (c. 1495–1522), Cortés successfully conquered Mexico-Tenochtitlán on August 13, 1521.

Cortés quickly moved to control the rest of the central valley of Mexico but made Mexico-Tenochtitlán the capital city of the new Spanish territory. Roman Catholic churches were built on top of the ruins of Aztec temples, and the new government buildings replaced other sacred Aztec constructions. The Mexican presidential palace, the city's cathedral, and the main central square were located exactly in the same place where the Aztec's most important buildings were erected. That gives Mexico City a profound sense of the dramatic changes that occurred with the arrival of the Spanish conquistadores. It also reflects the deep history of a city that has been one of the world's greatest cities for centuries. Most of the people of Mexico are mestizo (mixed Amerindian and European descent). They are like Mexico City, where two rich and expanding civilizations came together.

After Cortés conquered it, Mexico-Tenochtitlán (now Mexico City) became the center of colonial rule—through the 16th, 17th, and 18th centuries, and through the heart of the independence movement between 1810 and 1821. It was at the center of the political instability that characterized Mexico between 1823 and 1867. It was the place where president Benito Juárez (1806–1872) began adopting his celebrated reforms. Mexico City was the main objective of the revolutionary leaders of 1910.

Plaza de la Constitución, the square in the center of the city (commonly referred to as the Zócalo), symbolizes the three cultures of Mexico City: the original Aztec, the invading Spanish, and the resulting Mexican culture that blends the two. The Distrito is one of the most populated cities in the world. It was the site of the Olympic Games in 1968, when drug testing was first introduced. The city experienced rapid growth in the 1960s, 1970s, and 1980s.

Into the first decade of the 21st century, the Distrito continues to experience a number of problems. Among them were: extreme air pollution; official and police corruption; traffic congestion; and a sharp increase in violent crimes such as murder, robbery and kidnapping.

In July of 2006, the Distrito also became the center for the nation's disputed presidential election, in which Party of the Democratic Revolution (PRD) candidate Andrés Manuel López Obrador contested the vote count that gave victory to his opponent, National Action Party (PAN) candidate Felipe Calderon, claiming that massive election fraud had taken place.

Then in November of 2006, the Distrito's legislators passed a law that would give same-sex couples, as well as unmarried heterosexual couples, civil union status, thus allowing them to gain access to pension and inheritance rights.

9 State and Local Government

The chief of government is the chief executive (or mayor) in the Distrito Federal. Previously appointed by the president as a cabinet minister, since 1997 the chief executive has been democratically elected, by those residing in the Distrito Federal, for a six-year, nonrenewable term. The first elected chief of government was Cuauhtémoc Cárdenas Solórzano (b.1934). The legislative assembly of the Distrito is comprised of 66 members, 40 elected in single member districts and 26 elected by proportional representation. The chief of government of the Distrito is elected concurrently with the president of Mexico on a separate ballot. As in other federal districts, the federal government retains some authority to decide on matters that pertain to financial and administrative issues.

The local and state governments are the same, since the Distrito Federal is the local government of the capital city of Mexico. The Distrito is divided into 16 political delegations.

10 Political Parties

The three main political parties in all of Mexico are the Institutional Revolutionary Party (PRI), the National Action Party (PAN), and Party of the Democratic Revolution (PRD). These three parties have a strong presence in the Distrito. Voters first democratically elected their chief of government in 1997. Former PRD presidential candidate Cuauhtemoc Cárdenas Solórzano won the election. The PRD's Andrés Manuel López Obrador won the 2000 election and emerged as one of the most important contenders for the 2006 presidential election. He was succeeded by Alejandro Encinas Rodríguez in 2005. In the

The Mexico City skyline. AP IMAGES.

2006 elections, Marcelo Luis Ebrard Casaubon of the PRD was elected the chief of government (mayor) for the Distrito.

The PRD is strongest in the Distrito, but the PAN has also made inroads. Since the PRI has mostly lost support in urban areas, its strength in the Distrito has also diminished significantly since the mid-1980s.

11 Judicial System

The Superior Tribunal of Justice is the highest court in the Distrito Federal. Its members are appointed by the chief of government, with congressional approval, for renewable six-year terms. Although there is also an electoral tribunal and lower courts, the presence of the national Supreme Court and the Federal Electoral Tribunal usually render the Distrito Federal Superior Tribunal and Electoral Tribunal less important than its counterparts in the other 31 states. Yet, as the Distrito Federal slowly changes from being a bureaucracy highly controlled by the federal government into a more state-like autonomous entity, the independence, the autonomy, and the importance of the Distrito judicial system will become more important.

12 Economy

The economy of the Distrito Federal is marked by its position as the nation's capital, housing the nation's ministries, and most of its government agencies. But the Distrito and the 21 principal municipalities in the State of México that surround the capital account for a major portion of the nation's industrial base. Many manufacturing concerns are headquartered in the Distrito. It is also a major distribution center, and a center for Mexico's tourism industry. Some 400,000 firms are located in the Distrito.

13 Industry

Major industries located in the Distrito Federal include the manufacture of auto parts, food and beverages, tobacco products, textiles, clothing, electrical equipment, electronics, machine tools, heavy machinery, paper and wood products, and chemicals. Overall, the Distrito and the 21 principal municipalities in the State of México that surround the capital, account for 40% of the nation's industrial base.

Handicrafts are also produced in the Distrito. These include Judas dolls, piñatas, paper cuttings, and basketwork.

14 Labor

As of 2005, the Distrito Federal had 3,983,540 eligible workers. Some 3,769,550 were listed as employed and 213,990 were listed as unemployed. Unemployed workers in rural areas may not be counted, however. The unemployment rate that year was reported to be 5.3%. Of those who were working, services employed 57.8%, followed by commerce at 22.3%, and manufacturing at 13.1%.

The US Bureau of Labor Statistics reported that Mexican workers saw their wages increase from $2.49 per hour in 2003 to $2.50 per hour in 2004. (The average US worker earned $15.70 per hour in 2004.) The maximum work week is set at 48 hours by law. The average worker spends 40 to 45 hours per week on the job. Workers earn twice their regular hourly rate for up to nine hours a week of overtime. When a worker works more than nine hours overtime in a week, he or she earns three times the regular hourly rate. After one year, workers are entitled by law to six days paid vacation.

15 Agriculture

A few small dairy farms lie on the outskirts of the city, with the milk and cheese sold locally. Some families also raise pigs and chickens in backyard pens. A typical family might keep three pigs, and one or two dozen chickens. Some of the animals are consumed by the family, but most are raised to be sold by local butcher shops. Vegetables and fruits are also raised. These include corn, spinach, oats, animal feed, as well as roses, nopal (a kind of prickly pear cactus), and maguey (a spiney plant used in the production of mezcal, a colorless liquor).

Corn was the most common crop raised by residents living in the Distrito. In 2004 residents there produced 9,411 tons of corn. Livestock products from the Distrito that same year included: 797 tons of beef, 2,542 tons of pork, 536 tons of poultry, and 148 tons of lamb. Milk production from dairy cows totaled 13 million liters (3 million gallons), while egg production stood at 699 tons in 2004.

16 Natural Resources

While most of the forests are protected, oyamel (a fir tree) and pine are still harvested for sale. The total value of forest wood production in 2003 was about $1.8 million.

17 Energy and Power

In 2005, there were 2,745,605 users of electricity in the Distrito Federal. There were 2,384,995 residential customers. Sales of electricity that same year totaled 13,366,503 megawatt hours, of which the largest users were medium-sized industrial firms at 5,980,420 megawatt hours. Electricity is provided and distributed by the Federal Electricity Commission, and Central Light and Power. Both utilities are run by the Mexican government.

18 Health

In 2003, the Distrito Federal had 81 hospitals and 554 outpatient centers that were part of the national health system. In 2004, the Distrito Federal had the highest number of medical personal in the country. There were about 13,921 doctors, 30,880 nurses, and 1,201 dentists working in these health centers. There were an additional 309 independent health centers in the state in 2004.

Most of the Mexican population is covered under a government health plan. The IMSS (Instituto Mexicano de Seguro Social) covers the general population. The ISSSTE (Instituto de Seguridad y Servicios Sociales de Trabajadores del Estado) covers state workers.

19 Housing

Housing in the Distrito varies from luxury townhouses and apartments to housing built from poor quality materials. Most homes are built with solid materials such as concrete, stone, or brick. In 2000, about 71% of all homes were owner-occupied. In 2005, there were an esti-mated 2,287,189 residential housing units in the state. About 51% of these units were single-family detached homes. About 30% were units in apartment buildings. The average household was estimated at 3.8 people.

20 Education

Public education in Mexico is free for students from ages 6 to 16 and most students in the Distrito attend public schools. However, in 2002/03, about 21% of primary school students, 15% of secondary school students, and 26% of high school students were enrolled in private schools. In 2004/05, it was estimated that 93.9% of age-eligible students completed primary school, which includes six years of study. About 81.5% of eligible students completed secondary school, which includes three years of study after primary school. About 61.6% of eligible students completed the *bachillerato*, which is similar to a high school diploma. The national average for completion of the *bachillerato* was 60.1%.

There are 44 institutions of higher education in the Distrito. The Universidad Nacional Autónoma de México (National University of Mexico–UNAM) is located in the Distrito, as are El Colegio de Mexico (College of Mexico) and the Instituto Politécnico Nacional (National Polytechnic Institute). There are also several specialty colleges such as the Institute of Social Science, Economics, and Administration; the National Institute of Anthropology and History, and the National Institute of Fine Arts and Literature. In 2005, there were about 446,168 students ages 20 and older who were enrolled in some type of higher education program. The

Mosaics depicting Mexico's history and future cover the central library of the Universidad Nacional Autónoma de México (UNAM) in Mexico City. The mosaics, listed in the **Guinness Book of World Records** *as the largest in the world, measure over 40,000 square feet (4,000 square meters).* PETER LANGER.

overall literacy rate was estimated at 96.2% in 2005.

21 Arts

Mexico City is home to many dance and music performing arts groups. The Ballet Folklórico Nacional de Mexico (National Folk Ballet of Mexico) performs in the Palacio de Bellas Artes. Three other companies—Ballet Independiente, Ballet Neoclásico, and Ballet Contemporánea—perform in Mexico City. There are three major orchestras, including a children's symphony orchestra. The Mexico City Philharmonic Orchestra (established by the government in

1978) was nominated for Best Recording in the 2001 Grammy Latino Awards. ¡Que Payasos! (Clowns) is a popular rock-and-roll group that performs at festivals, especially for young people. There are at least 85 theaters and auditoriums sponsoring plays, concerts, and other types of performances. There are also over 500 registered movie theaters, including multiscreen theaters and single-screen galleries.

22 Libraries and Museums

In 2003, there were 1,103 libraries in the Distrito with a combined stock of 17,051,117. The Biblioteca Nacional (National Library of Mexico), containing over 1,250,000 volumes, is located on the campus of the National Autonomous University of Mexico and contains over 1,250,000 volumes. The Hemeroteca Nacional (National Newspaper and Periodical Library) is also a part of the university and serves as is a depository library of the United Nations.

In 2003, there were 88 active museums registered in the Distrito that had permanent exhibits. The most important museums are the government sponsored National Museum of Art, the National Museum of Anthropology, the Museum of Modern Art, and the National Museum of Popular Culture. The former home of artist Frida Kahlo (1907–1954) is open as a museum as is the former art studio of famous painter Diego Rivera (1886–1957). The Palace of Fine Arts and the Basilica of the Virgin of Guadalupe (patron saint of Mexico) are popular sites as well. The former home and studio of architect Luis Barragán (1902–1988) was designated as a UNESCO World Heritage site in 2005.

23 Media

In 2005, there were at least 18 daily newspapers published in the district. The largest were *La Prensa* (*The Press*, with a circulation of about 275,000), *El Universal* (*The Universe*, circulation 170,000) and *Esto* (*This*, circulation 150,000). Others included *El Dia* (*The Day*), *El Financiero* (*The Financer*), and *Tribuna* (*Tribune*).

In 2004, there were 15 television stations and 61 radio stations (29 AM, 28 FM, and 5 shortwave). In 2005, there were about 749,312 subscribers to cable and satellite television stations. Also in 2005, there were about 2,451,646 residential phone lines, with about 41.1 main-line phones in use for every 100 people. This was the highest number of phones per population in the nation that year.

24 Tourism, Travel, and Recreation

Alameda Central, dating from the 17th century, is the oldest park in the country. The floating gardens of Xochimilco may be viewed by boat. University City houses the Universidad Autónoma de México (UNAM); its modern campus buildings feature murals and mosaics by Diego Rivera on their outer walls. The Palacio de Bellas Artes has murals by Diego Rivera and David Alfaro Siqueiros (1896–1974) and crystal carvings of Mexico's famous volcanoes, Popocatépetl and Iztaccihuatl.

The Zona Rosa (Pink Zone), a famous shopping area, also has two beautiful statues, La Diana Cazadora and the statue of Cristóbal Colón (Christopher Columbus). Chapultepec Park houses the castle of the former emperor Maximilian (1832–1867) and empress Carlotta (1840–1927), a zoo and botanical gardens, and the famous Museum of Anthropology, which has the old Aztec calendar and a huge statue of Tlaloc, the Aztec rain god. The beautiful baroque cathedral called the Catedral Metropolitana is a popular site for visitors of all faiths. The main avenue of Mexico City is La Avenida de la Independencia, featuring the statue of the Angel of Independence, a famous landmark of the city. The shrine of Our Lady of Guadalupe, the patron saint of Mexico, is visited by thousands of pilgrims each year.

Bullfighting is popular in Mexico City. Spectators may choose to pay higher prices to guarantee seats in the shade, since the sun in Mexico City can be scorching.

25 Sports

Soccer is the most popular sport and Mexico City has six soccer stadiums. The Atlante and América are First Division soccer teams in the Mexican Football Association (commonly known as Femexfut). Both teams play home games at Estadio Azteca (Aztec Stadium, seating 104,000). The Pumas from the Universidad Autónoma de México, also a First Division team, play in the 62,000-seat Olympic Stadium, built for the 1968 Olympics. Another First Division soccer team, Cruz Azul (Blue Cross), plays in the 36,000-seat Azul Stadium.

The Diablos Rojos (Red Devils) is a professional AAA minor league baseball team of the Mexican League. La Ola is a South Zone team of the National Professional Basketball League (LNBP). Mexico City also hosts bullfighting in the 40,000-seat Plaza Mexico and in the 10,000-seat Plaza de Toreo Cuatro Caminos. In 2004, there were a total of nine sports arenas in the Distrito.

The International Mexico City Marathon has been an annual event since 1983. The race is considered to be one of the most challenging marathons in the world because of the city's altitude.

26 Famous People

Hernán Cortés (1485–1547) was a Spanish conquistador who conquered Aztec emperor Montezuma II to become the founder of Spanish Mexico. Though born in Spain, after his death his remains were placed in a vault at the Hospital de Jesus chapel, which he helped build.

Octavio Paz (1914–1998), winner of the 1990 Nobel Prize for Literature, was born in Mexico City. Mario Jose Molina (b.1943) shared the 1995 Nobel Prize in Chemistry with colleagues Paul J. Crutzen and F. Sherwood Rowland for their study of the effects of chlorofluorocarbon gases (CFCs) on the ozone layer.

Carlos Fuentes (b.Panama, 1928) is a renowned writer, editor, and diplomat. He was head of the department of cultural relations in Mexico's ministry of foreign affairs from 1956 to 1959 and Mexican ambassador to France from 1975 to 1977. His fiction works deal with Mexican history and identity and include *A Change of Skin, Terra Nostra,* and *The Years with Laura Díaz* (all of which have been translated into English from Spanish). José Joaquín Fernández de Lizardi (1776–1827) was a journalist, satirical novelist, and dramatist, known by his pseudonym El Pensador Mexicano. His best known work is *El Periquillo Sarniento* (*The Itching Parrot*). Manuel Gutiérrez Nájera (1859–1895) is considered to be one of the first Mexican modernist poets.

Composer Carlos Chávez (1899–1978) produced works that combined Mexican, Indian, and Spanish-Mexican influences. Agustín Lara (1900–1970) was a popular composer who made his mark in the film industry from 1930 to 1950, a period known as the Golden Age of Mexican cinema.

Cantinflas (Mario Moreno Reyes 1911–1993) was a popular comedian, film producer, and writer who appeared in more than 55 films, including a role as Passepartoute in the 1956 version of *Around the World in Eighty Days.* The life of painter Frida Kahlo (1907–1954) was the subject of a 2002 feature film, *Frida,* starring Salma Hayek.

Carlos Slim Helú (b.1940) is a Mexican businessman who was listed as the third richest man in the world by *Forbes Magazine* in 2006. He controls three major telecommunication companies: Teléfonos de México (Telmex), Telcel, and América Móvil. Maria Asunción Aramburuzabala (b.1963) is the richest woman in Mexico. She has major holdings in Grupo Modelo, a brewing company known for Corona beer.

27 Bibliography

BOOKS

Aykroyd, Clarissa. *The Government of Mexico.* Philadelphia, PA: Mason Crest Publishers, 2003.

Carew-Miller, Anna. *Famous People of Mexico.* Philadelphia: Mason Crest Publishers, 2003.

Lourie, Peter. *Hidden World of the Aztec.* Honesdale, PA: Boyds Mills Press, 2006.

Morrison, Marion. *Mexico City.* Milwaukee, WI: World Almanac Library, 2004.

Gruber, Beth. *Mexico.* Washington, DC: National Geographic, 2006.

Zronik, John. *Hernando Cortes: Spanish Invader of Mexico.* New York: Crabtree Publishing Co., 2006.

WEB SITES

Government of Mexico. *Mexico for Kids.* www.elbalero.gob.mx/index_kids.html (accessed on March 30, 2007).

Mexico City. www.mexicocity.com (accessed on March 30, 2007).

Durango

PRONUNCIATION: doo-RAHN-goh.

ORIGIN OF STATE NAME: The name is believed to have been given to the region by Spanish settlers from the Basque region of Spain. It means "fertile land, with rivers surrounded by mountains."

CAPITAL: Durango.

ENTERED COUNTRY: 1825.

COAT OF ARMS: The oak tree with two wolves represents Biscay, the home province of many of the Spanish settlers; the crown above the coat of arms represents the king of Spain.

HOLIDAYS: Año Nuevo (New Year's Day—January 1); Día de la Constitución (Constitution Day—February 5); Benito Juárez's birthday (March 21); Primero de Mayo (Labor Day—May 1); Anniversary of the Battle of Puebla (1862), May 5; Revolution Day, 1910 (November 20); and Navidad (Christmas—December 25).

FLAG: There is no official flag.

TIME: 6 AM = noon Greenwich Mean Time (GMT).

1 Location and Size

Durango is located in northern Mexico and covers an area of 123,444 square kilometers (47,662 square miles), about the same size as the US state of Mississippi. It ranks as fourth in size among the states and covers about 6.3% of the total land area of Mexico. Durango is bordered by the state of Chihuahua on the north, by Nayarit and Jalisco on the south, by Zacatecas and Coahuila on the east, and by Sinaloa on the west. Durango is divided into 39 municipalities (similar to US counties). The capital is also called Durango.

The Sierra Madre Occidental, a large mountain range which crosses most of Mexico, runs through the state from north to south in the west. The highest peak is Cerro Gordo with an elevation of about 3,340 meters (10,958 feet). This region extends to the border states of Coahuila and Chihuahua. Deep canyons and plains are located between the mountains and semidesert regions. Valleys run through the center of the state between the Sierra del Oso, Sierra de Guajalotes, Sierra de la Magdalena, Sierra Coneto, and Sierra del Gamón. The fertile Comarca Lagunera region, which extends into neighboring Coahuila, lies near the east-central border.

Rock outcroppings. © ROBERT FRERCK/WOODFIN CAMP.

Most of the state's rivers and streams run down from the mountains toward the Pacific Ocean. These include Tamazula, Los Remedios, San Diego, and Mezquital rivers. The Nazas and Aguanaval rivers flow into the Bolsón de Mapimí, a semidesert region in the northeast. Bolsón de Mapimí is part of the larger region known as the Chihuahuan Desert, which extends northward through Mexico to the United States between the Sierra Madre Occidental and the Sierra Madre Oriental. Laguna Santiaguillo, in the center of the state, is one of the largest natural lakes. There are several lakes created by river dams, such as Presa Lázaro Cardenas.

2 Climate

The tropic of Cancer, a line of latitude at 23°27' north of the equator, passes through the state.

The climate regions to the north of the tropic of Cancer are generally known as the northern temperate zone. The regions of the state to the south are considered to be the torrid zone (or tropical zone). However, variations in altitude and rainfall also have a great effect on the climate in different regions the state.

Average temperature is 21°C (70°F). Average annual rainfall is 283 millimeters (11.2 inches). Monthly average rainfall in winter (November to April) is 8 millimeters (0.3 inch); monthly average rainfall in summer (May to October) is 36 millimeters (1.4 inches).

3 Plants and Animals

Durango has huge evergreen forests and also a large section of the Chihuahuan Desert (Bolsón de Mapimí) where many varieties of cactus

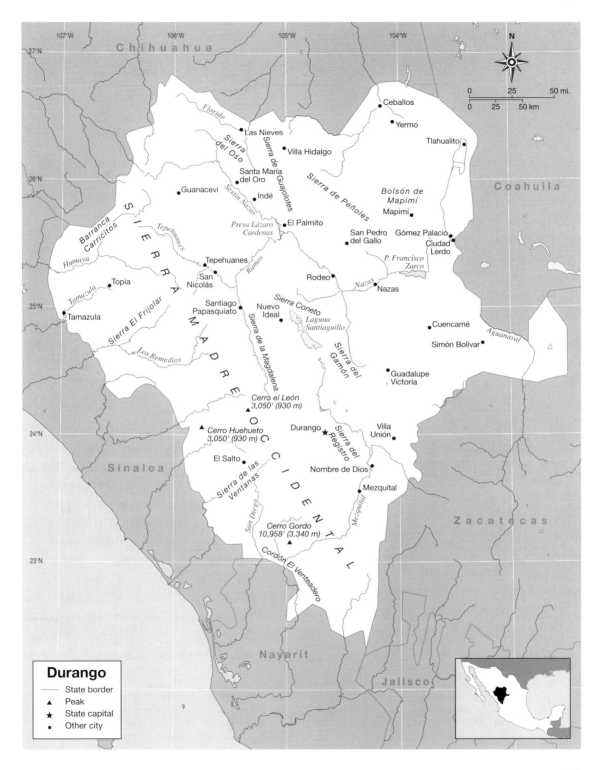

Durango

- State border
- ▲ Peak
- ★ State capital
- • Other city

thrive. The desert turtle was once fairly common but is now endangered in the state of Durango. Guayule, a source of rubber, is native to the state. Common plants of the desert include the fragrant gobernadora, ocotillo (with thorny branches growing toward the sky), yucca (with tall flower spikes in the spring), and candelilla (with a wax-like coating on its leaves to preserve water). Nopal cacti and mesquite (a common desert shrub) are plentiful.

Hundreds of species of butterflies are native to the state. Native animals include deer, badger, foxes, coyotes, squirrels, rabbits, kangaroo rats, and mice.

4 Environmental Protection

Durango began a program in 2003 to require industry within the state to track pollutants they generate through manufacturing. In 2004, the state had 114 municipal wastewater treatment plants in operation with a combined installed capacity of 3,313 liters per second (875 gallons per second). The volume of treated wastewater that year was estimated at 2,434 liters per second (632 gallons per second). There were also 34 industrial wastewater treatment plants in operation that year. As of 2004, about 93.6% of the population had access to safe drinking water.

In 2003, the state had about 5.4 million hectares (13.5 million acres) of woodland, including 495,020 hectares (1.2 million acres) of rain forest. In 2004, about 494 hectares (1,220 acres) of woodland were damaged or destroyed by forest fires. An additional 2,948 hectares (7,284 acres) of pasture and brush lands were also damaged by fires.

There is a forest preserve, La Michilía Biosphere Reserve, on the eastern side of the Sierra Madre Occidental. The Mapimí Biosphere reserve was established in 2000 to protect the distinctive plants and animals of this part of the Chihuahuan Desert region.

5 Population, Ethnic Groups, Languages

Durango had an estimated total population of 1,531,200 in 2006, ranking 24th among the states and the Distrito Federal. About 49% of the population were men and 51% were women. About 63% of the population lived in urban areas. The population density was 12.8 people per square kilometer (33 people per square mile). In 2005, the capital, Durango, had an estimated population of 526,659. Almost all citizens in Durango speak Spanish, but nearly 2% of the population speaks one of the indigenous languages, such as Tepehuano de Durango.

6 Religions

According to the 2000 census, 90.4% of the population, or 1.1 million people, were Roman Catholic. About 3.9%, or 48,794 people, were mainline or evangelical Protestants. About 1.8% were counted as other Biblical faiths, including 2,984 Latter-day Saints (Mormons) and 19,515 Jehovah's Witnesses. About 2.9% of the population claimed to have no religious affiliation. The Catedral Basílica de la Asunción de Maria (Cathedral Basilica of the Assumption of Mary) in the capital city is the seat of the Roman Catholic archdiocese of Durango.

7 Transportation

Durango has 10,477 kilometers (6,548 miles) of roads providing links to the Pacific coast and to inland cities such as Monterrey, Nuevo Léon, and Saltillo, Coahuila. The two primary roads crossing the state are the Pan-American Road (running from México state to Ciudad Juárez, Chihuahua) and the Transoceanic Road (from the Mexican state of Tamaulipas through Matamoros, Coahuila, to Mazatlan, Sinaloa).

In 2004, there were 158,158 automobiles registered in the state, along with 2,111 passenger trucks, 138,805 freight trucks, and 2,627 motorcycles.

There is an international airport serving the capital, Durango, with flights to about a dozen cities in Mexico and to Los Angeles and Chicago in the United States. There are also rail links connecting the state to border cities with the United States to the north and with many other cities in Mexico.

8 History

The Tepehuano, an indigenous group, inhabited Durango when the Spaniards first arrived in the 16th century. Captain Francisco de Ibarra was the first Spaniard to visit the region. The city of Durango was founded in 1563. Several indigenous revolts aimed at protesting the abuses and oppression by Spanish colonizers threw the region into turmoil for much of the 17th century.

Franciscan and Jesuit priests (from different orders of the Roman Catholic Church) built missions and sought to convert and work with the indigenous people of the area. Tensions with indigenous groups, including Apache and Comanche warriors, lasted well into the 19th century. This made it difficult for colonizers to promote economic development and introduce new agricultural technology to the region. Yet,

the tensions also reflected the poor living conditions that the native inhabitants of the region experienced during the colonial period and throughout most of the 19th century.

Mexico witnessed the independence revolt led by Miguel Hidalgo (1753–1811) in 1810. Several local priests in Durango supported the revolt and attempted to rally the population. But local authorities, loyal to Spain, firmly opposed any uprising. Eventually, in the late 1810s, Pedro Celestino Negrete defeated the Spanish royalists in Durango and consolidated support for independence. Durango joined other states in signing the Plan of Iguala in 1821, which secured Mexico's independence.

Durango was officially recognized as a Mexican state in 1825 and the first state constitution was written in 1825. Santiago Baca Ortíz became the first constitutional governor of Durango. The conflicts between liberal and conservative factions reached Durango in the mid-1850s. The conservatives managed to control the state during most of the period, but eventually liberal forces won control. The leaders in Durango united behind Porfirio Díaz (1830–1915). As president, Díaz in turn promoted economic and infrastructure development in the state.

In 1909, wealthy and powerful citizens in Durango began to doubt that Díaz could continue to be effective as president. They supported Francisco Madero (1873–1913) in leading a revolution to oppose a new presidential term for the aging Díaz. Revolutionary leaders successfully gained control of Durango in 1911. It was not until 1917, however, that Domingo Arrieta successfully led the state to adopt a new constitution. Under his leadership, peace and order was restored to the state. Durango aligned with the winning faction of the Mexican Revolution (1910–20) and signed the new 1917 constitution. But peace would not last long.

Francisco "Pancho" Villa (1878–1923), the legendary revolutionary leader, attempted a new uprising in 1923 in the Tepehuanes region in Durango but was quickly defeated. Yet four years later, Durango was involved in the Cristero War (1926–29). This war was launched by Roman Catholic militants who opposed the restrictions placed on the Catholic Church by the federal government. The "cristero" resistance was eventually defeated, but post-revolutionary peace arrived in Durango a couple of decades after it reached the rest of Mexico.

Following the passage of the North American Free Trade Agreement (NAFTA), a trade agreement between Mexico, the United States, and Canada, significant economic development took place in the state. The government invested significantly in new roads, upgrading of water systems, education and training, and improved health care systems.

Durango has been dominated by the Institutional Revolutionary Party (PRI) since the end of the revolution. In the 1980s, 1990s, and early 2000s, other parties were gaining strength in Mexico and elections in Durango were becoming more competitive. In the July 2004 election for the governorship, the PRI retained its hold on the office, with Ismael Hernández Deras winning the governorship with 54% of the votes cast.

9 State and Local Government

The state governor is elected for non-renewable six-year terms. Durango has a unicameral (one chamber) state congress comprised of 25 deputies elected for nonrenewable three-year terms. Fifteen deputies are elected in single-member districts and 10 by proportional representation. Although formal separation of powers and check-and-balance provisions exist in the constitution, the overwhelming power exercised by the PRI and the strong formal and informal attributions of the governor have limited the power and influence of the state legislature.

Comprised of 39 municipalities, local governments in Durango are relatively weak and their attributions are mostly limited. Elections take place every three years for municipal presidents and council members. Immediate re-election is not allowed.

10 Political Parties

The three main political parties in all of Mexico are the Institutional Revolutionary Party (PRI), the National Action Party (PAN), and the Party of the Democratic Revolution (PRD). Durango's politics have been dominated by the influential and powerful PRI. All of Durango's governors have belonged to the PRI since the end of the revolution. In the 1990s, Durango witnessed the emergence and consolidation of the PAN and PRD. Yet, as of 2004, those two parties had failed to transform their growing appeal into a statewide electoral victory. Ismael Alfredo Hernández Deras was elected governor in 2004.

11 Judicial System

The Superior Tribunal of Justice is Durango's highest court. Its eight members are elected for six-year, nonrenewable terms by the governor with legislative approval. Appointees must meet a number of stringent qualification require-

This Volkswagen dealership is in the city of Gomez Palacio. Most industrial activity is centered around three cities: the capital (Durango), Gomez Palacio, and Lerdo. © SUZY MOORE/WOODFIN CAMP.

ments. In addition, an electoral tribunal and a number of local courts and tribunals comprise the judiciary system in Durango. Because of the dominance of one political party (PRI), the judiciary may not operate with total independence.

12 Economy

The economy of Durango was once limited to agriculture and mining. Since the passage of the North American Free Trade Agreement (NAFTA) in 1992, however, hundreds of maquiladoras (assembly plants) have developed. Among the companies that operate in Durango are LG Philips, Sumitomo, Levi Strauss, and Sun

Apparel. Mining of silver and gold continue to be important economic activities as well.

13 Industry

Most industrial activity is centered around the capital, Durango, or in the eastern region known as Comarca Lagunera, around the cities of Gómez Palacio and Ciudad Lerdo.

As of 2004, there were nearly 4,000 industrial enterprises employing more than 100,000 workers. The main industries represented in Durango are textiles and clothing, wood products, auto parts, mining, food processing, and electronics.

The state's handicraft industries are centered on basketworks and wood carvings.

14 Labor

As of 2005, the state of Durango had 542,538 eligible workers. Some 524,535 were listed as employed and 18,003 were listed as unemployed. Unemployed workers in rural areas may not be counted, however. The unemployment rate that year was reported to be 3.3%. Of those who were working, services employed 35.9%, followed by agriculture at 20.8% and manufacturing at 17.1%.

The US Bureau of Labor Statistics reported that Mexican workers saw their wages increase from $2.49 per hour in 2003 to $2.50 per hour in 2004. (The average US worker earned $15.70 per hour in 2004.) The maximum work week is set at 48 hours by law. The average worker spends 40 to 45 hours per week on the job. Workers earn twice their regular hourly rate for up to nine hours a week of overtime. When a worker works more than nine hours overtime in a week, he or she earns three times the regular hourly rate. After one year, workers are entitled by law to six days paid vacation. Durango collects a 2% payroll tax from all wage earners.

Union activity in the state is mostly found in the capital city of Durango, in the La Laguna area around the cities of Lerdo and Gomez Palacio, and in the city of Torreon, which is across the border in the state of Coahuila. There are several unions in these cities, including the Mexican Workers Confederation (CTM), the Revolutionary Confederation of Workers and Farmers (CROC), the National Confederations of Popular Organizations (CNOP), and the Electricity Workers Confederation of the Mexican Republic (SUTERM).

15 Agriculture

In 2004, Durango ranked first among Mexico's states in the production of kidney beans (176,992 tons), second in the production of goat's milk (39 million liters/10 million gallons), third in the production of cow's milk (959 million liters/253 million gallons), and fourth in the production of poultry (195,673 tons).

In rural areas, many families carry out small-scale agriculture on small plots, growing food for their own consumption or to sell locally. In the early 2000s, family farmers were concerned about the impact of genetically engineered maize (corn) on their crops.

Agriculture in Durango is based on crops like corn, beans, chilies, alfalfa, apples, zacate (a type of hay), sorghum, and oats for animal feed. The Guadiana Valley is known for its aquaculture (cultivating products from the water) and the production of carp and mojarra (a silvery fish). In 2004, Durango produced 374,632 tons of corn and 33,636 tons of green chilies.

16 Natural Resources

Mexico is the largest silver producer in the world and the state of Durango is the third largest producer of silver (after the Mexican states of Zacatecas and Chihuahua). The cities of Durango, San Dimas, and Otáez are known for their gold and silver mining activities, while lead is produced at Cuencamé and Guanaceví. Zinc, copper, and fluorite are also produced in various parts of the state.

Durango also is a leading producer of pine and encino (a type of oak) lumber. In 2003, the value of forest wood was estimated at about $212.5 million, the highest value in the country.

The total fish catch in 2003 was about 3,943 tons, all of which was for human consumption.

17 Energy and Power

In 2005, there were 408,622 users of electricity in the state of Durango. Of that total, the largest number were residential customers at 360,686. Sales of electricity that same year totaled 2,598,918 megawatt hours, of which the largest users were medium-sized industrial firms at 939,082 megawatt hours. Electricity produced in the state of Durango comes from gas-turbine, steam, and combined cycle (using gas-turbine and steam technologies) plants. Electricity is provided and distributed by the Federal Electricity Commission and Central Light and Power. Both utilities are run by the Mexican government.

Demand for electricity in Durango grew rapidly (from 1,321 gigawatt hours in 1993 to nearly 2,000 gigawatt hours by 2000) after the North American Free Trade Agreement (NAFTA) went into effect in 1992. There is potential for development of hydroelectric power along the western slopes of the mountains.

18 Health

In 2003, the state had 22 hospitals and 482 out-patient centers that were part of the national health system. In 2004, there were about 1,641 doctors, 3,285 nurses, and 79 dentists working in these health centers. There were an additional 39 independent health centers in the state in 2004.

Most of the Mexican population is covered under a government health plan. The IMSS (Instituto Mexicano de Seguro Social) covers the general population. The ISSSTE (Instituto de Seguridad y Servicios Sociales de Trabajadores del Estado) covers state workers.

19 Housing

The most popular building materials for walls and floors are concrete, brick, stone, and adobe. Most homes have flat roofs made of some type of brick or stone. In 2000, about 83% of all homes were owner-occupied. In 2005, there were an estimated 358,302 residential housing units in the state. About 96% of these units were single-family detached homes. The average household was estimated at 4.2 people.

20 Education

Public education in Mexico is free for students from ages 6 to 16 and most students in the state attend public schools. In 2004/05, it was estimated that 90% of age-eligible students completed primary school, which includes six years of study. About 77.5% of eligible students completed secondary school, which includes three years of study after primary school. About 58.4% of eligible students completed the *bachillerato*, which is similar to a high school diploma. The national average for completion of the *bachillerato* was 60.1%.

There are at least six institutes of higher learning in Durango. The capital city is host to the Universidad Autónoma de Durango, the Instituto Tecnológico de Durango, and the

Durango movie set where many Hollywood Westerns were filmed. © ROBERT FRERCK/WOODFIN CAMP.

Universidad Juárez del Esatdao de Durango. In 2005, there were about 40,830 students ages 20 and older who were enrolled in some type of higher education program. The overall literacy rate was estimated at 93.5% in 2005.

21 Arts

Durango has many galleries selling local handicrafts. In the capital, Durango, there is an art school where students may study painting and sculpture. The Durango Performing Arts area is on the north side of the capital. There, footprints of many famous Hollywood movie stars who came to Mexico to film have been preserved. In 2004, there were at least four major theaters for the performing arts. There were also about 30 registered movie theaters, including multiscreen theaters and single-screen galleries.

22 Libraries and Museums

In 2003, there were 275 libraries in the state with a combined stock of 1,164,398 volumes. There were 20 museums registered in the state that had permanent exhibits, including the Cultural Institute of Durango, the Durango Regional Museum, and the Museum of Archeology. Other popular sites are the Museum of Popular Culture and the Museum of Thematic Films, which features antique cameras and photographs as well as memorabilia of movies that were filmed at locations within the state.

23 Media

In 2005, the capital city of Durango had five daily newspapers. The two largest were *La Voz de Durango* (*Durango Voice*) and *El Sol de Durango* (*Durango Sun*). The others were *Diario de Durango* (*Durango Daily*), *El Siglo de Durango* (*The Durango Century*), and *Victoria de Durango* (*Victory of Durango*).

In 2004, there were 78 television stations and 23 radio stations (19 AM and 4 FM). In 2005, there were about 32,203 subscribers to cable and satellite television stations. Also in 2005, there were about 208,804 residential phone lines, with about 15.6 mainline phones in use for every 100 people.

24 Tourism, Travel, and Recreation

The capital, Durango, has been the set for many cowboy movies. Some movie sets in locations such as Puebla del Oeste, Chupaderos, and Rancho La Joya, are still in operation. Guadiana Park has an artificial lake. Adventure sports enthusiasts may visit the caverns of the Sierra del Rosario and Espinazo del Diablo for hiking and cave diving. La Ferreria Archaeological Zone, south of Durango, is an ancient settlement site of the Chalchihuites of Zacatecas, featuring pyramids, small temples, and stone altars.

25 Sports

The Alacranes (Scorpions) play in the First Division "A" of the Mexican Football (soccer) Association (commonly known as Femexfut). Their home field is at the 14,000-seat Francisco Zarco stadium. The Lobos Grises (Gray Wolves) play as part of the North Zone of the National Professional Basketball League (LNBP).

26 Famous People

Famous citizens born in Durango include composer Silvestre Revueltas (1899–1940), who drew on Mexican folk music themes in his works for orchestra. Francisco "Pancho" Villa (1878–1923), though not born in the state, was known as a revolutionary bandit in Chihuahua and Durango.

27 Bibliography

BOOKS

Carew-Miller, Anna. *Famous People of Mexico.* Philadelphia: Mason Crest Publishers, 2003.

Day-MacLeod, Deirdre. *The States of Northern Mexico.* Philadelphia, PA: Mason Crest Publishers, 2003.

Gruber, Beth. *Mexico.* Washington, DC: National Geographic, 2006.

Marcovitz, Hal. *Pancho Villa.* Philadelphia, PA: Chelsea House Publishers, 2003.

WEB SITES

Government of Mexico. *Mexico for Kids.* www.elbalero.gob.mx/index_kids.html (accessed on March 30, 2007).

Government of the State of Durango. *Durango.* www.promociondurango.gob.mx/english.html (accessed on March 30, 2007).

Guanajuato

PRONUNCIATION: gwah-nah-WHAH-toh.

ORIGIN OF STATE NAME: From an Amerindian word that means "hill of frogs."

CAPITAL: Guanajuato.

ENTERED COUNTRY: 1824.

COAT OF ARMS: The coat of arms is supported by a base of colored marble with gold decoration. The base is a shell held by two laurel branches bound with a blue ribbon. The shell linking with the coat of arms symbolizes a stable home, opening to welcome guests. The gold background signifies nobility and represents the wealth of precious metals found in the state. The laurels stand for victory, and the acanthus flowers signify loyalty. This crest originally represented the city of Guanajuato but was later adopted by the state.

HOLIDAYS: Año Nuevo (New Year's Day—January 1); Día de la Constitución (Constitution Day—February 5); Benito Juárez's birthday (March 21); Primero de Mayo (Labor Day—May 1); Anniversary of the Battle of Puebla (1862), May 5; Revolution Day, 1910 (November 20); and Navidad (Christmas—December 25).

FLAG: There is no official state flag.

TIME: 6 AM = noon Greenwich Mean Time (GMT).

1 Location and Size

Guanajuato is in the center of Mexico. It covers an area of 30,608 square kilometers (11,817 square miles). It ranks as 22nd in size among the states and covers about 1.6% of the total land area of Mexico. Guanajuato is slightly larger than the US state of Maryland. It is bordered on the north by San Luis Potosí and Zacatecas, on the east by Querétaro, on the west by Jalisco, and on the south by Michoacán. Guanajuato is divided into 46 municipalities (similar to US counties). The capital, the city of Guanajuato, is located in approximately the center of the state.

Part of the Sierra Madre Oriental mountain range crosses the northeastern corner of the state. The great Central Plateau of Mexico covers much of the north-central portion of the state where fertile valleys lie. The southern portion of the state is crossed by the Sierra Volcánica Transversal (also known as the Cordillera Neovolcánica). The highest point in the state is Cerro Los Rosillos with an elevation of 3,810 meters (12,500 feet).

One of the most important rivers is the Lerma River. The Lerma River rises in México state and crosses Michoacán in the north to loop into southern Guanajuato. The Laja and Guanajuato Rivers feed into Lerma Rivers. Laguna de Yuriria in the south covers an area of about 80 square kilometers (30.8 square miles). It is the largest lake in the state and one of the most important lakes in the country. Presa Solís and Presa Begonias are lakes created by river dams.

A wide, fertile plains region known as El Bajio covers the southern part of the state and stretches into Querétaro. This region is extremely important for agriculture. The Valle de La Piedad and the Valle de Santiago are located in this region.

2 Climate

The climate is fairly dry. Average monthly rainfall from November to April is 1 centimeter (0.4 inches). Most of the rainfall occurs between May and September, when the average monthly rainfall is 9.5 centimeters (3.75 inches). The average temperature is 19°C (66°F). In the capital city of Guanajuato, the average temperature is 17°C (62°F) and average precipitation is 66.9 centimeters (26.3 inches) per year.

3 Plants and Animals

Trees in Guanajuato include oak, pine, birch, eucalyptus, guava, lemon, and many types of cactus and nopal (a type of cactus). Common animals include rabbits, armadillos, eagles, lizards, squirrels, deer, snakes, skunks, owls, heron, and quail.

4 Environmental Protection

In 2004, the state had 20 municipal wastewater treatment plants in operation with a combined installed capacity of 3,963 liters per second (1,046 gallons per second). The volume of treated wastewater that year was estimated at 2,879 liters per second (760 gallons per second). There were also 56 industrial wastewater treatment plants in operation that year. As of 2004, about 94.3% of the population had access to safe drinking water.

In 2003, the state had about 412,810 hectares (1 million acres) of woodland, including 18,141 hectares (44,827 acres) of rain forest. In 2004, about 67 hectares (165 acres) of woodland were damaged or destroyed by forest fires. An additional 209 hectares (516 acres) of pasture and brush lands were also damaged by fires.

There are few protected regions in the state. The Laguna de Yuriria, the largest lake in the state, was designated as a Ramsar Wetland of International Importance in 2004 to protect the endangered species of fish, birds, amphibians, and plants that are found in the area.

5 Population, Ethnic Groups, Languages

Guanajuato had an estimated total population of 4,967,500 in 2006, ranking sixth among the states and the Distrito Federal. About 48% of the population were men and 52% were women. About 68% of the population lived in urban areas. The population density was 162 people per square kilometer (420 people per square mile). In 2005, the capital, Guanajuato, had a population of 153,364. Almost everyone speaks Spanish, with a small percentage speaking one of

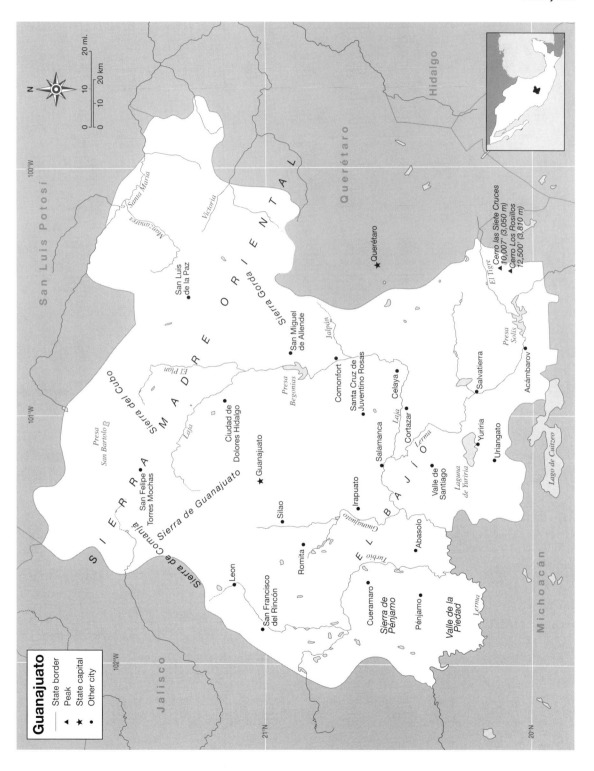

Guanajuato

— State border
◄ Peak
★ State capital
● Other city

20 mi.

20 km

N

San Luis Potosí

Querétaro

Hidalgo

Santa María

Manantiales

Victoria

Sierra Gorda

San Luis
de la Paz

San Miguel
de Allende

Jalpán

El Tigre

Cerro las Siete Cruces
10,007' (3,050 m)
Cerro Los Rosillos
12,500' (3,810 m)

★ Querétaro

Presa
Solís

Sierra del Cubo

El Plan

Presa
Begonias

Comonfort

Santa Cruz de
Juventino Rosas

Celaya

Salvatierra

Acámbaro

Presa
San Bartolo

Ciudad de
Dolores Hidalgo

Laja

Salamanca

Laja

Cortazar

Lerma

Yuriria

Uriangato

S   I   E   R   R   A

Sierra de Guanajuato

★ Guanajuato

San Felipe
Torres Mochas

Sierra de Comanja

Silao

Irapuato

E   L   B   A   J   Í   O

Guanajuato

Abasolo

Valle de
Santiago

Laguna
de Yuriria

Lago de Cuitzeo

Leon

Romita

Turbio

San Francisco
del Rincón

Cueramaro

Sierra de
Pénjamo

Pénjamo

Valle de la
Piedad

Lerma

Michoacán

San Luis Potosí

Jalisco

100°W

101°W

102°W

21°N

20°N

Monument to local hero in the battle for independence, Juan José de los Reyes Martínez (known as "Pipila"). © ROBERT FRERCK/WOODFIN CAMP.

the indigenous languages, such as Náhuatl and Otomi.

6 Religions

According to the 2000 census, 96.4% of the population, or 3.9 million people, were Roman Catholic; about 1.3%, or 53,390 people, were mainline or evangelical Protestants. Less than 1% were counted as other Biblical faiths, including 2,872 Latter-day Saints (Mormons) and 24,020 Jehovah's Witnesses. Less than 1% of the population claimed to have no religious affiliation.

There are many religious sites within the state. One of the most prominent is the Sanctuary of Cristo Rey, a church built on Cerro del Cubilete,

a mountain just outside of the capital city. The church serves as the base for one of the largest statues of Jesus in the world.

7 Transportation

Highways were constructed in the 1980s, helping the economy to grow by allowing goods to be transported. About 50% of all the people in Mexico live within 400 kilometers (250 miles) of Guanajuato, the capital of the state.

In 2004, there were 442,678 automobiles registered in the state, along with 19,665 passenger trucks, 397,826 freight trucks, and 27,422 motorcycles.

8 History

The first human settlements in Guanajuato date back to 500 BC. The Chupicuaro culture populated the region and left considerable cultural, religious, and traditional legacies. Before the arrival of the Spaniards, the region was inhabited by Guamare, Guaxabana, and Copuce indigenous groups. Prolonged human presence had left indelible traces of different cultures, often in tension with each other. Well-established settlements were also evident.

The first Spanish expedition arrived in 1522 led by Cristóbal de Olid (1488–1524). A year later, Spanish explorer Hernán Cortés (1485–1547) distributed some of the lands in the region to several of the lieutenants of his conquest expedition. In 1529, another Spanish explorer, Nuño de Guzmán (d. 1544), led an infamous expedition that killed many indigenous people and pillaged indigenous communities in the region. His pillaging included some communities that had already been conquered and assigned to colonizers under the *encomienda* (land tenure) system.

The discovery of silver mines in Zacatecas and Guanajuato helped promote Spanish settlements in the region in the late 16th and early 17th centuries. The city of Guanajuato was founded in 1557, two years after San Miguel (also in present-day Guanajuato) was founded, and 14 years before the foundation of Celaya. León, Guanajuato, was founded in 1574, reflecting the growing economic activity resulting from the exploitation of silver and other minerals. In 1762, the first inquisition official arrived in the region. The inquisition officials were priests appointed by the Catholic Church to combat followers of non-Catholic religions, particularly Protestants. The expulsion of the Jesuits (an order of the Roman Catholic Church) in 1767 provoked additional conflicts between local elites and the Catholic Church.

Guanajuato was one of the 12 regions that comprised Mexico in the 18th century, reflecting the economic and social importance of the agricultural and mineral producing region. The independence movement, which began in 1810, started in the city of Dolores, Guanajuato (known today as Dolores Hidalgo). Priest Miguel Hidalgo (1753–1811) called on peasants and patriots to revolt against the Spanish crown. A local hero, a miner named Juan José de los Reyes Martínez, is known by his nickname "Pipila." He was a hero in a battle in Guanajuato, and a statue commemorates his place in the state's history. Hidalgo organized an army that marched towards Mexico City. Although the rebellion was eventually defeated, the independence movement remained active in Guanajuato. In 1821 Guanajuato joined the rest of Mexico in signing the Plan of Iguala that secured the country's independence.

In the Mexican-American War (1846–48), a Guanajuato army fiercely fought the US occupation. During the political conflicts for power in the 1850s, Mexican revolutionary and later president Benito Juárez (1806–1872) made Guanajuato the provisional capital of his government. During the short French occupation (from 1863 to 1867) under the monarchy of Maximilian (1832–1867), Guanajuato was the most populated state of Mexico. Under Juárez, Guanajuato remained an economic and political power in Mexico. Benito Juárez and later President Porfirio Díaz (1830–1915) promoted economic development and improvements in infrastructure.

A plaza in the capital, Guanajuato. © ROBERT FRERCK/WOODFIN CAMP.

The Mexican Revolution, which started in 1910, was fiercely fought in Guanajuato. Revolutionary leaders organized militias and different factions faced each other in bloody battles. Francisco "Pancho" Villa (1878–1923) and other revolutionary leaders occupied different cities during the revolt. However, no group dominated the entire state. After the end of the revolution, the Cristero War (1926–29) brought new confrontations to the state. The Catholic Church's militant opposition to some of the policies of the new government and the uprising of Catholic loyalists generated much tension in Guanajuato. Eventually, the government made peace with the Catholic Church, but religious tensions remained present in the state.

Since the mid 1950s, the consolidation of anti-clerical (anti-Catholic) Institutional Revolutionary Party (PRI) rule in Mexico promoted the growth of the pro-Catholic National Action Party (PAN) party in Guanajuato. The election of PAN gubernatorial candidate Vicente Fox in 1995 represented the first state-wide electoral defeat for the PRI. Fox's gubernatorial victory in 1995 made Guanajuato the first state to elect a non-PRI governor since the end of the Mexican Revolution. Fox went on to become president of Mexico in 2000.

In the first decade of the 21st century, Guanajuato continued to grow economically. Politically, the National Action Party (PAN) retained its hold on the state's governorship in the 2006 elections.

9 State and Local Government

The governor is the most important and powerful figure in the state. With strong powers and attributions, the governor can assume an influential leadership role. The state governor is elected for non-renewable six-year terms. The state congress is comprised of 36 deputies, 22 elected in single member districts and 14 by proportional representation, for nonrenewable three-year terms.

The 46 municipalities of the state elect municipal presidents and council members every three years for nonrenewable terms. The powers and attributions of the municipal governments are strong because of historical tradition and the importance of local governments during the colonial period.

10 Political Parties

The three main political parties in all of Mexico are the Institutional Revolutionary Party (PRI), the National Action Party (PAN), and the Party of the Democratic Revolution (PRD). Although the PRI was the sole political party during much of the post revolution 20th century, PAN became a strong contender for political power and representation in the mid 1980s. PAN's Vicente Fox was the first non-PRI governor of the state. He went on to become the first non-PRI president of Mexico in 2000. Juan Carlos Romero Hicks of PAN was elected as governor in 2000. He was replaced by Juan Manuel Oliva Ramírez of PAN in 2006.

Balance of power provisions existing in the constitution were first implemented when a PAN candidate won the governorship in 1994. Democratic consolidation in Guanajuato has resulted in lively debates between two strong

The Hidalgo Market in the capital, Guanajuato, was built in the late 1800s. © ROBERT FRERCK/WOODFIN CAMP.

political parties. However, executive powers are now checked by the legislature.

11 Judicial System

The Supreme Tribunal of Justice is the highest court of the state. Members are appointed by the governor with congressional approval. The president of the Supreme Tribunal is elected from among its members for a renewable two-year period. The state legal system is also comprised of an electoral tribunal and local courts with different powers and attributions. The

The Valenciana silver mine operated for over 250 years. © ROBERT FRERCK/WOODFIN CAMP.

process of democratization experienced in the mid 1980s and 1990s has helped strengthen the independence and autonomy of the Guanajuato judiciary.

12 Economy

The state of Guanajuato's economy has been enhanced through the construction of dams and highways, the growth of the manufacturing sector, mining, trade, and tourism. As of 2003, 75% of the state's workforce was employed in non-agricultural activities, of which services accounted for 24%, industry 22%, and commerce 20%.

Although Guanajuato is best known as a center for the manufacture of footwear, the state is also home to one of Latin America's most important refineries. The state capital of Guanajuato has also become a center for tourism.

13 Industry

Industry is centered in cities such as León, Salamanca, and Irapuato. The main industries are silver and gold mining, oil, footwear, fabric and apparel manufacturing, A total of 13 industrial parks are located in Guanajuato, while the city of Leon is the nation's premier shoe manufacturing center. The city produces more than 100 million pairs of shoes annually, with more than 25 million pairs exported each year. In the city of Silao, General Motors has a light truck assembly plant. Textiles and clothing are manufactured in Salvatierra, Moroleon, and Uriangato.

The state's handicrafts industry is known for its pottery, toys, wax figures, leatherworks, woolen textiles, woodwork, and objects made from tin, copper and brass.

14 Labor

Guanajuato has the lowest unemployment rate in Mexico. Workers are engaged in mining, agriculture, manufacturing, and tourism.

As of 2005, the state of Guanajuato had 1,829,447 eligible workers. Some 1,754,175 were listed as employed and 75,272 were listed as unemployed. Unemployed workers in rural areas may not be counted, however. The unemployment rate that year was reported to be 4.2%. Of those who were working, services employed 31.8% followed by manufacturing at 23.4%, and commerce at 21.4%.

The US Bureau of Labor Statistics reported that Mexican workers saw their wages increase from $2.49 per hour in 2003 to $2.50 per hour in 2004. (The average US worker earned $15.70 per hour in 2004.) The maximum work week is set at 48 hours by law. The average worker spends 40 to 45 hours per week on the job. Workers earn twice their regular hourly rate for up to nine hours a week of overtime. When a worker works more than nine hours overtime in a week, he or she earns three times the regular hourly rate. After one year, workers are entitled by law to six days paid vacation.

Union activity in the state of Guanajuato is based mostly in the cities of Celaya, Leon, Silao, Irapuato, and the state capital of Guanajuato. All of Mexico's national unions are represented in at least one these cities. These unions include the Mexican Workers Confederation (CTM), the Revolutionary Confederation of Mexican Workers (CROM), and the Revolutionary Confederation of Workers and Farmers (CROC).

15 Agriculture

Guanajuato's farms produce corn, wheat, strawberries, mangoes, bananas, oats, sorghum, chilies, onions, cauliflower, broccoli, asparagus, potatoes, peas, tomatoes, and alfalfa. Farmers also grow flowers such as roses and *cempasúchil*, a special flower used in the celebration for the Day of the Dead, an ancient festival honoring the dead that is held on November 1st and 2nd.

In 2004, Guanajuato was a leading producer of corn at 1,638,580 tons, sorghum at 1,616,255 tons, potatoes at 113,265 tons, and Mexico's second-largest producer of wheat at 540,562 tons.

In some parts of the state, cattle, pigs, sheep, goats, and poultry are raised. In 2004, beef cattle brought to market totaled 199,375 head, while pigs totaled 365,100 head, and sheep 12,460 head. The state that year also produced 34,501 tons of beef, 94,499 tons of pork, and 133,343 tons of poultry. In 2004 the state produced 633 million liters (167 million gallons) of milk from dairy cows and 23.4 million liters (6 million gallons) of goat's milk. The state also ranked fifth among Mexico's states in the production of eggs at 78,292 tons.

16 Natural Resources

Mexico is the largest silver producer in the world. Silver has been mined in the state since the 1500s. Guanajuato ranks fourth among the country's silver-producing states (after

Zacatecas, Chihuahua, and Durango). Together the four states produce three-fourths of Mexico's silver output. The Los Torres mine is a major producer.

In 2003, the total value of forest wood production was estimated at about $604,672. Conifers were the primary harvest woods. Also in 2003, the total fish catch was included 2,888 tons, all for human consumption.

17 Energy and Power

In 2005, there were 1,395,341 users of electricity in the state of Guanajuato. Of that total, the largest number were residential customers at 1,193,271. Sales of electricity that same year totaled 7,575,147 megawatt hours, of which the largest users were medium-sized industrial firms at 2,388,568 megawatt hours. Power in Guanajuato is provided by a single 866 megawatt power plant located at Salamanca.

All of Mexico's electricity is provided and distributed by the Federal Electricity Commission, and Central Light and Power. Both of which are run by the Mexican government.

18 Health

In 2003, the state had 37 hospitals and 591 outpatient centers that were part of the national health system. In 2004, there were about 3,271 doctors, 7,016 nurses, and 195 dentists working in these health centers. There were an additional 217 independent health centers in the state in 2004.

Most of the Mexican population is covered under a government health plan. The IMSS (Instituto Mexicano de Seguro Social) covers the general population. The ISSSTE (Instituto de Seguridad y Servicios Sociales de Trabajadores del Estado) covers state workers.

19 Housing

Most homes are built of permanent materials such as brick, stone, or concrete, with floors, walls, and flat roofs of similar materials. There are several homes made of adobe walls and floors with sheet metal roofs. In 2000, about 81% of all homes were owner-occupied. In 2005, there were an estimated 1,048,543 residential housing units in the state. About 93% of these units were single-family detached homes. The average household was estimated at 4.7 people.

20 Education

Public education in Mexico is free for students from ages 6 to 16. While most students in the state attend public schools, in 2003/04, the state had the highest percentage of students attending private high schools at 38%. In 2004/05, it was estimated that 84.3% of age-eligible students completed primary school, which includes six years of study. About 78.2% of eligible students completed secondary school, which includes three years of study after primary school. About 55.9% of eligible students completed the *bachillerato*, which is similar to a high school diploma. The national average for completion of the *bachillerato* was 60.1%.

There are at least eight institutes of higher learning in the state. The Universidad de Guanajuato (University of Guanajuato) is located in the capital. There are technological institutes in Celaya, León, and Irapuato. In 2005, there were about 126,207 students ages 20 and older who were enrolled in some type of higher educa-

Homes on a hillside near the capital, Guanajuato. © ROBERT FRERCK/WOODFIN CAMP.

tion program. The overall literacy rate was esti-mated at 88.7% in 2005.

21 Arts

The state of Guanajuato sponsors the Ballet Folklórico of Guanajuato. The Universidad de Guanajuato (University of Guanajuato) has a symphony orchestra. There is also a choir called the Voces of Guanajuato. The theatrical group, Cornisa 20, participates in many cultural fairs. There is also the more formal Ludus Teatro. In 2004, there were at least 14 theaters for the per-forming arts. There were also at least 12 regis-tered movie theaters, including multiscreen the-aters and single-screen galleries.

The Cervantes International Festival of the Arts (established in 1972) is a month long festi-val held each year to promote the arts of theatre, music, literature, and visual arts. The annual Running of the Bulls at San Miguel includes concerts and theatrical events, as well as the run-ning of the bulls through town.

22 Libraries and Museums

In 2003, there were 344 libraries in the state with a combined stock of 1,944,632 volumes. The same year, there were 27 museums reg-istered in the state that had permanent exhib-its. The Mummy Museum, featuring over 100 mummies, is in Celaya. The Casa Museo Diego Rivera is the birthplace of this famous artist. In the capital, Guanajuato, there is a museum dedicated to Spanish novelist Miguel de Cervantes's work *Don Quijote* (Don Quixote).

23 Media

In 2005, there were at least 11 daily newspapers in the state. The newspaper, *AM Guanajuato,* is published in the capital city of Guanajuato. Celaya had *El Sol de Bajio* (*Bajio Sun*) and *AM*. Irapuato had three papers: *El Sol de Irapuato* (*Irapuato Sun*), *El Heraldo de Irapuato* (*Irapuato Herald*), and *El Centro* (*The Center*). León had four papers, with the largest being *El Sol de León* (*León Sun*).

In 2004, there were 27 television stations and 55 radio stations (38 AM and 17 FM). In 2005, there were about 174,394 subscribers to cable and satellite television stations. Also in 2005, there were about 564,679 residential phone lines, with about 14 mainline phones in use for every 100 people.

24 Tourism, Travel, and Recreation

The capital city is best-known as a colonial silver mining town, where visitors can tour the silver mines. The historic town and adjacent mines are designated as UNESCO World Heritage sites. Two main museums, a mummy museum and the museum of famous muralist and painter Diego Rivera (1886–1957), are major tourist attractions. In mid-October, the Festival Cervantina honoring the works of Miguel de Cervantes (1547–1616), who wrote *Don Quixote*, is a huge tourist attraction requiring reservations in advance. Nearby, on the mountain of Cerro del Cubilete, many visitors come to see the towering statue of Jesus that stand on top of the Sanctuary of Cristo Rey.

25 Sports

The Leon (Lions) and the Petroleros (Oilers) of Salamanca are both First Division "A" soccer teams in the Mexican Football association (commonly known as Femexfut). The Nou Camp stadium in Leon holds 31,350 people. The Olimpico stadium in Salamanca holds 6,000 spectators. The Lechugueros of Leon play in the South Zone of the National Professional Basketball League (LNBP).

In 2004, there were three bullfighting rings in the state, including the 15,000-seat Plaza de Toros at the Plaza Revolución.

26 Famous People

Famous people from the state include Miquel Hidalgo y Costilla (1753–1811), a priest and revolutionary who fought for the rights of native peoples and published the *Grito de Dolores* (*Cry of Pain*), a pamphlet that helped to trigger the fight for independence in 1810. Diego Rivera (1886–1957) was a world-famous painter and muralist. His works include the fresco *The Great City of Tenochtitlán* at the National Palace in Mexico City, *The Allegory of California* at the San Francisco Stock Exchange, and a series of murals at the Detroit Institute of Art. Vicente Fox (b.1942) was born in Mexico City but moved with his family to Guanajuato early in his childhood. He was governor of the state before being elected president of Mexico in 2000. José Alfredo Jiménez (1926–1973) was a well-known Mexican folk singer-songwriter in the *ranchera* style.

27 Bibliography

BOOKS

Day-MacLeod, Deirdre. *The States of Central Mexico*. Philadelphia, PA: Mason Crest Publishers, 2003.

DeAngelis, Gina. *Mexico*. Mankato, MN: Blue Earth Books, 2003.

Gaines, Ann. *Vicente Fox: The Road to the Mexican Presidency*. Chanhassen, MN: Child's World, 2003.

Gruber, Beth. *Mexico*. Washington, DC: National Geographic, 2006.

WEB SITES

Government of Mexico. *Mexico for Kids*. www.elbalero.gob.mx/index_kids.html (accessed on March 30, 2007).

Government of the State of Guanajuato. *Guanajuato Contigo Vamos*. www.guanajuato.gob.mx/ (accessed on March 30, 2007).

Guerrero

PRONUNCIATION: geh-REH-roh.

ORIGIN OF STATE NAME: Honors the memory of Vicente Guerrero Saldaña (1783–1831) who took part in the independence movement.

CAPITAL: Chilpancingo de los Bravo (typically called Chilpancingo).

ENTERED COUNTRY: 1849.

COAT OF ARMS: The upper section is formed by a headdress with eleven colored feathers. The central blue background represents the sky and water. A warrior displays a mace (clublike weapon) horizontally with his right hand. In his left hand, he holds a shield, which is a Náhuatl (language of the Aztec Indians) symbol for power, decorated in red, green, purple, and yellow. The warrior wears a tiger skin with spots denoting the stars that represent Tezcatlipoca, Lord of the Night. In the lower part of the shield, nine feathers form a fan.

HOLIDAYS: Año Nuevo (New Year's Day—January 1); Día de la Constitución (Constitution Day—February 5); Benito Juárez's birthday (March 21); Primero de Mayo (Labor Day—May 1); Anniversary of the Battle of Puebla (1862), May 5; Revolution Day, 1910 (November 20); and Navidad (Christmas—December 25).

FLAG: There is no official flag.

TIME: 6 AM = noon Greenwich Mean Time (GMT).

1 Location and Size

Guerrero is located in southern Mexico. It covers an area of 63,620 square kilometers (24,563 square miles), slightly larger than the US state of West Virginia. It ranks as 14th in size among the states and covers about 3.2% of the total land area of Mexico. It is bordered on the north by the states of Michoacán, México, and Morelos; on the east by the states of Puebla and Oaxaca; and on the south by the Pacific Ocean. Guerrero is divided into 80 municipalities (similar to US counties). The capital, Chilpancingo de los Bravos (typically called Chilpancingo), is located approximately in the center of the state.

Guerrero is one of the most mountainous states in Mexico. Its mountain ranges (sierras) include the Sierra Madre del Sur and the Sierras del Norte. The highest point in the state is Cerro Tiotepec at about 3,550 meters (11,646 feet).

Laguna de Coyuca bird sanctuary in Acapulco. © ROBERT FRERCK/WOODFIN CAMP.

Between these two mountain ranges is the warm and dry valley region surrounding the Río Balsas (Balsas River). Agriculture and livestock thrive in the interior valleys. The state is also known for its coastal plain along the coastline of the Pacific Ocean. The coastline stretches for 485 kilometers (301 miles).

The basin of the Río Balsas is formed by dozens of small rivers (tributaries) that rise in the Sierras del Norte and in the Sierra Madre del Sur and eventually flow into the Río Balsas. The Rio Balsas itself rises in the state of Tlaxcala and runs through Puebla and Guerrero to empty into the Pacific at Bahía de Petacaclo. The Presa del Infiernillo along the border with Michoacán is the third largest dam-built reservoir in the coun-try. Acapulco, established in 1550 by Spanish settlers, is one of Mexico's oldest resorts. Cliffs surround the natural Pacific coast harbor there.

2 Climate

Acapulco on the coast is generally hot and fairly humid. Most of the rain falls from June to October, when there are light showers each day, with occasional tropical storms. A damaging hurricane, Hurricane Pauline, caused several hundred deaths when it struck Guerrero and Oaxaca in October 1997.

The winter months (December to April) are slightly cooler with less rainfall. The average winter temperature ranges from 25°c to 27°c (77°F to 81°F). The average summer temperature

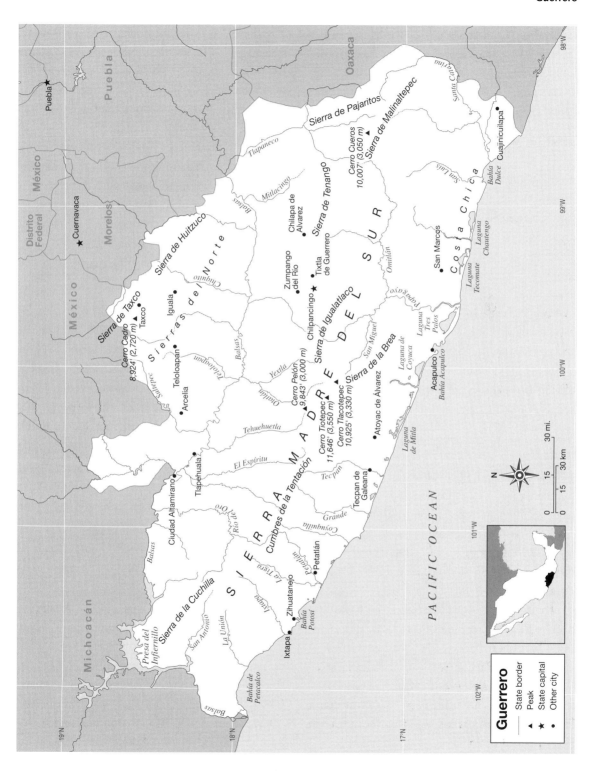

Guerrero

— State border
▲ Peak
★ State capital
• Other city

ranges from 28°C to 29°C (82°F to 84°F). In the coastal city of Acapulco, the average temperature ranges from 23°C to 31°C (75°F to 88°F).

3 Plants and Animals

There are tropical forests and mangroves along the Pacific Ocean. Oak and pine forests are found in the mountain areas. The valley around the Río Balsas has small, scrubby shrubs. Exotic tropical trees like the amate (umbrella plant), organ cactus, and many varieties of palm trees are common.

Native animals include iguanas and other lizards, snakes, rabbits, and coyotes. Animals that are endangered or whose habitat is threatened by development include jaguar, eagle, turtle, and iguana.

4 Environmental Protection

In 2004, the state had 26 municipal wastewater treatment plants in operation with a combined installed capacity of 2,891 liters per second (763 gallons per second). The volume of treated wastewater that year was estimated at 1,663 liters per second (439 gallons per second). There were also seven industrial wastewater treatment plants in operation that year. As of 2004, about 72.3% of the population had access to safe drinking water.

In 2003, the state had about 3.5 million hectares (8.7 million acres) of woodland, including 1.6 million hectares (3.9 million acres) of rain forest. In 2004, about 1,466 hectares (3,622 acres) of woodland were damaged or destroyed by forest fires. An additional 7,594 hectares (18,765 acres) of pasture and brush lands were also damaged by fires.

There are three national parks in the state. The largest is El Veladero National Park, in the mountain range that surrounds Acapulco Bay, which is home to many tropical trees and some wildlife. The Grutas (Grottos) de Cacahuamilpa national park can be found in the north near the town of Taxco. Playa Tortuguera Tierra Colorado, located along the southern coast near the city of Cuajinicuilapa, was designated as a Ramsar Wetland of International Importance in 2003.

5 Population, Ethnic Groups, Languages

Guerrero had an estimated total population of 3,152,800 in 2006, ranking 12th among the states and the Distrito Federal. About 48% of the population were men and 52% were women. Only about 45% of the population lived in urban areas. The population density was 49 people per square kilometer (129 people per square mile). In 2005, the capital of Chilpancingo had an estimated population of 214,219.

Almost everyone speaks Spanish, and about 13% of the population speaks one of the indigenous languages, such as Náhuatl, Tlapaneco, and many languages of the Mixtecas ethnic groups.

6 Religions

According to the 2000 census, 89.2% of the population, or over 2.3 million people, were Roman Catholic; about 4.4%, or 117,511 people, were mainline or evangelical Protestants. About 2% were counted as other Biblical faiths, including 43,320 Jehovah's Witnesses, 3,329 Latter-day Saints (Mormons), and 6,467 Seventh-day Adventists. About 3.1% of the population claimed to have no religious affiliation. The Cathedral Nuestra Señora de la Soledad is the seat of the Roman Catholic archdiocese of Acapulco.

7 Transportation

There are 8,146 kilometers (5,091 miles) of paved roads and 94 kilometers (58 miles) of railroad in the state. A four-lane highway connects Mexico City and Acapulco. International airports in Zihuatanejo and Acapulco, both near the Pacific coast, provide flights to and from Guerrero. In 2004, there were 298,795 automobiles registered in the state, along with 48,636 passenger trucks, 185,688 freight trucks, and 20,826 motorcycles.

8 History

The oldest evidence of human presence in Guerrero dates back to 300 BC, when the Olmec inhabited central and southern Mexico. In the 10th century, Teotihuacan groups built pyramids in Texmelincan and Teloloapan. Tepaneca Indians and others also built human settlements on the Pacific coast. Náhuatl (Aztec) groups eventually invaded the well-populated region in the 11th century. When the Aztecs conquered central Mexico, they divided the region that constitutes modern-day Guerrero into seven entities. Tax collection mechanisms were introduced, and centralized Aztec government exerted influence over the local natives.

When the Spanish arrived, they conquered the Aztec. The Spanish then replaced the Aztec in dominating the indigenous populations. In 1523, Juan Rodríguez led an expedition to the region. In 1527, Alonso de Saavedra Cerón

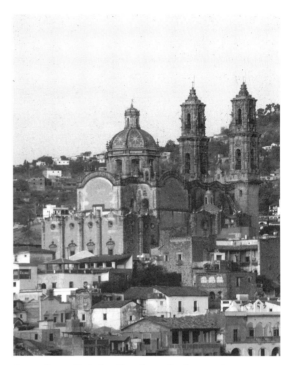

Santa Prisa Catholic Church was built in 1748. © ROBERT FRERCK/WOODFIN CAMP.

sailed off the Pacific coast towards the Molucas Islands but his expedition never returned.

In 1534, Spanish expeditions discovered silver in Taxco. Mineral production attracted more Spanish settlers. This radically changed the lives of indigenous communities. Trade with Asia was possible because the natural harbor at Acapulco made a great Pacific coast port. The tough and dangerous trip between Acapulco and Mexico City required twelve days to complete. But the prospects of lucrative trade routes with Asia converted it into one of the busiest colonial roads in Mexico.

Slave trade was also practiced in Acapulco during that period. Runaway slave communities formed in the mountain region and remained active until the mid-19th century. Modern-day descendants of African slaves live along the southern Pacific coast.

During the movement to gain independence for Mexico from imperialist Spain, José Morelos (1765–1815) was commissioned by Mexican priest and revolutionary Miguel Hidalgo (1753–1811) to form an independence army in Guerrero. More than three thousand soldiers joined Morelos. They liberated Chilpancingo from Spanish control and declared it the nation's capital in 1813 after the Anahuac Congress (the meeting at which regional leaders decided to fight for Mexican independence). After Morelos's death, the struggle for independence continued. Vicente Guerrero (1783–1831) emerged as the strongest independence leader and the movement eventually succeeded with the implementation of the Plan of Iguala in 1821, which freed Mexico from Spanish control.

Guerrero was appointed as chief of the southern region of Mexico, where he fiercely fought for the establishment of a federal republic. The political instability in the country led Guerrero to undertake a number of armed battles. He eventually became president of Mexico in 1829 but was assassinated nine months after taking office.

Indigenous rebellions and discontent with Antonio Lopez de Santa Anna (1794–1876), who served as president of Mexico from 1833 to 1836, helped worsen the political and military instability of the region. Many constitutionalist and liberal leaders sought refuge in Guerrero and attempted to reorganize their opposition to French emperor Maximilian (1832–1867). France had conquered and ruled parts of Mexico from 1864 to 1866. During the Porfiriato period, when Porfirio Diáz was in power (1877–80 and

1884–1911), conflicts between caudillo (politically powerful) leaders and military strongmen made it difficult for Guerrero to be fully controlled by the state authorities. The presence of militias and the weak state government made it easier for the Mexican Revolution to take hold in Guerrero starting in 1910.

When the revolution came to an end, the Institutional Revolutionary Party (PRI) emerged as the national political force. Allegiance to the PRI helped reduced old conflicts between local caudillo families in Guerrero. The presidency of Miguel Alemán from 1946 to 1952 helped promote economic development, particularly in Acapulco.

Widespread poverty and inequality helped fuel support for different guerrilla groups in the 1960s and 1970s. Economic development in the 1980s and the consolidation of Acapulco, Ixtapa, and Taxco as tourism attractions have benefited the economy of the state. Rural violence by insurgent groups continues in the early years of the 21st century. Guerrero is among the states with high numbers of insurgent groups operating in the countryside. Insurgents are small groups that rebel against the government, but who are not large enough or well organized enough to carry out a revolution.

During the first decade of the 21st century, the state of Guerrero has continued to struggle with issues of poverty, political instability, and crime. In a 2004 report by the United Nations, the town of Metlatonoc in Guerrero was found to be one of the poorest in all of Mexico. Making matters worse, the state has had to deal with rising criminal activity fueled by the illegal drug trade, whose violence had threatened the state's tourist resort of Acapulco.

9 State and Local Government

A powerful state governor is democratically elected every six years for a non-renewable term. A unicameral (one chamber) state congress is comprised of a 46-member assembly. Twenty-eight representatives are elected in single member districts and 18 by proportional representation.

Guerrero is comprised of 81 municipalities. Local governments in Guerrero have varying powers and attributions. Larger and more populated municipalities are more autonomous and independent of the state government. Municipal presidents and council members are elected for three-year nonrenewable terms.

10 Political Parties

The three main political parties in all of Mexico are the Institutional Revolutionary Party (PRI), the National Action Party (PAN), and the Party of the Democratic Revolution (PRD). The PRD traces its roots to revolutionary activities of the 1960s.

The PRI dominated politics in Guerrero after the end of the Mexican Revolution. All governors from the end of the Mexican Revolution (1910–20) until 2005 belonged to the Institutional Revolutionary Party (PRI). PRI governors from Guerrero have been important actors at the national level. Guerrero is one of the most populated states and a PRI stronghold. Candidates for president of Mexico seek the active support of the Guerrero governor. That dominance was broken by the election of Carlos Zeferino Torreblanca Galindo of the PRD in 2005.

11 Judicial System

The Superior Tribunal of Justice is the state's highest court. Comprised of 16 members appointed by the governor with congressional approval, the justices can be re-appointed after their six-year terms expire. There is a mandatory retirement provision for all those age 65. In addition, there are local and state level appeals courts as well as an electoral tribunal.

12 Economy

The state of Guerrero's economy is marked by its reliance upon tourism, agriculture, and mining, although the manufacturing sector has been growing. The state is the site of three important tourist resorts, Acapulco, Ixtapa-Zihuatanejo, and Taxco, which are said to comprise the Triangle of the Sun.

13 Industry

Historically, Guerrero never had much in the way of large-scale industry. The state has many small establishments, such as blacksmith shops, carpenter shops, and hat factories, all of which provide products and services to a local market. There are some manufacturing facilities that process products made from palm leaves and fibers. There are also a few assembly plants that produce clothing for export, and many of the soccer and volleyballs used throughout the world are made in Chichihualco.

Owing to the passage of the North American Free Trade Agreement (NAFTA) in 1992, many new maquiladoras (assembly plants) were established, especially in the northern region of the state.

Storefronts on the Plaza Borda in Taxco. © ROBERT FRERCK/WOODFIN CAMP.

The state's handicraft industry produces pottery, woolen and cotton textiles, wood and leather products, artistic paintings, lacquer work, and silver items.

14 Labor

As of 2005, the state of Guerrero had 1,126,326 eligible workers. Some 1,113,378 were listed as employed and 12,948 were listed as unemployed. Unemployed workers in rural areas may not be counted, however. The unemployment rate that year was reported to be 1.1%. Of those who were working, services employed 36.2%, followed by agriculture at 26.8%, and commerce at 16.9%.

The US Bureau of Labor Statistics reported that Mexican workers saw their wages increase from $2.49 per hour in 2003 to $2.50 per hour in 2004. (The average US worker earned $15.70 per hour in 2004.) The maximum workweek is set at 48 hours by law. The average worker spends 40 to 45 hours per week on the job. Workers earn twice their regular hourly rate for up to nine hours a week of overtime. When a worker works more than nine hours overtime in a week, he or she earns three times the regular hourly rate. After one year, workers are entitled by law to six days paid vacation.

15 Agriculture

Agriculture is a key part of Guerrero's economy, but the rough terrain and a lack of farm machinery have hampered development. As result, most of the state's farmers practice traditional agriculture. Crops include corn, sorghum, rice, soy, sesame, bananas, tomatoes, melons, lemons, coffee, green chilies, grapefruit, peanuts, mangoes, and vegetables. In recent years, the breeding of livestock has undergone significant development.

Corn was the most abundant crop. In 2004, the state produced 1,146,194 tons, in addition to 80,236 tons of sorghum, 20,489 tons of red tomatoes, and 63,491 tons of bananas.

In that same year, 81,059 head of beef cattle were brought to market, along with 155,049 pigs. In 2004, the state also produced 36,350 tons of beef, 22,934 tons of pork, and 13,083 tons of poultry.

16 Natural Resources

Many of the forests in the inland regions have been cut down by international timber companies. In 2003, forest wood production was valued at about $13.9 million. Pine was the primary type of wood harvested. In 2003, the World Bank invested in a program to help indigenous people manage the forests on their lands in Guerrero. The total fish catch in 2003 was about 6,153 tons, all for human consumption. Taxco is in the center of the silver mining region of Mexico.

17 Energy and Power

In 2005, there were 811,491 users of electricity in the state of Guerrero. Of that total, the largest number were residential customers at 729,836. Sales of electricity that same year totaled 2,574,410 megawatt hours, of which the largest users were medium-sized industrial firms at 1,041,874 megawatt hours. There are five operating electric power plants in the state of Guerrero, four are hydroelectric, and one is a gas-turbine facility. Electricity is provided and distributed by the Federal Electricity Commission, and Central Light and Power. The Mexican government runs both utilities.

18 Health

In 2003, the state had 27 hospitals and 1,007 outpatient centers that were part of the national health system. In 2004, there were about 2,661 doctors, 5,210 nurses, and 201 dentists working in these health centers. There were an additional 98 independent health centers in the state in 2004.

Most of the Mexican population is covered under a government health plan. The IMSS (Instituto Mexicano de Seguro Social) covers the general population. The ISSSTE (Instituto de Seguridad y Servicios Sociales de Trabajadores del Estado) covers state workers.

19 Housing

About half of all homes are built of concrete, brick, stone, or similar materials. There are, however, a large number of homes built with adobe walls and flooring and tile roofs. At the last census, only about 53% of all homes had an adequate drainage system, with only about 71% having piped water. In 2000, about 84% of all homes were owner-occupied. In 2005, there were an estimated 701,656 residential housing units in the state. About 91% of these units were single-family detached homes. The average household was estimated at 4.4 people.

Masks used for religious festivals. © MIREILLE VAUTIER/WOODFIN CAMP.

20 Education

Public education in Mexico is free for students from ages 6 to 16 and most of the students in the state attend public schools. In 2004/05, it was estimated that 81.7% of age-eligible students completed primary school, which includes six years of study. About 65.7% of eligible students completed secondary school, which includes three years of study after primary school. These were the lowest percentages for completion in the country that year. However, 64.8% of the eligible students completed the *bachillerato*, which is similar to a high school diploma. The national average for completion of the *bachillerato* was 60.1% that year.

Universidad Autónoma de Guerrero (Autonomous University of Guerrero) is in the capital, Chilpancingo. The state is also home to the Instituto Tecnológico de Acapulco (Technological Institute of Acapulco) and the Universidad Americana de Acapulco (American University of Acapulco). In 2005, there were about 70,752 students ages 20 and older who were enrolled in some type of higher education program. The overall literacy rate was estimated at 80% in 2005.

21 Arts

Acapulco and Taxco both have several theaters. Many craft galleries and artisans' workshops are open to the public throughout the state. There are at least 30 registered movie theaters, including multiscreen theaters and single-screen galleries. The Acapulco Philharmonic Orchestra was established in 1998 through a government initiative. Their home base is the Juan Ruiz de Alarcon Theatre, which seats about 1,100. The Alarconian Theatrical festival is a 10-day event held each year in Taxco to celebrate music, theater, dance, opera, and visual arts. The National Silver Fair (established 1948) in Taxco honors the regions history as a silver mining center by featuring arts and crafts made by silversmiths. Concerts and dance performances round out the festival.

22 Libraries and Museums

In 2003, there were 351 libraries in the state with a combined stock of 1,287,413 volumes. The same year, there were six museums registered in the state that had permanent exhibits. The Acapulco History Museum focuses on local interests. The Miguel Aleman Archeological Museum is also located in Acapulco. There is a Regional Museum of Chilpancingo and a Regional Museum of Guerrero.

23 Media

In 2005, there were about 16 daily papers in the state. Acapulco had four daily newspapers, including *El Sol de Acapulco* (*Acapulco Sun*), *Diario El Pacifico* (*The Pacific Daily*), *Tropico* (*Tropical*), and *Ultima Hora* (*Last Hour*). An English-language daily, *Acapulco Newspaper*, has been published for tourists, with information on shopping, dining, and other tourist attractions. Chilpancingo had nine daily papers, including

A diver leaps from the La Quebrada Cliff in Acapulco. AP IMAGES.

Diario de Guerrero (*Guerrero Daily*) and *Pueblo* (*Town*).

In 2004, there were 112 television stations and 42 radio stations (30 AM and 12 FM). In 2005, there were about 64,822 subscribers to cable and satellite television stations. Also in 2005, there were about 297,876 residential phone lines, with about 11 mainline phones in use for every 100 people.

24 Tourism, Travel, and Recreation

Acapulco is one of Mexico's oldest and best-known resort areas. The city lies around the spectacular Acapulco Bay. Visitors enjoy water sports, beaches, deep-sea fishing, and golf. A major tourist attraction is the cliff divers, who plunge from high rocky cliffs into deep water pools. San Diego Fort, built to defend the area against pirates, dates from 1616. Other cities that attract tourists are Ixtapa and Zihuanatejo, both of which lie on the ocean coast that is known as the Mexican Riviera (after the resort area on the south coast of France). Taxco, a colonial city located in the mountains at an altitude of 3,000 meters (6,000 feet), is famous for its hundreds of small shops that sell silver jewelry. The Cacahuamilpa Caverns near Taxco are popular for cave divers.

25 Sports

Acapulco has a bullfighting ring at the Plaza Caletilla. The Mexican Tennis Open, the most important tennis tournament in Latin America, is held annually in Acapulco. The Balsas River Nautical Marathon, held annually in November, is a six-day, 500-mile jet boat race.

26 Famous People

The state is named for Vicente Guerrero Saldaña (1783–1831), a leader in the independence movement. Cuauhtémoc (c.1495–1522), the last Aztec ruler, was hung by order of Spanish conqueror Hernán Cortés (1485–1547) and is buried in Ixcateopan. Poet and playwright Juan Ruiz de Alarcón (c.1580–1639) was born in Taxco. Rodolfo Neri Vela (b.1952) is a NASA payload specialist who was the first Mexican astronaut to fly in space.

27 Bibliography

BOOKS

Gruber, Beth. *Mexico.* Washington, DC: National Geographic, 2006.

Nantus, Sheryl. *The Pacific South States of Mexico.* Stockton, NJ: Mason Crest Publishers, 2003.

Vincent, Theodore G. *The Legacy of Vicente Guerrero: Mexico's First Black Indian President.* Gainesville, FL: University Press of Florida, 2001.

Whipperman, Bruce. *Pacific Mexico: Including Acapulco, Puerto Vallarta, Oaxaca, Guadalajara and Mazatlán,* 5th edition. Emeryville, CA: Avalon Travel Pub., 2001.

WEB SITES

Government of Mexico. *Mexico for Kids.* www.elbalero.gob.mx/index_kids.html (accessed on March 30, 2007).

Mexican Tourism Board. *Visit Mexico: Guerrero.* www.visitmexico.com/wb/Visitmexico/Visi_Guerrero (accessed on March 30, 2007).

Hidalgo

PRONUNCIATION: ee-DAHL-goh.

ORIGIN OF STATE NAME: Named for the priest, Father Miguel Hidalgo y Costilla (1753–1811), who launched the movement for independence from Spanish rule.

CAPITAL: Pachuca de Soto (often shortened to Pachuca).

ENTERED COUNTRY: 1862.

COAT OF ARMS: The upper half of the seal symbolizes the landscape before the arrival of the Spaniards. The bell on the left represents the call for independence made in 1810. The red cap signifies Hidalgo's status as a free and independent state. The lower half of the seal symbolizes military actions. Flanking the seal on the left is the banner of the Virgin of Guadalupe and on the right is the national flag of Mexico.

HOLIDAYS: Año Nuevo (New Year's Day—January 1); Día de la Constitución (Constitution Day—February 5); Benito Juárez's birthday (March 21); Primero de Mayo (Labor Day—May 1); Anniversary of the Battle of Puebla (1862), May 5; Revolution Day, 1910 (November 20); and Navidad (Christmas—December 25).

FLAG: There is no official flag.

TIME: 6 AM = noon Greenwich Mean Time (GMT).

1 Location and Size

Hidalgo lies in the center of Mexico. It covers an area of 20,842 square kilometers (8,047 square miles), about the same size as the US state of New Jersey. It ranks as 26th in size among the states and covers about 1% of the total land area of Mexico. Hidalgo is bordered on the north by the state of San Luis Potosí; on the east by the states of Veracruz and Puebla; on the south by the states México and Tlaxcala; and on the west by the state of Querétaro. Hidalgo is divided into 84 municipalities (similar to US counties). The capital is Pachuca.

La Huasteca, a fertile lowland area, can be found in the far north. The north-central part of the state is crossed by the Sierra Madre Oriental and the southern part of the state is crossed by part of the Sierra Volcánica Transversal (also known as the Cordillera Neovolcánica). The Sierra de Pachuca is the largest individual range of the mountain regions. The highest peak in the state is the Cerro la Peñuela at 3,350 meters (10,990 feet). There is a nearly flat southern highland pla-

La Huasteca, a lowland region that covers the northern part of the state, has fertile soil and adequate rain for agriculture.
© KAL MULLER/WOODFIN CAMP.

teau. The northern border of the state is part of La Huasteca, a gulf coast plains region of fertile land that is shared by San Luis Potosí, Veracruz, and Tamaulipas. The Amajac, Claro, Candelaria, Hules, and Calabozos Rivers are all a part of this region. They serve as tributaries for the Pánuco River, which eventually flows into the Gulf of Mexico. The Moctezuma River runs along the border with Querétaro. There are many rivers in the sierras. The Tula River crosses the Mezquital Valley and empties into the manmade reservoir of Presa Endho. Lago de Metztitlán, which is fed by the Rio Grande de Tulacingo, is one of the largest lakes.

2 Climate

The average temperature is 16°C (61°F). The temperature ranges from a high of 32°C (90°F) and a low of 9°C (48°F). Average annual rainfall at elevations around 2,000 meters (660 feet) is 57.8 centimeters (23 inches). In the capital city of Pachuca, the annual average temperature is 13°C (55°F) and average precipitation is about 39.2 centimeters (15.4 inches) per year.

3 Plants and Animals

In the mountains, the trees include fir, pine, oak, and juniper. There are also exotic hardwood trees, such as mahogany, ebony, rosewood, and mesquite. Coffee also grows in the mountains. Other plants range from nopal cacti and yucca to a variety of azaleas and roses. Native animals include the white-tailed deer, jaguar, coyote, porcupine, and skunk. Rattlesnakes are native to the state, along with several species of lizard.

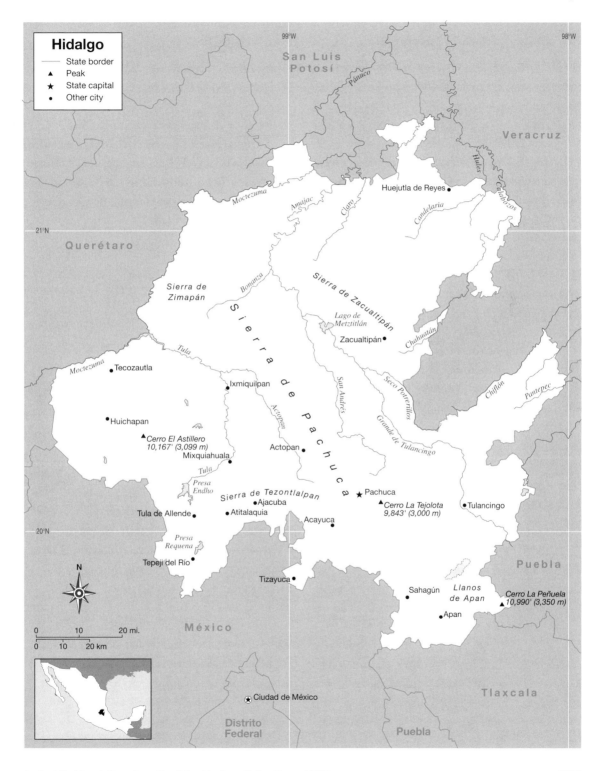

Hidalgo

--- State border
▲ Peak
★ State capital
● Other city

San Luis Potosí

Veracruz

Querétaro

99°W   98°W

Pánuco

21°N

Moctezuma   *Amajac*   *Claro*

Candelaria

Huejutla de Reyes ●

Hules

Calabozos

Sierra de Zimapán

Bonanza

Sierra de Zacualtipán

Lago de Metztitlán

Zacualtipán ●

Chahuatán

Moctezuma   *Tula*

Tecozautla ●

Ixmiquilpan ●

S i e r r a   d e   P a c h u c a

Actopan

San Andrés

Seco Potrerillos

Chiflon

Pantepec

Huichapan ●

▲*Cerro El Astillero*
10,167' (3,099 m)

Mixquiahuala ●

Actopan ●

Grande de Tulancingo

Tula

Presa Endho

Sierra de Tezontlalpan

● Ajacuba

★ Pachuca

▲*Cerro La Tejolota*
9,843' (3,000 m)

● Tulancingo

Tula de Allende ●

● Atitalaquia

Acayuca ●

20°N

Presa Requena

Tepeji del Río ●

Tizayuca ●

Puebla

Sahagún ●

Llanos de Apan

▲*Cerro La Peñuela*
10,990' (3,350 m)

Apan ●

México

N

0   10   20 mi.
0   10   20 km

Tlaxcala

★ Ciudad de México

Distrito Federal

Puebla

4 Environmental Protection

In 2004, the state had seven municipal wastewater treatment plants in operation with a combined installed capacity of 54 liters per second (14 gallons per second). The volume of treated wastewater that year was estimated at 48 liters per second (12.6 gallons per second). There were also 41 industrial wastewater treatment plants in operation that year. As of 2004, about 87.9% of the population had access to safe drinking water.

In 2003, the state had about 403,685 hectares (997,527 acres) of woodland, including 172,942 hectares (427,348 acres) of rain forest. In 2004, about 33 hectares (81.5 acres) of woodland were damaged or destroyed by forest fires. An additional 343 hectares (847 acres) of pasture and brush lands were also damaged by fires.

There are three national parks in the state: El Chico, Tula, and Los Mármoles. Lago de Metztitlán and Lago de Tecocomulco are Ramsar Wetlands of International Importance.

5 Population, Ethnic Groups, Languages

Hidalgo had an estimated total population of 2,381,600 in 2006, ranking 19th among the states and the Distrito Federal. About 48% of the population were men and 52% were women. Only about 47% of the population lived in urban areas. The population density was 113.5 people per square kilometer (293 people per square mile). In 2005, the capital Pachuca had a population of 275,578. Almost all residents speak Spanish. About 14% speak one of the indigenous (native) languages, such as Náhuatl, Otomi, and Tephua.

6 Religions

According to the 2000 census, 90.8% of the population, or over 1.7 million people, were Roman Catholic; about 5.2%, or 102,748 people, were mainline or evangelical Protestants. About 1.3% were counted as other Biblical faiths, including 16,767 Jehovah's Witnesses and 6,625 Latter-day Saints (Mormons). There were about 391 Jews. About 1.6% of the population claimed to have no religious affiliation.

7 Transportation

The state has about 4,858 miles (7,822 kilometers) of roads and 546 miles (879 kilometers) of railroads. In 2004, there were 300,466 automobiles registered in the state, along with 3,297 passenger trucks, 260,515 freight trucks, and 1,574 motorcycles. There is one international airport and one domestic airport.

8 History

There is evidence in Huapalcalco of a human presence in Hidalgo as early as 7000 BC. Ruins from the Tehotihuacano period (150 BC–750 AD) are scattered throughout the region. The Mixcóatl settled in the region around 900 AD. Indigenous Toltec leader Topiltzin, also known as Quetzalcóatl, assumed power in 977. He promoted architecture and the arts and banned human sacrifices. Defeated later, Quetzalcóatl escaped towards the north and is believed to have founded the Aztec empire. The Toltec escaped attacks from other indigenous groups and eventually abandoned the city of Tula in 1156. The Mexicas crossed Hidalgo before founding and settling in Mexico-Tenochtitlán. With the emergence of the Aztec empire, Hidalgo was conquered by the Aztecs, but some parts of the region remained independent.

Because of its geographical location in the central valley of Mexico, Hidalgo became an integral part of the Aztec empire and a central access route to the capital city from the Caribbean coast and northern Mexico. Hidalgo's strategic location made it a prized trophy for all those who sought to control the central valley of Mexico. From the Aztec empire until the Mexican Revolution of 1917, Hidalgo was a prime battleground for the control of access to the central valley of Mexico.

Spanish conqueror Hernán Cortés (1485–1547) traveled through Hidalgo on his way to conquer the Aztec empire in 1519. Spanish settlements in the region first introduced cattle and some agricultural crops in the mid-16th century. Franciscan (an order of the Roman Catholic Church) missions were established to convert the indigenous populations. Large silver mines and other minerals were discovered in the late 16th century. Mining activity eventually facilitated the development of an early working-class movement. Miners organized a group in the late 18th century to demand better wages and better working conditions.

The independence movement was pushed for by patriots and priests loyal to Miguel Hidalgo. An army of more than six thousand was formed in Hidalgo and headed by two priests. Indigenous revolts also added fuel to the political instability that characterized Mexico during the 1810s. Eventually, independence leaders prevailed, but personal disputes remained and political instability characterized much of 19th-century life in Hidalgo. During the Mexican-American War (1846–48), US troops occupied Hidalgo and

The Toltecs abandoned the city of Tula in 1156. © ROBERT FRERCK/WOODFIN CAMP.

defeated a Mexican loyalist army from Tampico in the Mexican state of Tamaulipas. When the Mexican Republic was restored, Hidalgo was converted into a state in 1869.

Political conflicts did not disappear, but peace was more common during the Porfiriato period, when Porfirio Díaz (1830–1915; president from 1877 to 1880 and again from 1884 to 1911) took power. Agriculture and mineral production remained central to the state's economy. When opposition leader Francisco Madero (1873–1913) announced his presidential campaign in 1908, Hidalgo leaders supported him.

When Porfirio Díaz (1830–1915) decided to run for reelection in 1910, Hidalgo joined the revolutionary forces. Madero's troops occupied Pachuca in 1911. A number of battles occurred in Hidalgo until years after the 1917 constitution was approved and passed into law for Mexico. The revolution ended in Hidalgo years after the rest of the country was pacified. In the 1920s and 1930s, the Roman Catholic Church and the Mexican government struggled over who would control the people and the economy of the country. This conflict, known as the Cristero War, reached Hidalgo. Some Roman Catholic loyalists attempted to oppose the revolutionary government's effort to restrict the power of the church.

In the first decade of the 21st century, the state of Hidalgo had become a major industrial center, much of which was based on heavy industry, such as the manufacturing of railway equipment, motor vehicles, and machinery. But agriculture remained an important part of the state's economy.

9 State and Local Government

A state governor is elected every six years for a nonrenewable term. A legislature comprised of a 29-seat congress, 18 elected in single member districts and 11 by proportional representation, serve for nonrenewable three-year terms and have formal check-and-balance powers. However, existing separation of power provisions have not been enforced since the state legislature and state governorship have always been controlled by the Institutional Revolutionary Party (PRI).

The 84 municipalities that exist in the state have limited but considerable formal attributions and powers. Municipal presidents and council members are elected for nonrenewable three-year terms. Some opposition party candidates have won a number of municipal presidencies in recent years.

10 Political Parties

The three main political parties in all of Mexico are the Institutional Revolutionary Party (PRI), the National Action Party (PAN), and Party of the Democratic Revolution (PRD). The PRI has controlled the state governorship since the early 1900s. Manuel Ángel Nuñez won the 1999 elections. Miguel Ángel Osorio Chong of the PRI was elected in 2005. The conservative PAN and left-wing PRD have grown in recent years, but only the PAN has a statewide organization capable of challenging the PRI.

11 Judicial System

A Superior Tribunal of Justice is the state's highest court. Its members are appointed by the president with legislative approval. If they are ratified after their six-year terms expire, they serve until the mandatory retirement age of 65. The president of the Superior Tribunal is appointed by its members. Membership in the Superior Tribunal is restricted to qualified attorneys. In addition, the judicial system is comprised of an electoral tribunal and lower courts.

12 Economy

The economy of the state of Hidalgo is centered upon heavy industry, mining, textiles, food processing, machine tools, petroleum refining, petrochemicals and agricultural products. A key factor in the state's industrial development has been its proximity to Mexico City. In 2003, manufacturing accounted for 24.36% of the state's economic activity, trade accounting for 12.01%, transport and communications for 7.41%, construction for 5.18%, and mining for 1.6%. Agriculture and livestock accounted for 10.01%.

13 Industry

Most of the state's industry, and over 26,000 businesses, are centered around the industrial cities of Tepeji del Río, Sahagún, Tula de Allende, Pachuca, Tulancingo, and Ixmiquilpan, which are concentrated in the western half of the state. In Sahagún, factories turn out subway and railroad cars, automobiles, trucks, tractors, and heavy machinery. Tula de Allende produces refined petroleum, while fabrics are made in Tepeji del Río.

14 Labor

As of 2005, the state of Hidalgo had 959,438 eligible workers. Some 927,222 were listed as employed and 32,216 were listed as unemployed. Unemployed workers in rural areas may not be counted, however. The unemployment rate that year was reported to be 3.4%. Of those who were working, services employed 29.3%, followed by agriculture at 26.7%, and commerce at 18.5%.

The US Bureau of Labor Statistics reported that Mexican workers saw their wages increase from $2.49 per hour in 2003 to $2.50 per hour in 2004. (The average US worker earned $15.70 per hour in 2004.) The maximum work week is set at 48 hours by law. The average worker spends 40 to 45 hours per week on the job. Workers earn twice their regular hourly rate for up to nine hours a week of overtime. When a worker works more than nine hours overtime in a week, he or she earns three times the regular hourly rate. After one year, workers are entitled by law to six days paid vacation.

15 Agriculture

La Huasteca, a lowland region that covers the northern part of Hidalgo, has fertile soil and adequate rain for agriculture. However, many farms in dry areas use irrigation systems such as canals, wells, and drip irrigation. Crops include corn, oats, barley, beans, chilies, coffee, tomatoes, potatoes, and chick peas, in addition to fruits such as apples, plums, cherries, mangos, mamey (similar to an apricot), bananas, and nuts. Livestock production includes cattle, sheep, goats and poultry. The state is the main supplier of meat and dairy products to Mexico City.

In 2004, the state of Hidalgo produced 618,153 tons of corn, 14,858 tons of green chilies, and 35,014 tons of kidney beans. In that same year, the state brought to market 90,031 tons of beef cattle, 161,297 pigs, and 7,568 sheep. It also produced 29,320 tons of beef, 18,995 tons of pork, 5,501 tons of lamb, and 61,400 tons of poultry. Milk production from dairy cows totaled 411 million liters (108 million gallons), while 10,754 tons of eggs were produced.

In arid and rocky areas where there is no irrigation for crops, a hardy cactus known as the maguey (agave cactus) is grown. A liquid, called *agua miel* (honey water), accumulates in the center of the plant. This liquid is collected and fermented to make a popular drink known as *pulque*. The plant also produces grubs (*chinicuiles*) that are gathered, cooked, and eaten. Ant larvae (*escamoles*), harvested from the roots of

Aqueduct, Los Arcos del Padre. © ROBERT FRERCK/WOODFIN CAMP.

the maquey, are considered to be a delicacy in Mexico.

16 Natural Resources

Hidalgo is rich in mineral deposits, including lead, iron, manganese, and zinc. There is also production of precious metals and minerals, such as gold, silver, and opals. Stone and marble, used to decorate churches and other buildings, is also quarried in the state.

In 2003, forest wood production was valued at about $8 million. The pine harvest accounted for most of that total. The fish catch in 2003 was estimated at about 5,401 tons.

17 Energy and Power

In 2005, there were 625,192 users of electricity in the state of Hidalgo. Of that total, the largest number were residential customers at 550,611. Sales of electricity that same year totaled 2,958,517 megawatt hours, of which the largest users were medium-sized industrial firms at 1,264,195 megawatt hours. There are three electric power plants in the state of Hidalgo. A 1,500 megawatt thermal (non-coal) plant, and a 489 megawatt combined cycle (gas-turbine and steam) plant are located in the city of Tula de Allende. A third facility, a 292 megawatt hydroelectric station, is located in Zimapan. Electricity is provided by the Federal Electricity Commission, and Central Light and Power. Both utilities are run by the Mexican government.

There is also an oil refinery in Tula de Allende.

18 Health

In 2003, the state had 28 hospitals and 716 outpatient centers that were part of the national health system. In 2004, there were about 1,862 doctors, 4,096 nurses, and 164 dentists working in these health centers. There were an additional 89 independent health centers in the state in 2004.

Most of the Mexican population is covered under a government health plan. The IMSS (Instituto Mexicano de Seguro Social) covers the general population. The ISSSTE (Instituto de Seguridad y Servicios Sociales de Trabajadores del Estado) covers state workers.

19 Housing

Most homes are built with materials such as stone, concrete, or bricks. About 20% of homes have roofs of some type of sheet metal. In 2000, about 84% of all homes were owner-occupied. In 2005, there were an estimated 558,448 residential housing units in the state. About 92% of these units were single-family detached homes. The average household was estimated at 4.2 people.

20 Education

Public education in Mexico is free for students from ages 6 to 16. In 2004/05, it was estimated that 95.7% of age-eligible students completed primary school, which includes six years of study. About 82.8% of eligible students completed secondary school, which includes three years of study after primary school. About 56.6% of eligible students completed the bachillerato, which is similar to a high school diploma. The national average for completion of the bachillerato was 60.1% that year.

The Universidad Autónoma de Hidalgo (Autonomous University of Hidalgo) is located in the capital. There is a technological institute in Pachuca. In 2005, there were about 66,328 students ages 20 and older who were enrolled in some type of higher education program. The overall literacy rate was estimated at 87.7% in 2005.

21 Arts

Hidalgo has six local cultural centers, including one at the Universidad Autónoma de Hidalgo. There are also several theaters, including El Teatro de la Ciudad de San Francisco. Handicrafts produced by the artisans of Hidalgo include wool and cotton textiles, pottery, mats, and other items made from ixtle fiber of the maguey plant. There are over 40 registered movie theaters, including multiscreen theaters and single-screen galleries.

22 Libraries and Museums

In 2003, there were 525 libraries in the state with a combined stock of 2,058,569 volumes. Prominent museums include both the Museum of Mineralogy and the Museum of Mining. The state also hosts the National Museum of Photography and the Museum of Religion and Ethnography.

23 Media

In 2005, the capital city, Pachuca, had three daily newspapers: *El Sol de Hidalgo* (*Hidalgo Sun*), *Nuevo Grafico* (*New Graphic*), *and Avazando* (*Advance*). Other papers in the state included *El Sol de Tulancingo* (*Tulancingo Sun*).

A high-powered antenna is located in Tulancingo. It provides satellite communications, connecting Mexico to many other parts of the world. In 2004, there were 24 television stations and 22 radio stations (13 AM and 9 FM). In 2005, there were about 64,281 subscribers to cable and satellite television stations. Also in 2005, there were about 203,274 residential phone lines, with about 10.2 mainline phones in use for every 100 people.

24 Tourism, Travel, and Recreation

Pachuca, the capital, has a cathedral and many marketplaces. The main fairs are the San Francisco Fair (October 4) and the Virgin de Guadalupe (December 12). In Tula de Allende, there is the Huapalcalco archeological site. El Chico National Park near Pachuca offers mountain climbing.

25 Sports

Pachuca, the capital, claims to be the first city in Mexico where soccer was played. Pachuca has a First Division soccer team in the Mexican Football Association (commonly known as Femexfut) that plays in the 30,000-seat Hidalgo stadium. The Garzas Plata (Silver Herons) are a basketball team at the Universidad Autónoma de Hidalgo.

26 Famous People

The state was named for Miguel Hidalgo y Costilla (1753–1811), who is known for issuing the call for independence on September 16, 1810. Manuel Ángel Nuñez (b.1951) was elected governor in 1999.

27 Bibliography

BOOKS

Carew-Miller, Anna. *Famous People of Mexico.* Philadelphia: Mason Crest Publishers, 2003.

Day-MacLeod, Deirdre. *The States of Central Mexico.* Philadelphia, PA: Mason Crest Publishers, 2003.

Lourie, Peter. *Hidden World of the Aztec.* Honesdale, PA: Boyds Mills Press, 2006.

Gruber, Beth. *Mexico.* Washington, DC: National Geographic, 2006.

WEB SITES

Government of Mexico. *Mexico for Kids.* www.elbalero.gob.mx/index_kids.html (accessed on March 30, 2007).

Mexican Tourism Board. *Visit Mexico: Hidalgo.* www.visitmexico.com/wb/Visitmexico/Visi_ Hidalgo (accessed on March 30, 2007).

Jalisco

PRONUNCIATION: hah-LEES-koh.

ORIGIN OF STATE NAME: The name Jalisco comes from the Náhuatl words *xali ixco* (sandy surface).

CAPITAL: Guadalajara.

ENTERED COUNTRY: 1824.

COAT OF ARMS: At the center is a dark blue shield with gold borders, accented with red x-shapes. Two golden lions face a tree in the center. Above the shield, there is a helmet with a red pennant flying from its top.

HOLIDAYS: Año Nuevo (New Year's Day—January 1); Día de la Constitución (Constitution Day—February 5); Benito Juárez's birthday (March 21); Primero de Mayo (Labor Day—May 1); Anniversary of the Battle of Puebla (1862), May 5; Revolution Day, 1910 (November 20); and Navidad (Christmas—December 25).

FLAG: There is no official flag.

TIME: 6 AM = noon Greenwich Mean Time (GMT).

1 Location and Size

Jalisco is located in the center of Mexico. It has an area of 78,609 square kilometers (30,351 square miles), which is a little smaller than the US state of South Carolina. It ranks seventh in size among the states and covers about 4% of the total land area of Mexico. Jalisco is bordered to the northwest by the state of Nayarit; to the north by the states of Zacatecas, Aguascalientes, and San Luis Potosí; to the east by the states of Guanajuato and Colima; and to the west by the Pacific Ocean. Jalisco is divided into 124 municipalities. Its capital is Guadalajara.

Jalisco lies at a meeting point between the Sierra Madre Occidental to the north and the Sierra Madre del Sur to the south. These north-south mountain ranges are separated by an east-west belt known as the Sierra Volcánica Transversal (also known as the Cordillera Neovolcánica). Some of the highest peaks in the country are found in this region, including the point in the state at Nevado de Colima (4,240 meters/13,911 feet) and Volcán de Colima. The Sierra Los Huicholes, Sierra de Bolaños, and Sierra de Pinabete o Buenavista are all part of the Sierra Madre Occidental. Other mountains include the Sierra de Cacoma, Sierra Manantlán, and Sierra de las Bufas.

The most important river system in Jalisco include the Lerma–Santiago, which crosses the central part of the state. The Lerma River begins in México state and runs through Michoacán then to Jalisco, where it flows into Lago de Chapala (Lake Chapala). The Rio Grande de Santiago flows out of Lago de Chapala and across the state into Nayarit on its way to the Pacific. Lago de Chapala, the largest natural lake in Mexico, covers an area of about 1,116 square kilometers (430 square miles). The Laguna San Marcos and Laguna de Sayula are smaller lakes also found in Jalisco. The Pacific coastline stretches a distance of 342 kilometers (212 miles).

2 Climate

In the capital, Guadalajara, the January temperature averages 15°C (60°F). In June, the average is 23°C (74°F). Rainfall is heaviest between June and September. The average annual rainfall in the capital is 90 centimeters (35.8 inches). Puerto Vallarta on the Pacific Ocean is warmer, with average January temperatures of 25°C (77°F) and August average temperatures of 28°C (83°F).

3 Plants and Animals

There are tropical forests with mahogany, rosewood, and cedar trees, mosses, and orchids. There are also lemon, coconut, and banana trees. In the cooler regions, there are white pine (and other species of pine), oak, fir, birch, and hazelnut trees. Native animals include pumas, jaguars, wolves, coyotes, wildcats, badgers, foxes, deer, eagles, doves, grouse, sparrow hawks, and many types of snakes. Small animals such as squirrels and raccoons also find habitats in Jalisco.

4 Environmental Protection

In 2004, the state had 83 municipal wastewater treatment plants in operation with a combined installed capacity of 3,081 liters per second (813 gallons per second). The volume of treated wastewater that year was estimated at 2,721 liters per second (718 gallons per second). There were also 54 industrial wastewater treatment plants in operation that year. As of 2004, about 92.9% of the population had access to safe drinking water.

Lago de Chapala, the most important and largest natural lake in the country, covers an area of about 1,116 square kilometers (430 square miles) and provides water for two of the nation's biggest cities, Mexico City and Guadalajara. The lake also supports a delicate ecosystem that is important for migratory bird populations. The water of Lago de Chapala has become polluted by heavy metals and other toxic substance due to inadequate wastewater treatment. Mismanagement of water resources and erosion of the shoreline have also caused the water level of the lake to drop. State and national officials, as well as some foreign environmental groups, are working on ways to preserve and protect the lake from further damage while promoting new ecological growth.

In 2003, the state had about 3 million hectares (7.4 million acres) of woodland, including 1 million hectares (2.6 million acres) of rain forest. In 2004, about 639 hectares (1,579 acres) of woodland were damaged or destroyed by forest fires. An additional 5,450 hectares (13,467 acres) of pasture and brush lands were also damaged by fires.

Sierra de Manantlan Biosphere Reserve is located between the states of Jalisco and Colima.

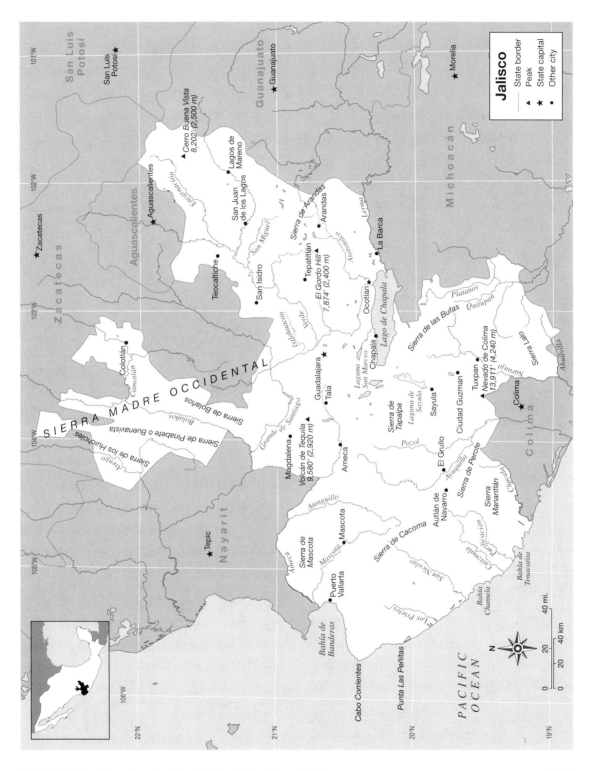

Jalisco

— State border
▲ Peak
★ State capital
● Other city

San Luis Potosí
★ San Luis Potosí

Guanajuato
★ Guanajuato

Michoacán
★ Morelia

Aguascalientes
★ Aguascalientes

Zacatecas
★ Zacatecas

▲ Cerro Buena Vista
8,202' (2,500 m)

Lagos de Mareno

Drenación

San Juan de los Lagos

San Miguel

Sierra de Arandas

Arandas

Lerma

La Barca

San Isidro

Teocaltiche

Tepatitlán

El Gordo Hill
7,874' (2,400 m)

Atotonilco

Ocotlán

Chapala

Lago de Chapala

Platanos

Quitupan

Sierra de las Bufas

Verde

Bolaños

Huiluacan

Laguna San Marcos

Tuxpan

Nevado de Colima
13,911' (4,240 m)

Naranjo

Sierra Lajo

Colima

Colotlán

Camotlán

SIERRA MADRE OCCIDENTAL

Sierra de Bolaños

Sierra de Pinabete o Buenavista

Grande de Santiago

Guadalajara

Tala

Sierra de Tapalpa

Laguna de Sayula

Sayula

Ciudad Guzmán

Ahuijilla

Sierra de Perote

Sierra de los Huicholes

Atengo

Volcán de Tequila
9,580' (2,920 m)

Magdalena

Ameca

Pozol

El Grullo

Autlán de Navarro

Sierra Manantlán

Chacala

Calcificación

Atenguillo

Mascota

Mascota

Sierra de Mascota

Mascota

Sierra de Cacoma

San Nicolás

Bahía de Tenacatita

Nayarit
★ Tepic

Ameca

Puerto Vallarta

Los Prietos

Bahía Chamela

Bahía de Banderas

Cabo Corrientes

Punta Las Peñitas

PACIFIC OCEAN

N

40 mi.

40 km

20

20

0

0

The Guadalajara Cathedral. AP IMAGES.

The reserve protects the Jalisco dry forests and shelters over 2,700 species of plants and 560 species of vertebrates. Neighboring the Manantlan reserve is the Chamela-Cuixmala Biosphere, which protects the coastal ecosystem and was designated as a Ramsar Wetland of International Importance in 2004. Laguna de Atotonilco, Laguna de Sayula, and Laguna de Zapotlán are also Ramsar sites. Several islands in Bahía Chamela were designated protected lands in 2002. Volcán Nevado de Colima National Park, located along the border with Colima, features the most active volcano in Mexico. The volcano frequently emits ash plumes and clouds that drift to local areas, affecting both the air and soil.

5 Population, Ethnic Groups, Languages

Jalisco had an estimated total population of 6,843,500 in 2006, ranking fourth among the states and the Distrito Federal. About 49% of the population were men and 51% were women. About 79% of the population lived in urban areas. The population density was 85 people per square kilometer (221 people per square mile). In 2005, the capital of Guadalajara had a population of 1,600,940. Almost all residents of Jalisco speak Spanish. A very small percentage of the population speak one of the indigenous (native) languages, such as Huichol and Náhuatl.

6 Religions

According to the 2000 census, 95.4% of the population, or about 5.2 million people, were Roman Catholic; about 2%, or 110,413 people, were mainline or evangelical Protestants. Less than 1% were counted as other faiths, including 40,646 Jehovah's Witnesses and 5,284 Latter-day Saints (Mormons). There were about 983 Jews. Less than 1% of the population claimed to have no religious affiliation.

The Cathedral Basilica of the Assumption of Mary in Guadalajara is the seat of the Roman Catholic archdiocese of Guadalajara. The Guadalajara México Temple of the Church of Jesus Christ of Latter-day Saints was dedicated in 2001.

7 Transportation

Guadalajara-Don Miguel Hidalgo Airport and Puerto Vallarta International-Gustavo Diaz Ordaz Airport provide international flights to and from Jalisco. The Guadalajara airport is the second-busiest airport (after Mexico City) in Mexico.

In 2004, there were 1,081,386 automobiles registered in the state, along with 10,996 passenger trucks, 761,760 freight trucks, and 85,987 motorcycles.

8 History

The first human settlements date back to more than ten thousand years ago. In 300 AD, the Mexican states of Nayarit, Colima, and Jalisco witnessed the emergence of a sedentary civilization near the Pacific Ocean. Towards the interior, more than a dozen different groups lived by

Iglesia del Carmen (del Carmen Church) in Guadalajara, one of the more than 50 Roman Catholic churches in Guadalajara. PETER LANGER.

the time the Spaniards first arrived in Mexico in 1519.

First invaded by Spaniard Alonso de Avalos in 1522, the area that now constitutes Jalisco, together with Aguascalientes and Zacatecas, was later named Nueva Galicia. Spanish conqueror Nuño de Guzmán (d. 1544) gained control of the region in 1536, but an indigenous rebellion in 1541 evolved into the Mixton War. Eventually, the Spaniards defeated the indigenous rebels and successfully incorporated the region into the colonial economy. Its capital city, Guadalajara, was founded in 1531. Many of the more than 50 Catholic churches in Guadalajara date from the colonial period, and its cathedral was finished in 1618. Indigenous revolts in 1593 and 1601 brought instability and generated a violent reprisal by the Spanish colonizers. A university was created in 1792, some 25 years after the expulsion of the Jesuits (an order of the Roman Catholic Church). The first printing press was brought to Guadalajara in 1793.

In November 1810, Guadalajara fell under the siege of the independence insurgents, who fought against Spanish control of Mexico. Father Miguel Hidalgo (1753–1811), one of the leaders of the independence movement, decreed the end of slavery there. Bishop Juan Cruz Ruiz de Cabañas y Creso, a priest who was a part of the independence movement, excommunicated (banned from the church) Hidalgo. After Hidalgo's assassination royalist forces moved to defeat the pro-independence insurgents and retake Guadalajara. Eventually, Jalisco joined other Mexican states in the formal declaration of independence under the Plan of Iguala agreement in 1821 and a new state constitution was passed into law in 1825. However, military uprisings and epidemic outbreaks hurt the economy and the consolidation of Jalisco as a powerful state during the mid-19th century.

Benito Juárez (1806–1872), the leader of the liberal faction that was seeking to establish a strong central government, was captured in Guadalajara in 1858 and almost killed. Eventually, Juárez and his allies emerged as the victor of the war between the liberals and the conservatives (who supported French colonial rule), but Jalisco initially supported the conservative forces and French emperor Maximilian

(1832–1867). (France had conquered and ruled parts of Mexico from 1864 to 1866.) Eventually, the liberal forces gained control of Jalisco and Porfirio Díaz (1830–1915) governed with the acquiescence of the Jalisco elite until the Mexican Revolution broke out in 1910.

Split among the different factions, Jalisco militias loyal to Díaz overpowered the revolutionaries early on in the Mexican Revolution. Later, revolutionary leader Francisco "Pancho" Villa (1878–1923) entered Guadalajara with his legendary Northern Division. Villa demanded land distribution and recognition of the peasants as legitimate actors in Mexican politics. After peace was mostly achieved in 1917, the revolutionary victors did not easily control Jalisco. Conflict raged between the Roman Catholic Church and the new government throughout the 1920s and 1930s. This conflict, known as the Cristero War, was launched by conservative Roman Catholics who opposed the anti-clerical positions of the new government. The conflict originated in Jalisco, where most of the fierce battles were fought.

Eventually, the revolutionary government made peace with the Roman Catholic Church. Conservative Jalisco leaders coexisted with revolutionary governors. Jalisco soon evolved to become a major industrial center.

Beginning in the 1930s, the Institutional Revolutionary Party (PRI) exercised control in Jalisco. Many believed the PRI maintained control of the country by discouraging debate. The late 1960s and early 1970s were characterized by unrest and demands for government reforms throughout Mexico. Several guerrilla groups (radical political groups) were operating in Jalisco during this period. In 1973, they kidnapped the father-in-law of then Mexican president Luis Echeverría (1970–1976) and former Jalisco governor José Guadalupe Zuno. As in the rest of the country, guerrilla activity decreased in the late 1970s.

In the 1980s, the conservative National Action Party (PAN) emerged as the main threat to the control that the PRI had successfully achieved over Jalisco. PAN continued to grow in influence through the 1980s, 1990s, and 2000s, winning the state's governorship in 1994, 2000, and 2006.

In the first decade of the 21st century, the state of Jalisco appeared peaceful and its economy was growing. But as with other states in Mexico, crime and official corruption plagued the state, due in large part to the influence of illegal drug trafficking. In 2003, Mexican president Vicente Fox ordered federal troops to raid 11 offices of Mexico's anti-drug police, one of which was in Jalisco.

9 State and Local Government

A state governor is democratically elected for a nonrenewable six-year term. The state congress is comprised of 40 deputies. Twenty are elected in single member districts, and twenty are elected by proportional representation, all for nonrenewable three-year terms. Separation of power and check-and-balance provisions were first fully exercised after PAN candidate Alberto Cárdenas became state governor in 1995.

There are 124 municipal governments in Jalisco. They have varying degrees of informal independence. The larger municipalities have more control over their own budgets. Municipal presidents and council members are elected for nonrenewable three-year terms.

10 Political Parties

The three main political parties in all of Mexico are the Institutional Revolutionary Party (PRI), the National Action Party (PAN), and the Party of the Democratic Revolution (PRD). As in most other Mexican states, the PRI exercised absolute control of state level politics from the end of the Mexican Revolution until the late 1980s. PAN victories in local elections prepared the way for an impressive PAN triumph at the gubernatorial race in 1994. PAN again won the 2000 gubernatorial election with former Guadalajara mayor Francisco Ramírez Acuña and in 2006 with Emilio Gonzalez Marquez, also a former mayor of Guadalajara. The PRD has limited presence in the state.

11 Judicial System

The Supreme Tribunal of Justice is the highest court in Jalisco. Its members are appointed by a two-thirds majority in congress from a list presented by the judiciary. Members are appointed for seven-year terms. Appointees must meet strict qualification requirements. Separation of power between the executive, legislative, and judicial is provided for in detail in the state constitution. In addition, Jalisco has an electoral tribunal and local courts.

12 Economy

As of 2003, Jalisco's economy was highly diversified and ranked third in size among Mexican states. Although 85% of businesses in the state were small and family-owned, large manufacturing plants were appearing at a growing rate. The state capital of Guadalajara is the nation's second-largest city. It is a retail and distribution center, in addition to being a major manufacturing center. The city also has developed a highly integrated banking and financial services sector. The state's proximity to the Pacific coast port of Manzanillo in the state of Colima provides Jalisco with access to key trans-Pacific routes to Asian countries such as China and Japan, as well as to northern Mexico. Tourism along the Pacific Ocean coastline, especially around the resort of Puerto Vallarta, is an important segment of the state's economy.

In 2003, the largest portion of the state's workforce was employed in manufacturing at 24%, followed by the services and commerce sectors at 19%, and agriculture and livestock at 10%.

13 Industry

Jalisco is a leader in the manufacture of computers. Some 60% of the nation's computer production is centered in Guadalajara. Other industrial products produced in the state include petrochemicals, footwear, leather goods, photographic equipment, iron and steel products, dairy products, and tequila, an alcoholic beverage sold domestically and for export. Petróleos Mexicanos, the state petroleum company, was exploring for oil in the southeast part of the state. Embroidery, formerly done by hand, is now mechanized. Embroidered garments are produced for export, especially to Asia through the port of Manzanillo in neighboring Colima. Jalisco beekeepers also produce commercial quantities of honey.

14 Labor

As of 2005, the state of Jalisco had 2,862,977 eligible workers. Some 2,778,509 were listed as employed and 84,468 were listed as unemployed. Unemployed workers in rural areas may not be counted, however. The unemployment rate that year was reported to be 3%. Of those who were working, services employed 40.3%, followed by commerce at 21.6%, and manufacturing at 20%.

The US Bureau of Labor Statistics reported that Mexican workers saw their wages increase from $2.49 per hour in 2003 to $2.50 per hour in 2004. (The average US worker earned $15.70 per hour in 2004.) The maximum work week is set at 48 hours by law. The average worker spends 40 to 45 hours per week on the job. Workers earn twice their regular hourly rate for up to nine hours a week of overtime. When a worker works more than nine hours overtime in a week, he or she earns three times the regular hourly rate. After one year, workers are entitled by law to six days paid vacation.

Labor unions in the state of Jalisco are found mostly in the capital city of Guadalajara. Among those present are the Mexican Workers Confederation (CMT), the Revolutionary Confederation of Workers and Farmers (CROC), the National Confederation of Popular Organizations (CNOP), and the Electricity Workers Confederation of the Mexican Republic (SUTERM).

15 Agriculture

Jalisco is the country's leading producer of corn, sugar, milk, and poultry. Other crops grown in the state include beans, oats, alfalfa, chilies, sorghum, wheat, onions, tomatoes, bananas, and chickpeas. Farmers also raise cattle, pigs, sheep, and goats. Crops that are processed include peanuts and agave for the production of tequila, an important commodity in the state.

In 2004, Jalisco produced 3,351,592 tons of corn, second among all of Mexico's states. It also produced 301,555 tons of sorghum, 157,868 tons of wheat, 109,930 tons of red tomatoes, 77,097 tons of green chilies, and 93,390 tons of bananas.

Livestock brought to market in 2004 included 502,134 head of beef cattle, 827,662 pigs, 43,624 goats, and 18,553 sheep. Jalisco also was first in the production of milk from dairy cows at 1.7 billion liters (449 million gallons) and eggs at 831,645 tons. The state was third in production of honey at 5,698 tons. The state ranked second in the production of beef at 178,486 tons and in poultry at 240,671 tons. It was also first in the production of pork at 208,072 tons.

16 Natural Resources

In the state's southern coastal regions, there is a thriving fishing industry. In 2003, the total fish catch was at about 11,291 tons. There are silver and gold mines in northern Jalisco. The dry forests thrive in regions when there is rain during four or five months of the year. During the dry periods, the trees of the dry forests lose their leaves. Jalisco's dry forests grow in the region around the Volcán de Colima. In 2003, forest wood production was valued at about $76.7 million. Pine accounted for most of that total, but encino (a type of oak), oyamel (a type of fir), and common tropical woods were also harvested.

17 Energy and Power

In 2005, there were 2,050,571 users of electricity in Jalisco. Of that total, the largest number were residential customers at 1,748,993. Sales of electricity that same year totaled 10,049,967 megawatt hours, of which the largest users were medium-sized industrial firms at 4,028,885 megawatt hours. Jalisco's electric power came from eight power plants, six of which were hydroelectric, one was gas-turbine, and one diesel powered. Electricity is provided and distributed by the Federal Electricity Commission, and Central Light and Power. Both utilities are run by the Mexican government.

18 Health

In 2003, the state had 52 hospitals and 948 outpatient centers that were part of the national health system. In 2004, there were about 5,497 doctors, 13,368 nurses, and 425 dentists working in these health centers. There were an additional 175 independent health centers in the state in 2004. There is also an AmeriMed hospital in Puerto Vallarta.

Most of the Mexican population is covered under a government health plan. The IMSS (Instituto Mexicano de Seguro Social) covers the general population. The ISSSTE (Instituto de Seguridad y Servicios Sociales de Trabajadores del Estado) covers state workers.

19 Housing

Most homes are built with materials such as concrete, brick, or stone. Adobe is a popular construction material in some areas. In 2000, about 69% of all homes were owner-occupied. In 2005, there were an estimated 1,582,089 residential housing units in the state. About 85% of these units were single-family detached homes. The average household was estimated at 4.2 people.

20 Education

Public education in Mexico is funded by the state and is free for all students ages 6 to 16. While most students in the state attend public school, in 2003/04 about 25% of high school students attended private schools. In 2004/05, it was estimated that 89.3% of age-eligible students completed primary school, which includes six years of study. About 74.5% of eligible students completed secondary school, which includes three years of study after primary school. About 58.5% of eligible students completed the *bachillerato*, which is similar to a high school diploma. The national average for completion of the *bachillerato* was 60.1% that year.

There are at least eight major institutions of higher learning in the state. The Universidad de Guadalajara (University of Guadalajara) is located in the capital. In 2005, there were about 235,334 students ages 20 and older who were enrolled in some type of higher education program. The overall literacy rate was estimated at 92.8% in 2005.

21 Arts

Jalisco has almost 70 local cultural institutions. In 2004, there were at least 16 theaters for the performing arts, including the Lakeside Little Theater, which sponsors works in English. The Jalisco Philharmonic Orchestra plays regularly at the Teatro Degollado in Guadalajara, which features theater and opera productions as well.

The annual San Pedro Fair (June) in Tlaquepaque offers a combination of art, culture, and sporting events. The annual International Mariachi and Charro Festival (September) began in 1993 and attracts musicians from across Mexico and around the world. The Feistas de Octubre (October Festivals) in Guadalajara involve concerts, dances, and mini fairs that take place throughout the entire month. The Festival del Gourmet, held in Puerto Vallarta, draws guest chefs from around the world for an annual food festival. The International Book Fair in Guadalajara has been held annually since 1987 at the University of Guadalajara and has become on of the largest celebrations of Spanish-language literature. The National Tequila Fair features rodeo events and mariachi concerts as well as demonstrations on the production of the city's most famous drink.

There are over 200 registered movie theaters, including multiscreen theaters and single-screen galleries. An annual Puerto Vallarta Film festival of the Americas features a variety of independent North American and Latin American films, as well as art exhibits and concerts.

22 Libraries and Museums

In 2003, there were 671 libraries in the state with a combined total of 4,263,876 volumes. The same year, there were 27 active museums registered in the state that had permanent exhibits. Cocula has a museum dedicated to the art of the *mariachi* (traditional Mexican music). The Museo Nacional de la Cerámica (National Ceramics Museum) features paintings as well as traditional pottery and masks. The Instituto de las Artesanías Jaliscienses (Arts and Crafts Institute of Jalisco) is in the capital, Guadalajara.

Fountain in Guadalajara. PETER LANGER.

Guadalajara is also home to the Ripley's Museum of the Incredible, the Wax Museum, and the Globo Children's Museum.

23 Media

In 2005, the capital, Guadalajara, had five daily newspapers: *El Informador* (*The Informer*), *El Occidental* (*The Western*), *El Sol de Guadalajara* (*Guadalajara Sun*), *Ocho Columnas* (*Eight Columns*) and *El Financiero* (*The Financer*). There were three daily papers in Puerto Vallarta: *Meridiano* (*Meridian*), *Tribuna de la Bahia* (*Bay Tribune*), and *Vallarta Opina* (*Vallarta Opinion*).

In 2004, there were 168 television stations and 84 radio stations (46 AM and 38 FM). In 2005, there were about 381,816 subscribers to cable and satellite television stations. Also in 2005, there were about 1,166,076 residential phone lines, with about 22 mainline phones in use for every 100 people.

24 Tourism, Travel, and Recreation

The capital, Guadalajara, is known as the Pearl of the West because of its beautiful architecture and geographic location. It is also the home of many festive mariachi bands that play at weddings and other festivals. Along with golf and tennis, Guadalajara also hosts *charro* (rodeos), where cowboys compete in roping and riding events.

Zoológico Guadalajara is a major zoo in the capital. The Hospicio Cabañas in Guadalajara, a residential hospital built in the early 19th century to serve orphans, the handicapped, and

Nuevo Vallarta is only about 7 miles (11 kilometers) from the Puerto Vallarta Airport. PETER LANGER.

the elderly, has been designated as a UNESCO World Heritage site because of architectural design and the artwork that was incorporated into the building.

Puerto Vallarta is the state's best-known resort. Tourists enjoy sport fishing, rock climbing, and mountain biking. Zapopan has the Museo de Casa Albarrón, featuring taxidermy (stuffed and mounted animals) exhibits of the great hunters. The Agave Landscape and Ancient Industrial Facilities of Tequila, found near the foothills of Volcán de Tequila, was established as UNESCO World Heritage site in 2006. The famous "Mexican hat dance" originated in the city of Guadalajara.

25 Sports

Soccer is extremely popular. There are six soccer teams in the state that compete in the Mexican Football Association (commonly known as Femexfut). Club Guadalajara and Atlas are First Division teams and the Academicos and Tapatio are First Division "A" teams. The Universidad Autónoma de Guadalajara (UAG) sponsors teams in both the First Division and the First Division "A;" both teams are known as the Owls. Most soccer matches are played in the 63,163-seat Estadio Jalisco (Jalisco Stadium). The university's soccer teams in Guadalajara play in the 23,000-seat 3 de Marzo stadium.

In 2004, there were seven bullfighting rings in the state, including a 20,000-seat bullfighting ring in Guadalajara. Zapopan has a basketball team, the Tecos de la Universidad Autónoma de Guadalajara, which plays in the 40,000-seat Gimnasio Universitario.

The annual International Half Marathon held in November begins in Puerto Vallarta, Jalisco, and ends in Nuevo Vallarta, Nayarit. Another popular half marathon is held in Guadalajara each February. An annual golf tournament was established in 2001 at the Nicklaus Vista Vallarta and Mayan Palace Golf Courses in Puerto Vallarta. The International Puerto Vallarta Sailfish and Marlin Tournament has been held annually since 1955.

26 Famous People

Notable Jalisco citizens include Bishop Juan Cruz Ruiz de Cabañas y Crespo (b. Spain, 1752–1824), who directed the construction of the Hospicio Cabañas for homeless people and orphans. The Cabañas became the headquarters for the state secretary of culture in 1992. Artist Gerardo Murillo (1875–1964) was born in Guadalajara and used the pseudonym Dr. Atl. Muralist José Clemente Orozco (1883–1949) was born in Ciudad Guzmán. His *Man of Fire* may be seen in the Cabañas Institute in Guadalajara. Novelist Agustín Yáñez (1904–1980) wrote about myths of the indigenous people and the Spanish colonial era. His works include the novels *The Edge of the Storm* and *The Lean Lands*. Popular writer Juan Rulfo (1918–1986) is best-known for his works *The Burning Plain* and *Pedro Páramo*.

José Pablo Moncayo (1912–1958) was a well-known composer of classical music who also served as the conductor of the National Symphony in Mexico City. Carlos Santana (b.1947), leader of the band Santana, is a famous Mexican rock-and-roll guitarist born in Autlan De Navarro. He was inducted into the Rock and Roll Hall of Fame in the United States in 1998. Luis Barragán (1902–1988) was considered to be one of the most important Mexican architects of the 20th century. He became the second winner of the Pritzker Prize in 1980. His home and studio in Mexico City were designated as a UNESCO World Heritage site in 2005. Jose Vergara is a prominent film producer and the owner of three soccer teams.

27 Bibliography

BOOKS

Carew-Miller, Anna. *Famous People of Mexico*. Philadelphia: Mason Crest Publishers, 2003.

Day-MacLeod, Deirdre. *The States of Central Mexico*. Philadelphia, PA: Mason Crest Publishers, 2003.

Gruber, Beth. *Mexico*. Washington, DC: National Geographic, 2006.

Valenzuela-Zapata, Ana Guadalupe, and Gary Paul Nabhan. *Tequila: A Natural and Cultural History*. Tucson: University of Arizona Press, 2004.

Whipperman, Bruce. *Pacific Mexico: Including Acapulco, Puerto Vallarta, Oaxaca, Guadalajara and Mazatlán*, 5th edition. Emeryville, CA: Avalon Travel Pub., 2001.

WEB SITES

Government of Mexico. *Mexico for Kids*. www.elbalero.gob.mx/index_kids.html (accessed on March 30, 2007).

Mexican Tourism Board. *Visit Mexico: Jalisco*. www.visitmexico.com/wb/Visitmexico/Visi_Jalisco (accessed on March 30, 2007).

State of México

PRONUNCIATION: MEH-hee-koh.

ORIGIN OF STATE NAME: The state (and country) name comes from words in the language of the indigenous Náhuatl people: *metztli* (moon), *xictli* (center), and *co* (place).

CAPITAL: Toluca.

ENTERED COUNTRY: 1824.

COAT OF ARMS: A shield surrounded by gold trim and a red border with the words "Libertad Travajo Cultura" (Spanish for "Freedom Work Culture"). In the upper left is a pyramid, representing the historic Aztec civilization; in the upper right, commemorating the Battle of Cross Mountain in the war for independence, two crosses rise above a green peak. A cannon is firing in front of the peak. The lower half of the shield features an open book with a pick and a spade, representing the rich ores found in the state. The yellow and brown rays in the background represent agriculture.

HOLIDAYS: Año Nuevo (New Year's Day—January 1); Día de la Constitución (Constitution Day—February 5); Benito Juárez's birthday (March 21); Primero de Mayo (Labor Day—May 1); Anniversary of the Battle of Puebla (1862), May 5; Revolution Day, 1910 (November 20); and Navidad (Christmas—December 25).

FLAG: There is no official state flag.

TIME: 6 AM = noon Greenwich Mean Time (GMT).

1 Location and Size

México state is bordered on the north by Querétaro and Hidalgo; on the east by Tlaxcala and Puebla; on the south by Distrito Federal (Federal District), Morelos, and Guerrero; and on the west by Michoacán. It has an area of 22,357 square kilometers (8,632 square miles), a little larger than the US state of Massachusetts. It ranks as 25th in size among the states and covers about 1.1% of the total land area of Mexico. The State of México is divided into 125 municipalities (similar to US counties). Its capital, Toluca de Lerdo, lies near the center of the state.

Much of the northern part of the state is crossed by the east-west belt of mountains known as the Sierra Volcánica Transversal (also know as the Cordillera Neovolcánica). This region has some of the highest mountains in the country. Volcán Popocatépetl, along the southeast border with Puebla, is the highest point in the state and the second-highest peak in the country at an elevation of about 5,465 meters (17,930 feet). Volcán Iztaccíhuatl is the third-highest peak in the country at about 5,230 meters (17,454 feet). Volcán Nevado de Toluca, in the south-central portion of the state, is the fourth-highest point in the country and the highest peak that is completely within the borders of the State of México. The Sierra Madre del Sur cross the southwest portion of the state. The southeast edge of the state is part of the Balsas River basin that stretches into the state of Guerrero. The Sierra Nevada are also located here.

The State of México's rivers include the Lerma, the Tula, and the Moctezuma. Some areas of the state, such as the valley of Cuautitlán-Texcoco near the border with the Distrito Federal, have no water resources. Laguna de Zumpango is one of the largest natural lakes. There are several lakes created by river dams, including the Presa Valle de Bravo and the Presa Villa Victoria.

2 Climate

The climate varies considerably by region. In the valley regions, the climate is hot and dry. Around the capital, Toluca de Lerdo, the climate is cooler. The average annual temperature range in Toluca de Lerdo is 12°C to 17°C (54°F to 63°F). Rainfall in Toluca de Lerdo averages 800 to 900 millimeters (31 to 35 inches).

3 Plants and Animals

In the eastern part of the state, the mountains of the Sierra Nevada are covered with pine, oak, white cedar, and fir trees. Plants native to the valleys are cactus, nopal (similar to prickly pear), copal trees (a type of tree with heavy, thick resin), and gourds.

Native animals include coati (a raccoon-like animal) and deer. There are many bird species native to the state, including the sparrow hawk. The State of México and its southern neighbor, Michoacán, are winter homes to hundreds of thousands of migrating monarch butterflies.

4 Environmental Protection

In 2004, the state had 67 municipal wastewater treatment plants in operation with a combined installed capacity of 6,879 liters per second (1,817 gallons per second). The volume of treated wastewater that year was estimated at 4,451 liters per second (1,175 gallons per second). There were also 225 industrial wastewater treatment plants in operation that year. As of 2004, about 90.6% of the population had access to safe drinking water.

In 2003, the state had about 645,858 hectares (1.5 million acres) of woodland, including 87,789 hectares (216,931 acres) of rain forest. In 2004, about 300 hectares (741 acres) of woodland were damaged or destroyed by forest fires. An additional 2,092 hectares (5,169 acres) of pasture and brush lands were also damaged by fires.

There are several protected areas in the state, including eight national parks. Iztaccíhuatl and Popocatépetl National Park is the largest national park in the state. It covers the terrain around the volcanic peaks of Popocatépetl and Iztaccíhuatl, the second- and third-highest peaks in the country. The Ciénegas del Lerma, located in the eastern portion of the state, was designated as a Ramsar Wetland of International Importance in 2004.

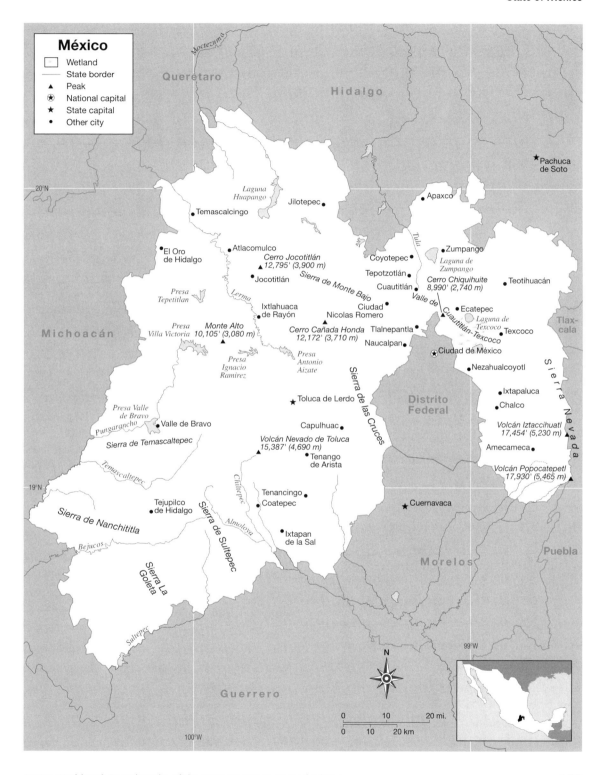

México

- Wetland
- State border
- ▲ Peak
- ✪ National capital
- ★ State capital
- • Other city

Querétaro

Hidalgo

★ Pachuca de Soto

Moctezuma

20°N

Laguna Huapango

• Temascalcingo

• Jilotepec

• Apaxco

• El Oro de Hidalgo

• Atlacomulco

Cerro Jocotitlán ▲ *12,795' (3,900 m)*

• Coyotepec

• Zumpango

Laguna de Zumpango

• Tepotzotlán

Cerro Chiquihuite 8,990' (2,740 m)

• Teotihuacán

• Jocotitlán

Sierra de Monte Bajo

• Cuautitlán

Lerma

Presa Tepetitlan

• Ixtlahuaca de Rayón

• Ciudad Nicolas Romero

Valle de

• Ecatepec

Cuautitlán-Texcoco

Laguna de Texcoco

Michoacán

Presa Villa Victoria

Monte Alto 10,105' (3,080 m) ▲

Cerro Cañada Honda 12,172' (3,710 m)

• Tlalnepantla

• Texcoco

Tlax-cala

Presa Ignacio Ramirez

Presa Antonio Aizate

• Naucalpan

✪ Ciudad de México

• Nezahualcoyotl

Sierra Nevada

Presa Valle de Bravo

★ Toluca de Lerdo

Sierra de las Cruces

Distrito Federal

• Ixtapaluca

• Chalco

Volcán Iztaccihuatl 17,454' (5,230 m)

Pungarancho

• Valle de Bravo

• Capulhuac

Sierra de Temascaltepec

Volcán Nevado de Toluca 15,387' (4,690 m)

• Tenango de Arista

• Amecameca

Volcán Popocatepetl 17,930' (5,465 m) ▲

19°N

Temascaltepec

• Tejupilco de Hidalgo

Sierra de Nanchititla

Sierra de Sultepec

Chilitepec

Almoloya

• Tenancingo
• Coatepec

★ Cuernavaca

• Ixtapan de la Sal

Morelos

Puebla

Bejucos

Sierra La Goleta

Sultepec

Guerrero

100°W

N

99°W

0   10   20 mi.

0   10   20 km

A plume of smoke and steam rises from the Popocatépetl volcano. AP IMAGES.

5 Population, Ethnic Groups, Languages

México had an estimated total population of 14,224,800 in 2006, ranking first among the states and the Distrito Federal. About 49% of the population were men and 51% were women. About 87% of the population lived in urban areas. The population density was 662 people per square kilometer (1,711 people per square mile), which was the second-highest population density in the nation (after the Distrito Federal). In 2005, the capital of Toluca de Lerdo had a population of 747,512.

Almost all citizens speak Spanish as their first language. In 2005, there were about 312,319 people who spoke indigenous (native) languages such as Mazahua, Otomi, Náhuatl, and the languages of the Mixtec and Zapotec ethnic groups.

6 Religions

According to the 2000 census, 91.2% of the population, or about 10 million people, were Roman Catholic; about 3.8%, or 423,068 people, were mainline or evangelical Protestants. The state had the largest population of Jehovah's Witnesses at 134,468 members. The state also had the largest Latter-day Saints (Mormon) community with 25,491 members. The Jewish community of 14,084 was the second-largest in the country with 14,084 (following the Distrito

Temple of the Moon, at the head of the Street of the Dead, includes ruins that date to 100 BC. © ROBERT FRERCK/ WOODFIN CAMP.

Federal). About 1.8% of the population claimed to have no religious affiliation.

The Catedral de Corpus Christi in Tlalnepantla is the seat of the Roman Catholic archdiocese of Tlalnepantla.

7 Transportation

There are international airports in Toluca de Lerdo (Toluca–Alfonso Lopez Airport) and Mexico City that provide international flight service to México state. There are 1,227 kilometers (762 miles) of railroad tracks. A system of 9,510 kilometers (5,907 miles) of highways links the state with the rest of the country. In 2004, there were 998,407 automobiles registered in

the state, along with 3,027 passenger trucks, 223,029 freight trucks, and 4,836 motorcycles.

8 History

First inhabited around 5000 BC, the central valley of México was the home to several different civilizations before the Aztecs settled in the region around the 13th century. Among the early civilizations, Olmec and Toltec groups built towns and religious centers. Perhaps the most important pre-Aztec constructions, the pyramids of the Sun and the Moon, belong to the Teotihuacan culture (200 to 800 AD). By the time the Spaniards arrived, Toltec groups inhabited the valley surrounding the capital city, Tenochtitlán, where the Aztecs ruled.

Spanish conqueror Hernán Cortés (1485–1547) organized in Texcoco the attack on México-Tenochtitlán in 1521. Dutch Franciscan priests (from an order of the Roman Catholic Church) first settled in the region in 1523 to convert the large indigenous population that inhabited the central valley of México. Jesuits, Agustines, and Dominican priests (from other orders of Catholicism) joined the Catholic conversion efforts starting in the 1530s. The Tepozotlán convent was one of the most important Jesuit centers in the entire continent during the Spanish conquest of Mexico.

Yet, the diseases brought by the Spaniards and the oppression imposed upon the indigenous communities brought the population down from two million at the time of the conquest to about two hundred thousand a century later. Agricultural production and services to the growing capital city of México, one of the most important centers of Spanish colonial presence in the Americas, represented the region's main economic activities during the 17th and 18th centuries.

The independence movement quickly reached the then province of México. The independence army overpowered the royalists (loyal to Spain) in Toluca de Lerdo and then moved on to Mexico City. The royalist opposition to independence was defeated in a bloody battle at Las Cruces Mountain in 1810. After the execution of independence leader José Morelos (1765–1815), the region was once again controlled by the royalist forces. Yet, the new independence movement in 1821 was finally successful in freeing the province from Spanish colonial rule. In 1827,

the separation of Mexico City as the nation's capital forced the province of México to establish Toluca de Lerdo as the new state capital.

US troops briefly occupied the state in 1847. Constant administrative and political reforms assigned former State of México territories to newly created provinces and states during much of the 19th century. The state became a central fighting ground for the civil war between liberals and conservatives in the 1860s. Yet, after the liberals were victorious, the state was peacefully controlled, first by liberal president Benito Juárez (1806–1872) and later by President Porfirio Díaz (1830–1915). During the years that Porfirio Díaz was in power, roads, bridges, and other structures were built. He also consolidated the central government and made it strong enough to begin to challenge the influence of the Roman Catholic Church and the large landowners. The years that Porfirio Díaz was in power (1877–80 and 1884–1911) came to be known as the Porfíriato period.

Another revolution began in 1910 and became known as the Mexican Revolution. This new conflict caused friction in the state between large landowners and landless peasants. The creation of the Mexico Distrito Federal, as the nation's capital, at the end of the revolution in 1917, was the last time the state lost territory to newly created entities. Rapid urbanization and industrial development characterized the state's economy during most of the 20th century.

Although it is formally and legally a different state, with a significant rural population, a large portion of the state's population inhabits the areas that surround Distrito Federal and are thus considered today part of the larger metropolitan area of one of the most populated cities in the world.

In the first decade of the 21st century, the State of México remained one of Mexico's most industrially developed states. Despite this, poverty, official corruption, and crime remain problems for the state.

9 State and Local Government

The powerful state governor is elected democratically every six years for a nonrenewable term. The legislature is unicameral (one chamber) comprised of 45 members elected in single-member districts and 30 members elected by proportional representation. Deputies serve for three-year terms and cannot be immediately reelected.

The 125 municipal governments that comprise the State of México hold municipal president and council member elections every three years. Immediate reelection is prohibited. Larger municipalities have more resources, especially those that border Mexico City.

10 Political Parties

The three main political parties in the country of Mexico are the Institutional Revolutionary Party (PRI), the National Action Party (PAN), and the Party of the Democratic Revolution (PRD). The PRI has controlled politics in the State of México since the end of the revolution. No other party has succeeded in winning a gubernatorial race in that state, although the PAN and the PRD have won important municipal presidencies. Enrique Peña Nieto of the PRI was elected for a six-year term in 2005.

Because the Institutional Revolutionary Party (PRI) has dominated the executive and legislative branches throughout most of the 20th century, existing division of power and check-and-balances provisions have only been recently utilized as opposition parties have increased their presence in the legislature.

11 Judicial System

The Superior Tribunal of Justice is the highest court of the State of México. Its members are appointed by a special council of the judiciary and their nonrenewable term lasts for fifteen years. The renewal of justices is staggered to provide continuity to the high court. Only qualified and experienced attorneys can be appointed to the high court by the council of the judiciary. In addition, an electoral court and various local courts also constitute the state judicial system.

12 Economy

The economy of the State of México is marked by a high degree of industrial development and its proximity to the nation's capital, the Distrito Federal, which the state surrounds. The state's 150,000 firms are primarily based on industry and commercial activities, with tourism and handicrafts acting as complementary industries. The Teotihuacan pyramids are an international tourist destination.

13 Industry

The State of México's chief industries are food processing, motor vehicles, chemicals, textiles, paper, and machinery assembly. Companies such as Daimler Chrysler, Ford, General Motors, Kimberly Clark, and Celanese operate a number of industrial parks throughout the state, of which three are in the capital city of Toluca de Lerdo. Handicrafts, such as woolen and cotton textiles, wooden carvings, pottery, metal, basketwork, paper lampshades, onyx and obsidian figures, and stone mortars of the Zumpango region are produced in México state.

14 Labor

As of 2005, the State of México had 6,159,172 eligible workers. Some 5,821,960 were listed as employed and 337,212 were listed as unemployed. Unemployed workers in rural areas may not be counted, however. The unemployment rate that year was reported to be 5.4%. Of those who were working, services employed 43.5%, followed by commerce at 21.7% and manufacturing at 19%.

The US Bureau of Labor Statistics reported that Mexican workers saw their wages increase from $2.49 per hour in 2003 to $2.50 per hour in 2004. (The average US worker earned $15.70 per hour in 2004.) The maximum work week is set at 48 hours by law. The average worker spends 40 to 45 hours per week on the job. Workers earn twice their regular hourly rate for up to nine hours a week of overtime. When a worker works more than nine hours overtime in a week, he or she earns three times the regular hourly rate. After one year, workers are entitled by law to six days paid vacation.

The unions in the State of México are mostly based around the state's capital city of Toluca de Lerdo. They include the Mexican Workers Confederation (CTM), the Revolutionary Confederation of Workers and Farmers (CROC), and the Revolutionary Confederation of Mexican Workers (CROM).

15 Agriculture

Crops are grown in the State of México on large and small farms, some of which are irrigated while others are not. Crops grown include mangos, avocados, oranges, plums, nuts, mamey (similar to an apricot), papaya, corn, wheat, alfalfa, maguey (cactus), tomatoes, potatoes, and various types of beans.

In 2004, crop production for the State of México included: 1,680,872 tons of corn, 111,837 tons of potatoes, 42,590 tons of wheat, 37,320 tons of red tomatoes, and 20,817 tons of avocados. Livestock brought to market in 2004 included: 316,702 head of beef cattle, 704,763 pigs, 20,716 goats, and 56,670 sheep. In that same year, the state produced 480 million liters (126 million gallons) of milk from dairy cows and 37,267 tons of eggs. Meat production included: 40,438 tons of beef, 27,690 tons of pork, 574 tons of goat, 7,165 tons of lamb, and 117,308 tons of poultry.

16 Natural Resources

The state's natural resource base is centered on its nine national parks. Visitors to the state's national parks can enjoy mountain climbing, fishing, camping, or horseback riding. In Nevado de Toluca National Park, there is a volcanic crater with two deep lakes. Scuba divers and hikers enjoy the natural environment of these crater lakes. Bird watching, especially hummingbirds, is popular in Zoquiapan y Anexas National Park. Sacramonte National Park features views of the Popocatépetl and Iztaccíhuatl volcanoes from the top of Sacramonte Hill.

In 2003, forest wood production was valued at about $15.2 million. Most of that value came from the harvest of pine. The fish catch in 2003 was about 7,347 tons, all for human consumption.

17 Energy and Power

In 2005, there were 2,748,806 users of electricity in the State of México. Of that total, the largest number were residential customers at 2,461,993. Sales of electricity that same year totaled 15,441,616 megawatt hours, of which the largest users were medium-sized industrial firms at 6,885,903 megawatt hours. The State of México has two operating power plants, a 549 megawatt combined cycle (combined gas-turbine and steam) facility and a 450 megawatt thermal (non-coal) plant, both of which are at Acolman. Electricity is provided by the Federal Electricity Commission and Central Light and Power. Both utilities are run by the Mexican government.

18 Health

In 2003, the state had 64 hospitals and 1,212 outpatient centers that were part of the national health system. In 2004, there were about 7,544 doctors, 15,255 nurses, and 810 dentists working in these health centers. Though the total number of medical personnel seems higher than other states, the doctor to patient ratio is the lowest in the country with about 73.4 doctors for every 100,000 people. There were an additional 539 independent health centers in the state in 2004.

Most of the Mexican population is covered under a government health plan. The IMSS (Instituto Mexicano de Seguro Social) covers the general population. The ISSSTE (Instituto de Seguridad y Servicios Sociales de Trabajadores del Estado) covers state workers.

19 Housing

Most homes are built with materials such as concrete, brick, and stone. In some areas there are homes with adobe walls and floors and tile or sheet metal roofs. In 2000, about 79% of all homes were owner-occupied. The State of México has more housing units than any other state in the country. In 2005, there were an estimated 3,243,566 residential housing units. About 76% of these units were single-family detached homes. About 10% were units in apartment buildings. The average household was estimated at 4.3 people.

20 Education

Public education in Mexico is free for students from ages 6 to 16. While most students in the state attend public schools, in 2002/03 about 25% of high school students attended private schools. In 2004/05, it was estimated that 93.8% of age-eligible students completed primary school, which includes six years of study. About 79.6% of eligible students completed secondary school, which includes three years of study after primary school. About 56.3% of eligible students completed the *bachillerato*, which is similar to a high school diploma. The national average for completion of the *bachillerato* was 60.1% that year.

There are over 15 institutions of higher learning in the state. Universidad Autónoma del Estado de México (Autonomous University of the State of México) is in Toluca de Lerdo. In 2005, there were about 431,736 students ages

20 and older who were enrolled in some type of higher education program. The overall literacy rate was estimated at 94% in 2005.

21 Arts

The State of México has its own Ballet Folklórico company. The Symphonic Orchestra of the State of México was founded in 1971 and is based at Sala Felipe Villanueva Hall in Toluca de Lerdo. There are over 15 theaters and 39 cultural centers. There are also several chapters of the French cultural society Alianza Francesa. There are over 230 registered movie theaters, including multi-screen theaters and single-screen galleries.

22 Libraries and Museums

In 2003, there were 1,479 libraries in the state with a combined stock of 6,736,993 volumes. The same year, there were 34 active museums in the state that had permanent exhibits. The Mexican Cultural Center complex in Toluca de Lerdo contains a large library as well as the Modern Art Museum, the Museum of Anthropology and History, and the Museum of Popular Culture. The city of Teotihuacán, an excavated ruin, showcases the pyramids and city structure of the Aztec civilization. The archeological site houses at least three museums on the art, culture, and history of the Aztec.

23 Media

In 2005, the capital city, Toluca de Lerdo, had 11 daily newspapers. The largest were *El Manana* (*The Morning*), *El Sol de Toluca* (*Toluca Sun*), *El Vespertino* (*The Evening*), and *El Diario* (*The Daily*).

In 2004, there were 79 television stations and 23 radio stations (15 AM and 8 FM). In 2005, there were about 210,593 subscribers to cable and satellite television stations. Also in 2005, there were about 2,175,384 residential phone lines, with about 17.4 mainline phones in use for every 100 people.

24 Tourism, Travel, and Recreation

The capital city, Toluca de Lerdo, is mainly an industrial city. Tourists often stay in Toluca de Lerdo hotels when they travel to visit the ruins of the Aztec ceremonial city Teotihuacán. At Teotihuacán, the famous Pyramids of the Sun and the Moon are located. Teotihuacán means "the place where men become gods." Ixtapán de la Sal is famous for its spas and thermal baths. The Parque Nacional Izta-Popo (Izta-Popo National Park) is the home of México's two famous volcanoes, Popocatépetl and Iztaccíhuatl. The Cosmovitral in Toluca de Lerdo is one of the largest botanical gardens in the nation.

25 Sports

There are two soccer teams in the state that compete in the Mexican Football Association (commonly known as Femexfut). The Club Toluca plays in the First Division and Atlético Mexiquense plays in the First Division "A." El Potros (Colts) is the soccer team at the Universidad Autónoma del Estado de México. In 2004, the State of México had seven sports arenas. There was one bullfighting ring.

26 Famous People

Juana Inés de la Cruz (1651–1695) was a nun who became a well-known poet and outspoken supporter of women's rights. His Eminence Javier Lozano Barragán (b.1933) is a Mexican Cardinal Deacon of San Michele Archangelo and president of the Pontifical Council for the Pastoral Care of Health Care Workers in the Roman Catholic Church.

27 Bibliography

BOOKS

Carew-Miller, Anna. *Famous People of Mexico.* Philadelphia: Mason Crest Publishers, 2003.

Day-MacLeod, Deirdre. *The States of Central Mexico.* Philadelphia, PA: Mason Crest Publishers, 2003.

George, Lynn. *Teotihuacan: Designing an Ancient Mexican City.* New York: Rosen Pub. Group's PowerKids Press, 2004.

Gruber, Beth. *Mexico.* Washington, DC: National Geographic, 2006.

WEB SITES

Government of Mexico. *Mexico for Kids.* www.elbalero.gob.mx/index_kids.html (accessed on March 30, 2007).

Mexican Tourism Board. *Visit Mexico: State of México.* www.visitmexico.com/wb/Visitmexico/Visi_Mexico (accessed on March 30, 2007).

Michoacán

PRONUNCIATION: mee-CHO-ah-CAHN.

ORIGIN OF STATE NAME: Probably comes from the native word Mechoacan, which means "place of the fishermen."

CAPITAL: Morelia (moh-REH-lee-ah).

ENTERED COUNTRY: October 3, 1824.

COAT OF ARMS: The fish at the top of the state coat of arms refers to Michoacán as the "place of fishermen." The picture of a man on horseback represents Generalísimo José María Morelos y Pavón (1765–1815), for whom the capital city of Morelia was named. The three crowns symbolize the history of the region as part of the Purépecha empire. The buildings pictured are meant to represent industry and culture. Blue is used to depict the sky and water.

HOLIDAYS: Año Nuevo (New Year's Day—January 1); Día de la Constitución (Constitution Day—February 5); Benito Juárez's birthday (March 21); Primero de Mayo (Labor Day—May 1); Anniversary of the Battle of Puebla (1862), May 5; Revolution Day, 1910 (November 20); and Navidad (Christmas—December 25).

FLAG: There is no official state flag.

TIME: 6 AM = noon Greenwich Mean Time (GMT).

1 Location and Size

Michoacán is located in west-central Mexico. It has an area of 58,644 square kilometers (22,642 square miles), which is a little smaller than the US state of West Virginia. It ranks as 16th in size among the states and covers about 2.9% of the total land area of Mexico. Michoacán is bordered on the north and west by Jalisco; on the north by Guanajuato; on the northeast by Querétaro; on the east by the states of México and Guerrero; on the west by Colima and the Pacific Ocean; and on the south by Guerrero and the Pacific Ocean. Michoacán has 113 municipalities (similar to US counties). Its capital is Morelia.

Michoacán is formed in part by two large mountain ranges, the Sierra Volcánica Transversal in the north and the Sierra Madre del Sur in the south. There are more than 80 volcanoes in the state, including Pico de Tancítaro at 3,845 meters (12,615 feet), which is the highest point in the state. There are 55 volcanic craters near Pico de Tancítaro. Other important volcanoes include Patamban (3,750 meters/12,303 feet) and Paricutín (2,775 meters/9,100 feet).

This waterfall is found in Eduardo Ruiz National Park, named for historian Eduardo Ruiz. The park lies near Uruapan, about 120 kilometers (75 miles) from the capital, Morelia. PETER LANGER.

There are 26 volcanic craters in the vicinity of Paricutín.

In the far north, the land is generally flat; the Maravatío and Zamora valleys are located in this region.

Lago de Chapala (Lake Chapala) lies on the border with Jalisco. It is Mexico's largest natural lake. Lago de Chapala has an area of about 1,686 square kilometers (651 square miles). Other large lakes in the state include Lago de Cuitzeo, Lago de Pátzcuaro, and Laguna de Zirahuén. Presa del Infiernillo, a large reservoir created by a river dam, is the third-largest manmade lake in the country. The Lerma River rises in México state and crosses Michoacán in the north. The Duero River in the north flows into the Lerma. The Balsas River runs along the border with Guerrero. The Pacific coastline stretches a distance of 247 kilometers (153 miles).

2 Climate

The climate varies widely from place to place depending on altitude and prevailing winds. The coast enjoys a tropical climate with an average temperature of about 28°C (82°F). The central region has a milder climate, with an average temperature of about 22°C (71°F). The high-altitude regions can experience freezing temperatures.

The average temperature in the state ranges from a minimum of 18°C (64°F) to a maximum of 28°C (83°F). The average precipitation ranges

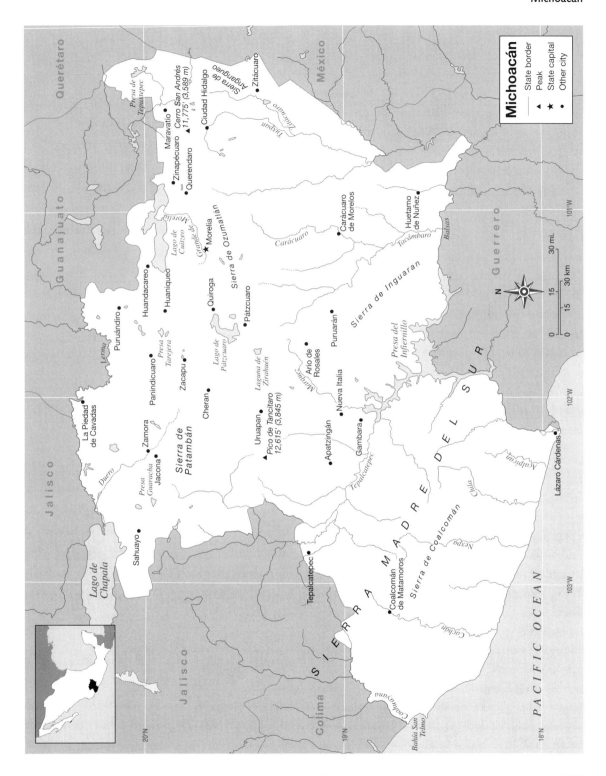

from a minimum of 64 centimeters (25 inches) to a maximum of 162 centimeters (64 inches). In the capital city of Morelia, the average temperature ranges from 14°c (57°F) in January to 20°c (68°F) in June. The average precipitation rate in the capital is 78.1 centimeters (30.7 inches) per year.

3 Plants and Animals

The state has a wide variety of tree species, including forests of oak, cedar, and pine. Mango trees can be found in the eastern and western regions. Common animals include coyotes, skunks, armadillos, squirrels, and lynxes. Eagles and parrots are found in the tropical regions. Pelicans and seagulls are found in the coastal lagoon regions. Sharks, whales, and porpoises inhabit the waters of the coast. There are more species of whales and porpoises here than in any other part of the world. Marine life includes about 900 fish species and 34 species of marine mammals.

4 Environmental Protection

In 2004, the state had 20 municipal wastewater treatment plants in operation with a combined installed capacity of 1,735 liters per second (458 gallons per second). The volume of treated wastewater that year was estimated at 1,052 liters per second (277 gallons per second). There were also 34 industrial wastewater treatment plants in operation that year. As of 2004, about 91% of the population had access to safe drinking water.

Lago de Chapala, the most important and largest natural lake in the country, is located along the border with Jalisco and covers an area of about 1,116 square kilometers (430 square miles). The lake supports a delicate ecosystem that is important for migratory bird populations. The water of Lago de Chapala has become polluted by heavy metals and other toxic substance due to inadequate wastewater treatment. Mismanagement of water resources and erosion of the shoreline have also caused the water level of the lake to drop. State and national officials, as well as some foreign environmental groups, are working on ways to preserve and protect the lake from further damage while promoting new ecological growth.

In 2003, the state had about 2.6 million hectares (6.4 million acres) of woodland, including over 1 million hectares (2.6 million acres) of rain forest. In 2004, about 1,232 hectares (3,044 acres) of woodland were damaged or destroyed by forest fires. An additional 5,172 hectares (12,780 acres) of pasture and brush land were also damaged by fires.

In the eastern region of the state, north of Zitácuaro, the Mariposa Monarca Biosphere Reserve is the winter home for the monarch butterflies of North American. Each year, tens of millions of monarch butterflies migrate to the high-altitude fir forests from Canada and the United States. In 2005, the biosphere covered an area of about 56,259 square kilometers (21,721 square miles).

There were six national parks in the state in 2005. The Humedales del Lago Pátzcuaro, Laguna Costera El Caimán, Laguna de Zacapu, and Playón Mexiquillo are listed as Ramsar Wetlands of International Importance.

Janitzio Island lies in Pátzcuaro Lake. Its buildings have white walls and red-tiled roofs. A 40-meter (132-foot) monument of Mexican patriot José Morelos, sculpted from pink stone, stands on the island's highest point. © KAL MULLER/WOODFIN CAMP.

5 Population, Ethnic Groups, Languages

Michoacán had an estimated total population of 4,003,700 in 2006, ranking ninth among the states and the Distrito Federal. About 48% of the population were men and 52% were women. About 51% of the population lived in urban areas. The population density was 66 people per square kilometer (173 people per square mile). In 2005, the capital, Morelia, had an estimated population of 684,145. Almost all citizens speak Spanish as their first language. About 3% of the population speaks an indigenous (native) language, such as Purépecha and Náhuatl.

6 Religions

According to the 2000 census, 94.8% of the population, or 3.2 million people, were Roman Catholic; nearly 2%, or 63,726 people, were mainline or evangelical Protestants. About 1% were counted as other Biblical faiths, including 31,787 Jehovah's Witnesses and 3,889 Seventh-day Adventists. About 1.3% of the population claimed to have no religious affiliation. The Catedral de las Monjas in Morelia is the seat of the Roman Catholic archdiocese of Morelia.

7 Transportation

Uruapan Airport provides international flights to and from Michoacán. There are about 8,618

The aqueduct in the capital, Morelia, was built in 1785. It stretches for more than one mile (1.6 kilometers) through the city. PETER LANGER.

kilometers (3,353 miles) of roads in the state and 1,275 kilometers (792 miles) of railroads. In 2004, there were 444,862 automobiles registered in the state, along with 8,756 passenger trucks, 487,309 freight trucks, and 30,404 motorcycles.

8 History

Olmec and Náhuatl groups inhabited the region since 200 BC. Indigenous Quechua groups migrated to the region around 500 AD and eventually dominated the other groups. The Quechua established the capital city in Pátzcuaro, one of the oldest indigenous cities built in Mexico. Later, another indigenous leader, Tariácuri, con-

quered new land. He founded the Purépecha empire. His descendants established the capital city in Tzintzuntzán and expanded the empire. They challenged the influence of the Aztec empire in central Mexico before the arrival of the Spanish conquistadors (Spanish conquerors of the Americas).

Emperor Zuuangua defeated an invading Aztec army led by Montezuma II (Moctezuma II; 1466–1520). He secured his empire and kept out Aztec rule. Spanish conqueror Hernán Cortés (1485–1547) arrived in the region in 1519. Zuuangua later rejected a plea to fight the Spanish conquistadors. He tried to remain neutral. But he died of smallpox, a disease brought by the Spaniards. Eventually, his empire was conquered by the Europeans.

In 1522, Spanish soldier Cristobal de Olid (1488–1524) peacefully conquered the Purépecha empire for the Spanish crown. The population was already decimated by diseases brought by the Spaniards. The military might of the conquistadors overpowered all indigenous resistance efforts. Spanish leader Nuño Beltrán de Guzmán summoned Purépecha emperor Tangáxoan to Mexico City for talks. But instead of talking, he kidnapped him. Beltrán de Guzmán asked for a large ransom of gold before he would set Tangáxoan free. Beltrán de Guzmán later launched a conquest of Michoacán in 1530. It ended with the torture and execution of Tangáxoan and the Spanish occupation of the region.

In 1533 Vasco de Quiroga initiated the conversion of the indigenous communities to the teachings of the Roman Catholic Church. He was made bishop of Michoacán in 1538. The city of Morelia was founded in 1541.

Agricultural activity characterized much of the colonial period (period of Spanish rule). Frequent volcanic eruptions caused the deaths of thousands of indigenous people.

When the independence movement began in Mexico (about 1810), Mexican priest and revolutionary Miguel Hidalgo y Costilla (1753–1811) entered Morelia without much resistance. Royalists (those loyal to Spain) had abandoned the city a few days earlier. During Hidalgo's stay in Morelia, the newly appointed governor declared the end of slavery. The independence fighters were eventually defeated by Royalists in 1811 at a battle at Calderón Bridge, however, and true independence was not achieved until 1821.

Political instability characterized much of the 19th century, until Mexican general and later president Porfirio Díaz (1830–1915) brought peace to the country. He took control after the death of President Benito Juárez (1806–1872). Porfirio Díaz initiated a long period of liberal authoritarian rule known as "Porfiriato." The revolution of 1910 brought an end to Porfiriato. Michoacán became a central battleground for revolutionaries who wanted land reform. Several revolutionary leaders fought in Michoacán. Thousands of landless peasants joined armies and militias to win more rights and land for peasants.

The most important 20th-century Mexican president, Lázaro Cárdenas (1895–1970), was a native of Michoacán. Cárdenas was named president in 1934. He adopted land reforms and gave millions of peasants the right to farm on communal (shared) lands. Cárdenas also nationalized the oil companies. This provided the government with money for education, health care, and public services. Cárdenas also brought political stability and formed the Institutional Revolutionary Party (PRI). Cárdenas is known as the father of present-day Mexico. He is revered as the man who brought stability to the country. His land distribution policies improved the standards of living for a majority of Mexicans.

In the first decade of the 21st century Michoacán remained one of Mexico's poorest states, with many of its people heavily reliant on money sent to them by family members working in the United States. In addition to poverty, violent crime also troubled the state, fueled in large part by the traffic in illegal drugs, for which the state's long Pacific coastline served as a haven for narcotics smugglers. Labor unrest also troubled the state. In April 2006, workers at a steel mill

The picturesque town of Angangueo, the center of the area where monarch butterflies migrate each year. © ROBERT FRERCK/
WOODFIN CAMP.

went on strike over the refusal of the government to recognize a union official that was accused of being corrupt. Adding to the labor unrest were protests by mine workers over safety issues, following a mine explosion that killed 65 miners.

9 State and Local Government

The state governor is elected every six years for a nonrenewable term. In relative terms, the executive has enormous powers and attributions. The legislative assembly is comprised of a unicameral (single) chamber with 40 deputies (24 are elected from single member districts and 16 are elected by proportional representation). Checks and balances and separation of powers provisions were not fully enforced until 2001, when the Party of the Democratic Revolution (PRD) won the state gubernatorial race and no party won absolute majority in the state legislature.

The 113 municipal governments in Michoacán democratically elect their municipal presidents and council members every three years. Immediate re-election is not allowed. Municipal governments in more populated cities have more influence, resources, and leverage than governments in largely rural areas.

10 Political Parties

The three main political parties in all of Mexico are the Institutional Revolutionary Party (PRI), the National Action Party (PAN), and the Party of the Democratic Revolution (PRD). The PRI

Fishers on Pátzcuaro Lake use butterfly-shaped nets. WOODFIN CAMP.

historically dominated Michoacán politics. The PRD has emerged as the strongest party in recent years. In 2002, the PRD's candidate, Lázaro Cárdenas Batel, was the first man to defeat a PRI candidate for governor. He is the grandson of Lázaro Cárdenas, the founder of the PRI and former president of Mexico, and the son of Cuauhtemoc Cárdenas, the founder of the PRD. Lázaro Cárdenas Batel capitalized on the strength of the left in Michoacán and his family name recognition.

11 Judicial System

The Supreme Tribunal of Justice is the highest court in the state. Its seven members are elected for three-year terms and can be re-elected. Justices must retire when they reach the age of 70. New appointments are made by the legislature from a three-person list submitted by the governor. Other judicial bodies are the electoral tribunal and local courts. Although judicial independence was nominally established in the state constitution, the excessive influence exerted by the PRI over local authorities in the past prevented the full autonomy of the state judicial system.

12 Economy

As of 2003, Michoacán economy was geared toward the production and processing of foodstuffs for the domestic economy and for export, as well as for the production of steel and nonfuel minerals. Agriculture accounted for the largest portion of the state's workforce at 29%, followed by 23% in the services sector, 16% in commerce, and 14% in industry.

13 Industry

Michoacán is Mexico's leading state for the production of iron, and has one of Latin America's largest steel mills located in the port city of Lazaro Cardenas, where a major new port has been under construction. Food processing for export is also an important industry. The state's handicraft industry produces carved wooden instruments, lacquer work, metal items, and pottery.

14 Labor

Michoacán citizens have migrated in large numbers to work in the United States and elsewhere. As of 2005, Michoacán had 1,599,256 eligible workers. Some 1,577,885 were listed as employed and 41,371 were listed as unemployed. Unemployed workers in rural areas may not be counted, however. The unemployment rate that year was reported to be 2.5%. Of those who were working, services employed 34.9%, followed by agriculture at 20.7%, and commerce at 20.2%.

The US Bureau of Labor Statistics reported that Mexican workers saw their wages increase from $2.49 per hour in 2003 to $2.50 per hour in 2004. (The average US worker earned $15.70 per hour in 2004.) The maximum work week is set at 48 hours by law. The average worker spends 40 to 45 hours per week on the job. Workers earn twice their regular hourly rate for up to nine hours a week of overtime. When a worker works more than nine hours overtime in a week, he or she earns three times the regular hourly rate.

After one year, workers are entitled by law to six days paid vacation.

15 Agriculture

Michoacán is Mexico's largest producer of avocados and strawberries. The state also ranks third in the production of chickpeas and lemons, and fourth in the production of sesame and sorghum. Sugarcane, corn, wheat, mangoes, strawberries, papaya, and limes are grown as well.

In 2004, crop production for the state included: 1,267,501 tons of corn; 569,777 tons of sorghum; 202,118 tons of wheat; 162,476 tons of red tomatoes; 146,463 tons of sugar; and 864,069 tons of avocados.

The breeding of livestock is important in Michoacán. Pork, beef, and poultry are the main meat products. The state is also known for its production of milk, eggs, honey, and beeswax.

Livestock brought to market in 2004 included: 270,766 head of beef cattle; and 300,640 pigs. In that same year, the state produced 312 million liters (82 million gallons) of milk from dairy cows, 26,428 tons of eggs, and 1,776 tons of honey. Meat production included: 50,529 tons of beef; 46,347 tons of pork; and 43,837 tons of poultry.

16 Natural Resources

Michoacán produces about 15% of Mexico's timber. In 2003, the value of forest wood was estimated at $54.4 million. Pine and encino (a type of oak) were the primary woods.

Mining has played a significant role in the state's economy. About 32 cities have substantial deposits of iron ore. In the Angangueo region, gold, silver, lead, zinc, and barite are produced.

In the Coalcoman region, silver, lead, copper, zinc, and barite are produced. Gold is also produced in Churumuco de Morelos, while copper is also produced in Tingambato.

The fishing industry provides mojarra (small silvery fish), carp, red snapper, shark, turtles, crabs, and oysters. In 2003, the total fish catch was about 22,824 tons.

17 Energy and Power

In 2005, there were 1,305,146 users of electricity in the state of Michoacán. Of that total, the largest number were residential customers at 1,115,182. Sales of electricity that same year totaled 7,071,697 megawatt hours, of which the largest users were large industrial firms at 3,946,303 megawatt hours. Electric power in Michoacán is produced by 12 generating stations, including a single 195 megawatt capacity geothermal plant and 11 hydroelectric plants with a combined capacity of 438 megawatts.

Electricity is provided and distributed by the Federal Electricity Commission, and Central Light and Power. Both utilities are run by the Mexican government.

18 Health

In 2003, the state had 50 hospitals and 899 outpatient centers that were part of the national health system. In 2004, there were about 2,732 doctors, 5,699 nurses, and 192 dentists working in these health centers. There were an additional 198 independent health centers in the state in 2004.

Most of the Mexican population is covered under a government health plan. The IMSS (Instituto Mexicano de Seguro Social) covers the general population. The ISSSTE (Instituto de Seguridad y Servicios Sociales de Trabajadores del Estado) covers state workers.

19 Housing

Most homes are built with materials such as brick, concrete, or stone with flat roof constructions. There are a large number of homes built with adobe walls and floors and tile or sheet metal roofs. In 2000, about 80% of all homes were owner-occupied. In 2005, there were an estimated 913,390 residential housing units in the state. About 93% of these units were single-family detached homes. The average household was estimated at 4.3 people.

20 Education

Public education in Mexico is free for students from ages 6 to 16. While most students attend public schools, in 2003 about 26% of high school students attended private schools. In 2004/05, it was estimated that 82.5% of age-eligible students completed primary school, which includes six years of study. About 68.5% of eligible students completed secondary school, which includes three years of study after primary school. Only 48.6% of eligible students completed the *bachillerato*, which is similar to a high school diploma. This was the lowest rate of graduation in the country that year. The national average for completion of the *bachillerato* was 60.1% that year.

Both El Colegio de Michoacán and the Universidad Michoacana are located in Michoacán. The oldest university on the American continent, Universidad Michoacana de San Nicolás de Hidalgo, was founded in

Masks made from vegetables are seen during a festival in Uruapan. © KAL MULLER/WOODFIN CAMP.

1540. (It was known as Colegio de San Nicolás Hidalgo at that time.) In 2005, there were about 99,994 students ages 20 and older who were enrolled in some type of higher education program. The overall literacy rate was estimated at 87.2% in 2005.

21 Arts

Michoacán has a contemporary dance company and a musical group called Ensamble de las Rosas. There is a symphony orchestra in Morelia. A children's chorus, Niños Cantores de Morelia, is also based in Morelia. The city also hosts the annual International Guitar Festival of Morelia and the International Organ Festival, both of which have gained popularity with musicians from around the world. The Miguel Bernal Jiminez International Musical Festival of Morelia was established in 1989 in honor of one of Mexico's famous composers. The Paracho Guitar festival celebrates the city where some of the most famous Mexican guitars are made.

In 2004, there were at least five major theaters for the performing arts. Most communities have local cultural centers. There are over 70 registered movie theaters, including multiscreen theaters and single-screen galleries. The annual Morelia Film Festival was established in 1996. An Avocado Festival is held in Uruapan each November.

22 Libraries and Museums

In 2003, there were 466 libraries in the state with a combined stock of 2,341,394 volumes. There were 14 active museums registered in the state that had permanent exhibits. The capital, Morelia, has the State Museum (focusing on anthropology), the Michoacán Regional Museum, the Museum of Colonial Art, the Museum of Contemporary Art, the Mask Museum, and the Candy Museum. The city of Aquila has a museum dedicated to sea turtles.

23 Media

In 2005, the capital city, Morelia, had two daily newspapers: *El Sol de Morelia* (*Morelia Sun*) and *La Voz de Michoacán* (*The Michoacán Voice*). The city of Zamora also published two daily papers: *El Sol de Zamora* (*Zamora Sun*) and *El Heraldo de Zamora* (*Zamora Herald*).

In 2004, there were 110 television stations and 53 radio stations (40 AM and 13 FM). In 2005, there were about 195,920 subscribers to cable and satellite television stations. Also in 2005, there were about 421,177 residential phone lines, with about 11.9 mainline phones in use for every 100 people.

24 Tourism, Travel, and Recreation

Morelia is a main tourist attraction. People living in Morelia enjoy spring-like temperatures year-round. There are communities of retired American and Canadian citizens in Morelia. These communities sponsor courses for those who wish to study Spanish. Morelia is a beautiful colonial city offering museums and shopping. One of the main attractions is the planetarium.

The historic city center of Morelia was established as a UNESCO World Heritage site in 1991. There are archeological sites at Tzintzuntzan and Ihuatzio. The Mariposa Monarca Biosphere Reserve, a sanctuary for migrating monarch butterflies, is also a popular tourist spot.

25 Sports

The Monarcas (Monarchs) Morelia play in the First Division of the Mexican Football (soccer) Association (commonly known as Femexfut). Their home field is at the 38,000-seat Morelos stadium. The Guerreros (Warriors) Morelia compete as part of the South Zone of the National Professional Basketball League (LNBP). The 15,000-seat Plaza Monumental in Morelia is a bullfighting ring. There is a smaller ring, the Palacio del Arte, which holds 4,000 people.

26 Famous People

José María Morelos y Pavón (1765–1815) was born in the city of Vallatoid, which has since been renamed Morelia in his honor. He was a priest and soldier who served as a popular revolutionary leader. Lázaro Cárdenas (1895–1970) was president of Mexico from 1934 to 1940 and became known as a champion for the working class. Alfonso García Robles (1911–1991) was a Mexican statesman. He received the Noble Peace Prize in 1982 for his work toward nuclear disarmament.

27 Bibliography

BOOKS

Andrade, Mary J. *The Vigil of the Little Angels: Day of the Dead in Mexico.* San Jose, CA: La Oferta Review, 2001.

Day-MacLeod, Deirdre. *The States of Central Mexico*. Philadelphia, PA: Mason Crest Publishers, 2003.

DeAngelis, Gina. *Mexico*. Mankato, MN: Blue Earth Books, 2003.

Gruber, Beth. *Mexico*. Washington, DC: National Geographic, 2006.

Laufer, Peter. *Made in Mexico*. Washington, D.C.: National Geographic Society, 2000.

WEB SITES

Government of Mexico. *Mexico for Kids*. www.elbalero.gob.mx/index_kids.html (accessed on March 30, 2007).

Mexican Tourism Board. *Visit Mexico: Michoacán*. www.visitmexico.com/wb/Visitmexico/Visi_Michoacan (accessed on March 30, 2007).

Morelos

PRONUNCIATION: moe-RAY-lohss.

ORIGIN OF STATE NAME: Named for the military hero José María Morelos y Pavón (1765–1815), who fought in the war for Mexican independence.

CAPITAL: Cuernavaca (kwair-nah-VAH-kah).

ENTERED COUNTRY: April 1869.

COAT OF ARMS: The green field in the center features a cornstalk, symbolizing the fertility of the land. The silver banner above the cornstalk contains the Spanish words for land and freedom. Around the border is a slogan from revolutionary leader Emiliano Zapata (1879–1919): "The land will be returned to those who work it with their hands."

HOLIDAYS: Año Nuevo (New Year's Day—January 1); Día de la Constitución (Constitution Day—February 5); Benito Juárez's birthday (March 21); Commemoration of the Free and Sovereign State of Morelos (April 16); Primero de Mayo (Labor Day—May 1); Anniversary of the Battle of Puebla (1862), May 5; Revolution Day, 1910 (November 20); and Navidad (Christmas—December 25).

FLAG: There is no official state flag.

TIME: 6 AM = noon Greenwich Mean Time (GMT).

1 Location and Size

Morelos is located in south-central Mexico. The region is known as the "Central Breadbasket" because it is an important center for agriculture. The state has an area of about 4,893 square kilo-meters (1,889 square miles), a little smaller than the US state of Delaware. It ranks as 30th in size among the states and covers about 0.3% of the total land area of Mexico. It is bordered on the north by the Distrito Federal (Federal District), on the northwest and northeast by the state of México, on the southeast by Puebla, and on the west and southwest by Guerrero. Morelos is divided into 33 municipalities (similar to US counties). The capital is Cuernavaca.

The northern and eastern regions of Morelos are crossed by the east-west belt known as the Sierra Volcánica Transversal (also known as the Cordillera Neovolcánica). Some of the highest peaks in the country are found in this region, including Volcán Popocatépetl along the northeast border with Puebla. It is the highest point in the state and the second-highest peak in the country at an elevation of about 5,465 meters

(17,930 feet). The Sierra Madre del Sur reach into the southwest region of the state.

Most of the rivers of Morelos are formed by rainwater that runs off the northern mountains. The Amacuzac River crosses the southwestern part of the state. The Yantepec and Chinameca Rivers cross north-south through the center of the state and the Tepalcingo River is in the southeastern part of the state.

The largest lake is Laguna Tequesquitengo, with an area of about 124 square kilometers (48 square miles). Many popular hunting and fishing resorts are found there.

2 Climate

The country is divided into three basic climatic regions: Sierra Alta, Piedemonte, and Los Valles. Los Valles (the valleys) covers most of the state and has hotter temperatures. The small Sierra Alta and Piedemonte regions are in the higher elevations of the north, which generally have cooler temperatures.

Temperatures in the state range from a minimum of about 10°C (49°F) to a maximum of about 23°C (74°F). The capital city of Cuernavaca is known worldwide as "The City of Eternal Spring" because of its temperate climate. The average year-round temperature in Cuernavaca is 21°C (69°F). The main rainy season is from the end of May until September. Annual precipitation ranges from 87 centimeters (34 inches) in some regions to 183 centimeters (72 inches) in other areas. In Cuernavaca, the average precipitation is 94.4 centimeters (37.1 inches) per year.

3 Plants and Animals

In the Sierra Alta region, there are forests of pine, fir, and oak. Other plants include madrona (a shrub with yellow berries) and ferns. Carnations, lilies, violets, and marigolds are common flowers. In the Piedemonte region, there are nopal (a type of cactus), cactus, mesquite, and maguey. In the valleys, there are willows and amates. Poinsettias, the official flower of Cuernavaca, are grown in some regions. Bougainvillea is common throughout the state.

Common bird species include quail, eagles, sparrow hawks, and doves. The gallina de monte, an endangered bird species, is found in Morelos as well. Coyotes, badgers, and tlacuaches (Mexican opossum) are found throughout state, as are chameleons and iguanas.

4 Environmental Protection

In 2004, the state had 24 municipal wastewater treatment plants in operation with a combined installed capacity of 1,320 liters per second (348 gallons per second). The volume of treated wastewater that year was estimated at 1,076 liters per second (284 gallons per second). There were also 70 industrial wastewater treatment plants in operation that year. As of 2004, about 91% of the population had access to safe drinking water.

In 2003, the state had about 88,488 hectares (218,658 acres) of woodland, including 62,127 hectares (153,519 acres) of rain forest. In 2004, only 4 hectares (9.8 acres) of woodland were damaged or destroyed by forest fires. An additional 205 hectares (506 acres) of pasture and brush land were also damaged by fires.

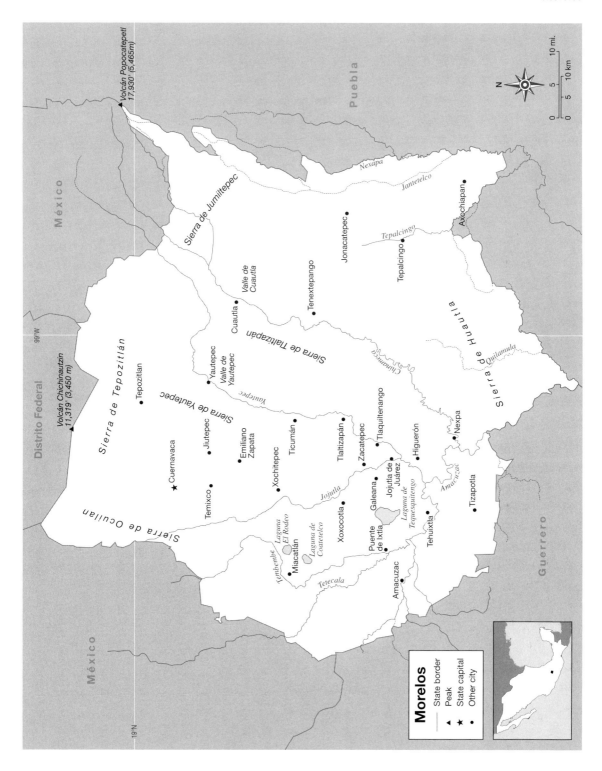

Volcán Popocatepetl
17,930' (5,465m)

Puebla

México

Nexapa

Jantetelco

Axochiapan

Sierra de Jumiltepec

Jonacatepec

Tepalcingo

Tepalcingo

Valle de
Cuautla

Cuautla

Tenextepango

99°W

Sierra de Tlaltizapán

Sierra de Huautla

Volcán Chichinautzin
11,319 (3,450 m)

Distrito Federal

Sierra de Tepozitlán

Tepoztlan

Yautepec

Valle de
Yautepec

Sierra de Yautepec

Yautepec

Chinameca

Quilamula

Sierra de

Cuernavaca

Jiutepec

Emiliano
Zapata

Ticumán

Tlaltizapán

Zacatepec

Tlaquiltenango

Higuerón

Nexpa

Xochitepec

Jojutla

Galeana

Jojutla de
Juárez

Amacuzac

Tizapotla

Temixco

Sierra de Ocuilan

Laguna
El Rodeo

Tenbembé

Miacatlán

Laguna de
Coatetelco

Xoxocotla

Puente
de Ixtla

Laguna de
Tequesquitengo

Tehuixtla

Tetecala

Amacuzac

México

Guerrero

10 mi.

10 km

N

Morelos

State border —
Peak ◀
State capital ★
Other city •

19°N

Cuernavaca Cathedral. PETER LANGER.

Lagunas de Zempoala National Park lies in northwest Morelos near Cuernavaca. It features three volcanic crater lakes. El Tepozteco National Park is located in the southwest region of the state. The region linking the two national parks is known as the Ajusco–Chchinautzin Biological Corridor, which is also a protected area.

5 Population, Ethnic Groups, Languages

Morelos had an estimated total population of 1,634,700 in 2006, ranking at 22nd among the states and the Distrito Federal. About 48% of the population were men and 52% were women. About 79% of the population lived in urban areas. The population density was 330 people per square kilometer (856 people per square mile). In 2005, the capital, Cuernavaca, had an estimated population of 349,102. Almost all citizens speak Spanish as their first language. A small percentage of the population speaks an indigenous (native) language, such as Náhuatl.

6 Religions

According to the 2000 census, 83.6% of the population, or 1.1 million people, were Roman Catholic; 7.3%, or 97,860 people, were mainline or evangelical Protestants. About 3.1% were counted as other Biblical faiths, including 9,455 Seventh-day Adventists, 4,719 Latter-day Saints (Mormons), and 27,084 Jehovah's Witnesses.

There were 1,788 Jews. About 4.3% of the population claimed to have no religious affiliation.

There are several religious sites in the state. On the slopes of Volcán Popocatépetl, there are several old monasteries from the 16th century. These were once inhabited by the Franciscan, Dominican, and Augustinian priests who converted the indigenous population to Christianity. The monasteries have been designated as UNESCO World Heritage sites.

7 Transportation

Cuernavaca Airport provides international flights to and from Morelos. The state has about 1,819 kilometers (1,130 miles) of roads and 246 kilometers (153 miles) of railroads. In 2004, there were 174,085 automobiles registered in the state, along with 4,357 passenger trucks, 71,523 freight trucks, and 5,754 motorcycles.

8 History

The first human settlements in Morelos date back to 2000 BC. Toltec groups inhabited the land and started farms in the area. Around 600 AD, Xichicalco became the region's largest settlement. According to some historians, the worshiping of Quetzalcóatl (believed to be the father of civilization) was first started there. In the 12th century, the end of the Toltec empire allowed for the settlement of different groups in the region. In the 14th century, the Tlahuicas became the largest group in the region. In the late 1420s, the Tlahuicas were overpowered despite fierce resistance and were then absorbed by the Aztec empire.

When the Spaniards arrived, Spanish conqueror Hernán Cortés (1485–1547) sent Gonzalo de Sandoval to conquer the region in 1521. In 1523, Sandoval settled in the region. He established North America's first sugar cane mill at Tlaltenango. The first Franciscan priests arrived in 1529 to convert the indigenous people to the Roman Catholic faith. Diseases and mistreatment by Spanish settlers drastically reduced the indigenous population during the 16th and 17th centuries. Later in the 17th century, African slaves were brought to work on the sugar cane and other plantations. The region became an important route to connect the capital city of Mexico with the southern provinces during the colonial period.

The independence movement did not reach Morelos until 1811, a year after the historic uprising initiated by Mexican priest and revolutionary Miguel de Hidalgo y Costilla (1753–1811). Cuernavaca, the most important city in the region, became a center of independence revolt. Priest José Morelos (1765–1815) fought for independence in the state until he was killed in 1815. Yet, resistance against Spanish rule persisted in the region. When independence was finally achieved for the entire country in 1821, Cuernavaca joined in.

As in the rest of Mexico, political instability characterized much of the 19th century. Morelos continued to be one of the largest producers of sugar cane in the world. The large landowners and the plantation economy combined to create enormous inequalities between the wealthy and the working peasants. Morelos lies close to the capital of the country. Because of this, Morelos also became a strategic battleground for all those who sought to overthrow the national government during the 19th century. During this period, the region was given the name Morelos after independence leader José Morelos.

In 1910, when the Mexican Revolution began, several leaders who sought to promote land distribution revolted against the government. Emiliano Zapata (1879–1919) was among them. Together with revolutionary Francisco "Pancho" Villa (1878–1923), Zapata is one of the best known heroes of the Mexican Revolution. Zapata was leader of the Southern Liberation Army. He fought fiercely alongside the ever-changing factions of the revolution to demand peasant rights and land reform. After the new constitution was approved in 1917, Zapata continued fighting to improve the lives of peasants. He was captured and killed in 1919.

Several uprisings demanding land reform and vindicating peasants' rights took place during the 20th century after the revolution. But the central government successfully maintained order and peace. A rapid industrialization process and ambitious development of the infrastructure helped Morelos become an industrial, agricultural, and tourist center in the decades after the end of the revolution.

In the first decade of the 21st century, the state of Morelos continued to develop industrially, and in other areas. However, crime and official corruption continue to trouble the state. In April 2004, the state's entire 552-person police force was dismissed over claims that it was protecting drug smugglers. The state's governor, Sergio Estrada, said that new recruits would face regular lie-detector tests as well as be tested for alcohol and dug use.

9 State and Local Government

The governor is elected for a nonrenewable six-year term and exerts an enormous influence over state matters. The legislature is comprised of a 30-member state congress. Deputies are elected for nonrenewable three-year terms—18 members are elected from single member districts and 12 are elected for proportional representation.

The 33 municipalities that comprise the state of Morelos elect their municipal presidents and council members every three years, for nonrenewable terms. Larger municipalities have more leeway to decide their own budget and make administrative decisions.

10 Political Parties

The three main political parties in all of Mexico are the Institutional Revolutionary Party (PRI), the National Action Party (PAN), and the Party of the Democratic Revolution (PRD). Despite the historical predominance of the PRI in the state, the emergence of strong opposition in the 1990s in the rest of Mexico reached Morelos, too. For the first time since the end of the revolution, a party other than the Institutional Revolutionary Party (PRI) won the gubernatorial race in 2000. Sergio Estrada Cajigal Ramírez, a member of the National Action Party (PAN), was elected for a six-year term ending in 2006. The PAN is now the strongest party in the state, but the PRD has a growing presence as well. The PRI continues to exert influence in local governments.

11 Judicial System

The Superior Tribunal of Justice is comprised of justices appointed by the state congress from a three-person list presented by the Council of the Judiciary. Justices are elected for an initial six-year period. If they are ratified, they cannot be removed until they reach the mandatory retirement age of 65. Only highly qualified attorneys

A street scene in the capital, Cuernavaca. PETER LANGER.

familiar with state legislation can be included on the list presented by the Council of the Judiciary.

12 Economy

The economy of Morelos has been marked by rapid industrialization. The ambitious development of the state's transportation infrastructure has helped Morelos become an important center for industry, agriculture, and tourism. The non-agricultural economy is dominated by the state's three largest cities, Cuernavaca (the state capital), Cuautla, and Jiutepec. Agriculture has been moving toward meeting commercial needs rather than those of subsistence farming.

The state's tourism sector is built around archeological sites and monasteries and convents converted to meet the needs of tourists.

The state's main exports are motor vehicles, tomatoes, sugar cane, honey, and flowers.

13 Industry

Industry is largely centered on the state's three largest cities: Cuernavaca (the state capital), Cuautla, and Jiutepec. As of 2003, each of these cities had at least two modern industrial parks. The state capital was home to over 25,000 companies involved in the production of textiles, auto parts, pharmaceuticals, processed foods, electrical and electronic equipment, machine tools, cosmetics, and industries associated with agriculture. Nissan Mexicana, Upjohn, Beecham de México, and Firestone all have large facilities in the state, mostly near Cuernavaca.

The state's handicraft industry produces pottery, ritual ceramics, items made from ixtle fiber, as well as pots and pans, ponchos, shawls, hats, crosses, and sandals.

14 Labor

As of 2005, the state of Morelos had 704,427 eligible workers. Some 685,021 were listed as employed and 19,406 were listed as unemployed. Unemployed workers in rural areas may not be counted, however. The unemployment rate that year was reported to be 2.7%. Of those who were working, services employed 44.3%, followed by commerce at 20.9%, and agriculture at 11.9%.

The US Bureau of Labor Statistics reported that Mexican workers saw their wages increase from $2.49 per hour in 2003 to $2.50 per hour in 2004. (The average US worker earned $15.70 per hour in 2004.) The maximum work week is set at 48 hours by law. The average worker spends 40 to 45 hours per week on the job. Workers earn twice their regular hourly rate for up to nine hours a week of overtime. When a worker works more than nine hours overtime in a week, he or she earns thee times the regular hourly rate. After one year, workers are entitled by law to six days paid vacation.

15 Agriculture

Morelos is considered to be one of Mexico's most important agricultural states. Agriculture there is built along three natural regions (Sierra Alta, the Piedemonte, and Los Valles), each with its own types of soil, animal species, and vegetation.

Flowers such as carnations, bird of paradise, and chrysanthemums are grown for export in the Los Valles region, while the Sierra Alta and Los Valles regions also raise livestock, such as cows, pigs, horses, sheep, goats, and poultry. The Piedemonte region cultivates fruit trees, in addition to crops such as corn, beans, tomatoes, chilies and squash. Other crops grown in Morelos are oats, sorghum, avocados, figs, onion, and sugarcane.

In 2004, crop production for the state of Morelos included: 83,965 tons of corn, 229,626 tons of sorghum, 57,598 tons of red tomatoes, 163,834 tons of sugar, and 30,948 tons of avocados. Livestock brought to market included: 50,641 head of beef cattle, 132,987 pigs, 6,830 goats, and 813 sheep. In that same year, the state produced 17.7 million liters (4.6 million gallons) of milk from dairy cows and 931 tons of eggs. Meat production included: 4,788 tons of beef, 2,747 tons of pork, 362 tons of goat, 375 tons of lamb, and 45,616 tons of poultry.

Aquaculture or fish farms are also important contributors to the agricultural sector. These are divided into two groups, those that provide ornamental fish, for which the state is Mexico's leading producer, and those that provide fish for human consumption, which include lobster, tilapia, trout, and catfish.

16 Natural Resources

The production of cement has become an important sector in the economy of Morelos with the construction of one of the world's most modern cement plants, Cementos Moctezuma. Forestry is a fairly insignificant industry, with only about $132,663 worth of forest wood produced in

Lagoons near Cuernavaca. © ROBERT FRERCK/WOODFIN CAMP.

2003. The fish catch in 2003 was about 540 tons, all for human consumption.

17 Energy and Power

Morelos does not generate its own electricity, and as a result, it must rely on power imports from surrounding states.

In 2005, there were 499,965 users of electricity in the state. Of that total, the largest number were residential customers at 438,114. Sales of electricity that same year totaled 2,116,621 megawatt hours, of which the largest users were medium-sized industrial firms at 686,417 megawatt hours. Electricity is provided and distributed by the Federal Electricity Commission, and

Central Light and Power. Both utilities are run by the Mexican government.

18 Health

In 2003, the state had 12 hospitals and 259 outpatient centers that were part of the national health system. In 2004, there were about 1,484 doctors, 2,995 nurses, and 113 dentists working in these health centers. There were an additional 72 independent health centers in the state in 2004.

Most of the Mexican population is covered under a government health plan. The IMSS (Instituto Mexicano de Seguro Social) covers the general population. The ISSSTE (Instituto de

Seguridad y Servicios Sociales de Trabajadores del Estado) covers state workers.

19 Housing

Most homes are built with materials such as stone, concrete, or brick with flat roof constructions. Adobe homes with sheet metal or tile roofs can be found in some areas. In 2000, about 77% of all homes were owner-occupied. In 2005, there were an estimated 403,054 residential housing units in the state. About 85% of these units were single-family detached homes. The average household was estimated at four people.

20 Education

Public education in Mexico is free for students from ages 6 to 16. While most students attend public schools, in 2002/03 about 25% of high school students attended private schools. In 2004/05, it was estimated that 93% of age-eligible students completed primary school, which includes six years of study. About 85.8% of eligible students completed secondary school, which includes three years of study after primary school. About 61% of eligible students completed the *bachillerato*, which is similar to a high school diploma. The national average for completion of the *bachillerato* was 60.1% that year.

The Universidad Autónoma del Estado de Morelos (Autonomous University of Morelos) and the National Center for Technological Research and Development are in Cuernavaca. There are technological institutes in Zaratepec and Cuernavaca. In 2005, there were about 51,516 students ages 20 and older who were enrolled in some type of higher education program. The overall literacy rate was estimated at 91% in 2005.

21 Arts

Morelos has several theaters, many of them open air. There is a French Alliance chapter in Cuernavaca. Also in Cuernavaca there is a cultural center named after the famous muralist David Alfaro Siqueiros (1896–1974). Two musical groups, Mitote Jazz and Banda de Música Santamaría, are famous in Morelos. There are two puppet theaters: Artimañas and Groupo Gente (which cater to hospitals and social interaction groups). There are over 40 registered movie theaters, including multiscreen theaters and single-screen galleries.

22 Libraries and Museums

In 2003, there were 246 libraries in the state with a combined stock of 1,336,000 volumes. The same year, there were 10 museums registered in the state that had permanent exhibits. In Cuernavaca, there is a museum of herbal medicine, which has a medicinal herb garden. Cuernavaca's Palacio de Cortes has some murals by Mexican artist Diego Rivera (1886–1957). The archeological site at Xochicalco has a museum of artifacts.

23 Media

In 2005, the capital, Cuernavaca, had three daily newspapers: *El Sol de Cuernavaca* (*Cuernavaca Sun*), *El Regional del Sur* (*Regional Sun*), and *El Financiero* (*The Financer*). The city of Cuautla had *El Sol de Cuautla* (*Cuautla Sun*).

In 2004, there were 8 television stations and 23 radio stations (5 AM and 18 FM). In 2005, there were about 65,410 subscribers to cable and satellite television stations. Also in 2005, there were about 310,402 residential phone lines, with about 21 mainline phones in use for every 100 people.

24 Tourism, Travel, and Recreation

Morelos has a temperate climate. There are many golf courses, national parks, and spas catering to tourists. There are also many archeological sites, including Las Pilas at Chalcatzingo and the Pyramid of Tepozteco. The archeological zone of Xochicalco is a UNESCO World Heritage site. A favorite site with tourists is the San Anton waterfall. Fairs and festivals include the Feast for Our Lady of the Miracles (late August–early September). Cuernavaca has many language schools catering to American and Canadian tourists wishing to study Spanish. Volcán Popocatépetl is a popular spot for hikers and religious tourists who visit the 16th-century monasteries built along the slopes of the volcano.

25 Sports

There are no major stadiums or sports teams in Morelos. Spectators enjoy sports in Mexico City.

26 Famous People

Emiliano Zapata (1879–1919) was a revolutionary who led the native peoples of Morelos to fight for their right to own their own land. The troops who fought with him were called *zapatistas*. The state was named for José María Morelos y Pavón (1765–1815), a priest and soldier, born in Vallatoid (now the city of Morelia in Michoacán) who served as a popular revolutionary leader.

27 Bibliography

BOOKS

Carew-Miller, Anna. *Famous People of Mexico.* Philadelphia: Mason Crest Publishers, 2003.

Day-MacLeod, Deirdre. *The States of Central Mexico.* Philadelphia, PA: Mason Crest Publishers, 2003.

Gruber, Beth. *Mexico.* Washington, DC: National Geographic, 2006.

Stein, R. Conrad. *Emiliano Zapata: Revolutionary and Champion of Poor Farmers.* Chanhassen, MN: Child's World, 2004.

WEB SITES

Government of Mexico. *Mexico for Kids.* www.elbalero.gob.mx/index_kids.html (accessed on March 30, 2007).

Mexican Tourism Board. *Visit Mexico: Morelos.* www.visitmexico.com/wb/Visitmexico/Visi_Morelos (accessed on March 30, 2007).

Nayarit

PRONUNCIATION: nah-yah-REET.

ORIGIN OF STATE NAME: The state was named in honor of Nayar, a sixteenth-century governor of the Cora (Nayari) people, an indigenous group native to the state.

CAPITAL: Tepic (teh-PEEK).

ENTERED COUNTRY: February 5, 1917.

COAT OF ARMS: The coat of arms of Nayarit is made up of three sections. A corn stalk appears on the left, weapons appear on the right, and a mountain landscape lies across the lower section. In the center is a small shield surrounded by a white border with seven footprints, symbols of the seven tribes of the Nahuatl, or Aztecs. An illustration of the Eagle of Aztlan is in the center of the shield. Green, blue, and gold are used to represent the colors of the Nayarit landscape.

HOLIDAYS: Año Nuevo (New Year's Day—January 1); Día de la Constitución (Constitution Day—February 5); Benito Juárez's birthday (March 21); Primero de Mayo (Labor Day—May 1); Anniversary of the Battle of Puebla (1862), May 5; Revolution Day, 1910 (November 20); and Navidad (Christmas—December 25).

FLAG: There is no official state flag.

TIME: 5 AM = noon Greenwich Mean Time (GMT).

1 Location and Size

Nayarit is located on the western coast of Mexico. It covers an area of 27,825 square kilo-meters (10,743 square miles), which is a little larger than the US state of Maryland. It ranks as 23rd in size among the states and covers about 1.4% of the total land area of Mexico. Nayarit is bordered on the north by the states of Sinaloa and Durango, on the south by Jalisco, on the east by Zacatecas and Jalisco, and on the west by the Pacific Ocean. Nayarit is divided into 20 municipalities (similar to US counties). The capital is Tepic.

Most of the population lives in the broad valleys of the state. Tepic and Xalisco are located in the Matatipac Valley and Compostela lies in the Coatlán valley. The northwestern coastal plain has several marshes and lagoons. The northern and eastern portion of the state are crossed by the Sierra Madre Occidental. In the southern part of this range is the highest point in the state, Cerro El Vigia, at an elevation of about 2,740 meters (8,990 feet). Individual ranges in this area of the state include the Sierra de Huajicori, Sierra Pajaritos, and the Sierra de Huanacaxtle.

Nayarit has 300 kilometers (186 miles) of Pacific coastline. There are clusters of islands in the Pacific Ocean that belong to Nayarit. These include a group of four islands known as the Islas Marietas and Isla Isabela.

The main rivers are the Grande de Santiago, San Pedro, and Acaponeta. The Ameca River forms the southern border with Jalisco. There are a number of lagoons along the coast, including Laguna Agua Brava and Laguna Mexcalititlán.

2 Climate

The climate in the valley and coastal regions is typically warm. The average year-round temperature in Tepic is 20°C (68°F). However, there are cooler temperatures in the mountain regions. The statewide average high temperature is 27°C (80°F). The average low temperature statewide is 21°C (69°F). Annual rainfall ranges from a minimum of 77 centimeters (30 inches) in some regions to a maximum of 264 centimeters (104 inches) in other parts of the state. In Tepic, the average rainfall is 125.5 centimeters (49.3 inches per year).

Hurricanes are one of the natural hazards occurring in the state. In 2002, Hurricane Kenna swept through San Blas with wind speeds of up to 230 kilometers per hour (143 miles per hour).

3 Plants and Animals

There are mangrove trees along the coast and pastures across the valleys. Coconut palms and guava trees can be found in the state. Pine and oak trees grow in the mountain regions.

Common animals include white-tailed deer, wildcats, pumas, coyote, and wild boars. Smaller mammals include skunks, badgers, rabbits, and armadillos. Mountain doves, cojólite (a kind of pheasant), and the bobo bird live in the state as well.

4 Environmental Protection

In 2004, the state had 56 municipal wastewater treatment plants in operation with a combined installed capacity of 1,834 liters per second (484 gallons per second). The volume of treated wastewater that year was estimated at 1,467 liters per second (387 gallons per second). There were also four industrial wastewater treatment plants in operation that year. As of 2004, about 93.8% of the population had access to safe drinking water.

In 2003, the state had over 1.2 million hectares (3.2 million acres) of woodland, including 487,580 hectares (1.2 million acres) of rain forest. In 2004, about 154 hectares (380 acres) of woodland were damaged or destroyed by forest fires. An additional 1,955 hectares (4,830 acres) of pasture and brush land were also damaged by fires.

El Manglar is an organization that was formed in 1993 to protect the mangroves and rain forests. The forests were threatened by rapid growth of tourism and shrimp farming. Isla Isabel and Islas Marietas are national park sites, both of which have also been designated as Ramsar Wetlands of International Importance.

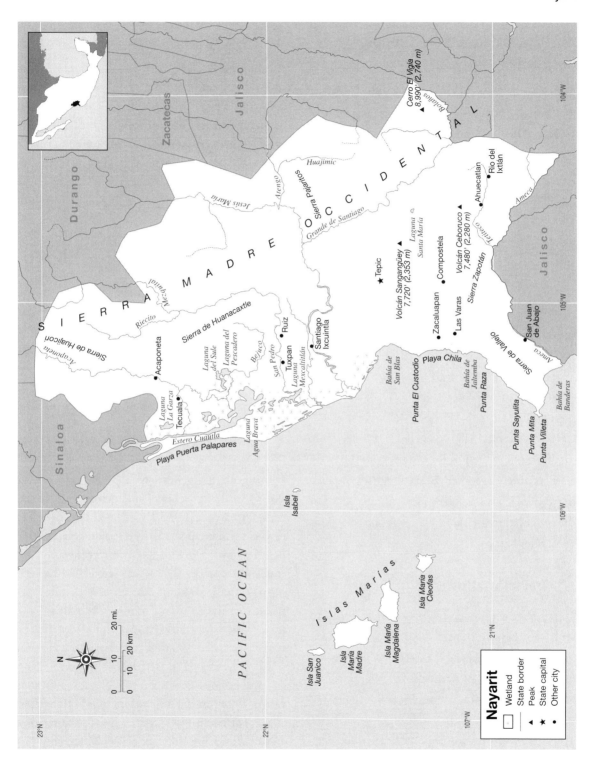

5 Population, Ethnic Groups, Languages

Nayarit had an estimated total population of 961,400 in 2006, ranking 29th among the states and the Distrito Federal. About 49% of the population were men and 51% were women. About 59% of the population lived in urban areas. The population density was 34 people per square kilometer (90 people per square mile). In 2005, the capital, Tepic, had a population of 336,403. Almost all citizens speak Spanish as their first language. A small percentage of the population speaks indigenous (native) languages, such as Cora, Huichol, and Tepehuano.

6 Religions

According to the 2000 census, 91.8% of the population, or 748,579 people, were Roman Catholic. About 3%, or 24,313 people, were mainline or evangelical Protestants. About 1.3% were counted as other Biblical faiths, including 8,686 Jehovah's Witnesses. About 2.9% of the population claimed to have no religious affiliation.

7 Transportation

Tepic Airport provides international flights to and from Nayarit. There are about 3,089 kilometers (1,919 miles) of roads and 245 miles (395 kilometers) of railroads in the state. In 2004, there were 90,291 automobiles registered in the state, along with 1,477 passenger trucks, 108,278 freight trucks, and 3,920 motorcycles.

8 History

Although there is scattered evidence that points to human settlements as early as 5000 BC, it was only around 400 AD that the Cora civilization originated in the region. The Cora reached their most impressive level of development around 1200.

The first Spaniard to arrive in Nayarit was Hernán Cortés (1485–1547), who visited the region in an expedition in 1523. Five years later, Nuño Beltrán de Guzmán conquered the different villages that existed in the region. Famous for his ruthless behavior and his will to overpower indigenous leaders, Beltrán de Guzmán built the Espíritu Santo village on top of the ruins of the indigenous city of Tepic. Cortés visited Tepic in 1531 and attempted to take control of the region, but Beltrán de Guzmán successfully convinced the Spanish crown to name him governor of a newly created province for the territories he had conquered.

Beltrán de Guzmán was replaced in 1536 by Diego Pérez de la Torre, who died in 1538 fighting an indigenous revolt. The new governor, Cristobal de Oñate, changed the provincial capital to a valley near Tepic. Several indigenous revolts threatened the Spanish colonizers' control of the region. The most famous revolt was led by indigenous leader Tenamaxtli in 1548. During most of the 16th and 17th centuries, Franciscan priests (of the Roman Catholic Church) sought to convert the indigenous Cora, but many fiercely resisted Spanish occupation. Only in 1722 did the Spaniards succeed in conquering the indigenous rebels in the Nayar mountain range. Economic development was experienced in the 18th century primarily due to the region's strategic location for trade with California.

As an independence movement began to take shape in 1810, local priest and leader José María Mercado rose to control most of the region. A royalist army (loyal to Spain) recaptured most of Nayarit a year later. A few years later, the independence movement had completely disappeared in the region.

National independence in 1821 did not bring many changes to Nayarit. The 1830s and 1840s were characterized by conflicts between centralists and federalists, whereas the 1850s and 1860s witnessed war between liberals and conservatives. The national victory of the liberals, led by Benito Juárez (1806–1872) first and by Porfirio Díaz (1830–1915) later, brought peace and some economic development to Nayarit. The region was first made an autonomous entity in 1860.

During the Mexican Revolution, which started in 1910, different factions fought in Nayarit. Factions were loyal to Mexican revolutionaries Francisco Madero (1873–1913), Porfirio Díaz (1830–1915), Victoriano Huerta (1854–1916), and Venustiano Carranza (1859–1920). Some militias loyal to revolutionary Francisco "Pancho" Villa (1879–1923) also fought in the region. When the Carranza forces emerged as victorious, they quickly controlled Nayarit. The 1917 constitutional convention declared Nayarit as a federal state. A new state constitution was passed into law in 1918.

The revolutionary army was led by Lázaro Cárdenas (1895–1970) in Nayarit. Some battles were also fought in Nayarit during the Cristero war, where Roman Catholic loyalists revolted against the anti-clerical policies of the revolutionary government in the late 1920s.

There was some economic development resulting from ambitious agriculture promotion policies undertaken by the government in the 1950s and 1960s, but Nayarit remained one of the poorest and least developed states in Mexico.

In the first decade of the 21st century Nayarit remained one of Mexico's poorest states, its economy based largely on agriculture and the extraction of natural resources. Like many of Mexico's other states, crime and official corruption continued to trouble Nayarit. In January 2003, the office of the state's anti-narcotics police force was raided by Mexican troops due to claims that the unit was involved in drug smuggling.

9 State and Local Government

The legislature is comprised of a 30-seat congress. Eighteen deputies are elected in single-member districts and twelve are elected by proportional representation. Although historically the Institutional Revolutionary Party (PRI) governors exercised overwhelming influence over the legislature, after the PRI lost the governorship to the National Action Party (PAN) in 1999, provisions for separation of powers and checks and balances have been generally enforced. Yet, the governor continues to enjoy much power and excessive influence, curtailing the oversight power of the legislature. The state governor is elected for nonrenewable six-year terms.

The 20 municipalities that comprise Nayarit hold regular democratic elections for municipal presidents and council members every three years. Immediate re-election is not allowed. Highly centralized budgetary and administrative decision making at the state level hinder the development and consolidation of local governments.

10 Political Parties

The three main political parties in all of Mexico are the Institutional Revolutionary Party (PRI), the National Action Party (PAN), and the Party of the Democratic Revolution (PRD). The PRI controlled state-level politics since the end of the Mexican Revolution (1910–20). All state governors were PRI members until Antonio Echevarría Domínguez, of the PAN, won the 1999 election. However, Ney González Sánchez of the PRI was elected after him in 2005.

11 Judicial System

The Superior Tribunal of Justice is the highest court in the state. It is comprised of seven justices appointed for nonrenewable ten-year terms by the congress from a list submitted by the state governor. Only qualified and well-respected attorneys familiar with state laws and regulations can be appointed. In addition, an electoral tribunal and local courts also comprise the state's legal system.

12 Economy

The economy of Nayarit is heavily dependent upon agriculture. Important products are tobacco, fishing, livestock, and aquaculture (fish farms). Mining is also important. There is also a growing forestry sector. In terms of employment, Nayarit's economy is dominated by the service sector which accounts for 29% the labor force, followed by agriculture at 26%, commerce with 19%, and industry at 12%. Overall, the state's industrial development has been very limited.

13 Industry

The tobacco industry has been one of the most significant contributors to the state's economy. This involves the manufacture of cigarettes, for which Tepic is the site of a major factory. Small factories in the southern region of the state produce processed meats (cold cuts) and tequila, while craftsmen make leather goods and saddles. The sugarcane industry is also prominent in the state. There is also an oyster research center in the coastal town of San Blas.

The state's handicraft industry produces woolen and cotton textiles, paper masks, and articles from yarn.

14 Labor

As of 2005, the state of Nayarit had 398,934 eligible workers. Some 389,745 were listed as employed and 9,189 were listed as unemployed. Unemployed workers in rural areas may not be counted, however. The unemployment rate that year was reported to be 2.3%. Of those who were working, services employed 39.1%, followed by agriculture at 24.6% and commerce at 18.6%.

The US Bureau of Labor Statistics reported that Mexican workers saw their wages increase from $2.49 per hour in 2003 to $2.50 per hour in 2004. (The average US worker earned $15.70 per hour in 2004.) The maximum work week is set at 48 hours by law. The average worker spends 40 to 45 hours per week on the job. Workers earn twice their regular hourly rate for up to nine hours a week of overtime. When a worker works more than nine hours overtime in a week, he or she earns three times the regular hourly rate. After one year, workers are entitled by law to six days paid vacation.

15 Agriculture

Nayarit is Mexico's leading tobacco growing state. Both tobacco and sugarcane are the primary export crops of the state. Fruit growing is a major part of agriculture and includes production of avocados, mango, papaya, bananas, and tamarind. Other major crops include corn, beans, sorghum, rice, tomatoes, peanuts, and squash. Cows, sheep, pigs, chickens, and goats, are the main livestock animals. However, deer, iguana, raccoons, and rabbits are also used for meat. The southern region of the state is known for its honey production.

In 2004, crop production included: 204,071 tons of corn, 258,657 tons of sorghum, 39,793 tons of rice, 30,493 tons of red tomatoes, 217,162 tons of sugar, and 93,239 tons of bananas. Livestock brought to market that year included: 54,147 head of beef cattle, 69,604 pigs, and 45 goats. The state also produced: 66.4 million liters (17.5 million gallons) of milk from dairy cows, 14,462 tons of eggs, and 421 tons of honey. Meat production included: 22,648 tons of beef, 4,844 tons of pork, 543 tons of goat, 164 tons of lamb, and 26,474 tons of poultry.

16 Natural Resources

The coastal lake zone has an abundant amount of shrimp. Tuna and red snapper are also part of the ocean catch. The main fishing center is at San Blas, which is also the site of an oyster research center. In 2003, the fish catch was at about 30,276 tons.

Pine, coconut palms, and oak trees are cut for commercial use. In 2003, the value of forest wood production was at about $854,799. Gold, silver, and lead are found in the state and processed in two main facilities.

17 Energy and Power

In 2005, there were 316,125 users of electricity in Nayarit. Of that total, the largest number were residential customers at 278,733. Sales of electricity that same year totaled 972,578 megawatt hours, of which the largest users were residential customers at 428,689 megawatt hours. Nayarit has two power generating stations, both are hydroelectric and are located at the state capital of Tepic. The two stations have a combined capacity of 962 megawatts. Electricity is provided and distributed by the Federal Electricity Commission and Central Light and Power. Both utilities are run by the Mexican government.

As a small state whose economy has been based predominantly on agriculture, Nayarit's electricity consumption is among the lowest in Mexico.

18 Health

In 2003, the state had 14 hospitals and 336 outpatient centers that were part of the national health system. In 2004, there were about 963 doctors, 1,995 nurses, and 76 dentists working in these health centers. There were an additional 20 independent health centers in the state in 2004.

Most of the Mexican population is covered under a government health plan. The IMSS (Instituto Mexicano de Seguro Social) covers the general population. The ISSSTE (Instituto de Seguridad y Servicios Sociales de Trabajadores del Estado) covers state workers.

19 Housing

Most homes are built with materials such as stone, brick, or concrete with flat roof constructions. Adobe homes with sheet metal or tile roofs are common in some areas. In 2000, about 80% of all homes were owner-occupied. In 2005, there were an estimated 244,445 residential housing units in the state. About 94% of these units were single-family detached homes. The average household was estimated at 3.9 people.

20 Education

Public education in Mexico is free for students from ages 6 to 16 and most of the students in the state attend public schools. In 2004/05, it was estimated that 94.2% of age-eligible students completed primary school, which includes six years of study. About 83.1% of eligible students completed secondary school, which includes three years of study after primary school. About 61.1% of eligible students completed the *bachillerato*, which is similar to a high school diploma. The national average for completion of the *bachillerato* was 60.1% that year.

The Universidad Autónoma de Nayarit and the Instituto Tecnológico de Tepic are both located in Tepic. In 2005, there were about 33,583 students ages 20 and older who were enrolled in some type of higher education program. The overall literacy rate was estimated at 90% in 2005.

21 Arts

The state of Nayarit has a local ballet company, the Ballet de Cámara de Nayarit. The city of Tepic has two theaters. There are also over 25

Isla Isabela is one of the islands in the Pacific Ocean that belongs to Nayarit. © KAL MULLER/WOODFIN CAMP.

auditoriums and public venues throughout the state.

22 Libraries and Museums

In 2003, there were 118 libraries in the state with a combined stock of 592,777 volumes. The same year, there were six active museums registered in the state that had permanent exhibits. The Regional Museum of Anthropology and History is in Tepic. Tepic also has a Museum of Popular Arts, which is also called the Casa de los Cuatro Pueblos. The house of poet Amado Nervo (1870–1919) is open as a museum.

23 Media

In 2005, the capital city, Tepic, published four daily newspapers: *Meridiano, Express, Realidades (The Facts),* and *El Tiempo de Nayarit* (*Nayarit Times*).

In 2004, there were 61 television stations and 21 radio stations (18 AM and 3 FM). In 2005, there were about 37,309 subscribers to cable and satellite television stations. Also in 2005, there were about 130,151 residential phone lines, with about 15.6 mainline phones in use for every 100 people.

24 Tourism, Travel, and Recreation

The state beaches are very popular for both tourists and locals. There are national parks at Isla Isabel and Islas Marietas. Nayarit hosts festivals for *charros* (horsemen) and rodeos. Main celebrations in Tepic are those during Holy Week (the week before the Christian holiday Easter) and for Independence Day (mid-September).

25 Sports

Swimming, surfing, and fishing are popular water sports for residents and tourists alike. Soccer is a popular sport, particularly among school children. The Nicolas Alvarez Ortega Stadium (soccer) is located in Tepic. The International Regatta at Nueva Vallarta is a four-day sailing event in Bahía Banderas. The regatta has been held annually since 1993.

26 Famous People

The poet Amado Nervo (1870–1919) was born in Nayarit. Antonio Echevarría Domínguez was elected governor in 1999. Ney González Sánchez (b.1963) took the office of governor in 2005.

27 Bibliography

BOOKS

Burt, Janet. *The Pacific North States of Mexico.* Philadelphia: Mason Crest Publishers, 2003.

DeAngelis, Gina. *Mexico.* Mankato, MN: Blue Earth Books, 2003.

Gruber, Beth. *Mexico.* Washington, DC: National Geographic, 2006.

WEB SITES

Government of Mexico. *Mexico for Kids.* www. elbalero.gob.mx/index_kids.html (accessed on March 30, 2007).

Mexican Tourism Board. *Visit Mexico: Nayarit.* www.visitmexico.com/wb/Visitmexico/Visi_ Nayarit (accessed on March 30, 2007).

Nuevo León

PRONUNCIATION: noo-WAY-voh-lay-OWN.

ORIGIN OF STATE NAME: Nuevo León was named in honor of the Spanish kingdom of León.

CAPITAL: Monterrey (mohn-teh-REH-ee).

ENTERED COUNTRY: 1824.

COAT OF ARMS: The coat of arms of Nuevo León is made up by four squares. At the top, six bees represent the hard-working nature of the local citizens. The upper left square features a picture of the sun over La Silla Hill (a landmark that often symbolizes the state), with an orange tree. In the upper right-hand square, a crowned lion is ready to attack. In the lower left, there is a picture of the San Francisco convent. On the lower-right, five smoking chimneys represent industry. The weapons around the border represent both native warriors and Spanish conquerors. The banner displays the state motto, *Sempre Ascendens,* which means "always rising."

HOLIDAYS: Año Nuevo (New Year's Day—January 1); Día de la Constitución (Constitution Day—February 5); Benito Juárez's birthday (March 21); Primero de Mayo (Labor Day—May 1); Anniversary of the Battle of Puebla (1862), May 5; Revolution Day, 1910 (November 20); and Navidad (Christmas—December 25).

FLAG: There is no official state flag.

TIME: 6 AM = noon Greenwich Mean Time (GMT).

1 Location and Size

Nuevo León is located in northern Mexico. It covers an area of 64,220 square kilometers (24,795 square miles), or about half the size of the US state of New York. It ranks as 13th in size among the states and covers about 3.3% of the total land area of Mexico. The Río Bravo (or Río Bravo del Norte) separates the northern tip of Nuevo León from the US state of Texas. This river is known as the Río Grande in the United States. On the east the state is bordered by Tamaulipas, on the southwest by San Luis Potosí, and on the west by Coahuila and Zacatecas. Nuevo León is divided into 51 municipalities (similar to US counties). The capital is Monterrey.

There is a wide region of plains in the northeastern portion of the country. The Sierra Madre Oriental, one of Mexico's major mountain ranges, crosses the state through the western

The Río Bravo (or Río Bravo del Norte) separates the northern tip of Nuevo León from the US state of Texas. This river is known as the Río Grande in the United States. © ROBERT FRERCK/WOODFIN CAMP.

and southern borders. The highest point is Cerro Potosí at 3,635 meters (11,926 feet). A series of caves near Monterrey known as Grutas de García are accessible to the public.

The most important river in Nuevo León is the San Juan, which flows 121 kilometers (75 miles) northeast into Tamaulipas. The Río Salado flows from Coahuila through Nuevo León to join the Río Bravo.

2 Climate

The state has an extreme range of temperatures, but for most of the year the climate is generally hot. In the north, the climate is hot and dry. In the central region, by the Sierra Madre, temperatures are cooler. In the south, the climate is dry and desert-like.

In Monterrey, the lowest recorded temperature was about 0°C (32°F) and the highest was 44°C (111°F). The average temperature ranges from 14°C (58°F) in January to 29°C (85°F) in August. On average, the temperature in Monterrey is above 26°C (80°F) for about 238 days each year. The average temperatures for the entire state are a minimum of about 17°C (62°F) and a maximum of 23°C (74°F). Average precipitation for the state ranges from a minimum of 20 centimeters (8 inches) to a maximum of 100 centimeters (39 inches).

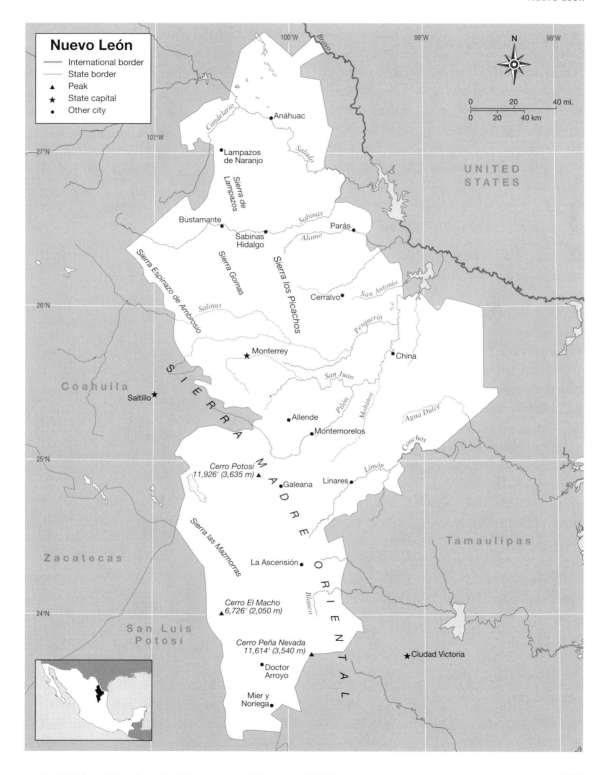

Nuevo León

- ——— International border
- ········ State border
- ▲ Peak
- ★ State capital
- ● Other city

100°W
99°W
98°W
101°W
27°N
26°N
25°N
24°N

N

0   20   40 mi.
0   20   40 km

Bravo

Candelario

Anáhuac

Lampazos
de Naranjo

UNITED
STATES

Sierra de
Lampazos

Salado

Sabinas

Bustamante

Parás

Sabinas
Hidalgo

Alamo

Sierra Gomas

Sierra los Picachos

Cerralvo

San Antonio

Salinas

Pesquería

Monterrey

China

Coahuila

San Juan

Saltillo

SIERRA

Allende

Pilón

Molinos

Agua Dulce

Montemorelos

Conchos

Cerro Potosí
11,926' (3,635 m) ▲

Galeana

Linares

Limón

Zacatecas

MADRE

Tamaulipas

Sierra las Mazmorras

La Ascensión

ORIENTAL

Blanco

Cerro El Macho
▲ 6,726' (2,050 m)

San Luis
Potosí

Cerro Peña Nevada
11,614' (3,540 m)

★Ciudad Victoria

Doctor
Arroyo

Mier y
Noriega

Sierra Espinazo de Ambrosio

3 Plants and Animals

Natural pastures and thickets cover some of the dry, low-altitude regions of the state. Forests of pine and oak trees can be found in areas with a greater level of humidity. Common animals in the state include *tlacuaches* (Mexican opossum), rabbits, coyotes, pumas, wild boar, and white-tailed deer.

4 Environmental Protection

Environmental concerns for the state include maintaining an adequate safe water supply and properly managing hazardous waste materials. In 2004, the state had 57 municipal wastewater treatment plants in operation with a combined installed capacity of 12,789 liters per second (3,378 gallons per second). The volume of treated wastewater that year was estimated at 9,754 liters per second (2,576 gallons per second). There were also 83 industrial wastewater treatment plants in operation that year. As of 2004, about 96.9% of the population had access to safe drinking water.

In 2003, the state had about 348,637 hectares (861,500 acres) of woodland. In 2004, only 7 hectares (17.3 acres) of woodland were damaged or destroyed by forest fires. An additional 66 hectares (163 acres) of pasture and brush land were also damaged by fires. There are two national parks in the state: Cumbres de Monterrey and El Sabinal.

5 Population, Ethnic Groups, Languages

Nuevo León had an estimated total population of 4,279,900 in 2006, ranking eighth among the states and the Distrito Federal. The population was almost evenly divided between men and women. About 93% of the population lived in urban areas. The population density was 66 people per square kilometer (171 people per square mile). In 2005, the capital, Monterrey, had an estimated population of 1,113,814. Almost all citizens speak Spanish as their first language. Less than 1% of the population speaks indigenous (native) languages, including Náhuatl, Huasteco, and Otomi.

6 Religions

According to the 2000 census, 87.9% of the population, or about 3 million people, were Roman Catholic; about 6.2%, or 211,402 people, were mainline or evangelical Protestants. About 2% were counted as other Biblical faiths, including 10,403 Seventh-day Adventists, 10,563 Latter-day Saints (Mormons), and 46,150 Jehovah's Witnesses. There were 665 Jews. About 2.8% of the population claimed to have no religious affiliation.

The Cathedral of Our Lady of Monterrey is the seat of the Roman Catholic archdiocese of Monterrey. A temple of the Church of Jesus Christ of Latter-day Saints was dedicated in Monterrey in 2002.

7 Transportation

Monterrey Airport provides international flights to and from Nuevo León. The state has about 8,664 kilometers (5,381 miles) of roads and 1,096 kilometers (681 miles) of railroads. In 2004, there were 983,132 automobiles registered in the state, along with 14,372 passenger trucks, 438,461 freight trucks, and 19,498 motorcycles.

8 History

There is scattered anthropological and archeological evidence of early nomad and hunter and gatherer indigenous groups during the first centuries. Yet, when the Spaniards arrived, there were no large human settlements in the region. Most of the native population was comprised of nomadic groups that traveled through the unfriendly Nuevo León terrain.

The first conquistadors (those who sought to conqueror Mexico for the Spanish crown) to visit the region were Alvar Nuñez Cabeza de Vaca (c. 1490-c. 1560) in around 1535 and Andrés de Olmos in around 1545. In 1575, Alberto del Canto found a valley that he called Extremadura, where the city of Monterrey was later founded. Farther north, he found the mineral deposits of San Gregorio. In 1579, King Felipe II (1527–1598) of Spain granted Luis Carvajal y de la Cueva the authorization to conquer those territories. Three years later, Carvajal initiated his expedition and founded the San Luis de Francia settlement. In the early 16th century, Diego de Montemayor was named governor of the region and he led a new colonization effort. Franciscan priests joined Montemayor with the intention of converting the indigenous population to Catholic faith. However, colonization efforts were mostly abandoned by the late 16th century.

Tlaxcala Amerindians were sent during the 16th century to help the colonization efforts and to help nomadic tribes learn the advantages of permanent settlements. Because of the lack of accessible cheap labor and the vast ter-ritorial extensions, cattle ranching became the most important economic activity in the region during the colonial period. The need to combat nomadic tribes, however, made it costly for cattle ranchers to consolidate their businesses. In the mid-1700s there was a short-lived mining fever resulting from the discovery of gold and silver mines. The mines were rapidly exploited to their limits and the fever subsided. During the late-1700s, Catholic convents and seminaries were built in the region, taking advantage of the large land entitlements given to the church and because population density remained low.

The independence movement caught on for a short period of time in Nuevo León in 1811. But after the execution of the extremely popular and powerful priest and revolutionary Miguel de Hidalgo y Costilla (1753–1811), the independence revolts were brought to a halt. Royalist forces, loyal to Spain, then regained control of the entire region. After the adoption of the Plan of Iguala in 1821, Nuevo León became a province of independent Mexico. Starting in 1824 it was made into a federal state, and a new state constitution was established.

Political instability characterized much of the 19th century. First, conflicts between centralists and federalists, and later, civil war between liberals and conservatives, prevented the economic development of the region. These continuing conflicts regularly threw social order into turmoil in Monterrey and other towns. The consolidation of a liberal regime after Mexico ceded its northern territories, including Texas, to the United States helped bring about much needed economic development. However, low population density remained a problem for Nuevo León. A new railroad between Mexico City and

Monterrey helped bring about industrialization towards the end of the 19th century.

The Mexican Revolution started early in Nuevo León. Mexican revolutionist Francisco Indalécio Madero (1873–1913) was arrested in Monterrey in 1910 during his failed presidential campaign. Accusations of fraud by incumbent president Porfirio Díaz (1830–1915) triggered the call for a revolution later that year. Eventually, the revolutionary victors controlled Nuevo León. The state participated in the writing and ratification of the Mexican Constitution of 1917. After the end of the revolution, Nuevo León consolidated as a cattle ranching state. In addition, Monterrey consolidated its position as the most important industrial and financial center of northern Mexico.

In the first decade of the 21st century, the residents of Nuevo Leon had one of the highest overall standards of living in Mexico. The state's location along to the border with the United States also ensured its economic prosperity. But its location along the United States border also meant that the state had become a crossing point for illegal narcotics entering the United States. As a result violent crime and official corruption became a problem for the state.

9 State and Local Government

The state governor is elected for a nonrenewable six-year term. The legislature is comprised of a 42-seat unicameral (one chamber) congress. Twenty-six deputies are elected from single member districts, and sixteen deputies are elected by proportional representation.

The 51 municipalities that comprise Nuevo León hold democratic elections for municipal presidents and council members every three years.

Immediate re-election is not allowed. Although some decentralization initiatives are producing positive results, the state still has a long way to go to achieve successful decentralization.

10 Political Parties

The three main political parties in all of Mexico are the Institutional Revolutionary Party (PRI), the National Action Party (PAN), and the Party of the Democratic Revolution (PRD). Although the PRI dominated state politics since the end of the Mexican Revolution, the PAN consolidated as a strong local party in Nuevo León since the mid 1950s. PAN candidates regularly won several municipal government elections. Then a PAN candidate, Fernando Canales Clariond, won the gubernatorial race in 1997. The PRI regained control of the governorship in 2003 with the election of José Natividad González Parás. The alternation in power and the strength of the PAN and PRI have called into play the implementation of separation-of-power and checks-and-balances provisions previously existing in the constitution.

11 Judicial System

The Superior Tribunal of Justice is the highest court in the state. Its members are appointed by the congress from a three-person list submitted by the state governor. The term of appointment is 10 years and justices can be re-elected only for an additional 10-year term. Only highly qualified attorneys can be appointed to the high court. A judicial council also plays a role in fostering the development of a high quality justice system. An electoral tribunal and other lower courts are also part of the Nuevo León judicial system.

12 Economy

Nuevo León is one of Mexico's leading industrial states. Which a gross domestic product of $48 billion (as of 2003), its capital city of Monterrey is the home base for some of Mexico's largest companies, as well as the financial and distribution center for northeast and north central Mexico. The state also has excellent road and rail connections, and one of the highest standards of living in Mexico.

13 Industry

Nuevo León was an early site for heavy industry (iron and steel) in Latin America. The state currently has a diversified industrial structure, that includes oil refining, along with heavy and light manufacturing. Nuevo León is a leading national producer of iron, steel, and chemicals. There are a total of 176 maquiladoras (foreign-owned industrial plants) located within the capital city of Monterrey. Also located in Monterrey are a number of Mexico's largest firms. These include Cemex, one of the world's largest cement companies; bakery product giant Bimbo; food and grain firm Maseca; banking firm Banorte (wholly owned by Mexicans); telecommunications firm Alestra; glass-maker Vitro; aluminum producer Hylsa; FEMSA (Coca-Cola in Latin America); and brewer Cervecería Cuauhtémoc-Moctezuma.

The state's handicraft industry sector produces blankets, ponchos, carved wooden items, reed lamps, and furniture.

14 Labor

As of 2005, the state of Nuevo León had 1,859,550 eligible workers. Some 1,771,542 were listed as employed and 88,008 were listed as unemployed. Unemployed workers in rural areas may not be counted, however. The unemployment rate that year was reported to be 4.9%. Of those who were working, services employed 45.3%, followed by manufacturing at 23.5%, and commerce at 19.4%.

The US Bureau of Labor Statistics reported that Mexican workers saw their wages increase from $2.49 per hour in 2003 to $2.50 per hour in 2004. (The average US worker earned $15.70 per hour in 2004.) The maximum work week is set at 48 hours by law. The average worker spends 40 to 45 hours per week on the job. Workers earn twice their regular hourly rate for up to nine hours a week of overtime. When a worker works more than nine hours overtime in a week, he or she earns three times the regular hourly rate. After one year, workers are entitled by law to six days paid vacation.

Nuevo León's workers are highly unionized, with many of them independent of Mexico's state-run labor organizations. In the capital city of Monterrey, more than 60% of the workforce belongs to a union.

15 Agriculture

Nuevo León has three distinct growing regions: the Northern Gulf Coastal Plain, the Sierra Madre Oriental region, and the Highland region. Agricultural products vary by region. The Northern Gulf Coastal Plain produces watermelon, pears, melons, squash, corn, beans, chili peppers, cotton, avocados, nuts, and sorghum.

A series of caves near Monterrey known as Grutas de García are accessible to the public. © KAL MULLER/ WOODFIN CAMP.

The Sierra Madre Oriental and the Highland regions both produce corn, wheat, avocado, carrots, beans, and potatoes. The Sierra Madre Oriental region also produces green tomatoes, while the Highland region produces onion, squash, and chili peppers.

In the Northern Gulf Coastal Plain the primary livestock are cattle, goats, pigs, sheep, and horses. Poultry farms produce chickens and eggs. Honey and honey products are also produced. In the Sierra Madre Oriental region, livestock is mostly goats and horses. In the Highland region, livestock consists mainly of goats, although horses, cows, and sheep are also raised.

In 2004, crops produced in the state of Nuevo Leon included: 70,312 tons of corn, 142,773 tons of potatoes, 51,163 tons of wheat, 124,052 tons of sorghum, and 2,991 tons of avocados. Livestock brought to market included: 72,163 head of beef cattle, 55,293 pigs, 8,022 goats, and 857 sheep. In that same year, the state produced 41.3 million liters (10 million gallons) of milk from dairy cows and 88,291 tons of eggs. Meat production included: 36,067 tons of beef, 17,593 tons of pork, 1,409 tons of goat, 394 tons of lamb, and 110,911 tons of poultry.

16 Natural Resources

Mining products include zinc, copper, lime, coal, iron, silver, and barite (used for drilling oil wells). In 2003, the value of forest wood production was estimated at about $1.8 million. Common tropical woods and pine were the primary woods harvested. The fish catch in 2003 was only about 216 tons, all of which was for human consumption.

17 Energy and Power

In 2005, there were 1,260,382 users of electricity in the state of Nuevo León. Of that total, the largest number were residential customers at 1,111,891. Sales of electricity that same year totaled 13,703,088 megawatt hours, of which the largest users were medium-sized firms at 6,029,797 megawatt hours. Nuevo León has seven power generating stations, of which five are gas-turbine operated, and two are combined cycle (gas-turbine and steam), with a total capacity of 1,064 megawatts. Electricity is provided and distributed by the Federal Electricity Commission, and Central Light and Power. Both utilities are run by the Mexican government.

18 Health

In 2003, the state had 29 hospitals and 527 outpatient centers that were part of the national health system. In 2004, there were about 3,186 doctors, 8,221 nurses, and 219 dentists working in these health centers. There were an additional 51 independent health centers in the state in 2004.

Most of the Mexican population is covered under a government health plan. The IMSS (Instituto Mexicano de Seguro Social) covers the general population. The ISSSTE (Instituto de Seguridad y Servicios Sociales de Trabajadores del Estado) covers state workers.

19 Housing

Most homes are built with materials such as concrete, stone, and brick. In 2000, about 80% of all homes were owner-occupied. In 2005, there were an estimated 1,014,042 residential housing units in the state. About 92% of these units were single-family detached homes. The average household was estimated at 4.1 people.

20 Education

Public education in Mexico is free for students from ages 6 to 16. While most students in the state attend public schools, in 2002/03 about 35% of high school students attended private schools. In 2004/05, it was estimated that 95% of age-eligible students completed primary school, which includes six years of study. About 85% of eligible students completed secondary school, which includes three years of study after primary school. About 61.5% of eligible students completed the *bachillerato*, which is similar to a high school diploma. The national average for completion of the *bachillerato* was 60.1% that year.

There are at least five major institutions of higher learning in the state, including the Universidad de Monterrey and the Universidad Autónoma de Nuevo León. In 2005, there were about 127,898 students ages 20 and older who were enrolled in some type of higher education program. The overall literacy rate was estimated at 95.5% in 2005.

21 Arts

In 2004, the state had at least 11 theaters for the performing arts. A theater group, Teatro Saltimbanque, and a musical group, Música Maestra, perform throughout the state. There are also cultural centers in most cities. There are over 300 registered movie theaters, including multiscreen theaters and single-screen galleries.

22 Libraries and Museums

In 2003, there were 452 libraries in the state with a combined stock of 2,835,840 volumes. The library of the Autonomous University of Nuevo Léon serves as a depository library for the United Nations. In 2003, there were 34 museums registered in the state that had permanent exhibits. In the capital, Monterrey, there is the Museo de Arte Contemporaneo (Contemporary Art Museum, or MARCO), the Museo de Historia Mexicana (Museum of Mexican History), Museo del Vidrio (Glass Museum), and the Museo Metropolitano de Monterrey (Monterrey

Waterfalls in Nuevo León. © KAL MULLER/WOODFIN CAMP.

Metropolitan Museum). There is also La Casa de los Titeres (the Puppet House) and the Mexican Professional Baseball Hall of Fame.

23 Media

In 2005, the capital, Monterrey, had eight daily newspapers. The two largest were *El Norte (The North),* with a circulation of about 133,872, and *Metro*, with a circulation of 62,000. Others included *El Porvenir* (*The Future*), *Extra*, and *El Sol* (*The Sun*).

In 2004, there were 69 television stations and 69 radio stations (29 AM, 39 FM, and 1 shortwave). In 2005, there were about 250,966 subscribers to cable and satellite television stations. Also in 2005, there were about 858,492 residential phone lines, with about 28.6 main-line phones in use for every 100 people.

24 Tourism, Travel, and Recreation

There is a park based on the television series *Sesame Street*. Birds and butterflies native to the western Sierra Madre region thrive in the habitat of Chipinque Park. Visitors can also hike and go rock climbing there. The city of Monterrey hosts a number of museums and other cultural sites popular for tourists. The national parks of Cumbres de Monterrey and El Sabinal draw both national and international tourists.

25 Sports

Monterrey's Fuerza Regia (Royal Force) is part of the National Professional Basketball League (LNBP). The team plays in the 4,200-seat Gimnasio Nuevo León. The AAA minor league baseball team, Sultanes (Sultans) de Monterrey, plays in the 27,000-seat Estadio Monterrey. There are three soccer teams competing in the Mexican Football Association (commonly known as Femexfut). Though two of the teams are known as the Rayados Monterrey, one team plays in the First Division and the other plays in the First Division "A." The Tigres of the Universidad Autónoma de Nuevo León are a First Division team. The primary soccer stadium is the 38,622-seat Tecnológico. The University's stadium seats over 39,000. In 2004, there was one bullfighting ring in the state. The Mexican Professional Baseball Hall of Fame is in Monterrey.

26 Famous People

Alfonso Reyes (1889–1959) was born in Monterrey. He was a diplomat and a teacher and was considered to be one of the greatest Spanish American writers of his time. One of his most famous prose poems was *Visión de Anáhuac.* Judith Grace Gonzalez Hicks (b.1960?) won the title of Miss Mexico in 1981 and hosts a popular television talk show, *Casos de Familia.*

27 Bibliography

BOOKS

Day-MacLeod, Deirdre. *The States of Northern Mexico.* Philadelphia, PA: Mason Crest Publishers, 2003.

Gruber, Beth. *Mexico.* Washington, DC: National Geographic, 2006.

Hernández, Marie Theresa. *Delirio—The Fantastic, the Demonic, and the Reél: The Buried History of Nuevo León.* Austin: University of Texas Press, 2002.

Mora-Torres, Juan. *The Making of the Mexican Border.* Austin: University of Texas Press, 2001.

WEB SITES

Government of Mexico. *Mexico for Kids.* www.elbalero.gob.mx/index_kids.html (accessed on March 30, 2007).

Mexican Tourism Board. *Visit Mexico: Nuevo Leon.* www.visitmexico.com/wb/Visitmexico/Visi_Nuevo_leon (accessed on March 30, 2007).

Oaxaca

PRONUNCIATION: wah-HAH-kah.

ORIGIN OF STATE NAME: The name of the state comes from the Náhuatl (the language of the Aztecs) word *Hauxyacac,* which means "on the top of the guaje tree." The guaje tree is common throughout the state.

CAPITAL: Oaxaca de Juárez (wah-HAH-kah deh HWAH-rehs), named for the former president Benito Juárez (1806–1872).

ENTERED COUNTRY: October 13, 1824.

COAT OF ARMS: An eagle perched on a cactus with a snake in its beak forms the top of the symbol. The shield below contains an oval encircled by the motto "El Respeto Al Derecho Ajeno es La Paz", with symbols of the state's archeology.

HOLIDAYS: Año Nuevo (New Year's Day—January 1); Día de la Constitución (Constitution Day—February 5); Benito Juárez's birthday (March 21); Primero de Mayo (Labor Day—May 1); Anniversary of the Battle of Puebla (1862), May 5; Revolution Day, 1910 (November 20); and Navidad (Christmas—December 25).

FLAG: There is no official state flag.

TIME: 6 AM = noon Greenwich Mean Time (GMT).

1 Location and Size

Oaxaca is located on the southern coast of Mexico. It is the fifth-largest state with an area of 93,793 square kilometers (36,213 square miles), which is a little smaller than the US state of Indiana. It covers about 4.8% of the total land area of Mexico. Oaxaca is bordered on the north by the states of Puebla and Veracruz, on the east by Chiapas, on the south by the Pacific Ocean, and on the west by Guerrero. Oaxaca is divided into 570 municipalities (similar to US counties). Its capital is Oaxaca de Juárez.

Oaxaca is part of the region known as the Isthmus of Tehuantepec. An isthmus is a narrow strip of land that is bordered by water and connects two larger land areas. The Isthmus of Tehuantepec is bordered by the Bay of Campeche on the north and the Gulf of Tehuantepec on the south. The states of Veracruz and Chiapas are also part of the Isthmus.

The Sierra Madre del Sur covers most of the western and central portion of the state. The highest point in the country, Cerro Nube (also known as Quie Yelaag) rises to an elevation of

This 2000-year-old ahuehuete (cypress) tree is known as El Tule. It is believed to be the world's largest tree, with a circumference of nearly 140 feet (42 meters). © ROBERT FRERCK/WOODFIN CAMP.

about 3,720 meters (12,205 feet). Canyons and caves also are found throughout the state. In the central Oaxaca Valley and along the coast, the land is flat.

There are many rivers in that state. In Oaxaca, the most beautiful waterfalls are the Salto de Conejo, Cabdadihui, Yatao, Salto de Fraile, and Apaola. Lagoons are found near the Pacific coast. They include Laguna Superior and Laguna Inferior on the southeast coast of the Isthmus of Tehuantepec and the much smaller Laguna Chacahua and Laguna Corralero on the southwest coast. Mar Muerto is a large lagoon along the border with Chiapas. The Pacific coast-line extends 598 kilometers (371 miles). Presa

Miguel Alemán in the north and Presa Benito Juárez are two major manmade reservoirs.

2 Climate

The climate is moderate all year. The average winter temperature is 17°C (63°F) in November, December, and January. From May to August, the average temperature is 22°C (72°F). Rainfall for the entire state ranges from a minimum average of about 42.7 centimeters (16.8 inches) to a maximum average of about 375 centimeters (147 inches).

The temperature in Oaxaca de Juárez can range from an average low temperature of 12°C (55°F) to an average high of 27°C (82°F). The aver-

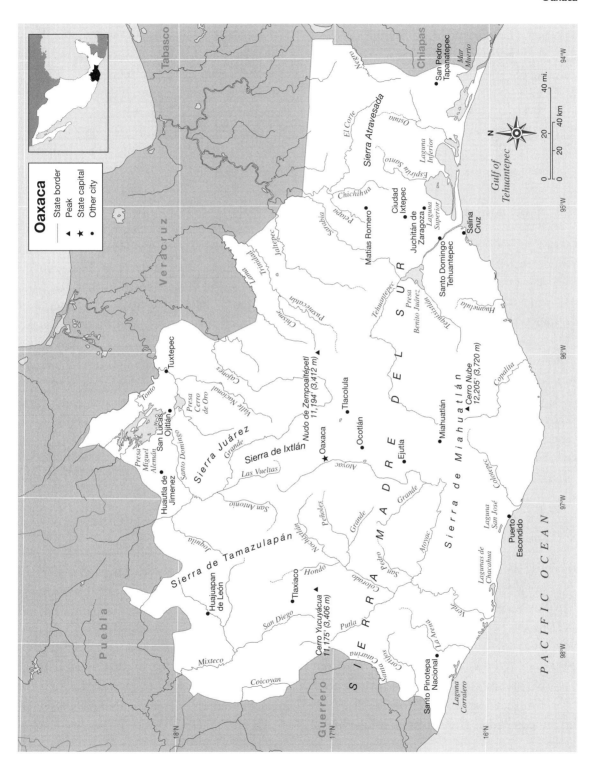

age rainfall in the capital is 69 centimeters (27.4 inches) per year. Oaxaca occasionally is struck by damaging hurricanes, such as Hurricane Pauline in October 1997. In the coastal city of Salina Cruz, the temperature ranges from an average low of 23°C (75°F) to an average high of 30°C (87°F). Annual precipitation in Salina Cruz is about 97 centimeters (38.5 inches).

3 Plants and Animals

Oaxaca has about 30,000 different plant species. Some of the most common trees are oyamel trees, ahuehuete (cypress), cedar, mahogany, ash, oak, and juniper. Coconut palms and mangroves (a tropical evergreen) are also found. Fennel, thyme, and laurel are common plants. Small animals include squirrels, tlacuaches (Mexican possums), and armadillos. Larger mammals include deer, wildcats, leopards, wild boar, tapirs, and spider monkeys. Some common birds include tzentzontles (the bird of a thousand voices), goldfinches, sparrows, hawks, and eagles. Fish species include lisa, red snapper, sailfish, carp, shrimp, and lobster.

4 Environmental Protection

In 2004, the state had 50 municipal wastewater treatment plants in operation with a combined installed capacity of 843 liters per second (222 gallons per second). The volume of treated wastewater that year was estimated at 640 liters per second (169 gallons per second). There were also 13 industrial wastewater treatment plants in operation that year. As of 2004, about 74.3% of the population had access to safe drinking water.

In 2003, the state had over 5.1 million hectares (12.6 million acres) of woodland, including over 2.3 million hectares (5.9 million acres) of rain forest. In 2004, about 1,117 hectares (2,760 acres) of woodland were damaged or destroyed by forest fires. An additional 4,659 hectares (11,512 acres) of pasture and brush land were also damaged by fires.

The Lagunas de Chacahua National Park is a protected area on the coast with many bamboo groves and mangrove swamps, as well as alligators, turtles, and tropical birds. There are two other national parks in the state: Benito Juárez and Huatulco. Part of Huatulco has been designates as a Ramsar Wetland of International Importance. Playa Tortuguera Cahuitán is also a Ramsar site.

In 2002, eight communities in Oaxaca began local conservation efforts as part of a Community Protected Areas program. These new Community Protected Areas are focused on efforts to preserve the Mexican dry forest on the Pacific coast and the Mesoamerican Pine-Oak forest in Sierra Norte.

5 Population, Ethnic Groups, Languages

Oaxaca had an estimated total population of 3,552,300 in 2006, ranking 10th among the states and the Distrito Federal. About 48% of the population were men and 52% were women. Among the states, Oaxaca has the highest percentage of people living in rural areas, at about 72%. The population density was 37 people per square kilometer (96 people per square mile). In 2005, the capital, Oaxaca de Juárez, had a population of 265,033.

The indigenous (native) population of Oaxaca is over 1 million, the highest number among the states. Indigenous groups include the Zapotec, Amuzgos, Chochos, Huaves, and others. There is also a group known as the Afromixtecas, who represent an ethnic mix of the Mixteca and the African slaves who were brought to Mexico by the Spanish. Most citizens speak Spanish as their first language. About 33% of the population speaks indigenous languages. This was the highest percentage in the country.

6 Religions

According to the 2000 census, 84.8% of the population, or about 2.56 million people, were Roman Catholic; about 7.8%, or 234,150 people, were mainline or evangelical Protestants. About 2.3% were counted as other Biblical faiths, including 25,986 Seventh-day Adventists, 2,828 Latter-day Saints (Mormons), and 37,504 Jehovah's Witnesses. There were 1,199 Jews. About 4% of the population claimed to have no religious affiliation.

The Metropolitan Cathedral of Our Lady of the Assumption in the capital city is the seat of the Roman Catholic archdiocese of Antequera. A temple of the Church of Jesus Christ of Latter-day Saints was dedicated in the capital city of Oaxaca in 2000.

7 Transportation

Oaxaca Airport provides international flights to and from Oaxaca. The state has about 15,569 kilometers (9,670 miles) of roads and 651 kilometers (450 miles) of railroads. In 2004, there were 122,610 automobiles registered in the state,

along with 3,105 passenger trucks, 109,373 freight trucks, and 8,143 motorcycles.

8 History

Some archeological ruins that date back to more than 11,000 BC make Oaxaca the first place where human settlements occurred in Mexico. Olmec culture developed in the region around 3,000 BC. Quiché culture first emerged around 2,000 BC. The archeological ruins of Monte Albán were built around 800 BC. Zapotec Indians built large irrigation systems in the Oaxaca Valley around 800 AD. Mexica Indians populated the region starting around 1200 AD. The Aztecs founded the city of Oaxaca and dominated the other indigenous groups and cultures in the mid-14th century.

When the Spaniards first arrived and Spanish conqueror Hernán Cortés (1485–1547) sought to defeat the Aztec empire in Tenochtitlán-Mexico (ancient name of Mexico City), some of Cortés' envoys went to the region and made peace with the Chinanteco Indians. Mexica Indians, however, continued to resist Spanish occupation until 1522. At that time Francisco de Orozco and Pedro de Alvarado (c. 1485–1541) completed the conquest of the region for the Spanish crown. Attempts to convert the native Oaxaca Indians to Christianity had begun in 1521. In 1529, Cortés, seeking to protect territories that he hoped to retain for himself, ordered the destruction of many villages that were founded by Spanish soldiers and conquistadors (those who sought to take control of Mexico for Spain). Internal land conflicts among the Spanish colonizers and the resistance of several indigenous groups made the region somewhat unstable for a few years after the conquest.

Cortés introduced sugarcane and wheat to his vast territories. Agricultural production soon consolidated as the main economic engine in the region.

By the 16th century, the indigenous population had been decimated. Diseases brought by the Europeans, overexploitation for agricultural purposes, and widespread famine brought defeat. Yet, agricultural production flourished as Oaxaca traded with Puebla and Mexico City. Silk was widely produced in the region. Silk production helped Oaxaca establish trade relations with places as distant as Peru through the Pacific ports of Huatulco and Tehuantepec. The capital city of the region, Antequera (later renamed Oaxaca), had more than six thousand inhabitants.

Mexican priest and revolutionist José María Morelos y Pávon (1765–1815) brought the independence movement to Oaxaca in 1812. A later attempt by a Spanish royalist army sent from Guatemala to regain control of Oaxaca failed. Defeat was at the hands of an army led by another Mexican priest and patriot Mariano Matamoros (1770–1814). Later, after Morelos's downfall, Spanish royalists regained control of Oaxaca until the region joined the rest of Mexico in declaring independence with the Plan of Iguala in 1821. Oaxaca became a federal state of Mexico in 1824.

The unstable period that marked the reign of Antonio López de Santa Anna (1794–1876), who was in and out of power from the early 1830s to the mid 1850s, ended when Benito Juárez (1806–1872), Oaxaca's most revered son, emerged as a local and national leader in the 1850s. (Juárez officially became president of Mexico in 1858). Another Oaxaca notable leader, Porfirio Díaz (1830–1915), successfully

resisted the efforts by French troops to take control of Oaxaca. (The French, under the leadership of Emperor Maximilian [1832–1867], briefly controlled parts of Mexico from 1863 to 1867.) With the triumph of the Reforma movement led by Juárez, Oaxaca joined the rest of Mexico in supporting the liberal government that brought about radical and profound reforms. Juárez, a native indigenous himself, died in 1872 while serving as president. Porfirio Díaz, Juárez's former ally and political opponent when Juárez last served as president, eventually became president himself in 1877. His rule came to an end with the Mexican Revolution of 1910.

During Juárez's and Díaz's tenures, Oaxaca developed as an agricultural, financial, and commercial center. Díaz extended the railroads well into the state and brought telegraph lines to the major cities. Toward the end of Díaz's reign, many of the leaders in Oaxaca supported him against the revolutionaries who were opposed to the aging president taking on yet another presidential term. However, a few revolutionary revolts sparked throughout the state. After Díaz abandoned the presidency and left Mexico, military conflicts reached Oaxaca as well.

After the revolution, Oaxaca evolved as a tourist, commercial, and agricultural center. Because of its extremely rich archeological heritage and numerous ancient religious and historic sites, Oaxaca is also considered the birthplace of much of Mexico's legendary history and traditions.

Oaxaca entered the first decade of the 21st century as the second poorest state in Mexico, surpassed only by Chiapas. Industrial development was extremely limited, with tourism the single most important source of income. In

Panoramic view of the capital. © CATHERINE KARNOW/WOODFIN CAMP.

addition to poverty, the state was also troubled by labor unrest, and political instability. In May 2006, the state's teachers went on a months-long strike demanding better pay, more help for poorer students, and the resignation of the state's governor, Ulises Ruiz.

9 State and Local Government

The state governor is democratically elected every six years for a nonrenewable term. The legislature is comprised of a 42-member unicameral (single chamber) congress. Twenty-five deputies are elected in single member districts, and 17 deputies are elected by proportional representation, all for three-year periods. Immediate re-election is not allowed.

The 570 municipalities that comprise Oaxaca hold democratic elections for municipal presidents and council members every three years. Immediate re-election is not allowed. Because of the widely varying size and financial resources of the different municipalities, decentralization efforts have produced mixed results in recent years.

10 Political Parties

The three main political parties in all of Mexico are the Institutional Revolutionary Party (PRI), the National Action Party (PAN), and the Party of the Democratic Revolution (PRD). The PRI has been the historically dominant party in state politics throughout the 20th century. Since the

A flower vendor balances her inventory on her head. PETER LANGER.

Mexican Revolution, only PRI candidates have won the gubernatorial races. Ulises Ruiz Ortiz of the PRI won the gubernatorial race in 2004, defeating PAN and PRD candidates. PAN and PRD have gained electoral strength in recent years and have successfully captured important municipal governments.

11 Judicial System

The Superior Tribunal of Justice is the highest court in the state. The governor appoints members for renewable 15-year terms, with legislative approval. Justices are not accountable to the executive or legislative branches, but they must pursue justice and defend the autonomy of the judiciary. The appointees must possess a number of stringent attorney qualifications. In addition, the state judicial system also is made up of lower courts and an electoral tribunal.

12 Economy

Oaxaca is one of Mexico's poorest states, ranking second only to the state of Chiapas which has the distinction of being the poorest. The state's economy is primarily based upon tourism, agriculture and resource extraction. Although most of the people in Oaxaca work in agriculture, tourism has become the single most important source of income to the state, with tourists visiting the coastal communities of Huatulco, Escondido, Puerto Angel, and the state capital of Oaxaca. Coffee is the second largest producer of income, and accounts for 30% of the state's exports. Oaxaca has become a leading supplier of organically grown coffee (chemical fertilizers and pesticides are not used). Forestry products are also a source of income, with the state a major producer of timber.

13 Industry

Most manufacturing in Oaxaca is small and at the handicraft level. However, there is a large oil refinery at Salina Cruz that supplies most of the oil and oil byproducts that are used by the Pacific coastal region. Another industry involves the production of mezcal, a liquor that is distilled from the heart of the agave plant. Oaxaca provides up to 60% of Mexico's mezcal output, with annual production around 5 million liters (1.3 million gallons), of which nearly 1.5 million liters (400,000 gallons) are exported, mostly to the United States.

Oaxaca is well-known for its handicrafts. These include clothing, pottery, wood and leather items. Handicrafts are usually produced by individual artists. Some communities have small-scale production of handicrafts by groups of workers.

14 Labor

As of 2005, the state of Oaxaca had 1,476,200 eligible workers. Some 1,454,516 were listed as employed and 21,684 were listed as unemployed. Unemployed workers in rural areas may not be counted, however. The unemployment rate that year was reported to be 1.5%. Of those who were working, agriculture employed 36.3%, followed by services at 27.1%, and commerce at 15.6%.

The US Bureau of Labor Statistics reported that Mexican workers saw their wages increase from $2.49 per hour in 2003 to $2.50 per hour in 2004. (The average US worker earned $15.70 per hour in 2004.) The maximum work week is set at 48 hours by law. The average worker spends 40 to 45 hours per week on the job. Workers earn twice their regular hourly rate for up to nine hours a week of overtime. When a worker works more than nine hours overtime in a week, he or she earns three times the regular hourly rate. After one year, workers are entitled by law to six days paid vacation.

15 Agriculture

Most of the citizens of Oaxaca are farmers. The most important crops are mangoes and coffee. Oaxaca produces more mangoes than any other Mexican state. Oaxaca is the third largest producer of coffee. Corn and beans are the major crops for local consumption. Other important crops include avocados, oranges, lemons, bananas, sugarcane, melons, rice, pineapple, sorghum, red tomatoes, and tobacco. Most of the livestock are beef and dairy cattle. A festival every December celebrates the radish, which was introduced to Mexico by the Spanish in the late 1500s.

In 2004, crops produced in the state included: 694116 tons of corn, 39,798 tons of sorghum, 53,847 tons of bananas, 14,649 tons of red tomatoes, 334,613 tons of sugar, and 3,014 tons of avocados. Livestock brought to market in 2004 included: 62,871 head of beef cattle, 72,207 pigs, 14,013 goats, and 12,063 sheep. In that same year, the state produced 143 million liters (37 million gallons) of milk from dairy cows and 7,164 tons of eggs. Meat production included: 39,153 tons of beef, 30,575 tons of pork, 4,270 tons of goat, 1,633 tons of lamb, and 7,985 tons of poultry.

16 Natural Resources

Though Oaxaca has a wide variety of fish, the fishing industry has not been developed to its full potential. Shrimp are a popular catch. In 2003, the total fish catch was about 14,957 tons. Forests cover about half of the land area in the state, with most forest areas belonging to local communities. Wood is cut primarily for fuel and building material, but there are some small businesses that produce furniture such as chairs and tables. In 2003, the total value of forest wood production was about $28.8 million. Gold, silver, lead, copper, zinc, graphite, stone and marble are all found in mines and quarries.

17 Energy and Power

In 2005, there were 955,146 users of electricity in the state of Oaxaca. Of that total, the largest number were residential customers at 838,243. Sales of electricity that same year totaled 2,141,923 megawatt hours, of which the largest users were residential at 856,242 megawatt hours. Electric power in Oaxaca is generated by three power stations, two of which are hydroelectric and one wind-driven. They have a combined capacity of 358 megawatts. Electricity is produced and distributed by the Federal Electricity Commission, and Central Light and Power. Both utilities are run by the Mexican government.

18 Health

In 2003, the state had 44 hospitals and 1,267 outpatient centers that were part of the national health system. In 2004, there were about 1,838 doctors, 4,923 nurses, and 168 dentists working in these health centers. There were an additional 85 independent health centers in the state in 2004.

Most of the Mexican population is covered under a government health plan. The IMSS (Instituto Mexicano de Seguro Social) covers the general population. The ISSSTE (Instituto de Seguridad y Servicios Sociales de Trabajadores del Estado) covers state workers.

19 Housing

Most homes are built with materials such as stone, brick, or concrete for both the walls and the roof. However, adobe homes with sheet metal or tile roofs are not uncommon. Also in 2000, Oaxaca had the highest percentage of home ownership with 87% of all homes owner-occupied. In 2005, there were an estimated 802,854 residential housing units in the state. About 94% of these units were single-family detached homes. The average household was estimated at 4.4 people.

20 Education

Public education in Mexico is free for students from ages 6 to 16 and most students in the state attend public schools. In 2004/05, it was estimated that 85.9% of age-eligible students completed primary school, which includes six years of study. About 76% of eligible students completed secondary school, which includes three years of study after primary school. About about 56% of eligible students completed the *bachillerato*, which is similar to a high school diploma. The

Examples of radish art displayed during El Festival de los Rábanos (Festival of the Radishes) held in December each year. ©
CATHERINE KARNOW/WOODFIN CAMP.

national average for completion of the *bachillerato* was 60.1% that year.

There are at least seven institutions of higher learning in the state, including the Benito Juárez Autonomous University of Oaxaca. In 2005, there were about 77,749 students ages 20 and older who were enrolled in some type of higher education program. The overall literacy rate was estimated at 81.2% in 2005.

21 Arts

Oaxaca has three local performing companies: the Contemporary Dance Company of Oaxaca; Mírame, a musical group; and Pasatono, a group performing indigenous music. There are also 35 theaters for the performing arts and dozens of local cultural centers. Oaxaca is also famous for its painted animals made of copal wood, native to the area. Also black clay pottery is a native craft. There are over 30 registered movie theaters, including multiscreen theaters and single-screen galleries.

The Fiestas de Noviembre (November Festivals) include a variety of cultural and sporting events that take place throughout the month, primarily in Puerto Esconcdido. The Dia de los Muertos (Day of the Dead) festivals held in the state have been particularly popular among tourists. The Fiestas of Lunes del Cerro is held during the last two weeks of July each year. The streets of the cities and towns are filled with music and

A woman with her pottery. © CATHERINE KARNOW/WOODFIN CAMP.

performers in this festival celebrating the state's heritage. The annual Festival de los Rábanos (Festival of the Radishes) in December is held in the capital and highlights the work of local artists and sculptures, who create works made entirely out of radishes and local flowers.

22 Libraries and Museums

In 2003, there were 531 libraries in the state with a combined stock of 2,054,896 volumes. The same year, there were 10 museums registered in the state that had permanent exhibits. One of the best known museums is part of the archeological site of Monte Albán, a pre-Columbian settlement. Oaxaca also has the Museum of Oaxacan Culture, The Manuel Alvarez Bravo

Photography Museum, the Oaxaca Museum of Contemporary Art, and a gallery at the Oaxaca Graphic Arts Institute.

23 Media

In 2005, the capital, Oaxaca, had four daily newspapers: *El Imparcial, Noticias, El Observador,* and *El Sur (The South). El Imparcial del Istmo (Isthmus Impartial)* is a special edition of *El Imparcial* published in Salina Cruz.

In 2004, there were 150 television stations and 50 radio stations (34 AM and 16 FM). In 2005, there were about 31,633 subscribers to cable and satellite television stations. Also in 2005, there were about 183,802 residential

Alameda Park in the capital surrounds the cathedral. Each December, it is filled with market stalls during El Festival de los Rábanos (Festival of the Radishes). © ROBERT FRERCK/WOODFIN CAMP.

phone lines, with about 6.4 mainline phones in use for every 100 people.

24 Tourism, Travel, and Recreation

The beaches of Huatulco, 40 minutes by airplane trip from the capital, Oaxaca, are clean and natural. Tangolunda Bay draws tourists interested in the environment. Visitors to the Huatulco area enjoy water sports, scuba diving, snorkeling, and fishing. The coastal village of Puerto Escondido is a main tourist resort.

The city of Oaxaca features beautiful colonial architecture. The historic town center and the nearby Archeological site on Monté Alban are UNESCO World Heritage sites. Oaxaca is also famous for its black clay pottery artifacts. The Fiestas of Lunes del Cerro and the Festival de los Rábanos (Festival of the Radishes) in December draw many visitors.

25 Sports

Oaxaca has a AAA minor league baseball team, the Guerreros (Warriors), which plays in the 8,000-seat L. E. Vasconcelos stadium. In 2004, there were four major sports arenas in the state.

26 Famous People

Benito Juárez (1806–1872) was a Zapotec Indian who was born on March 21, 1806, in the Oaxaca village of San Pablo Guelatao. He served as president of Mexico for two terms. He is considered to be one of the most beloved Mexican leaders. His birthday is a national holiday. Porfirio Díaz (1830–1915) was a dictator who ruled Mexico from 1877 until 1911. Juana Inés de la Cruz (1651–1695), a 17th-century feminist writer, and Rufino Tamayo (1899–1991), a renowned Zapotec painter, were also natives of Oaxaca.

27 Bibliography

BOOKS

Carew-Miller, Anna. *Famous People of Mexico.* Philadelphia: Mason Crest Publishers, 2003.

Gruber, Beth. *Mexico.* Washington, DC: National Geographic, 2006.

Haden, Judith Cooper. *Oaxaca: The Spirit of Mexico.* New York, NY: Artisan, 2002.

Nantus, Sheryl. *The Pacific South States of Mexico.* Stockton, NJ: Mason Crest Publishers, 2003.

Norget, Kristin. *Days of Death, Days of Life: Ritual in the Popular Culture of Oaxaca.* New York: Columbia University Press, 2006.

Whipperman, Bruce. *Pacific Mexico: Including Acapulco, Puerto Vallarta, Oaxaca, Guadalajara and Mazatlán,* 5th edition. Emeryville, CA: Avalon Travel Pub., 2001.

WEB SITES

Government of Mexico. *Mexico for Kids.* www.elbalero.gob.mx/index_kids.html (accessed March 30, 2007).

Mexican Tourism Board. *Visit Mexico: Oaxaca.* www.visitmexico.com/wb/Visitmexico/Visi_Oxaca (accessed on March 30, 2007).

Puebla

PRONUNCIATION: PWEH-blah.

ORIGIN OF STATE NAME: The state of Puebla was named for its capital city, which was established by the Spaniards. New settlements were often called pueblas.

CAPITAL: Puebla. The formal name, Heroica Puebla de Zaragoza, honors Ignacio Zaragoza who led the Mexican army to defeat the French.

ENTERED COUNTRY: October 13, 1824.

COAT OF ARMS: The coat of arms is a shield divided into four squares: one depicts a factory, representing progress; the hydroelectric dam represents Puebla's contribution to the supply of electricity; the rifle commemorates the Civil War that began November 20, 1910; the human hand holding a plant with farm land in the background represents agriculture. The smaller shield in the center features a mountain landscape with a rising sun, marked 5 Mayo 1862. (This is the date that the Mexican army defeated the French.) At the top of the shield is a native symbol for the sun. The snakes along the sides are symbols of the Tolteca culture. Around the shield is the state motto *unidos en el tiempo en el esfuerzo en la justicia y en la esperanza* (United in time, in effort, in justice, and in hope).

HOLIDAYS: Año Nuevo (New Year's Day—January 1); Día de la Constitución (Constitution Day—February 5); Benito Juárez's birthday (March 21); Primero de Mayo (Labor Day—May 1); Anniversary of the Battle of Puebla (1862), May 5; Revolution Day, 1910 (November 20); and Navidad (Christmas—December 25).

FLAG: There is no official state flag.

TIME: 6 AM = noon Greenwich Mean Time (GMT).

1 Location and Size

Puebla is part of the central region of the country that is known as the breadbasket of Mexico. The state has an area of 34,292 square kilometers (13,240 square miles), which is twice the size of the US state of Hawaii. It ranks as 21st in size among the states and covers about 1.8% of the total land area of Mexico. It is bordered by the states of México, Morelos, Guerrero, Oaxaca, Veracruz, Hidalgo, and Tlaxcala. Puebla is divided into 217 municipalities (similar to US counties). Its capital city is also called Puebla.

The landscape is mountainous. Most of the central region of the state is crossed by the east-west belt known as the Sierra Volcánica

Transversal (also known as the Cordillera Neovolcánica). Some of the highest peaks in the country are found in this volcanic region. Pico de Orizaba (also called Citlaltépetl), which lies on the border with Veracruz and has an elevation of 5,610 meters (18,406 feet), is the highest peak in the state and the country. Volcán Popocatépetl, which lies west of the capital on the border with the state of México, has an elevation of about 5,465 meters (17,930 feet) and is the second-highest point in the country. Volcán Iztaccihuatl is the third-highest peak in the country at about 5,230 meters (17,454 feet). Sierra Negra and Malinche are the fifth- and sixth-highest peaks in the country.

The Sierra Madre Oriental cross over part of the northern branch of the state. The Sierra Madre del Sur begin near the southeast corner of the state. Wide valleys, such as the one where the capital is located, lie at high elevations.

There are dozens of small rivers in Puebla. The Necaxa River flows for about 200 kilometers (125 miles) through Puebla and Veracruz to the Gulf of Mexico. It provides water for irrigation and hydroelectric power. Near the Veracruz border, the Necaxa Falls cascade over 165 meters (540 feet). The San Pedro and Apulco are also in the north. The Nexapa and Atoyac are two main rivers in the south. Presa Valsequillo is a major reservoir along the Atoyac River. The mineral waters of the state's natural springs are believed to have healing properties.

2 Climate

Temperatures are fairly constant year-round, with variation depending on elevation. The daytime temperatures range from 21°C to 27°C (70°F to 80°F). At night, the temperature drops to around 4°C (45°F). There is little rainfall from November to March, but from April through October heavy afternoon rains are common. In the capital city of Puebla, the temperature ranges from an average low of 11°C (53°F) to an average high of 20°C (69°F). The average rainfall in the capital is 84 centimeters (33.1 inches) per year.

3 Plants and Animals

Pine, willow, and oak trees are common throughout the state. There are large forest areas in the Huachinango region. Animals common to the state include hares, raccoons, rabbits, and eagles. The quetzal, a green-feathered bird, is found in the Tezuitlán region.

4 Environmental Protection

In 2004, the state had 29 municipal wastewater treatment plants in operation with a combined installed capacity of 2,837 liters per second (749 gallons per second). The volume of treated wastewater that year was estimated at 2,186 liters per second (577 gallons per second). There were also 99 industrial wastewater treatment plants in operation that year. As of 2004, about 83.7% of the population had access to safe drinking water.

In 2003, the state had about 768,226 hectares (1.8 million acres) of woodland, including 307,455 hectares (759,737 acres) of rain forest. In 2004, about 68 hectares (168 acres) of woodland were damaged or destroyed by forest fires. An additional 3,070 hectares (7,586 acres) of pasture and brush land were also damaged by fires.

La Malinche National Park is a protected area shared with the state of Tlaxcala. The park

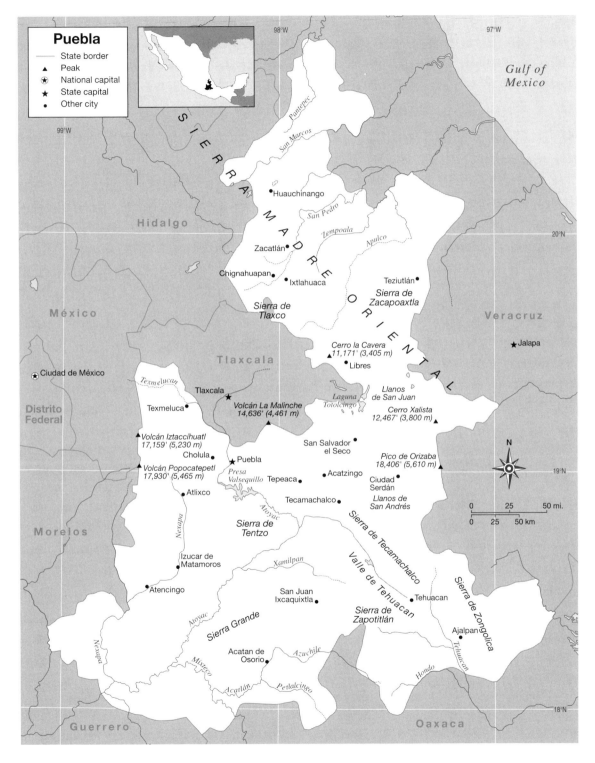

Puebla

- State border
- ▲ Peak
- ⊛ National capital
- ★ State capital
- • Other city

Gulf of Mexico

98°W

97°W

99°W

S I E R R A

Pantepec

San Marcos

Huauchinango

San Pedro

Hidalgo

Lempoala

20°N

Apulco

Zacatlán

M A D R E

Chignahuapan

Ixtlahuaca

Teziutlán

Sierra de Zacapoaxtla

México

Sierra de Tlaxco

O R I E N T A L

Veracruz

Cerro la Cavera
11,171' (3,405 m) ▲

★ Jalapa

Libres

Tlaxcala

Llanos de San Juan

Ciudad de México

Texmelucan

Tlaxcala ★

Laguna Totolcingo

Texmeluca

Volcán La Malinche
14,636' (4,461 m) ▲

Cerro Xalista
12,467' (3,800 m) ▲

Distrito
Federal

Volcán Iztaccíhuatl
17,159' (5,230 m) ▲

San Salvador
el Seco

Pico de Orizaba
18,406' (5,610 m) ▲

Cholula

★ Puebla

N

Volcán Popocatepetl
17,930' (5,465 m) ▲

Presa
Valsequillo

Tepeaca

Acatzingo

Ciudad
Serdán

19°N

Atlixco

Tecamachalco

Llanos de
San Andrés

0   25   50 mi.

0   25   50 km

Morelos

Atoyac

Sierra de
Tentzo

Sierra de Tecamachalco

Nexapa

Izucar de
Matamoros

Xamilpan

Valle de Tehuacan

Atencingo

San Juan
Ixcaquixtla

Tehuacan

Sierra de
Zapotitlán

Sierra de Zongolica

Atoyac

Sierra Grande

Ajalpan

Nexapa

Azuchile

Acatan de
Osorio

Tehuacan

Mixteco

Hondo

Acatlán

Petlalcingo

18°N

Guerrero

Oaxaca

is located at the base of the Malinche volcano (4,461 meters/14,636 feet). The Tehuacán-Cuicatlán Biosphere Reserve, with protected pine and oak forests, lies on the border with Oaxaca.

5 Population, Ethnic Groups, Languages

Puebla had an estimated total population of 5,478,900 in 2006, ranking fifth among the states and the Distrito Federal. About 48% of the population were men and 52% were women. About 52% of the population lived in urban areas. The population density was 161 people per square kilometer (418 people per square mile). The capital, Puebla, had a 2005 estimated population of 1,485,941. Almost all citizens speak Spanish as their first language. About 10% of the population speak indigenous (native) languages, including Náhuatl, Totoanac, and Mazateco.

6 Religions

According to the 2000 census, 91.6% of the population, or 3.9 million people, were Roman Catholic. About 4.3%, or 188,586 people, were mainline or evangelical Protestants. About 1.4% were counted as other Biblical faiths, including 42,415 Jehovah's Witnesses, 7,753 Seventh-day Adventists, and 12,601 Latter-day Saints (Mormons). There were 2,251 Jews. About 1.4% of the population claimed to have no religious affiliation.

There are several religious pilgrimage sites in the state. The Franciscan, Dominican, and Augustinian monks who converted the indigenous population to Christianity built monasteries along the slopes of Volcán Popocatépetl. These 16th-century monasteries have been preserved as UNESCO World Heritage sites. The Metropolitan Cathedral of Our Lady of the Immaculate Conception is the seat of the Roman Catholic archdiocese of Puebla.

7 Transportation

Puebla-Huejotsingo Airport provides international flights to and from Puebla. The state has about 8,046 kilometers (4,998 miles) of roads and 709 kilometers (440 miles) of railroads. In 2004, there were 420,082 automobiles registered in the state, along with 8,352 passenger trucks, 256,407 freight trucks, and 10,972 motorcycles.

8 History

Archeological evidence points to a civilization that developed agriculture and established sedentary human settlements in the region around 6000 BC. Olmec influence was clear in Puebla starting in 1000 BC. Around 300 AD. Teotihuacán culture was present in the region, especially in Cholula. The Totonaca culture developed in the northern part of Puebla. Mixtec Indians occupied Cholula starting in 900 AD. In the 12th century, an exiled Toltec-Chichimec group from Tula occupied the region. Mexicas occupied most of the region starting in the 14th century.

In 1519, on their way to Tenochtitlán, Mexico (present-day Mexico City), Spanish conqueror Hernán Cortés' (1485–1547) troops occupied Huejotzingo and Cholula. They killed most of the native people living there. In 1520, the Spanish conquistadors (those who sought to conqueror Mexico for Spain) controlled most important villages and human settlements in the region. After the fall of the Aztec empire, the Spaniards moved on to conquer the remaining indigenous territories in Puebla. In 1524, massive land grants, known as *encomiendas*, were assigned by the Spanish crown to the conquistadors. The purpose of the *encomiendas* was to promote the exploitation of the land for agricultural and mining. Cattle ranching and sugarcane and silk production were developed during the late 16th century. Franciscan priests initiated the conversion of indigenous groups to the Roman Catholic faith starting in 1524.

During the early 17th century, the most important textile factories of the Spanish American colonies were situated in the city of Puebla. A printing press brought in 1640 reflected Puebla's importance as a commercial, agricultural, and industrial center in Mexico. Yet, the indigenous population was decimated rapidly. They died from poor living conditions forced on them by the Spanish colonizers. They also died from diseases brought by the Spaniards to the new continent.

The independence movement came to Puebla in 1811. Fierce resistance from Spanish royalists (people loyal to Spain) prevented a decisive victory by the pro-independence fighters. The independence fighters were led by José Morelos (1765–1815). Neither side exercised definitive control of the state until Agustín de Iturbide (1783–1824) led his army into Puebla and declared independence in 1821.

Between the late 1820s and 1867, Puebla was characterized by constant conflicts between different factions and internal power disputes. First, federalists against centralists and later, liberals against conservatives faced off in confusing and often bloody battles for the control of one of the most economically and strategically impor-

tant states in the federation. The Battle of Puebla was one of the most symbolically important battles. It took place on May 5, 1862, when French troops invaded Mexico. They faced fierce resistance by Mexican patriots loyal to constitutional president Benito Juárez (1806–1872).

Porfirio Díaz (1830–1915) followed Juárez as president of Mexico. Díaz's reign in power is often referred to as the Porfiriato period. Puebla experienced healthy and sustained economic growth resulting from agriculture, cattle production, and textiles. As in the rest of the country, growth of the infrastructure was central to the economic development plan pushed for by authoritarian leader Porfirio Díaz.

The Mexican Revolution, which began in 1910, was fiercely fought in Puebla. Revolutionary leader Emiliano Zapata (1879–1919) fought against those opposed to land redistribution and peasants' rights. Eventually, the winners of the revolution imposed their more moderate views and the revolts were pacified.

After the revolution, Puebla evolved to become an industrial center, but its large rural population remained largely impoverished. People in rural areas had limited access to the benefits of economic development.

In the first decade of the 21st century, the state of Puebla was one of Mexico's chief industrial centers and accounted for an important share of Mexico's gross domestic Product (GDP). Although Puebla had a strong, diverse economy, the state, as with other Mexican states, faced problems with official corruption and rural poverty.

9 State and Local Government

The state governor is democratically elected every six years for a nonrenewable term. The legislature is comprised of a unicameral (single chamber) congress elected every three years, with no immediate re-election provisions. Its 41 members are made up of 26 legislators elected from single-member districts and 15 elected by proportional representation.

The 217 municipalities that comprise Puebla hold democratic elections for municipal presidents and council members every three years. Immediate re-election is not allowed. Because of the widely varying size and financial resources of the different municipalities, decentralization efforts have produced mixed results in recent years.

10 Political Parties

The three main political parties in all of Mexico are the Institutional Revolutionary Party (PRI), the National Action Party (PAN), and the Party of the Democratic Revolution (PRD). The PRI has historically dominated power in Puebla since the end of the Mexican Revolution. Puebla is one of the PRI strongholds. Governor Manuel Bartlett (1993–99) unsuccessfully sought the PRI presidential nomination in 2000. Mario Marín Torres of the PRI won the gubernatorial election of 2004. Although they have made electoral gains in the larger urban areas, the PAN and the PRD remain largely minority parties in Puebla.

Because the Institutional Revolutionary Party (PRI) continues to dominate the executive and legislative branches, constitutional provisions for separation of power have not been fully implemented.

11 Judicial System

The Superior Tribunal of Justice is the highest court in the state. Its members are appointed by the legislature from a three-person list presented to it by the state governor. Only highly qualified attorneys can be appointed to the highest court. Because Puebla has been ruled exclusively by the PRI since the end of the revolution, the judiciary has historically exercised little independence and autonomy.

12 Economy

Puebla's economy is highly diversified and it is one of Mexico's top seven states in contributions to the gross domestic product (GDP). As of 2003, there were some 80,000 firms in the state, of which 40% were located in the capital city of Puebla. Manufacturing, general service-based companies, trade activities, finance, insurance, and transportation and communication firms account for the majority of the state's economic activities, although there are vibrant agriculture and livestock sectors.

13 Industry

Puebla's manufacturing activity centers on the automotive and textile industries. Volkswagen is one of the major companies with facilities in the state, along with a number of primary and secondary suppliers to the plant. The textile industry is centered in the capital city of Puebla. Other industries in the state include petrochemicals, paper, and sugar processing.

The El Parian market in the capital, Puebla. © ROBERT FRERCK/WOODFIN CAMP.

The state's handicraft industry produces paintings, embroidered cloth, ceramics and pottery, and other items made from clay, stone, palm leaves, and reeds.

14 Labor

As of 2005, the state of Puebla had 2,282,864 eligible workers. Some 2,218,848 were listed as employed and 63,976 were listed as unemployed. Unemployed workers in rural areas may not be counted, however. The unemployment rate that year was reported to be 2.8%. Of those who were working, services employed 28.4%, followed by agriculture at 26.7% and manufacturing at 19.8%.

The US Bureau of Labor Statistics reported that Mexican workers saw their wages increase from $2.49 per hour in 2003 to $2.50 per hour in 2004. (The average US worker earned $15.70 per hour in 2004.) The maximum work week is set at 48 hours by law. The average worker spends 40 to 45 hours per week on the job. Workers earn twice their regular hourly rate for up to nine hours a week of overtime. When a worker works more than nine hours overtime in a week, he or she earns three times the regular hourly rate. After one year, workers are entitled by law to six days paid vacation.

In the capital city of Puebla, several labor unions are active. These include: the National Union of Workers (UNT), the Mexican Workers

Confederation (CTM), and the Revolutionary Confederation of Workers and Farmers (CROC). UNT's membership includes the Independent Union of Volkswagen workers, which represents 10,300 workers at the Volkswagen plant in Puebla.

15 Agriculture

The main agricultural crops throughout Puebla are corn, coffee, avocados, beans, wheat, onions, tomatoes, peanuts, oats, sorghum, sugar, and alfalfa. Apples are another important crop. The Huachinango region even hosts an annual apple fair. Other fruit crops produced in the state include mangos, grapes, oranges, lemons, and peaches. Potatoes are an important crop in the Ciudad Serdán region, which also hosts a regional fair to celebrate this crop.

Livestock includes cattle (for both meat and dairy products), pigs, and poultry. In some areas, donkeys are raised as well. The San Pedro Cholula region is known for its honey, milk, cream, and cheese production. The Tehuacán region is one of the nation's most important producers of poultry and eggs.

In 2004, crop production for the state of Puebla included: 855,354 tons of corn, 66,240 tons of potatoes, 44,177 tons of sorghum, 196,522 tons of sugar, 17,659 tons of red tomatoes, 33,169 tons of kidney beans, and 11,701 tons of avocados. Livestock brought to market included: 87,596 head of beef cattle, 298,940 pigs, 4,398 goats, and 15,299 sheep. In that same year, the state produced: 365 million liters (96 million gallons) of milk from dairy cows, 429,754 tons of eggs, and 3,231 tons of honey. Meat production included: 30,609 tons of beef,

75,742 tons of pork, 3,237 tons of goat, 2,592 tons of lamb, and 157,900 tons of poultry.

16 Natural Resources

As of 2006, the state of Puebla was known to have deposits of gold, silver, copper, and lead. However, the mining sector was not significantly developed. The state also has the potential to become a producer of lumber. In 2003, the value of forest wood production was about $16.8 million. Pine and oyamel (a type of fir) were the primary types of wood harvested. In 2003, the fish catch totaled at about 5,300 tons.

17 Energy and Power

In 2005, there were 1,385,529 users of electricity in the state of Puebla. Of that total, the largest number were residential customers at 1,202,394. Sales of electricity that same year totaled 6,462,136 megawatt hours, of which the largest users were medium-sized industrial firms at 2,343,270 megawatt hours. Electric power in Puebla is generated by five power plants: one gas-turbine, one geothermal, and three hydroelectric stations. They have a combined capacity of 524 megawatts. Electricity is provided by the Federal Electricity Commission and Central Light and Power. Both utilities are run by the Mexican government.

18 Health

In 2003, the state had 63 hospitals and 952 outpatient centers that were part of the national health system. In 2004, there were about 3,409 doctors, 7,786 nurses, and 331 dentists working in these health centers. There were an additional

128 independent health centers in the state in 2004.

Most of the Mexican population is covered under a government health plan. The IMSS (Instituto Mexicano de Seguro Social) covers the general population. The ISSSTE (Instituto de Seguridad y Servicios Sociales de Trabajadores del Estado) covers state workers.

19 Housing

Most homes are built with materials such as concrete, brick, and stone. Adobe homes with tile or sheet metal roofs are common in some areas. In 2000, about 79% of all homes were owner-occupied. In 2005, there were an estimated 1,207,470 residential housing units in the state. About 83% of these units were single-family detached homes. The average household was estimated at 4.5 people.

20 Education

Public education in Mexico is free for students from ages 6 to 16. While most students in the state attend public schools, in 2002/03 about 22% of high school students attended private schools. In 2004/05, it was estimated that 91% of age-eligible students completed primary school, which includes six years of study. About 83.6% of eligible students completed secondary school, which includes three years of study after primary school. About 68.1% of eligible students completed the *bachillerato*, which is similar to a high school diploma. The national average for completion of the *bachillerato* was 60.1% that year.

There are at least seven institutions of higher learning in the state, including the Universidad de las Américas, Puebla (University of the

The voladores *(people who fly) perform during the October* feria *(festival) in Cuetzalan.* © KAL MULLER/WOODFIN CAMP.

Americas, Puebla) and the National Institute of Astrophysics, Optics, and Electronics. In 2005, there were about 143,420 students ages 20 and older who were enrolled in some type of higher education program. The overall literacy rate was estimated at 86.9% in 2005.

21 Arts

Puebla has many cultural centers and theaters. The Teatro Carpa Carlos Ancira is a theater for the blind. The folk ballet company, Ballet Folklórico of Puebla, performs regularly. Local artisans produce handicrafts, including clay pottery, wooden masks, and fiber works. An annual Nopales Cactus Festival is held in Tlaxcalancingo, featuring foods made from this local plant. The annual Concert of the Bells in Cholula (November) celebrates the sound of the local church bells. The town is said to have the most churches and altars in Mexico, with 365—one for each day of the year.

In October, Cuetzalan hosts a *feria* (festival) that features *voladores* (people who fly). The *voladores* dress in colorful costumes, and climb to the top of a pole 150 feet (45 meters) tall. The *voladores* then tie their ankles to ropes wound around the pole and leap into the air. They fly around and around the pole as the rope unwinds. Their flight is accompanied by flute music.

There are over 100 registered movie theaters, including multiscreen theaters and single-screen galleries.

22 Libraries and Museums

In 2003, there were 595 libraries in the state with a combined stock of 2,866,980 volumes. The same year, there were 26 museums registered in the state that had permanent exhibits. Prominent museums include the Puebla Regional Museum of Anthropology and History, the Museum of Colonial Religious Art, and the Jose Luis Bello y Gonzalez Museum of Art.

23 Media

In 2005, the capital city, Puebla, had ten daily newspapers. *El Sol de Puebla* (*Puebla Sun*) was one of the largest with a circulation of about 67,000. Others included *El Heraldo*, *Cambio* (*Change*), *El Financiero* (*The Financer*), and *La Voz de Puebla*

(*Puebla Voice*). Tehuacan had two daily newspapers: *El Mundo de Tehuacan* (*Tehuacan World*) and *El Sol de Tehuacan* (*Tehuacan Sun*).

In 2004, there were 55 television stations and 38 radio stations (22 AM and 16 FM). In 2005, there were about 139,838 subscribers to cable and satellite television stations. Also in 2005, there were about 599,979 residential phone lines, with about 13.2 mainline phones in use for every 100 people.

24 Tourism, Travel, and Recreation

Buildings and ruins from the colonial and pre-Columbian period may be found in the city of Cholula, where there is a site with pre-Columbian pyramids and a church built in the 18th century. Tourists enjoy visiting the cathedral and the El Parian marketplace, both in the capital, Puebla. Tourists also enjoy sampling foods that originated in the state, including mole sauce (spicy chocolate sauce of Aztec origin) and chalupas. The historic town center of Puebla is a UNESCO World Heritage site. Tourists also are drawn to the mineral springs of Tehuacan and the thermal baths of Chignahuapan. Volcán Popocatépetl draws both hikers and religious tourists who come to visit the 16th-century monasteries built along the slopes of the volcano. La Malinche National Park also draws many visitors.

25 Sports

Los Lobos (Wolves) of the Benemérita Universidad Autónoma de Puebla and Club Puebla compete as First Division "A" teams in the Mexican Football (soccer) Association (commonly known as Femexfut). The home field for both teams is at the 42,684-seat Cuahutehmoc stadium. There are two Mexican League, AAA baseball teams, Los Pericos (Parrots) and Los Tigres (Tigers). Both teams play in the Estadio Hermanos Serdán. In 2004, there were seven sports arenas in the state.

26 Famous People

The ceramic artist Herón Martinez Mendozo is from Acatlán, Puebla. His work is included in the Nelson A. Rockefeller collection of Mexican art at California's Mexican Museum. His relatives in Acatlán continue to produce ceramic works from his designs.

27 Bibliography

BOOKS

Day-MacLeod, Deirdre. *The States of Central Mexico*. Philadelphia, PA: Mason Crest Publishers, 2003.

Gruber, Beth. *Mexico*. Washington, DC: National Geographic, 2006.

WEB SITES

Government of Mexico. *Mexico for Kids*. www.elbalero.gob.mx/index_kids.html (accessed on March 30, 2007).

Mexican Tourism Board. *Visit Mexico: Puebla*. www.visitmexico.com/wb/Visitmexico/Visi_Puebla (accessed on March 30, 2007).

Querétaro

PRONUNCIATION: keh-REH-taw-rwo.

ORIGIN OF STATE NAME: The name comes from the native word *queréndaro*, which means "the place of the crags" (rocky terrain).

CAPITAL: Santiago de Querétaro (The name was officially changed to Santiago de Querétaro from Querétaro in July 1996, but it is still commonly known as Querétaro.)

ENTERED COUNTRY: October 3, 1824.

COAT OF ARMS: The coat of arms features a shield divided into three sections. A picture of the Sun with a human face is at the top of the shield, underneath the symbol of the cross. A horseman carrying a flag is pictured next to a picture of a tree. The flags that surround the shield are Mexican flags. The figure on top of the shield is the Mexican coat of arms.

HOLIDAYS: Año Nuevo (New Year's Day—January 1); Día de la Constitución (Constitution Day—February 5); Benito Juárez's birthday (March 21); Primero de Mayo (Labor Day—May 1); Anniversary of the Battle of Puebla (1862), May 5; Revolution Day, 1910 (November 20); and Navidad (Christmas—December 25).

FLAG: There is no official state flag.

TIME: 6 AM = noon Greenwich Mean Time (GMT).

1 Location and Size

Querétaro is located in the central region of the country known as the breadbasket of Mexico. It covers an area of 11,684 square kilometers (4,511 square miles), which is about half the size of the US state of New Hampshire. It ranks as 27th in size among the states and covers about 0.6% of the total land area of Mexico. Querétaro is bordered on the north by San Luis Potosí, on the east by the states of México and Michoacán, and on the west by Guanajuato. Querétaro is divided into 18 municipalities (similar to US counties). The capital is Santiago de Querétaro.

The landscape is marked by the central highland plateau and two large mountain ranges (sierras). The Sierra Gorda in the north is part of the Sierra Madre Oriental; it is made up of high peaks, small valleys, and deep canyons. In the south, there are mountains of volcanic origin known as the Sierra Volcánica Transversal (also known as the Cordillera Neovolcánica). The Sierra de Amealco and the Sierra Pinal de Zamorano are part of this region. The highest point in the state is Cerro Zamorano, which rises to an elevation of about 3,360 meters (11,023 feet) near the border with Guanajuato.

The Moctezuma River, which flows along part of the southeastern border, is one of the largest rivers. The Lerma River flows along part of the southwest border. The largest lakes, including Presa Constitucíon de 1917 and Presa La Llave, are reservoirs created by river dams.

2 Climate

The climate in the south is usually cool and humid, with abundant rain in the summer, hail, and frequent frosts. In the central part of the state, the climate is dry or semi-dry, with very little rainfall. The northern region is sometimes referred to as the Querétaro desert zone because it is so dry.

In the capital city of Santiago de Querétaro, the average year-round temperature is 18°C (64°F). The temperature rarely goes below 10°C (50°F). Average rainfall is about 59.7 centimeters (23.5 inches) per year.

3 Plants and Animals

Thorny, sturdy plants grow in the dry regions of the state. These include ocotillo (a woody, thorny shrub) and nopal cactus (prickly pear). Pine and oak forests cover some of the highland region. White-tailed deer are common. Smaller mammals include raccoons, weasels, squirrels, skunks, and tlacuaches (Mexican opossum). Hawks, woodpeckers, sparrows, and doves are common birds.

4 Environmental Protection

In 2004, the state had 51 municipal wastewater treatment plants in operation with a combined installed capacity of 946 liters per second (249 gallons per second). The volume of treated wastewater that year was estimated at 657 liters per second (173 gallons per second). There were also 131 industrial wastewater treatment plants in operation that year. As of 2004, about 95.4% of the population had access to safe drinking water.

In 2003, the state had about 247,372 hectares (601,385 acres) of woodland, including 67,211 hectares (166,082 acres) of rain forest. In 2004, only 3 hectares (7.4 acres) of woodland were damaged or destroyed by forest fires. An additional 252 hectares (622 acres) of pasture and brush land were also damaged by fires.

The Sierra Gorda Biosphere Reserve covers about 383,567 hectares (947,814 acres) in Querétaro. The reserve is home to several endangered and threatened species, including black bears, jaguars, the green toucan, and the Humboldt butterfly. There are two national parks in the state: Cerro de las Campanas and El Cimatario. Presa Jalpan in the northern part of the state was designated as a Ramsar Wetland of International Importance in 2004, in part to protect the migratory bird population.

5 Population, Ethnic Groups, Languages

Querétaro had an estimated total population of 1,628,500 in 2006, ranking 23rd among the states and the Distrito Federal. About 49% of the population were men and 51% were women. About 66% of the population lived in urban

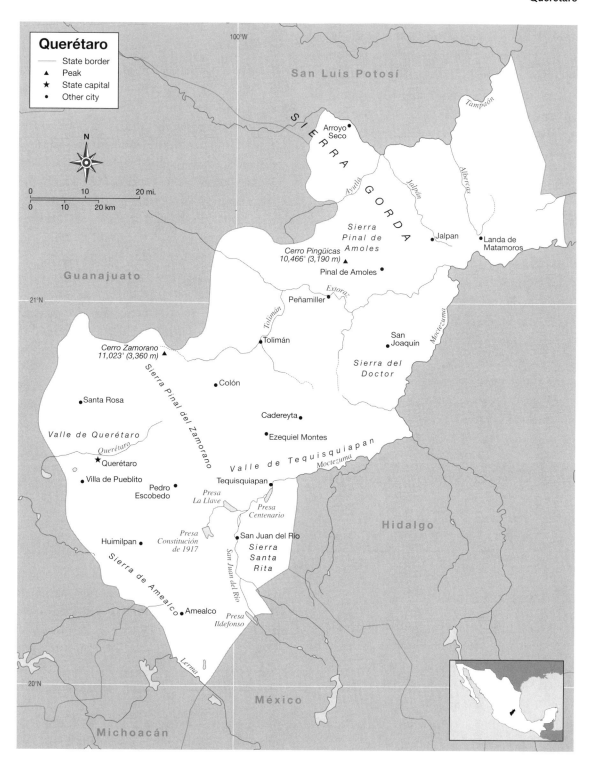

Querétaro

- —— State border
- ▲ Peak
- ★ State capital
- • Other city

N

0   10   20 mi.
0   10   20 km

San Luis Potosí

S I E R R A

G O R D A

Tampaón

Arroyo Seco

Ayutla

Jalpán

Alberca

Sierra Pinal de Amoles

Jalpan

Landa de Matamoros

Cerro Pingüicas
10,466' (3,190 m) ▲

Pinal de Amoles

Guanajuato

21°N

Extoraz

Peñamiller

Tolimán

Tolimán

San Joaquín

Moctezuma

Sierra del Doctor

Cerro Zamorano
11,023' (3,360 m) ▲

Colón

Santa Rosa

Cadereyta

Valle de Querétaro

Ezequiel Montes

Querétaro

Valle de Tequisquiapan

Moctezuma

★ Querétaro

Villa de Pueblito

Tequisquiapan

Pedro Escobedo

Presa La Llave

Presa Centenario

Hidalgo

Huimilpan

Presa Constitución de 1917

San Juan del Río

San Juan del Río

Sierra Santa Rita

Sierra de Amealco

Amealco

Presa Ildefonso

Lerma

20°N

México

Michoacán

100°W

areas. The population density was 138 people per square kilometer (358 people per square mile). In 2005, the capital, Santiago de Querétaro, had an estimated population of 734,139. Almost all citizens speak Spanish as their first language. A small percentage of the population, speaks indigenous (native) languages, including Otomi.

6 Religions

According to the 2000 census, 95.3% of the population, or 1.1 million people, were Roman Catholic; about 1.9%, or 23,461 people, were mainline or evangelical Protestants. Less than 1% were counted as other Biblical faiths, including 7,764 Jehovah's Witnesses, 1,657 Seventh-day Adventists, and 1,460 Latter-day Saints (Mormons). Less than 1% of the population claimed to have no religious affiliation.

There are many churches in the state and many religious festivals held throughout the year. One popular festival is the feast of San Miguel Arcángel, held on September 29 in San Miguel de Allende to celebrate the city's patron saint. There are five Franciscan mission sites located in the Sierra Gorda. Built in the mid-18th century, they were designated as UNESCO World Heritage sites in 2003.

7 Transportation

Querétaro Airport provides international flights to and from the state. The state has about 7,822 kilometers (4,858 miles) of roads and 879 kilometers (546 miles) of railroads. In 2004, there were 154,064 automobiles registered in the state, along with 3,984 passenger trucks, 88,831 freight trucks, and 4,377 motorcycles.

8 History

The first human settlements date back to around 400 AD. The Teotihuacán culture populated the area for several centuries. Later inhabited by the Otomi civilizations, the Mexicas conquered the region a couple of centuries before the arrival of the Spanish conquistadors (explorers and soldiers who sought to claim Mexico for Spain). The Otomi people became allies of the Spanish conquerors and joined forces to defeat the Mexicas in the Querétaro region. Cristóbal de Olid was the first Spaniard to visit the region in 1522.

Between 1522 and 1526, two Otomi leaders had converted to Roman Catholicism. They changed their names to Fernando de Tapia and Nicolás de San Luis Montañez. They founded the city of Santiago de Querétaro. The city grew and consolidated as an agricultural and commercial center during the 16th and 17th centuries. It was officially named the third city of the viceroyalty of Mexico in 1671. A famous and impressive aqueduct was built in Querétaro between 1726 and 1739.

National heroes Miguel Hidalgo y Costilla (1753–1811) and Mariano Matamoros (1770–1814) were priests in the region when they initiated the independence movement against Spanish rule in 1810. With the defeat of the independence forces two years later, the region was brought back into royalist rule, although some pro-independence militias remained active throughout the 1810s. With the formal declaration of independence in 1821, Querétaro was made a province. It achieved the status of federal state in 1824. The first state constitution dates back to 1825.

During the federalist-centralist and liberal-conservative conflicts of most of the 19th cen-

A famous and impressive aqueduct was built in Querétaro between 1726 and 1739. PETER LANGER.

tury, Querétaro experienced political and social instability. Different leaders revolted against state and national authorities, with varying levels of success. For a short period of time (from 1863 to 1867), Querétaro and much of Mexico was under French occupation and the rule of Emperor Maximilian (1832–1867). When Maximilian was forced to abandon Mexico City in 1867, he sought refuge in Querétaro. He was later defeated and arrested there. Monarchical rule was abolished. Emperor Maximilian was tried and sentenced to death. He was executed in Querétaro on June 19, 1867.

When the liberals, under the leadership of Benito Juárez (1806–1872), regained control of the country, Querétaro was occupied by liberal loyal troops. During the Porfiriato period (the years that Porfirio Díaz [1830–1872] was in power [1877–80 and 1884–1911]), Querétaro experienced economic and infrastructural development. Some Protestant churches, most notably the Methodist Church, also established a presence in the region during Porfirio Díaz's rule.

A strike by the railroad workers was violently repressed by the government in 1909. This growing tension between workers and the government partially led to the Mexican Revolution in 1910. Different factions fought for control of Querétaro during the first years of the revolution, which lasted from 1910 to 1920. When the Mexican constitution was ratified in 1917,

Querétaro was under the rule of the revolutionary victors.

The Cristero War was a conflict between those loyal to the Roman Catholic Church leadership and the revolutionary government. It affected Querétaro to a small degree. Its violence mostly ended with the end of the revolution in 1920. During the post-revolutionary decades, Querétaro evolved as an industrial center. It benefited from its proximity to the capital city of Mexico. Querétaro's economy was largely industrial. The Institutional Revolutionary Party (PRI) was powerful in rural Mexico, but it was not as effective in Querétaro. The National Action Party (PAN) emerged as a viable political alternative in Querétaro in 1997. Three years later, in 2000, the PAN candidate defeated the PRI candidate in the national presidential election for the first time.

In the first decade of the 21st century, the economy of Querétaro continued to benefit from Mexico's participation in the North American Free Trade Agreement (NAFTA). Politically, the state remained peaceful, while PAN continued to hold the state's governorship.

9 State and Local Government

The state governor is elected for a nonrenewable six-year term. The state legislature is a unicameral (single chamber) assembly comprised of 25 members. Fifteen members are elected in single member districts and 10 are elected by proportional representation. Legislators serve for three-year terms and immediate re-election is not allowed.

The 18 municipalities that comprise Querétaro hold democratic elections for municipal presidents and council members every three years. Immediate re-election is not allowed. Although some decentralization initiatives are producing positive results, the state still has a long way to go to achieve successful decentralization.

10 Political Parties

The three main political parties in all of Mexico are the Institutional Revolutionary Party (PRI), the National Action Party (PAN), and the Party of the Democratic Revolution (PRD). Although the PRI tightly dominated state politics throughout most of the 20th century, the PAN emerged as a powerful party in the late 1980s. The PAN first won a gubernatorial election in 1997. The PAN won its second consecutive gubernatorial election in 2003 when Francisco Garrido Patrón became state governor.

The Institutional Revolutionary Party (PRI) does not hold the governorship, but it maintains a strong presence in the legislature. Because no one party controls the executive and legislative branches of government, constitutional provisions for separation of power are put to work.

11 Judicial System

The Superior Tribunal of Justice is the highest court in the state. Its ten members are elected by the legislature from a three-person list presented to it by the governor. After their three-year terms expire, they can be reappointed. Only qualified attorneys can be appointed to the highest court. In addition, an electoral tribunal court and lower courts also comprise the state's judicial system.

12 Economy

The economy of the state of Querétaro has been increasingly based on manufacturing, although agriculture, livestock raising, and mining remain important sectors. The state's economy has also been affected by its proximity to the nation's capital and the location of Highway 57 (the NAFTA Highway) which runs through the state and its capital city of Querétaro, conveniently linking it to the United States border.

13 Industry

Industrial activity in Querétaro is centered on food processing industries (dairy products, baby food, canned vegetables and fruit), chemical fertilizers, and farm vehicles. Companies such as Kellogg, Delphi, Gerber, Nestle, Siemens, Kimberly Clark, and General Electric are among those firms that have operations in the state. Most manufacturing companies are in or around the capital city.

The state's handicrafts industry produces furniture, items made from reeds and wicker, stone and marble fountains, basketworks, pottery, woolen textiles, metalwork, and jewelry.

14 Labor

As of 2005, the state of Querétaro had 646,874 eligible workers. Some 621,504 were listed as employed, and 25,370 were listed as unemployed. Unemployed workers in rural areas may not be counted, however. The unemployment rate that year was reported to be 3.9%. Of those who were working, services employed 38.5%, followed by manufacturing at 22.2%, and commerce at 19.8%.

The US Bureau of Labor Statistics reported that Mexican workers saw their wages increase from $2.49 per hour in 2003 to $2.50 per hour in 2004. (The average US worker earned $15.70 per hour in 2004.) The maximum work week is set at 48 hours by law. The average worker spends 40 to 45 hours per week on the job. Workers earn twice their regular hourly rate for up to nine hours a week of overtime. When a worker works more than nine hours overtime in a week, he or she earns three times the regular hourly rate. After one year, workers are entitled by law to six days paid vacation.

Labor relations in the capital city of Querétaro generally are good and strikes are not frequent.

15 Agriculture

Agriculture is one of the main economic activities. Primary crops include beans, cabbage, alfalfa, onions, lettuce, animal feed, barley, green chilies, and sorghum. Livestock breeding, especially of dairy cows, is important in the pasturelands. The state of Querétaro is one of the leading milk producers in the country.

In 2004, crop production for the state of Querétaro included: 307,361 tons of corn, 64,773 tons of sorghum, 11,316 tons of red tomatoes, and 7,282 tons of green chilies. Livestock brought to market in 2004 included: 71,645 head of beef cattle, 175,153 pigs, 11,603 goats, and 3,265 sheep. In that same year, the state produced 209 million liters (55 million gallons) of milk from dairy cows, 621,000 liters of goat's milk, and 25,154 tons of eggs. Meat production included: 29,526 tons of beef, 15,148 tons of pork, 224 tons of goat, 699 tons of lamb, and 205,082 tons of poultry.

16 Natural Resources

Mineral resources include zinc, lead, and mercury. The state is also well-known for its fire opals and is a major center for amethysts and topaz cutting. The chief mining districts are in Cadereyta and Tolimán. The forest industry is fairly small. In 2003, the total value of forest wood was only about $331,259. Pine was the primary wood harvested. In 2003, the total fish catch was about 700 tons, all for human consumption.

17 Energy and Power

In 2005, there were 434,767 users of electricity in the state of Querétaro. Of that total, the largest number were residential customers at 377,042. Sales of electricity that same year totaled 3,374,595 megawatt hours, of which the largest users were medium-sized industrial firms at 1,412,587 megawatt hours. Electric power in Querétaro is generated from a single 620 megawatt capacity combined cycle (gas-turbine and steam) plant in Pedro Escobedo. Electricity is provided by the Federal Electricity Commission, and Central Light and Power. Both utilities are run by the Mexican government.

Querétaro's electricity consumption in the 1990s was low compared to the rest of Mexico. After the passage of the North American Free Trade Agreement (NAFTA)—a trade agreement between Mexico, the United States, and Canada—electricity consumption grew because of the manufacturing facilities that were built in the state.

18 Health

In 2003, the state had 9 hospitals and 288 outpatient centers that were part of the national health system. In 2004, there were about 1,243 doctors, 2,357 nurses, and 100 dentists working in these health centers. There were an additional 56 independent health centers in the state in 2004.

Most of the Mexican population is covered under a government health plan. The IMSS (Instituto Mexicano de Seguro Social) covers the general population. The ISSSTE (Instituto de Seguridad y Servicios Sociales de Trabajadores del Estado) covers state workers.

19 Housing

Most homes are built with materials such as concrete, stone, or brick. In 2000, about 82% of all homes were owner-occupied. In 2005, there were an estimated 359,953 residential housing units in the state. About 91% of these units were single-family detached homes. The average household was estimated at 4.4 people.

20 Education

Public education in Mexico is free for students from ages 6 to 16 and most students in the state attend public schools. In 2002/03, about 12% of primary and secondary school students and 27% of high school students attended private schools. In 2004/05, it was estimated that 95.8% of age-eligible students completed primary school, which includes six years of study. About 77.2% of eligible students completed secondary school, which includes three years of study after primary school. About 60.7% of eligible students completed the *bachillerato*, which is similar to a high

Tequisquiapan, about two hours' drive from Mexico City, is a popular weekend destination for residents of the congested city. Tequisquiapan has a central plaza with a church with a single bell tower on one side and shops and restaurants on the other three. PETER LANGER.

school diploma. The national average for completion of the *bachillerato* was 60.1% that year.

The Universidad Autónoma de Querétaro (Autonomous University of Querétaro) is located in the capital. There are at least three other major institutions of higher education in the state. In 2005, there were about 48,893 students ages 20 and older who were enrolled in some type of higher education program. The overall literacy rate was estimated at 90% in 2005.

21 Arts

Querétaro has nine local cultural centers and at least 20 theaters for the performing arts, including those located at the Universidad Autónoma

de Querétaro. Querétaro also hosts many musical, art, and dance presentations. The Escuela de Danza Nijinsky is a school of ballet. The city of San Miguel de Allende is home to many artists and writers. The San Miguel music festival in December is famous. There is also a festival on September 29 each year to honor San Miguel Arcángel, the city's patron saint. There are over 50 registered movie theaters, including multiscreen theaters and single-screen galleries.

22 Libraries and Museums

In 2003, there were 152 libraries in the state with a combined stock of 1,047,171 volumes. The same year, there were 18 museums registered in the state that had permanent exhibits. There is a Mathematics Museum located on the campus of the Autonomous University of Querétaro. The Art Museum of Querétaro is also located in the capital city, as is the Querétaro Regional Museum.

23 Media

In 2005, there were three major daily newspapers published in the state: *El Sol de San Juan del Río* (*San Juan del Rio Sun*), *El Financiero* (*The Financer*), and *Noticias* (*News*).

In 2004, there were 9 television stations and 19 radio stations (11 AM and 8 FM). In 2005, there were about 86,059 subscribers to cable and satellite television stations. Also in 2005, there were about 206,756 residential phone lines, with about 17.6 mainline phones in use for every 100 people.

24 Tourism, Travel, and Recreation

San Miguel de Allende attracts many foreign tourists. San Miguel is as the home of many artists and writers and is known for its excellent restaurants. Two points of interest in this colonial city are La Parroquia (a pink Gothic-style church) and El Chorro, a natural spring where women of the town still do laundry. The capital city, Santiago de Querétaro, has an archeological zone known as El Cerrito; ruins from pre-Hispanic civilizations dating from the first century may be viewed there. The city also has an aqueduct that was built in 1743. The historic monument zone of the city of Santiago de Querétaro was made a UNESCO World Heritage site in 1996.

25 Sports

The Santiago de Querétaro Cometas (Comets) play in the South Zone of the National Professional Basketball League (LNBP). The Querétaro Deportivo (Sports) compete in the First Division of the Mexican Football (soccer) Association (commonly known as Femexfut). Their home field is at the 40,785-seat La Corregidora stadium. There is a 12,000-seat bullfighting ring in the Plaza Santa María.

26 Famous People

Francisco Garrido Patrón became governor in 2003.

27 Bibliography

BOOKS

Day-MacLeod, Deirdre. *The States of Central Mexico*. Philadelphia, PA: Mason Crest Publishers, 2003.

Gruber, Beth. *Mexico*. Washington, DC: National Geographic, 2006.

WEB SITES

Government of Mexico. *Mexico for Kids*. www. elbalero.gob.mx/index_kids.html (accessed on March 30, 2007).

Mexican Tourism Board. *Visit Mexico: Queretaro*. www.visitmexico.com/wb/Visitmexico/Visi_ Queretaro (accessed on March 30, 2007).

Quintana Roo

PRONUNCIATION: keen-TAH-nah ROH-oh.

ORIGIN OF STATE NAME: The state was named after Andrés de Quintana Roo (1787–1851), who fought for Mexican independence.

CAPITAL: Chetumal (cheh-too-MAHL).

ENTERED COUNTRY: 1974.

COAT OF ARMS: A rising sun with seven rays represents the first seven municipalities of Quintana Roo. The symbol in the upper left represents a marine shell marking the state's position on the Caribbean. The five-pointed star symbolizes the "morning star," representing the planet Venus. It can generally be seen in the eastern sky just before sunrise and represents the state's position as the easternmost point of Mexico. The three triangles represent the forests of Quintana Roo. Red is the Mayan color to represent the east, yellow represents the south, white is the north, and black is the west. Green is a sacred color.

HOLIDAYS: Año Nuevo (New Year's Day—January 1); Día de la Constitución (Constitution Day—February 5); Benito Juárez's birthday (March 21); Primero de Mayo (Labor Day—May 1); Anniversary of the Battle of Puebla (1862), May 5; Revolution Day, 1910 (November 20); and Navidad (Christmas—December 25).

FLAG: There is no official state flag.

TIME: 6 AM = noon Greenwich Mean Time (GMT).

1 Location and Size

Quintana Roo is the easternmost state at the tip of the Yucatán Peninsula. Quintana Roo covers an area of 42,360 square kilometers (16,355 square miles), which is a little less than half the size of the US state of Maine. The island of Cozumel covers an additional area of 477 square kilometers (184 square miles). Quintana Roo ranks as 19th in size among the states and covers about 2.2% of the total land area of Mexico. It borders the states of Yucatán to the northwest, Campeche to the west, the Central American countries of Belize and Guatemala to the south, and the Gulf of Mexico and the Caribbean Sea to the east and north. The state is divided into eight municipalities (similar to US counties). Its capital is Chetumal.

Quintana Roo is situated on the Yucatán Peninsula, which is low and flat. The southwestern region of the peninsula is the highest, reaching an altitude of 230 meters (754 feet) at Cerro El Charro, the highest point in the state. The Meseta de Zohlaguna is a large plateau that stretches into Campeche to the west.

The Caribbean coastline is long and beautiful, with fine beaches. One important feature of this coastline is the coral reef. The total length of the coastline is 865 kilometers (537 miles). There are several islands off the coast, including the popular resort of Isla Cozumel.

The most important river is the Honda River, which forms the border with Belize. Lakes within the state are relatively small. There are also underground caves filled with water that has filtered through the porous rocks. These caves are known as *cenotes*.

2 Climate

The warm waters of the Caribbean Sea contribute to the climate, which is generally warm and humid. The average temperature range is 25.5°C to 26.5°C (78°F to 80°F), with maximum high temperatures between 36°C and 38°C (97°F and 100°F) and low temperatures ranging from 12°C to 14°C (54°F to 57°F). The highest monthly average rainfall, 17 centimeters (6.7 inches), occurs in September. Annual rainfall ranges from 1,100 to 1,500 millimeters (43 to 59 inches), with the average being 1,200 millimeters (47 inches).

In the capital city of Chetumal the temperature ranges from an average low of 22°C (72°F) to an average high of 30°C (86°F). Average precipitation in the capital is 119 centimeters (47.2 inches) per year. The temperature range in Cozumel is similar to that of the capital, but the average annual rainfall is higher at about 190 centimeters (74.9 inches).

The region is also frequently affected by tropical storms and hurricanes. In September 1989, Hurricane Hugo struck Cancún with 320-kilometer-per-hour (200-mile-per-hour) winds, causing major damage to the resort hotels there. Hurricane Keith hit Chetumal in 2000 with winds of 148 kilometers per hour (92 miles per hour). In 2005, Hurricane Emily swept through Cozumel in July with winds at a maximum 213 kilometers per hour (132 miles per hour). In October of the same year, Hurricane Wilma hit Cozumel with winds of 222 kilometers per hour (138 miles per hour).

3 Plants and Animals

There are four basic ecosystems, or natural environments, found in the state: forests, savanna, mangroves, and reefs. The forests contain mahogany, cedars, East Indian rosewoods, and palm trees. Common animals in this ecosystem are anteaters, spider monkeys, white-tailed deer, and tepezcuintles (a type of dog). Birds found here include turkeys, parrots, doves, and nightingales. The savanna region features pastureland and bushes. Mangroves are tropical evergreen trees that generally grow along the coast and have large, tangled root systems. Animals found in the mangroves include herons, pelicans, and ducks. Manatees and alligators are also found in the nearby waters. The limestone reef that lies along the coast is the home of lobsters, shrimp, sea snails, and other fish.

4 Environmental Protection

In 2004, the state had 20 municipal wastewater treatment plants in operation with a combined installed capacity of 1,881 liters per sec-

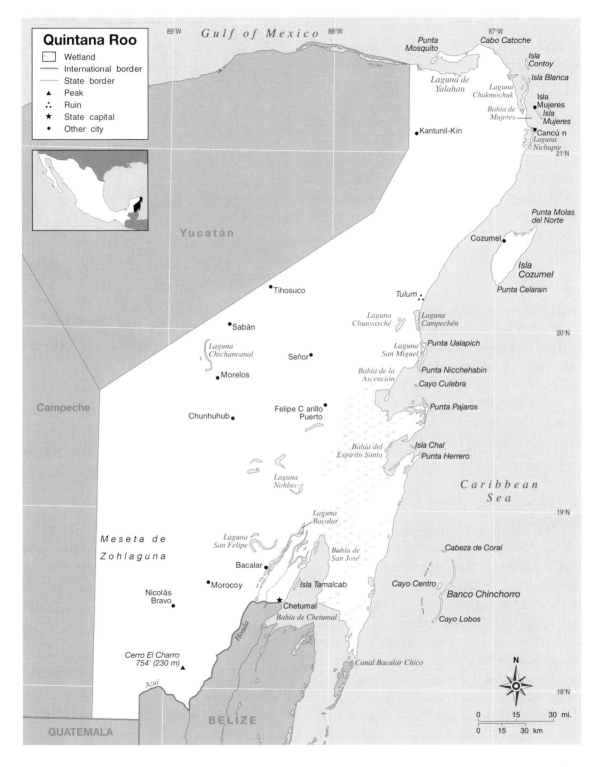

Quintana Roo

- Wetland
- International border
- State border
- ▲ Peak
- ∴ Ruin
- ★ State capital
- • Other city

Gulf of Mexico

89°W 88°W 87°W

Punta Mosquito

Cabo Catoche

Isla Contoy

Isla Blanca

Laguna de Yalahan

Laguna Chakmochuk

Isla Mujeres

Bahía de Mujeres

Isla Mujeres

•Kantunil-Kin

Cancún

Laguna Nichupte

21°N

Yucatán

Punta Molas del Norte

Cozumel

Isla Cozumel

Punta Celarain

•Tihosuco

Tulum

Laguna Chunyaxché

Laguna Campechén

•Sabán

20°N

Laguna Chichancanal

Señor•

Laguna San Miguel

Punta Ualapich

Punta Nicchehabin

•Morelos

Bahía de la Ascención

Cayo Culebra

Felipe C arillo Puerto

Punta Pajaros

Chunhuhub•

Bahía del Espíritu Santo

Isla Chal

Punta Herrero

Laguna Nohbec

Caribbean Sea

19°N

Laguna Bacalar

Laguna San Felipe

Cabeza de Coral

Meseta de Zohlaguna

Bacalar

Bahía de San José

Nicolás Bravo

•Morocoy

Isla Tamalcab

Cayo Centro

Banco Chinchorro

★Chetumal

Bahía de Chetumal

Cayo Lobos

Honda

Cerro El Charro 754' (230 m) ▲

Canal Bacalar Chico

Azul

N

Campeche

GUATEMALA

BELIZE

18°N

0 15 30 mi.

0 15 30 km

ond (496 gallons per second). The volume of treated wastewater that year was estimated at 1,350 liters per second (356 gallons per second). There were also two industrial wastewater treatment plants in operation that year. As of 2004, about 96.7% of the population had access to safe drinking water.

In 2003, the state had over 3.6 million hectares (9.1 million acres) of rain forest. In 2004, about 81 hectares (200 acres) of woodland were damaged or destroyed by forest fires. An additional 367 hectares (906 acres) of pasture and brush land were also damaged by fires.

There are several protected areas that are meant to preserve and sustain the diverse ecosystems of the state. There are six national parks located in the state, four of which are also designated as Ramsar Wetlands of International Importance: Cozumel, Puerto Morelos, Xcalak, and Isla Contoy. There are six other Ramsar sites in the state. One of them, Sian Ka'an, is also a UNESCO Natural World Heritage Site. Sian Ka'an (on Cozumel) serves as a habitat for over 300 species of bird.

5 Population, Ethnic Groups, Languages

Quintana Roo had an estimated total population of 1,175,800 in 2006, ranking 26th among the states and the Distrito Federal. About 51% of the population were men and 49% were women. About 79% of the population lived in urban areas. The population density was 23 people per square kilometer (60 people per square mile). In 2000, the capital, Chetumal, had a population of 121,602.

Most citizens speak Spanish as a first language. However, about 16% of the popula-

Mayan ruins of Chichen Itza. AP IMAGES.

tion speaks some indigenous (native) language, including Maya, Tzotzil, and Kanjobal. This is the fourth-highest percentage in the country (following Oaxaca, Yucatán, and Chiapas).

6 Religions

According to the 2000 census, 73.2% of the population, or 552,745 people, were Roman Catholic; about 11.2%, or 84,319 people, were mainline or evangelical Protestants. About 4.6% were counted as other Biblical faiths, including 14,285 Seventh-day Adventists, 3,415 Latter-day Saints (Mormons), and 16,919 Jehovah's Witnesses. There were 587 Jews. About 9.6% of the population claimed to have no religious affiliation.

7 Transportation

Cancún International Airport, Chetumal International Airport, and Cozumel Airport provide international flights to and from Quintana Roo. The state has about 5,302 kilometers (3,293 miles) of roads. In 2004, there were 119,875 automobiles registered in the state, along with 1,171 passenger trucks, 37,053 freight trucks, and 30,230 motorcycles.

8 History

Around 3000 BC, the proto-Mayan groups first populated the region. During the 10th century, a Mayan group known as the Itzáes built the cities of Chichén Itzá and Champotón, two of the most impressive Mayan ruins that still exist in Mexico. Together with other groups influenced by the Toltec and Chichimec cultures, the Itzáes formed the Mayapan League, a loose coalition of Mayan cities. In 1194, the Itzáes abandoned Chichén Itzá. They founded the city of Petén, another celebrated Mayan architectural wonder.

In 1502, the first contact with Spanish conquistadors (Spanish explorers who sought to conquer Mexico for Spain) took place off the coast of Quintana Roo, where some of the members of Christopher Columbus's (1451–1506) last expedition discovered native fishing boats. In 1511, a Spanish ship from Darien (Panama) was stranded near the coast. Several survivors were captured and executed in the region with the exception of Gonzalo Guerrero and Jerónimo de Aguilar, who were accepted and assimilated into Mayan culture.

In 1517, the Hernández de Córdoba expedition arrived in Cabo Catoche and later Juan de Grijalba (c. 1489–1527) arrived in Cozumel.

In 1519, Spanish conqueror Hernán Cortés (1485–1547) arrived in Chetumal and rescued Jerónimo de Aguilar. In 1526, Francisco de Montejo (c. 1479–1553) proposed to Spanish king Carlos V (1500–1558) the conquest of the Yucatán province. The conquest was started in 1527 and completed in 1546 by Montejo's son, Francisco Montejo y León.

During the 16th and 17th centuries, pirates operating in the Caribbean constantly attacked the coastal regions. In 1652, the city of Salamanca de Balacar was attacked by buccaneers and then abandoned. Efforts were made to prevent a possible English invasion from the Belize territories. Catholic conversion efforts were first launched in the 18th century, allowing for the Maya population to retain much of its original cultural heritage well into the independence period.

After independence, in 1823, Guatemala annexed much of the Petén-Itzá territory. In 1841, an effort by large landowners to declare the independence of the Yucatán Peninsula from Mexico failed because of the lack of international recognition. In 1847, an ethnic war brought instability and destruction to the region. Mexico and Britain signed the Marshal Saint John Treaty that established the Belize-Mexico border on the Hondo River.

In 1901, the last indigenous rebels were subdued. In 1902, Quintana Roo was made an independent territory, autonomous of the Yucatán state. After being incorporated with Yucatán and Campeche during different phases of the Mexican Revolution, Quintana Roo was made an independent entity by President Lázaro Cárdenas (1895–1970), who served as president of Mexico from 1934 to 1940. The region became a federal state in 1974.

The Labna Arch was the entrance to the city of Labna, which flourished around 700–800 AD. © ROBERT FRERCK/ WOODFIN CAMP.

Because of its innumerable natural beauties and its rich archeological and anthropological heritage, UNESCO incorporated the region into its Man and Biosphere Program in 1986. Aside from its growing and consolidating tourism industry, Quintana Roo remains scarcely populated, with little industrial and non-tourism related economic activities. Two major factors have influenced Quintana Roo's slow growth: the state's heavy reliance on tourism, which has been widely promoted by the national government, and its late achievement of federal statehood. As a result, Quintana Roo has been slow to develop a strong local economy and vibrant civil society.

9 State and Local Government

The state governor is elected for a six-year nonrenewable term. The state legislature is comprised of 25 deputies elected for nonrenewable three-year terms. Fifteen deputies are elected in single-member districts and 10 are elected by proportional representation. Although the constitution includes separation of power provisions, the governor exercises enormous influence over the legislature.

The eight municipalities that make up Quintana Roo hold democratic elections for municipal presidents and council members every three years. Immediate re-election is not allowed.

An aerial view of the famous beaches of Cancun. AP IMAGES.

10 Political Parties

The three main political parties in all of Mexico are the Institutional Revolutionary Party (PRI), the National Action Party (PAN), and the Party of the Democratic Revolution (PRD). The PRI has continued to dominate state politics, as it has in much of the country since the end of the Mexican Revolution. Although the PAN and PRD have received a considerable share of the vote in recent elections, the PRI remains as the strongest party in the state. Félix González Canto of the PRI took office as governor in 2005. Because the PRI continues to exercise strong power at the gubernatorial level, decentralization efforts have lagged behind in Quintana Roo.

11 Judicial System

The Superior Tribunal of Justice is the highest court in the state. Its members are appointed by the legislature from a three-person list submitted to them by the Superior Tribunal. Only qualified attorneys can be included in the list. There is a mandatory retirement age of 65. In addition, an electoral tribunal court and local courts complete the state's judicial system.

12 Economy

Tourism is the most important economic activity in Quintana Roo accounting for 80% to 90% of the economy. Cancún, once an uninhabited island, has grown to be one of the world's leading tourist destinations. In 2004, Quintana Roo accounted for 11 million tourists out of the 20 million that visited Mexico. In that same year, Cancún alone was visited by 3.4 million tourists. However, Playa del Carmen, located 80 kilometers from Cancún on the Riviera Maya, is expanding even faster than did Cancún at the beginning.

Agriculture, livestock breeding, forestry exploitation, apiculture (beekeeping), and fishing follow in importance. Industrial activities have barely gained a footing in the economy. Exports are chicle (a chief ingredient of chewing gum), honey, seafood, and fruit.

13 Industry

The industrial activities that take place in Quintana Roo are almost entirely tied to meeting the needs of the tourism industry. The state's large-scale industries are in sugar and construction materials. Small-scale industry is in tortillas, bread, purified water, and ice.

The state's handicrafts industry consists of jewelry made from black coral, items from sisal and palm fibers, lianas (a vine-like plant), and locally-made dresses.

14 Labor

As of 2005, the state of Quintana Roo had 525,215 eligible workers. Some 513,375 were listed as employed, and 11,840 were listed as unemployed. Unemployed workers in rural areas may not be counted, however. The unemployment rate that year was reported to be 2.2%. Of those who were working, services employed 57%, followed by commerce at 20.4% and construction at 8%.

The US Bureau of Labor Statistics reported that Mexican workers saw their wages increase from $2.49 per hour in 2003 to $2.50 per hour in 2004. (The average US worker earned $15.70 per hour in 2004.) The maximum work week is set at 48 hours by law. The average worker spends 40 to 45 hours per week on the job. Workers earn twice their regular hourly rate for up to nine hours a week of overtime. When a worker works more than nine hours overtime in a week, he or she earns three times the regular hourly rate. After one year, workers are entitled by law to six days paid vacation.

15 Agriculture

Farms in Quintana Roo grow corn, beans, rice, sugarcane, jalapeño chilies, and watermelon. Beekeeping products are honey and wax. Cattle, pigs, and sheep are the livestock bred.

In 2004, crop production for the state of Quintana Roo included: 16,782 tons of corn, 6,798 tons of bananas, 133,269 tons of sugar, 1,400 tons of rice, and 9,528 tons of green chilies. Livestock brought to market in 2004 included: 17,987 head of beef cattle, 113,221 pigs, and 1,582 sheep. In that same year, the state produced: 4.9 million liters (1.2 million gallons) of milk from dairy cows, 760 tons of eggs, and 2,573 tons of honey. Meat production included: 4,465 tons of beef, 8,751 tons of pork, 126 tons of lamb, and 6,663 tons of poultry.

16 Natural Resources

There is fishing for shrimp, lobster, and sea snails. In 2003, the total fish catch was about 4,107 tons. Mahogany, cedar, and common tropical woods are harvested. Chicle, a sticky white sap that may be used as the raw material for chewing gum and other products, is another forest product found in both the high and low stature semi-evergreen forests of Quintana Roo. In 2003, the value of forest wood was about $6.1 million.

17 Energy and Power

In 2005, there were 336,907 users of electricity in the state of Quintana Roo. Of that total, the largest number were residential customers at 297,358. Sales of electricity that same year totaled 2,475,236 megawatt hours, of which the largest users were medium-sized industrial firms at 1,396,334 megawatt hours. Electric power in the state is generated by six power stations: one diesel and five gas-turbine plants. Electricity is provided by the Federal Electricity Commission and Central Light and Power. Both utilities are run by the Mexican government.

18 Health

In 2003, the state had 19 hospitals and 183 outpatient centers that were part of the national health system. In 2004, there were about 984 doctors, 1,619 nurses, and 81 dentists working in these health centers. There were an additional 31 independent health centers in the state in 2004. There is also an AmeriMed center, an American hospital in Cancún geared towards tourists and their families.

Most of the Mexican population is covered under a government health plan. The IMSS (Instituto Mexicano de Seguro Social) covers the general population. The ISSSTE (Instituto de Seguridad y Servicios Sociales de Trabajadores del Estado) covers state workers.

19 Housing

Most homes are built with materials such as concrete, brick, and stone. Wood is the next most common construction material. In 2000, the state had the lowest percentage of home ownership at about 68% of all homes being owner-occupied. In 2005, there were an estimated 285,742 residential housing units in the state. About 62% of these units were single-family detached homes. The average household was estimated at four people.

20 Education

Public education in Mexico is free for students from ages 6 to 16 and most of the students in the state attend public schools. In 2004/05, it was estimated that 97.9% of age-eligible students completed primary school, which includes six years of study. About 80.8% of eligible students completed secondary school, which includes three years of study after primary school. About 58.7% of eligible students completed the *bachillerato*, which is similar to a high school diploma. The national average for completion of the *bachillerato* was 60.1% that year.

The Universidad de Quintana Roo and the Instituto Tecnológico are located in the capital, Chetumal. In 2005, there were about 24,612 students ages 20 and older who were enrolled in some type of higher education program. The overall literacy rate was estimated at 92% in 2005.

21 Arts

Quintana Roo has at least 14 theaters for the performing arts. A principal cultural center is

The ruins at Tulum are preserved as part of Tulum National Park. © ROBERT FRERCK/WOODFIN CAMP.

the Centro Cultural de Bellas Artes. There are displays of archeological artifacts from the city of Chetumal. The annual Cancún Jazz Festival features exhibits on Mexican and Mayan arts and culture, as well as music. There are over 50 registered movie theaters, including multiscreen theaters and single-screen galleries.

22 Libraries and Museums

In 2003, there were 121 libraries in the state with a combined stock of 885,767 volumes. The same year, there were 17 museums registered in the state that had permanent exhibits. There is the Museum of Popular Mexican Art in Cancún and the Museum of Musical Instruments in Cozumel.

23 Media

The *Diario de Quintana Roo* (*Quintana Roo Daily*) is published in Chetumal. In 2004, there were 18 television stations and 21 radio stations (14 AM and 7 FM). In 2005, there were about 65,703 subscribers to cable and satellite television stations. Also in 2005, there were about 148,843 residential phone lines, with about 20.1 mainline phones in use for every 100 people.

24 Tourism, Travel, and Recreation

The two main tourist attractions are the cities of Cancún and Cozumel. These are primarily tourist destinations, but they are also places from which people take off to visit famous archeological sites, such as Chichén Itzá in Yucatán. Cozumel, a small island with excellent beaches, has many Mayan archeological ruins at San Gervasio. The Chankanaab Lagoon is a natural aquarium popular with snorkelers. The archeological city of Tulum is one of the main tourist attractions of Quintana Roo. Tulum was a Mayan site built on a cliff overlooking the Caribbean. Isla Mujeres (Isle of Women) offers diving and snorkeling. There is a large stone cross in the water dedicated to those who lost their lives there. Quintana Roo was also the site of the pirate trade.

25 Sports

The Cancún Pioneros (Pioneers) and Inter Playa del Carmen are Second Division teams of the Mexican Football (soccer) Association (commonly known as Femexfut). Pioneros is also the name of Cancún basketball team of the National

Scuba gear hangs out to dry at the Dive Paradise resort in Cozumel. This island is renowned for its scuba diving.
COPYRIGHT © 2004 KELLY A. QUIN.

Professional Basketball League (LNBP). In 2004, the state had three major sports arenas.

Water sports are popular for both residents and tourists, who are drawn to the Caribbean beaches of the state.

26 Famous People

Quintana Roo was named after Andrés Quintana Roo (1787–1851), an early patriot of the Mexican Republic. Joaquín Ernesto Hendricks Díaz was elected governor of Quintana Roo in 1999. Félix González Canto (b.1968) became governor in 2005. He was a deputy in federal congress from 2003–05 and a Mexican representative to the Central American parliament in 2004.

27 Bibliography

BOOKS

Cancun and the Yucatan. London, Eng.: Dorling Kindersley, 2003.

Field, Randi. *The Gulf States of Mexico.* Philadelphia, PA: Mason Crest Publishers, 2003.

Gassos, Dolores. *The Mayas.* Philadelphia, PA: Chelsea House Publishers, 2005.

Green, Jen. *Caribbean Sea and Gulf of Mexico.* Milwaukee, WI: World Almanac Library, 2006.

Gruber, Beth. *Mexico.* Washington, DC: National Geographic, 2006.

WEB SITES

Government of Mexico. *Mexico for Kids.* www. elbalero.gob.mx/index_kids.html (accessed on March 30, 2007).

Mexican Tourism Board. *Visit Mexico: Quintana Roo.* www.visitmexico.com/wb/Visitmexico/ Visi_Quintana__Roo (accessed on March 30, 2007).

San Luis Potosí

PRONUNCIATION: sahn-loo-ees poh-toh-SEE.

ORIGIN OF STATE NAME: The Spaniards originally named the region Valle de San Luis, a name that was soon shortened to San Luis. After discovering large amounts of gold and silver, the Spaniards added the word Potosí (hill), which was a name they were applying to rich mining regions.

CAPITAL: San Luis Potosí.

ENTERED COUNTRY: 1824.

COAT OF ARMS: The coat of arms features San Luis Rey, the patron saint of the state, standing on top of San Pedro Hill, which has cave-like openings representing the mines of the state. Blue and yellow are used to represent night and day. Two silver and two gold bars represent the mining activities of the state.

HOLIDAYS: Año Nuevo (New Year's Day—January 1); Día de la Constitución (Constitution Day—February 5); Benito Juárez's birthday (March 21); Primero de Mayo (Labor Day—May 1); Anniversary of the Battle of Puebla (1862), May 5; Revolution Day, 1910 (November 20); and Navidad (Christmas—December 25).

FLAG: There is no official state flag.

TIME: 6 AM = noon Greenwich Mean Time (GMT).

1 Location and Size

San Luis Potosí covers an area of 60,982 square kilometers (23,545 square miles), which is slightly smaller than the US state of West Virginia. It ranks as 15th in size among the states and covers about 3.1% of the total land area of Mexico. It is surrounded by nine Mexican states, thereby being the state with the most states bordering on it. To the north are Coahuila and Nuevo León; on the northeast is Tamaulipas; on the east is Veracruz; on the south, Hidalgo, Querétaro, and Guanajuato; on the southwest, Jalisco; and on the west, Zacatecas. San Luis Potosí is divided into 58 municipalities (similar to US counties). The capital city is also called San Luis Potosí.

The Sierra Madre Oriental mountain range runs through the central and eastern portion of San Luis Potosí. The western portion of the state lies on the nation's Central Plateau. The highest point in the state, Cerro Grande, lies on the plateau at an elevation of about 3,180 meters (10,433 feet).

La Huasteca, a lowland region that covers the southeast part of the state, has fertile soil and adequate rain for agriculture.

Important rivers include the Santa María, which joins the Moctezuma River in Querétaro. The Verde is another southern river. There are spectacular waterfalls at Tamul and Micos.

2 Climate

The tropic of Cancer, a line of latitude at 23°27' north of the equator, passes through the state. The climate regions to the north of the tropic of Cancer are generally known as the northern temperate zone. The regions of the state to the south are considered to be the torrid zone (or tropical zone). However, variations in altitude and rainfall also have a great effect on the climate in different regions the state.

In regions of higher altitude, the climate is dry and desert-like. In the central region of the state, the climate may vary from cool to hot, but the lower regions of the state are generally hot and humid. In the capital city of San Luis Potosí, the average year-round temperature is about 18°C (64°F), ranging from an average of 12°C (55°F) in January to 22°C (72°F) in May. The average precipitation in the capital is 35 centimeters (13.9 inches) per year.

3 Plants and Animals

Some of the most common plants in the state are Chinese palm and yucca trees, organ cactus, nopal (prickly pear), and various ferns and mosses. Sapodilla, papaya, and banana trees are also found. Large mammals include wildcats and deer. Small mammals include prairie dogs, hares, tlacuaches (Mexican opossums), and tepezcuin-

tles (small dogs). Rattlesnakes and armadillos can also be found. Hawks and eagles are common birds.

4 Environmental Protection

In 2004, the state had nine municipal wastewater treatment plants in operation with a combined installed capacity of 812 liters per second (214 gallons per second). The volume of treated wastewater that year was estimated at 559 liters per second (147 gallons per second). There were also 61 industrial wastewater treatment plants in operation that year. As of 2004, about 80% of the population had access to safe drinking water.

In 2003, the state had about 822,044 hectares (2 million acres) of woodland, including 367,192 hectares (907,351 acres) of rain forest. In 2004, only 5 hectares (12.3 acres) of woodland were damaged or destroyed by forest fires. An additional 82 hectares (202 acres) of pasture and brush land were also damaged by fires. Protected areas in the state include El Potosí and Gogorrón, both national parks.

5 Population, Ethnic Groups, Languages

San Luis Potosí had an estimated total population of 2,448,300 in 2006, ranking 17th among the states and the Distrito Federal. About 48% of the population were men and 52% were women. About 54% of the population lived in urban areas. The population density was 39 people per square kilometer (101 people per square mile). In 2005, the capital, San Luis Potosí, had an estimated population of 730,950.

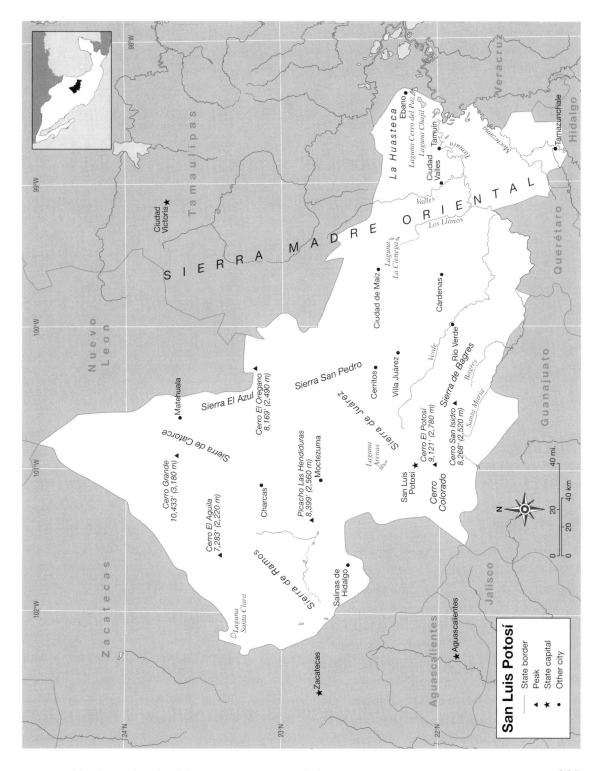

San Luis Potosí

Legend:
- State border
- ▲ Peak
- ★ State capital
- • Other city

Real de Catorce is located in the Catorce mountain range, one of the highest plateaus in Mexico. © DANNY LEHMAN/CORBIS.

Almost all citizens speak Spanish as their first language. About 9% of the population speaks indigenous (native) languages, including Náhuatl, Huasteco, and Pame.

6 Religions

According to the 2000 census, 92% of the population, or 1.8 million people, were Roman Catholic; about 4.6%, or 93,257 people, were mainline or evangelical Protestants. About 1% were counted as other Biblical faiths, including 14,365 Jehovah's Witnesses, 3,215 Seventh-day Adventists, and 2,435 Latter-day Saints (Mormons). About 1.5% of the population claimed to have no religious affiliation. The Cathedral of San Luis Rey is the seat of the Roman Catholic archdiocese of San Luis Potosí.

7 Transportation

The state has about 8,293 kilometers (5,151 miles) of roads and 1,280 kilometers (795 miles) of railroads. In 2004, there were 257,589 automobiles registered in the state, along with 3,117 passenger trucks, 207,223 freight trucks, and 17,384 motorcycles. There are two airports in the state, mostly for domestic flights.

8 History

Around 10,000 BC hunter and gatherer groups first visited the San Luis Potosí region. There are some archeological ruins that date back to 1200 BC in the region. Before the arrival of the Spanish conquistadors (those who sought to conqueror

This Roman Catholic cathedral in San Luis Potosí dates from the 18th century. © MIREILLE VAUTIER/WOODFIN CAMP.

Mexico for Spain), Chichimeco and Huasteco groups inhabited the area.

In October 1522, Spanish conqueror Hernán Cortés (1485–1547) initiated the conquest of the region. In 1524, Nuño Beltrán de Guzmán took possession of the territory as the crown-appointed governor. Another Spaniard, Beltrán de Guzmán, kidnapped thousands of native Amerindians. He sold them as slaves in other parts of Mexico. Around 1539, Franciscan priests Antonio de Roa and Juan Sevilla initiated a campaign to convert the Indians in the region to Roman Catholicism. The discovery of mineral deposits in San Luis Potosí and Zacatecas in 1546 attracted new settlers. The Chichimec Amerindians revolted against increased colonial presence and launched a military offensive

known as the Chichimec War toward the end of the 1500s.

Franciscan priest Diego de la Magdalena established a hospice for Indians in what later became the town of San Luis Potosí. In 1583, mestizo (person of mixed Spanish and indigenous heritage) military leader Miguel Caldera sought to bring an end to the Chichimec War. Viceroy Luis de Velasco (1511–1564) sent four hundred indigenous families who had converted to Catholicism to live among the Chichimec starting in 1591. In 1592, the discovery of new mineral deposits created a gold rush. The town of San Luis Potosí was formally founded in late 1592. Toward the turn of the century, new cattle ranches and agricultural fields emerged to service the growing mining industry. The Chichimec War ended in the 17th century. The indigenous populations were overpowered by the Spanish population's growth and the power of the colonizers. San Luis Potosí consolidated as a major mining center in Mexico during the 17th and 18th century.

The independence movement reached San Luis Potosí in 1810. Despite a number of bloody uprisings, the royalist forces (loyal to Spain) successfully maintained control of the region until 1821, when end to Spanish rule in the entire country came with a formal declaration of independence. San Luis Potosí became a federal state in 1824. Its new constitution was written in 1826.

A period of instability characterized much of Mexico between 1830 and 1870. After this period, forces loyal to President Porfirio Díaz (1830–1915) controlled San Luis Potosí. Economic development and improvements in infrastructure characterized much of the period. But uprisings by indigenous people continued. Different groups and different movements revolted demanding land distribution and improvements in the living conditions of peasants. A precursor of the Mexican Revolution was the first Liberal Congress organized in San Luis Potosí in 1901.

Revolutionary leader Francisco Indalécio Madero (1873–1913) was arrested in July 1910 and sent to San Luis Potosí. He escaped. He then issued the Plan of San Luis on October 5, 1910. This Plan encouraged Mexicans to take up arms against the government and marked the beginning of the Mexican Revolution (1910–20). Near the end of the revolution in 1917, the Cristero War, where Catholic loyalists revolted against the secular nature of the new govern-

ment, made it more difficult for revolutionary violence to be subdued.

The Institutional Revolutionary Party (PRI) ruled from 1934 to 2003. In 2003, Marcelo Santos of the National Action Party (PAN) was elected governor. During the early years of PRI control, San Luis Potosí emerged as one of the most troubled states in the union. A revolt against the land distribution programs championed by President Lázaro Cárdenas (1895–1970) in 1939 was violently repressed. The civic movement led by rightwing physician Salvador Nava generated political instability. This popular and relentless democratic leader challenged the domination of the PRI. Following the signing of the North American Free Trade Agreement (NAFTA), the economy of the state began to improve.

In the first decade of the 21st century, the economy of the state of San Luis Potosí continued to grow and diversify. The state's geographic location positions it well as a transportation center, which helps it take advantage of increased trade with the United States and Canada. With the end of PRI domination of the state's governorship in 2003, the state was poised for further change and growth.

9 State and Local Government

The state governor is democratically elected for a nonrenewable six-year term. The state legislature is comprised of 27 deputies elected for nonrenewable three-year terms. Fifteen deputies are elected in single member districts and 12 are elected by proportional representation.

The 58 municipalities that comprise San Luis Potosí hold democratic elections for municipal presidents and council members every three years.

Immediate reelection is not allowed. Although some decentralization initiatives are producing positive results, the state still has a long way to go to achieve successful decentralization.

10 Political Parties

The three main political parties in all of Mexico are the Institutional Revolutionary Party (PRI), the National Action Party (PAN), and the Party of the Democratic Revolution (PRD). Although the PRI dominated state politics after the end of the Mexican Revolution, a charismatic conservative leader, Salvador Nava of PAN, became mayor of San Luis Potosí in 1959. In 1991, Nava ran for governor and lost to the PRI amid accusations of massive fraud.

PRI control of the governorship lasted until 2003. Without being able to win the governor's office, PAN leaders worked to employ check-and-balance provisions against the governor. In 2003, PAN's candidate, Marcelo de los Santos Fraga, was elected governor.

11 Judicial System

The Supreme Tribunal of Justice is the state's highest court. Its 13 members are appointed by the legislature from a three-person list presented to them by the governor. Only qualified attorneys can be nominated. After their six-year terms expire, justices can be re-elected. Because of a strong self-governing legislature, an independent judiciary enforces formal separation of powers between the various branches of the government. In addition, an electoral tribunal court and lower courts are also components of the state's judicial system.

12 Economy

Manufacturing is the largest economic activity in San Luis Potosí. Most manufacturing is centered in the state's capital city, San Luis Potosí. The city of San Luis Potosí has long been an important railroad center. Its location along Mexico's main freight transportation corridor has helped generate strong economic growth and allowed the local economy to diversify. The city has also become a distribution site for domestic and foreign merchandise, due to its access to an extensive highway system.

13 Industry

Most industry is centered around the capital city. The primary industries are food processing, automobile manufacturing, non-metallic minerals, beverage production, metal smelting, textiles, mechanical, and other metal industries. In the state's Huasteca region, industries include sugar processing, cement, and meat products.

The state's handicraft industries produce musical instruments, cotton textiles, ceramics, basketwork, items made from leather, wood, and ixtle (a type of coarse plant fiber), jewelry, and ironwork.

14 Labor

As of 2005, the state of San Luis Potosí had 937,317 eligible workers. Some 913,817 were listed as employed, and 23,500 were listed as unemployed. Unemployed workers in rural areas may not be counted, however. The unemployment rate that year was reported to be 2.5%. Of those who were working, services employed

33.6%, followed by agriculture at 22%, and manufacturing at 18%.

The US Bureau of Labor Statistics reported that Mexican workers saw their wages increase from $2.49 per hour in 2003 to $2.50 per hour in 2004. (The average US worker earned $15.70 per hour in 2004.) The maximum work week is set at 48 hours by law. The average worker spends 40 to 45 hours per week on the job. Workers earn twice their regular hourly rate for up to nine hours a week of overtime. When a worker works more than nine hours overtime in a week, he or she earns three times the regular hourly rate. After one year, workers are entitled by law to six days paid vacation.

In the capital city of San Luis Potosí, unionized workers are represented by three unions: the Confederation of Mexican Workers (CMT), the Confederation of Mexican Workers and Farmers (CROC), and the Regional Confederation of Mexican Workers (CROM).

15 Agriculture

Most farms are found in the Huasteca region of the state, which is a fertile lowland area in the east. Fruit crops such as oranges, mangos, and guavas are important in this region. Sugarcane, sorghum, barley, and peanuts are also grown there. Fish farms that raise carp, catfish, and fresh water shrimp are also located in the Huasteca region. Corn and beans are primary crops throughout the state. Goats, sheep, and cattle are the primary livestock.

In 2004, crop production for the state of San Luis Potosí included 185,658 tons of corn, 159,330 tons of green chilies, 80,833 tons of sorghum, 125,123 tons of red tomatoes, 387,704 tons of sugar, and 72,316 tons of kidney beans.

Livestock brought to market in 2004 included 96,355 head of beef cattle, 109,905 pigs, 13,999 goats, and 3,908 sheep. In that same year, the state produced 144.5 million liters (38 million gallons) of milk from dairy cows, 3.4 million liters of goat's milk, and 2,563 tons of eggs. Meat production included 42,882 tons of beef, 8,317 tons of pork, 3,477 tons of goat, 2,284 tons of lamb, and 61,984 tons of poultry.

16 Natural Resources

Natural resources include deposits of silver and gold, plaster and tin, and fluorite, all of which are mined. Pine, oak, cedar, palo de rosa, lechuguilla, palm, and mesquite are harvested to make wood products. In 2003, the total value of forest wood production was about $199,303. In 2003, the total fish catch was about 177 tons, all for human consumption.

17 Energy and Power

In 2005, there were 691,808 users of electricity in the state of San Luis Potosí. Of that total, the largest number were residential customers at 592,894. Sales of electricity that same year totaled 4,820,857 megawatt hours, of which the largest users were large industrial firms at 2,421,834 megawatt hours. Electric power in San Luis Potosí is generated by four power plants: one 700 megawatt capacity thermal (non-coal) plant, and three hydroelectric stations with a combined capacity of 20 megawatts. Electricity is provided by the Federal Electricity Commission, and Central Light and Power. Both utilities are run by the Mexican government.

18 Health

In 2003, the state had 30 hospitals and 525 outpatient centers that were part of the national health system. In 2004, there were about 1,562 doctors, 3,994 nurses, and 190 dentists working in these health centers. There were an additional 44 independent health centers in the state in 2004.

Most of the Mexican population is covered under a government health plan. The IMSS (Instituto Mexicano de Seguro Social) covers the general population. The ISSSTE (Instituto de Seguridad y Servicios Sociales de Trabajadores del Estado) covers state workers.

19 Housing

Most housing is built with materials such as stone, brick, and concrete. Adobe homes with sheet metal roofs are common in some areas. In 2000, about 82% of all homes were owner-occupied. In 2005, there were an estimated 557,534 residential housing units in the state. About 93% of these units were single-family detached homes. The average household was estimated at 4.3 people.

20 Education

Public education in Mexico is free for students from ages 6 to 16 and most of the students in the state attend public schools. In 2004/05, it was estimated that 90% of age-eligible students completed primary school, which includes six years of study. About 81% of eligible students completed secondary school, which includes three years of study after primary school. About 66.8% of eligible students completed the *bachil-*

lerato, which is similar to a high school diploma. The national average for completion of the *bachillerato* was 60.1% that year.

Universidad Autónoma de San Luis Potosí (Autonomous University of San Luis Potosí) and the Universidad del Centro de México (University of Central Mexico) are located in the capital. In 2005, there were about 63,490 students ages 20 and older who were enrolled in some type of higher education program. The overall literacy rate was estimated at 89% in 2005.

21 Arts

The capital city is home to three local dance companies: the Ballet Provincial de San Luis Potosí, the Grupo de Danza Folklórica, and the Danza Contemporánea. Musical groups include La Banda de Música del Gobierno de San Luis Potosí and the San Luis Potosí Symphony Orchestra. San Luis Potosí also has at least four theaters for the performing arts. Most cities and towns have cultural centers. There are over 50 registered movie theaters, including multiscreen theaters and single-screen galleries.

22 Libraries and Museums

In 2003, there were 212 libraries in the state with a combined stock of 1,283,950 volumes. The same year, there were 19 museums in the state that had permanent exhibits. Museums in the capital city include the Museum of Popular Art, the National Mask Museum, and the San Potosí Regional Museum.

23 Media

In 2005, the capital city, San Luis Potosí, had five daily newspapers: *El Sol de San Luis Potosí*

(*The San Luis Potosí Sun*), *San Luis Hoy* (*San Luis Today*), *El Heraldo*, *Momento*, and *Pulso*. *El Manana* is published in Ciudad Valles.

In 2004, there were 38 television stations and 31 radio stations (21 AM, 9 FM, and 1 shortwave). In 2005, there were about 104,175 subscribers to cable and satellite television stations. Also in 2005, there were about 240,114 residential phone lines, with about 12.6 mainline phones in use for every 100 people.

24 Tourism, Travel, and Recreation

In the capital, San Luis Potosí, tourists often visit the Church of Nuestra Senora del Carmen because of its tiled domes and famous altars. The national fair of San Luis Potosí is celebrated in August. Santa María del Río has an ancient aqueduct that forms a waterfall. There is a spa with thermal baths nearby. The area around Santa María del Río is a popular resort area.

25 Sports

The Santos Reales (Royal Saints) of the capital city play in the North Zone of the National Professional Basketball League (LNBP). Club San Luis is the First Division soccer team of the Mexican Football Association (commonly known as Femexfut). Soccer is played in the 18,000-seat Alfonso Lastra Ramirez stadium. The Tuneros de San Luis compete in the Mexican League of AAA minor league baseball. In 2004, there were three major sports arenas and one active bullfighting ring in the state.

26 Famous People

Julián Carrillo Trujillo (1875–1965) was a well-known violinist, classical composer, and orchestra conductor. C. Marcelo de los Santos Fraga was elected governor in 2003.

27 Bibliography

BOOKS

DeAngelis, Gina. *Mexico*. Mankato, MN: Blue Earth Books, 2003.

Gruber, Beth. *Mexico*. Washington, DC: National Geographic, 2006.

WEB SITES

Government of Mexico. *Mexico for Kids*. Online www.elbalero.gob.mx/index_kids.html (accessed on March 30, 2007).

Mexican Tourism Board. *Visit Mexico: San Luis Potosí*. www.visitmexico.com/wb/Visitmexico/Visi_San_Luis_Potosi (accessed on March 30, 2007).

Sinaloa

PRONUNCIATION: see-nah-LOH-ah.

ORIGIN OF STATE NAME: The name Sinaloa comes from the Cahita language. It is a combination of the words *sina*, which means *pithaya* (a plant with thorny stalks), and *lobola,* which means rounded. The pithaya is a common plant throughout the region.

CAPITAL: Culiacán (coo-lee-ah-CAHN).

ENTERED COUNTRY: 1830.

COAT OF ARMS: The state coat of arms is an oval shield set on top of a solid rock base and crowned with a variation of the national emblem. There are five footprints in the border of the shield. Pictures inside the shield include a castle, anchors, and a deer head.

HOLIDAYS: Año Nuevo (New Year's Day—January 1); Día de la Constitución (Constitution Day—February 5); Benito Juárez's birthday (March 21); Primero de Mayo (Labor Day—May 1); Anniversary of the Battle of Puebla (1862), May 5; Revolution Day, 1910 (November 20); and Navidad (Christmas—December 25).

FLAG: There is no official state flag.

TIME: 5 AM = noon Greenwich Mean Time (GMT).

1 Location and Size

Sinaloa lies along the coast of the Gulf of California. It covers an area of 57,327 square kilometers (22,134 square miles), which is a little smaller than the US state of West Virginia. It ranks as 18th in size among the states and covers about 2.9% of the total land area of Mexico. The state is bordered on the north by Sonora and Chihuahua, on the south by Nayarit, and on the east by Durango. Sinaloa is divided into 18 municipalities (similar to US counties); its capital is Culiacán.

The Sierra Madre Occidental stretches down the eastern half of the state. The highest point in the state is at Picacho Los Frailes, with an elevation of about 2,510 meters (8,235 feet). A flat, coastal region lies along the west. Valleys lie between the ranges of mountains and the coastal plain, where the land is flat with few hills.

The rivers rise in the Sierra Madre Occidental and cross the state to flow into the Gulf of California and the Pacific Ocean. Major rivers are the Fuerte, Sinaloa, and San Lorenzo. The coastline extends for 640 kilometers (397 miles).

Laguna del Caimanero is a large lagoon along the southeaster border. Presa Miquel Hidalgo and Presa Adolfo López Mateos are two major inland reservoirs.

2 Climate

The tropic of Cancer, a line of latitude at 23°27' north of the equator, passes through the state. The climate regions to the north of the tropic of Cancer are generally known as the northern temperate zone. The regions of the state to the south are considered to be the torrid zone (or tropical zone). However, variations in altitude and rainfall also have a great effect on the climate in different regions the state. The climate along the coastal plains is generally hot. In the valleys, the climate can range from temperate to hot, while in the mountain regions temperatures range from temperate to cold.

In the summer months of June, July, and August, the daytime temperature averages 32°C (90°F); in the winter months of December, January, and February, the daytime temperature averages 27°C (80°F). Most of the rainfall occurs during July, August, and September. In the capital city of Culiacán, the average year-round temperature is 24°C (76°F) and the average rainfall is 54 centimeters (21.3 inches) per year.

3 Plants and Animals

Some of the most common trees in the state include oaks, poplars, ceiba, and mangroves (a tropical evergreen that usually grows along the coast). The pithaya (a plant with thorny stalks) is common throughout the state, as are laurels and bougainvilleas. Fruit trees such as lemons, peaches, and pears are found as well.

Some common mammals include deer, wildcats, badgers, wild boar, coyotes, and tlacuaches (Mexican possums). There are also many rabbits, squirrels, and raccoons. Sparrow hawks, buzzards, ducks, and swallows are common birds. Turtles, iguanas, and alligators also can be found.

4 Environmental Protection

In 2004, the state had 74 municipal wastewater treatment plants in operation with a combined installed capacity of 3,362 liters per second (888 gallons per second). The volume of treated wastewater that year was estimated at 2,793 liters per second (785 gallons per second). There were also 71 industrial wastewater treatment plants in operation that year. As of 2004, about 97% of the population had access to safe drinking water.

In 2003, the state had about 2.7 million hectares (6.6 million acres) of woodland, including 1.9 million hectares (4.8 million acres) of rain forest. In 2004, about 38 hectares (93.9 acres) of woodland were damaged or destroyed by forest fires. An additional 1,131 hectares (2,794 acres) of pasture and brush land were also damaged by fires.

Through the North American Commission for Environmental Cooperation (CEC), the state of Sinaloa has formed a partnership with the US state of Alaska in a project called the Western Hemisphere Shorebird Reserve Network. The Sinaloan wetlands serve as the winter home of over 30% of the Pacific Flyway shorebirds that breed in Alaska, Canada, and other West Coast regions of the United States. The Bahía de Santa Maria–Laguna Playa Colorada reserve area was designated as a Ramsar Wetland of International

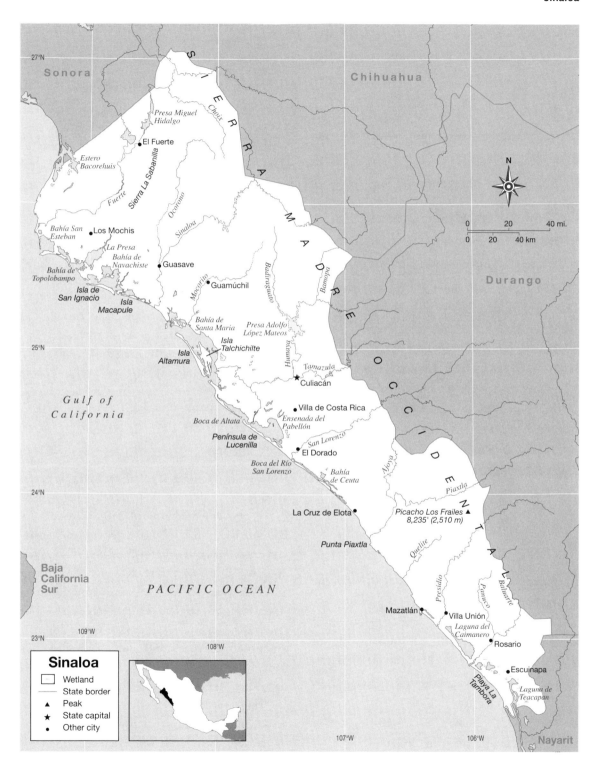

Sinaloa

☐ Wetland
— State border
▲ Peak
★ State capital
• Other city

Importance in 2004. Another Ramsar site, the Marismas Nacionales (National Marsh), stretches along a portion of the southern coast into the neighboring state of Nayarit. Playa El Verde Camacho is also a Ramsar site. The islands and protected areas within the Gulf of California were designated as UNESCO World Heritage sites in 2005.

5 Population, Ethnic Groups, Languages

Sinaloa had a total population of 2,637,700 in 2006, ranking 15th among the states and the Distrito Federal. The population was almost evenly divided between men and women. About 57% of the population lived in urban areas. The population density was 45 people per square kilometer (117 people per square mile). In 2005, the capital, Culiacán, had an estimated population of 793,730.

Almost all citizens speak Spanish as their first language. A small percentage of residents speak indigenous (native) languages such as Náhuatl and Mayo.

6 Religions

According to the 2000 census, 86.8% of the population, or about 1.9 million people, were Roman Catholic; almost 3%, or 65,346 people, were mainline or evangelical Protestants. About 2% were counted as other Biblical faiths, including 32,783 Jehovah's Witnesses, 6,305 Latter-day Saints (Mormons), and 6,275 Seventh-day Adventists. About 7.1% of the population claimed to have no religious affiliation.

7 Transportation

Sinaloa has three international airports: Mazatlán, Culiacán, and Los Mochis. There are 16,335 kilometers (10,146 miles) of roads. Culiacán has a highly developed highway network, including a four-lane highway direct to the United States. In 2004, there were 263,032 automobiles registered in the state, along with 5,641 passenger trucks, 257,567 freight trucks, and 11,035 motorcycles.

The railroad network links Sinaloa with the rest of Mexico and with key cities in the United States. There are about 1,234 kilometers (766 miles) of railway. There are major ports at Mazatlán and Topolobampo. The commercial route, CANMEX, that runs north and south from Alberta, Canada, through the United States to Mexico City, runs through the state. This is one of the most important routes for international trade in North America.

8 History

Some nomadic tribes regularly visited the region as early as 12,000 BC. Yet, the first permanent settlements emerged around 250 BC around the Baluarte River area. A Yuto-Aztec cultural renaissance took place at the northern end of the state around 900 AD in the settlements of Culiacán and Guasave. When the Spanish conquistadors (explorers who sought to claim Mexico for Spain) arrived, the region was inhabited by six different groups of sedentary and nomadic indigenous peoples. In 1529, Nuño Beltrán de Guzmán initiated the conquest of northern Mexico.

The slave trade of native Indians provoked revolts and uprisings that forced the Spaniards to relocate their main settlements. Indigenous leader Ayapín led one of the most notorious uprisings that forced Spaniards to request military support from neighboring Nueva Galicia (a former Spanish administrative region). Although that uprising was defeated, other indigenous uprisings forced the Spanish to abandon some settlements. Indigenous rebels executed Spanish conqueror Pedro de Montoya in 1583 when he attempted to colonize the area. Starting in 1591, a number of Jesuit missions won the sympathy of the otherwise resistant indigenous population. During most of the 17th century, colonial penetration was possible because of the successful Catholic conversion efforts by Jesuit priests. The province of Sinaloa was created in 1732 by royal decree. In 1767, a royal decree was issued to remove the Jesuits from Spanish America. This caused more problems for Sinaloa. Missions were abandoned and the indigenous people were robbed of their communal lands and forced to become feudal peasants and miners.

Although some independence leaders sought to provoke an uprising in the region, royalist forces (those loyal to Spain) soon controlled the revolts in 1810. During the decade-long independence quest, Sinaloa became a major center for contraband and illicit traffic. The states of Sonora and Sinaloa were initially part of the same federal entity, but they were formally separated into two different states in 1830. Local land-owning elites controlled state politics for much of the remaining 19th century, with little influence or authority from central Mexico.

During the liberal-conservative conflict of the 1860s, British and US troops attempted to invade the city of Mazatlán to protect the interest of foreign nationals. But conservative elites successfully subdued the challenge of those liberals loyal to President Benito Juárez (1806–

1872). As a result, most local leaders fought against the presence of foreign troops on nationalist grounds. After being occupied by French troops during the reign of Emperor Maximilian (1832–1867)—France briefly controlled parts of Mexico from 1863 to 1867—Sinaloa was freed. It was later controlled by the federal troops loyal to President Juárez.

During the Porfiriato period, from 1876 to 1910, when Porfirio Díaz (1830–1915) was in power as president of Mexico, Sinaloa experienced economic growth, but its small population hindered economic development and consolidation. Different factions fought in Sinaloa during the Mexican Revolution, which started in 1910, with some Francisco "Pancho" Villa (revolutionary leader, 1878–1923) loyalists claiming control of significant portions of the state. Yet, by 1917, forces loyal to the newly established constitutional government controlled the state. Some conflicts arose with the land reform initiatives promoted by the dominating political party, the Institutional Revolutionary Party (PRI), which affected large land estates owned by US companies. However, Sinaloa's scarce population prevented large land-related conflicts from emerging in the post-revolutionary period. The state's proximity to the United States, where there is a large market for illegal drugs, made it a prime candidate for the illegal production of the poppy, the plant used to produce opium.

In the first decade of the 21st century, the state of Sinaloa economically remained tied to agriculture. Industry has expanded, however, due in part to the state's network of modern roads, which provide access to the United States border, and ports capable of handling ocean-going freighters. Politically, the state remained under the control of the PRI. However, violent crime

The 18 municipalities that comprise Sinaloa hold democratic elections for municipal presidents and council members every three years. Immediate re-election is not allowed. Some decentralization initiatives are producing positive results.

10 Political Parties

The three main political parties in all of Mexico are the Institutional Revolutionary Party (PRI), the National Action Party (PAN), and the Party of the Democratic Revolution (PRD). The PRI continues to exercise strong control of state level politics. That party has never lost a gubernatorial election since the end of the Mexican Revolution. Jesús Alberto Aguilar Padilla of the PRI took office as governor in 2005. The fact that the PRI continues to control state level politics has prevented important decentralization initiatives from being implemented.

11 Judicial System

The Supreme Tribunal of Justice is the highest court in the state. Its 11 members are appointed for 15-year terms with no reelection provisions. There is a mandatory retirement age of 70. In addition, an electoral tribunal and local courts also comprise the state judicial system. The lack of alternation in power at the gubernatorial level has made it difficult for the Supreme Tribunal to become fully autonomous.

A basket vendor from Mazatlàn. © DANNY LEHMAN/ CORBIS.

and official corruption posed serious problems to the state.

9 State and Local Government

The state governor is democratically elected for six-year terms and cannot be reelected when the term expires. The legislature is comprised of a 40 member unicameral (single chamber) congress. Twenty-four members are elected in single member districts and 16 are elected by proportional representation. Congressional elections occur every three years and immediate re-election is not allowed.

12 Economy

As of 2003, the main economic activities of Sinaloa were agriculture, fishing, livestock breeding, commerce, and industry. Agriculture was the primary economic sector, covering over

75% of the state's total area. The state is well connected to the United States via four-lane highways and through its two ports, Mazatlán and Topolobampo, each of which provide access throughout the Pacific Basin. Topolobampo is connected by rail to the United States, and also has the capability to handle containerized freight, bulk agricultural products, and minerals. Tourism is also important to the state's economy, with the port of Mazatlán used as a port-of-call by cruise ships.

13 Industry

Sinaloa's industrial parks are scattered throughout the state, and are mainly tied to the processing of agricultural and seafood products through canning, packing, and frozen food plants. Processed food products from Sinaloa are tomato purée, flour, sugar, beer, edible oil, and chilorio (pork cooked in chili). Latin America's largest seafood canning facility is located in the port city of Mazatlán. The city of Los Mochis has developed a special ecological industrial park dedicated to housing nonpolluting industries.

Sinaloa's handicrafts industries produce high-quality furniture, as well as pottery, hats, sandals, baskets, saddles, belts, and objects made from shells.

14 Labor

As of 2005, the state of Sinaloa had 1,181,879 eligible workers. Some 1,143,227 were listed as employed, and 38,652 were listed as unemployed. Unemployed workers in rural areas may not be counted, however. The unemployment rate that year was reported to be 3.3%. Of those who were working, services employed 34.5%, followed by agriculture at 24.5%, and commerce at 21.4%.

The US Bureau of Labor Statistics reported that Mexican workers saw their wages increase from $2.49 per hour in 2003 to $2.50 per hour in 2004. (The average US worker earned $15.70 per hour in 2004.) The maximum work week is set at 48 hours by law. The average worker spends 40 to 45 hours per week on the job. Workers earn twice their regular hourly rate for up to nine hours a week of overtime. When a worker works more than nine hours overtime in a week, he or she earns three times the regular hourly rate. After one year, workers are entitled by law to six days paid vacation.

Some of the labor unions operating within the capital city of Culiacán are: the National Union of Workers (UNT), the Mexican Workers Confederation (CMT), and the Revolutionary Confederation of Workers and Farmers (CROC). Labor relations are reported to be good.

15 Agriculture

Sinaloa is considered to be the agricultural capital of Mexico. The cultivation of rice, sugarcane, wheat, vegetables, and fruit covers 75% of the state's total area. The state is Mexico's largest producer of vegetables and its second-largest producer of cereals. Other crops include tomatoes, beans, corn, sorghum, potatoes, soybeans, and squash. Crops are grown near sea level under irrigation in large fields using mechanized methods. Sinaloa is one of Mexico's leading sugarcane producers, which is a main source of income to Mexico.

Products that come from livestock breeding in Sinaloa are meat, sausage, cheese, and milk.

In 2004, the state of Sinaloa ranked first among all Mexican states in the production of corn at 4,004,140 tons, potatoes at 306,004 tons, and red tomatoes at 991,113 tons. The state was second in the production of green chilies at 319,841 tons, third in the production of kidney beans at 80,847 tons, and fourth in the production of sorghum at 423,892 tons. Farms in that state also produced 163,684 tons of sugar and 113,960 tons of wheat in that same year. Livestock brought to market in 2004 included: 120,467 head of beef cattle, 76,535 pigs, 15,394 goats, and 32,954 sheep. In that same year, the state produced 78.7 million liters (20.7 million gallons) of milk from dairy cows, and 35,062 tons of eggs. Meat production included: 73,359 tons of beef, 17,284 tons of pork, 1,767 tons of goat, 1,897 tons of lamb, and 109,195 tons of poultry.

16 Natural Resources

Fishing harvests include shrimp, tuna, sea bass, sardines, and marlin. Each year, Sinaloa produces and exports more than 22 million pounds of shrimp and 45,000 tons of tuna. In 2003, the total fish catch was about 233,256 tons, the second-largest catch in the country (after Sonora).

In 2003, the value of forest wood production was about $2 million. Pine was the primary wood harvested, but common tropical woods were also sold. Mineral resources include gold, silver, lead, and zinc. Nonmetallic minerals include limestone, talc, and salt.

17 Energy and Power

In 2005, there were 779,926 users of electricity in the state of Sinaloa. Of that total, the largest number were residential customers at 700,005. Sales of electricity that same year totaled 4,437,761 megawatt hours, of which the largest users were medium-sized industrial firms at 1,557,664 megawatt hours. Electricity is produced and distributed by the Federal Electricity Commission, and Central Light and Power. Both utilities are run by the Mexican government.

Sinaloa has six hydroelectric stations, two thermal power (non-coal) plants, and one gas-turbine plant with a total generating capacity of 1,853 megawatts.

18 Health

In 2003, the state had 38 hospitals and 399 outpatient centers that were part of the national health system. In 2004, there were about 2,654 doctors, 5,962 nurses, and 205 dentists working in these health centers. There were an additional 72 independent health centers in the state in 2004.

Most of the Mexican population is covered under a government health plan. The IMSS (Instituto Mexicano de Seguro Social) covers the general population. The ISSSTE (Instituto de Seguridad y Servicios Sociales de Trabajadores del Estado) covers state workers.

19 Housing

Most housing is built with materials such as brick, concrete, or stone. In 2000, about 83% of all homes were owner-occupied. In 2005, there were an estimated 642,114 residential housing units in the state. About 91% of these units were single-family detached homes. The average household was estimated at four people.

20 Education

Public education in Mexico is free for students from ages 6 to 16 and most of the students in the state attend public schools. In 2004/05, it was estimated that 86% of age-eligible students completed primary school, which includes six years of study. About 76.8% of eligible students completed secondary school, which includes three years of study after primary school. About 59.6% of eligible students completed the *bachillerato*, which is similar to a high school diploma. The national average for completion of the *bachillerato* was 60.1% that year.

The Universidad Autónoma de Sinaloa is located in Culiacán. There are technical institutes in Culiacán and Los Mochis. In 2005, there were about 86.166 students ages 20 and older who were enrolled in some type of higher education program. The overall literacy rate was estimated at 92.8% in 2005.

21 Arts

The state of Sinaloa has many performing musical groups. There is Ballet Folklórico (a contemporary dance group), an opera chorus, a percussion ensemble, and an orchestra. Sinaloa has at least five theaters for the performing arts including a Greek theater, several auditoriums, and various local cultural centers. The Sinaloa Symphony Orchestra in Mazatlán has been named the best regional orchestra in Mexico. It plays regularly at the Angela Peralta Theater.

The annual Sinaloa Arts Festival in Mazatlán (established 1993) includes dance, music, and visual arts with performers and artists from around the world. The Mazatlán Cultural festival (established 1994) features presentations of theater, dance, music, film, and literature. There are over 30 registered movie theaters, including multiscreen theaters and single-screen galleries.

22 Libraries and Museums

In 2003, there were 423 libraries in the state with a combined stock of 1,693,415 volumes. The same year, there were six museums registered in the state with permanent exhibits. The Sinaloa Museum of Art is in Culiacán. The Casa de la Cultura, a mansion once belonging to a prominent family, presents temporary exhibits on art and culture and serves as a local cultural center.

23 Media

In 2005, the capital, Culiacán, had three daily newspapers: *El Diario de Sinaloa* (*Sinaloa Daily*), *El Sol de Sinaloa* (*Sinaloa Sun*), and *El Sol de Culiacán* (*Culiacán Sun*). In Mazatlán, there were three daily newspapers: *El Sol del Pacífico* (*Pacific Sun*), *El Democrata Sinaloenese* (*Sinaloese Democrat*), and *Noroeste* (*Northwest*). There were also daily papers in Guamuchil, Guasave, and Los Mochis.

In 2004, there were 45 television stations and 49 radio stations (37 AM and 12 FM). In 2005, there were about 90,561 subscribers to cable and satellite television stations. Also in 2005, there were about 317,362 residential phone lines, with about 16.1 mainline phones in use for every 100 people.

24 Tourism, Travel, and Recreation

Founded in 1531, Culiacán is one of the oldest cities in Mexico. The city offers sport hunting and fishing for tourists. Many hunters come to shoot white-winged pigeon when in season.

Los Mochis is the point of origin of the railroad that connects the Sinaloan Coast with the Sierra Tarahumara. The Zona Dorado at the port city of Mazatlán is a major tourist resort area.

25 Sports

The state has four professional baseball teams that compete in the Mexican Pacific League. The Tomateros (Tomato Growers) of Culiacán won the Caribbean World Series in 2004. They play in the 16,000-seat General Angel Flores stadium. The Algodoneros (Cotton Growers) of Gusave play in the 8,000-seat Francisco Carranza Limón stadium. The Mazatlán Venados (Stags) were the 2005 series champions. They play in the 12,000-seat Teodoro Mariscal stadium. The Los Mochis Cañeros (Sugarcane Growers) won the 2003 Caribbean World Series.

Professional basketball teams in the state compete in the Pacific Coast Basketball League (CIBACOPA—Circuito de Baloncesto de las Costa del Pacifico). These include the Gusave Frayles, the Mazatlán Tiburones (Sharks), the Navolato Cañeros (Sugarcane Growers), Los Mochis Pioneros (Pioneers), and the Guamúchil Halcónes (Falcons).

The Dorados and Tigres Mochis are First Division "A" soccer teams competing in the Mexican Football Association (commonly known as Femexfut). In 2004, the state had three major sports arenas.

26 Famous People

Ramón F. Iturbe (1889–1953) was the first governor of the state. Juan S. Millán (b.1943) was elected as governor of Sinaloa in 1999. Jesús Alberto Aguilar Padilla (b.1952) became governor in 2005. Mexican singer and songwriter Chalino Sanchez died in Sinaloa in 1992. Laura Elena Martínez Herring (b.1964), born in Los Mochis, was the first Hispanic woman to win the title of Miss USA (1985). She has become a television and film actress in the United States.

27 Bibliography

BOOKS

Burt, Janet. *The Pacific North States of Mexico.* Philadelphia: Mason Crest Publishers, 2003.

DeAngelis, Gina. *Mexico.* Mankato, MN: Blue Earth Books, 2003.

Gruber, Beth. *Mexico.* Washington, DC: National Geographic, 2006.

Whipperman, Bruce. *Pacific Mexico: Including Acapulco, Puerto Vallarta, Oaxaca, Guadalajara and Mazatlán*, 5th edition. Emeryville, CA: Avalon Travel Pub., 2001.

WEB SITES

Government of Mexico. *Mexico for Kids*. www. elbalero.gob.mx/index_kids.html (accessed on March 30, 2007).

Mexican Tourism Board. *Visit Mexico: Sinaloa*. www.visitmexico.com/wb/Visitmexico/Visi_ Sinaloa (accessed on March 30, 2007).

Sinaloa State Secretariat of Economic Development. www.tsi.com.mx/Sde/ (accessed on March 30, 2007).

Sonora

PRONUNCIATION: soh-NOH-rah.

ORIGIN OF STATE NAME: There are conflicting stories about the origin of the state name. The name is probably from the word Señora (Our Lady), which refers to the Virgin Mary of Roman Catholicism, the religion brought to Mexico by Spanish explorers.

CAPITAL: Hermosillo (her-moh-SEE-yoh).

ENTERED COUNTRY: 1830.

COAT OF ARMS: The upper section is divided into three triangles. The center triangle depicts a picture of a Yaquí tribesman performing the Dance of the Deer. The left triangle represents the mining industry and the right triangle represents agriculture. The two squares at the bottom depict livestock and fish, representing other important industries in the state.

HOLIDAYS: Año Nuevo (New Year's Day—January 1); Día de la Constitución (Constitution Day—February 5); Benito Juárez's birthday (March 21); Primero de Mayo (Labor Day—May 1); Anniversary of the Battle of Puebla (1862), May 5; Revolution Day, 1910 (November 20); and Navidad (Christmas—December 25).

FLAG: There is no official state flag.

TIME: 5 AM = noon Greenwich Mean Time (GMT).

1 Location and Size

Sonora, Mexico's second largest state after Chihuahua, is located in the North Pacific region of the country. It covers an area of 179,503 square kilometers (69,306 square miles), which is a little smaller than the US state of North Dakota. Sonora borders the Mexican states of Sinaloa to the south, Chihuahua to the east, and Baja California to the northwest. The Gulf of California, which is sometimes called the Sea of Cortés, is located to the east. The US state of Arizona lies to the north. Sonora has 72 municipalities (similar to US counties). The capital is Hermosillo.

The mountain region of the Sierra Madre Occidental, which is known by different names as it crosses Sonora, begins near the border with the state of Chihuahua. The highest peak in the state is Cerro Pico Guacamayas at an elevation of 2,620 meters (8,595 feet). The western part of the state is an extensive plain that is wide in the north and narrows in the south. This region includes the Desierto de Altar, which is part of the Sonoran Desert that extends into the US

Blooming cactus. PETER LANGER.

states of Arizona and California. A low coastal plain stretches along the Gulf of California. The total length of the coastline is 1,208 kilometers (750 miles).

Sonora's rivers run into the Gulf of California. The Yaquí, which is the largest river in the state, begins near the US border and flows southwest to the Gulf. Its tributaries are Bavispe, Sahuaripa, and Moctezuma. The Mayo River, which is located in the southern part of the state, is about 400 kilometers (250 miles) and flows through Chihuahua and Sonora to the Gulf of California. The Colorado forms the natural border between Sonora and Baja California. Major inland lakes are the manmade reservoirs of Presa el Novillo, Presa Alvaro Obergón, and Presa Mocuzari. Isla Tiburón in the Gulf of California

is the largest island in the country, with an area of about 1,200 square kilometers (463 square miles).

2 Climate

The coastal regions of the state are generally warm and dry with a year-round average temperature of about 23°C (75°F). The northern part of the state is temperate and dry with an average year-round temperature of about 16°C (61°F). In the mountain regions, temperatures can be much cooler. In Hermosillo, the average year-round temperature is about 23°C (75°F). The average rainfall in the capital is about 24 centimeters (9.5 inches) per year. In the northern city of Nogales, the average year-round tempera-

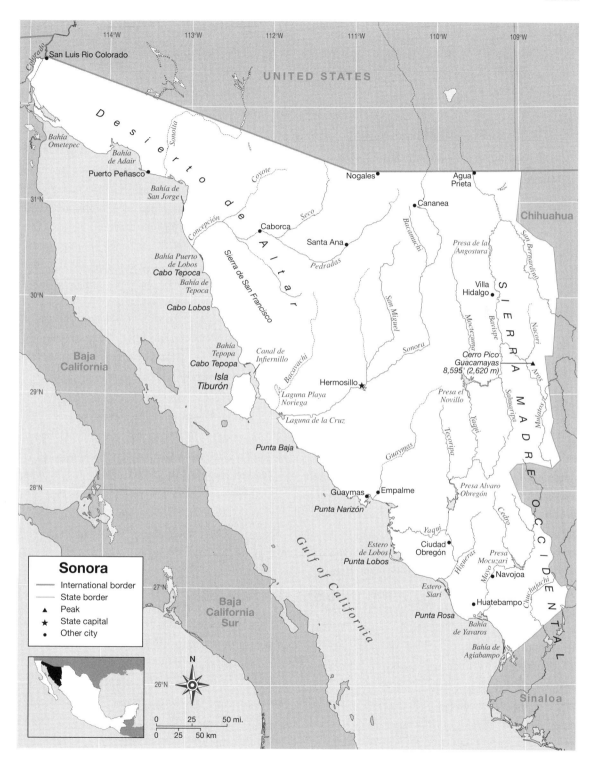

San Luis Rio Colorado

Colorado

UNITED STATES

Bahía
Ometepec

Bahía
de Adair

Puerto Peñasco

Bahía de
San Jorge

Nogales

Agua
Prieta

Chihuahua

Cananea

Caborca

Santa Ana

Presa de la
Angostura

San Bernardino

Bahía Puerto
de Lobos
Cabo Tepoca

Bahía de
Tepoca

Villa
Hidalgo

S
I
E
R
R
A

Cabo Lobos

Sierra de San Francisco

Cerro Pico
Guacamayas
8,595' (2,620 m)

Baja
California

Bahía
Tepopa
Cabo Tepopa

Isla
Tiburón

Canal de
Infiernillo

Presa el
Novillo

M
A
D
R
E

Hermosillo

Laguna Playa
Noriega

Laguna de la Cruz

Punta Baja

Guaymas

Presa Alvaro
Obregón

O
C
C
I
D
E
N
T
A
L

Guaymas

Empalme

Punta Narizón

Estero
de Lobos
Punta Lobos

Ciudad
Obregón

Yaqui

Presa
Mocuzari

Mayo

Navojoa

Estero
Siari

Huatebampo

27°N

Baja
California
Sur

Punta Rosa

Bahía
de Yavaros

Bahía de
Agiabampo

Sinaloa

Gulf of California

Sonora

International border
State border
▲ Peak
★ State capital
● Other city

N

0   25   50 mi.
0   25   50 km

ture is 16°c (62°F) and average rainfall is about 42 centimeters (16.9 inches) per year. The average snowfall in Nogales is 11 centimeters (4.5 inches) per year.

3 Plants and Animals

Palmilla, jojoba, pitahaya, and desert ironwood are plants common to the coastal regions of the state. In the mountain regions, forests of pine and oak are more common. Larger mammals found in the state include deer, wild boar, coyotes, pumas, wild rams, and bears. Smaller mammals include rabbits, hares, and squirrels. Chameleons, iguanas, and tarantulas are also found. Common birds include hawks and buzzards.

4 Environmental Protection

The state has experienced air pollution problems due to dusty roads, wood-burning for fuel, and automobile emissions. Maintaining an adequate, safe supply of drinking water is also a concern in some areas. In 2004, the state had 65 municipal wastewater treatment plants in operation with a combined installed capacity of 3,722 liters per second (983 gallons per second). The volume of treated wastewater that year was estimated at 2,575 liters per second (680 gallons per second). There were also 18 industrial wastewater treatment plants in operation that year. As of 2004, about 97.5% of the population had access to safe drinking water.

In 2003, the state had about 3.7 million hectares (9.3 million acres) of woodland, including 1.6 million hectares (4.1 million acres) of rain forest. In 2004, 542 hectares (1,339 acres) of woodland were damaged or destroyed by for-

est fires. An additional 4,127 hectares (10,198 acres) of pasture and brush land were also damaged by fires.

Protected areas in Sonora include the Sierra del Pincate and Gran Desierto de Altar Biosphere Reserve and the Cajon del Diablo Biosphere. Isla San Pedro Mártir was designated as a Ramsar Wetland of International Importance in 2004. The islands and protected areas of the Gulf of California were designated as UNESCO World Heritage sites in 2005.

5 Population, Ethnic Groups, Languages

Sonora had an estimated total population of 2,438,600 in 2006, ranking 18th among the states and the Distrito Federal. The population was almost evenly divided between men and women. About 76% of the population lived in urban areas. The population density was 13 people per square kilometer (34 people per square mile). In 2005, the capital, Hermosillo, had an estimated population of 701,834.

Almost all citizens speak Spanish as a first language. A small percentage of people speak indigenous (native) languages, such as Mayo and Yaquí.

6 Religions

According to the 2000 census, 87.9% of the population, or 1.7 million people, were Roman Catholic. About 4.8%, or 94,467 people, were mainline or evangelical Protestants. About 1.8% were counted as other Biblical faiths, including 7,290 Latter-day Saints (Mormons), 5,936 Seventh-day Adventists, and 22,231 Jehovah's

Witnesses. About 4.4% of the population claimed to have no religious affiliation.

A temple of the Church of Jesus Christ of Latter-day Saints was dedicated in Hermosillo in 2000. The Cathedral of the Ascension is the seat of the Roman Catholic archdiocese of Hermosillo.

7 Transportation

Ciudad Obregón Airport, Guaymas–General Jose Maria Yanez International Airport, and Nogales International Airport provide international flights to and from Sonora. The state has about 24,016 kilometers (14,917 miles) of roads and 1,958 kilometers (1,216 miles) of railroads. In 2004, there were 495,809 automobiles registered in the state, along with 7,609 passenger trucks, 296,380 freight trucks, and 5,012 motorcycles.

8 History

The first human presence in the state dates back to 30,000 BC when nomadic tribes of hunters and gatherers inhabited the region. The Pinacate Mountain region holds some ruins of settlements that are around 15,000 years old. Yet, more permanent human settlements first emerged around 1500 BC in the more fertile parts of the state, while the desert continued to house nomadic tribes. The Hohokam culture (originally from Arizona), the Mogollón culture (from New Mexico), and the Casas Grandes and Paquime cultures (from Chihuahua) influenced the region. Influence from Mesoamerican cultures that reached the region with trade and commercial interests were also strong during the first centuries AD. A massive migration from the Casa Grande region to the mountainous region gave birth to the Ópata tribes in 1340. At the arrival of the Spanish conquistadors (explorers who sough to claim Mexico for Spain), the different indigenous groups belonged to the Yuto-Náhuatl and Hokana linguistic families.

In 1531, Nuño Beltrán de Guzmán founded the city of San Miguel de Culiacán in what is now the neighboring state of Sinaloa. Sinaloa is where the Spanish initiated the search for mineral deposits, promoted slave trade, and fostered new colonization efforts in the region. In 1533, Diego Guzmán became the first Spaniard to enter what is now Sonora. He found resistance from indigenous populations near the Yaquí River and soon abandoned the region. In 1536, Spanish explorer Alvar Nuñez Cabeza de Vaca (c. 1490-c. 1560) and three other survivors of the failed Pánfilo de Narváez expedition passed through the region. In *Shipwreck,* his account of the years they wandered through indigenous territories before finding a Spanish settlement, Cabeza de Vaca, referred to two marvelous indigenous cities, Cíbola and Quivira. Several expeditions were launched to find those cities, but they apparently did not exist.

Because the region was slowly populated, it did not evolve into a major economic center in colonial Mexico. A prison was built in Sonora in 1586. New efforts to conquer indigenous territories drastically decimated the native population during the 17th century. The efforts by Jesuit priests to convert the indigenous population to Roman Catholicism and create sedentary settlements helped integrate the remaining native population to the colonial economy. The Jesuits created settlements where Indians could work the land and provide labor for mining enterprises. However, some Yaquí indigenous uprisings continued throughout the 17th century.

In 1810, Sonoran independence leaders revolted in an effort to join the independence movement launched elsewhere in Mexico. However, most landowners in Sonora were more concerned with keeping the attacks by the Apache Indians at bay.

It was only in 1821 that Sonora became incorporated into independent Mexico. Two years later, Sonora and Sinaloa were separated into two different states. After a period of political instability that characterized much of 19th century Mexico, Sonora was occupied by US troops in 1847. The Treaty of Hidalgo, where Mexico ceded territory to the United States, achieved peace between the two countries. This allowed for the exit of foreign troops. Yet, instability remained the dominant political culture in the region until the end of the Mexican Revolution in 1920.

Having consolidated as a cattle ranching and agricultural economy, Sonora remains a scarcely populated state with vast stretches of unpopulated desert areas. Its proximity to the United States has made the state an attractive port of entry for illicit drugs. Additionally, its location fosters a growing number of maquiladoras (manufacturing assembly plants) since the adoption of the North American Free Trade Agreement (NAFTA), a trade agreement between Mexico, the United States, and Canada, in 1994.

In the first decade of the 21st century, the state of Sonora's border with the United States continued to play a major role in the affairs of the state. Economically, the state's maquiladoras and farms retained their dependence upon markets in the United States. While this helped better the lives of the state's residents, there was a downside. The long, sparsely populated border region made Sonora a major gateway for the smuggling of illegal immigrants into the United States, as well as a transshipment point for illegal drugs. As a result, official corruption and crime became serious problems.

9 State and Local Government

A state governor is democratically elected every six years for a nonrenewable term. The legislature is comprised of a unicameral (one chamber) state congress with 27 members who serve nonrenewable three-year terms. Eighteen members are elected in single-member districts and nine are elected by proportional representation.

The 72 municipalities that comprise Sonora hold democratic elections for municipal presidents and council members every three years. Immediate re-election is not allowed.

10 Political Parties

The three main political parties in all of Mexico are the Institutional Revolutionary Party (PRI), the National Action Party (PAN), and the Party of the Democratic Revolution (PRD). The PRI has been the dominant party in the state since the end of the Mexican Revolution. All governors in Sonora have belonged to that party. In 1994, Sonora's favorite rising politician, Luis Donaldo Colosio (1948–1994), was appointed as the PRI presidential candidate, but he was assassinated before the election was held. Eduardo Bours Castelo of the PRI took office as governor in 2003. The PAN is the second-largest party in the state.

Adobe brick manufacturer. PETER LANGER.

Because the state has been ruled exclusively by the Institutional Revolutionary Party (PRI) since the end of the Mexican Revolution, formal separation of power provisions have not been effectively enforced. The PRI governor has exercised excessive influence over the PRI-controlled legislature.

11 Judicial System

The Supreme Tribunal of Justice is the highest court in the state. The state governor, with legislative approval, appoints seven members for renewable six-year terms. Only highly qualified attorneys with proven experience can be appointed to the Supreme Tribunal. Because the state has not experienced alternation in power since the Mexican Revolution, the formal autonomy and independence of the judiciary has not been enforced. In addition, an electoral tribunal and local courts also comprise the state's judicial system.

12 Economy

Geography plays a major role in the economy of Sonora. Because of its shared border with Arizona, the Sonoran economy has traditionally been tied to the United States, with more than 90% of its exports destined for the market there. This linkage has affected not only the state's manufacturing sector, but also its agricultural sector, both of which are heavily dependent upon exports to the United States. Since the mid-1980s, Sonora's export market has seen sustained growth due to the development of the *maquiladora* (assembly plant) and automotive industries in the border cities of Nogales and San Luis Rio Colorado, as well as in the state's capital city of Hermosillo.

The state's long coastline has also allowed a substantial fishing industry to develop, particularly in the port city of Guaymas, which has also generated considerable amounts of foreign currency earnings for Mexico. Although still in its infancy, the coastline's beaches have also allowed a tourism industry to develop, centered on the port city of Puerto Peñasco.

As of 2003, Sonora's gross domestic product (GDP) was $7 billion.

13 Industry

The state's manufacturing sector has been marked by the development of the so-called maquiladoras, or assembly plants, that produce items for companies such as Xerox, General Electric, and Bose. Most maquiladoras make electrical appliances and electronic equipment. These plants are labor-intensive assembly operations, relying on imports of parts from the United States. Some 71,000 people are employed by the maquiladoras, of which there are some 211, mostly located in Hermosillo and in Nogales and San Luis Rio Colorado, both of which are on the border with the United States.

14 Labor

As of 2005, the state of Sonora had 966,133 eligible workers. Some 935,301 were listed as employed and 30,832 were listed as unemployed. Unemployed workers in rural areas may not be counted, however. The unemployment rate that year was reported to be 3.1%. Of those who were working, services employed 38.3%, followed by commerce at 18.9% and manufacturing at 18.1%.

The US Bureau of Labor Statistics reported that Mexican workers saw their wages increase from $2.49 per hour in 2003 to $2.50 per hour in 2004. (The average US worker earned $15.70 per hour in 2004.) The maximum work week is set at 48 hours by law. The average worker spends 40 to 45 hours per week on the job. Workers earn twice their regular hourly rate for up to nine hours a week of overtime. When a worker works more than nine hours overtime in a week, he or she earns three times the regular hourly rate. After one year, workers are entitled by law to six days paid vacation.

In Hermosillo, the largest share of the city's unionized workforce are members of the Confederation of Mexican Workers (CTM), the revolutionary Confederation of Workers and Farmers (CROC), and the Regional Confederation of Mexican Workers. In the border city of Nogales, about 20% of the workforce is unionized. The unions there include CTM, CROC, and the Revolutionary Confederation of Mexican Workers (CROM).

15 Agriculture

Agricultural plays an important role in the economy of the state. In the north and northeast, where the climate is dry, irrigation systems are used and farmers produce alfalfa, asparagus, vegetables, fodder, grapes, dates, and olives. Livestock production is centered on cattle. The main crops in the central region include wheat, barley, alfalfa, and safflower. Cattle, poultry, and pigs are raised in the higher elevations.

The main crops in the east include corn, beans, chili, apples, and peaches. Pasture lands allow for the breeding of cattle, goats, horses, mules, and donkeys. In the south and southeast, the main crops are wheat, corn, beans, cotton, and soy. In the south, cotton and vegetables are also grown, while pigs, goats, cattle, sheep and poultry are raised. In the southeast, tomatoes, onions, lettuce and celery are also grown. A special regional cheese is produced in the southeast. It is spiced with *chiltepín* (piquín chile), which grows in the desert.

In 2004, the state of Sonora ranked second among all Mexican states in the production of wheat at 576,817 tons. Other crops produced in Sonora included: 75,989 tons of corn, 172,166 tons of potatoes, 51,339 tons of red tomatoes, and 35,982 tons of green chilies. Livestock brought to market in 2004 included: 53,304 head of beef cattle, 28,952 pigs, 454 goats, and 1,157 sheep. In that same year, the state produced: 136 million liters (35 million gallons) of milk from dairy cows, 974,000 liters (257,303 gallons) of goat's milk, and 144,432 tons of eggs. Meat production included: 74,971 tons of beef, 199,519 tons of pork, 412 tons of goat, 577 tons of lamb, and 6,094 tons of poultry.

16 Natural Resources

Sonora is Mexico's leading producer of copper, which is mined in the state's eastern region. Other mineral resources in the state include graphite, silver, gold, barite, zinc, and tungsten.

Fish species caught in the coastal and river waters of the state include shrimp, sardines, shark, sea bass, sole, and tuna. A total of about 7,000 fishing vessels operate off the Sonoran coast. In 2003, Sonora had the largest fish catch in the country at about 546,964 tons.

In 2003, the value of forest wood production was about $3.2 million. Pine was one of the primary types of wood harvested.

17 Energy and Power

In 2005, there were 775,111 users of electricity in the state of Sonora. Of that total, the largest number were residential customers at 693,553. Sales of electricity that same year totaled 9,030,242 megawatt hours, of which the largest users were large industrial firms at 2,552,734 megawatt hours. Electric power in Sonora is generated by 10 generating plants: one diesel, three gas turbine, two thermal (non-coal), three hydroelectric, and one combined cycle (gas-turbine and steam) plant. Electricity is produced and distributed by the Federal Electricity Commission and Central Light and Power. Both utilities are run by the Mexican government.

18 Health

In 2003, the state had 45 hospitals and 327 outpatient centers that were part of the national health system. In 2004, there were about 2,487 doctors, 5,601 nurses, and 184 dentists working in these health centers. There were an additional 53 independent health centers in the state in 2004.

Most of the Mexican population is covered under a government health plan. The IMSS (Instituto Mexicano de Seguro Social) covers the general population. The ISSSTE (Instituto de Seguridad y Servicios Sociales de Trabajadores del Estado) covers state workers.

19 Housing

Most homes are made with materials such as brick, concrete, and stone. Adobe homes with sheet metal roofs are found in some areas. In 2000, about 81% of all homes were owner-occupied. In 2005, there were an estimated 614,595 residential housing units in the state. About 91% of these units were single-family detached homes. The average household was estimated at 3.9 people.

20 Education

Public education in Mexico is free for students from ages 6 to 16 and most of the students in the state attend public schools. In 2004/05, it was estimated that 92% of age-eligible students completed primary school, which includes six years of study. About 83% of eligible students completed secondary school, which includes three years of study after primary school. About 58.6% of eligible students completed the *bachillerato*, which is similar to a high school diploma. The national average for completion of the *bachillerato* was 60.1% that year.

There are at least 10 main institutions of higher learning in the state. The main campus of the Universidad de Sonora, Universidad Kino, Universidad de Hermosillo, and El Colegio de Sonora are located in Hermosillo. In 2005, there were about 85,038 students ages 20 and older who were enrolled in some type of higher education program. The overall literacy rate was estimated at 94.2% in 2005.

21 Arts

Sonora has 26 local cultural centers including a French Alliance center in Ciudad Obregón. Three types of local music can be heard in towns throughout Sonora: *rancheras* recount lost loves, *corridos* are long narrative poems, and *huapangos* are rhythmic songs often heard at bullfights. Most activities are connected to Sonora's beautiful beaches. In 2004, there were at least three major theaters for the performing arts. There were also over 40 registered movie theaters, including multiscreen theaters and single-screen galleries.

22 Libraries and Museums

In 2003, there were 344 libraries in the state with a combined stock of 1,945,598 volumes. The same year, there were 19 museums registered in the state that had permanent exhibits. Hermosillo features the Museum of Sonora and the Regional Museum of the University of Sonora.

23 Media

In 2005, Hermosillo had five daily newspapers: *El Imparcial*, *El Independiente*, *Primera Plana* (*Front Page*), *Cambio* (*Change*), and *El Financiero* (*The Financer*). Ciudad Obregón published *Tribuna de Yaqui*. The city of San Luís Río Colorado has *Tribuna de San Luís*. There were also daily papers in Agua Prieta, Guaymas, Navojoa, and Nogales.

In 2004, there were 135 television stations and 110 radio stations (53 AM and 57 FM). In 2005, there were about 126,595 subscribers to cable and satellite television stations. Also

Desert sunset. PETER LANGER.

in 2005, there were about 343,310 residential phone lines, with about 16.9 mainline phones in use for every 100 people.

24 Tourism, Travel, and Recreation

The city of Hermosillo is on the Sea of Cortés, which has many beautiful beaches. Bahía Kino, in the town of Kino, is a great beach for snorkeling and swimming. Isla Tiburon (Shark Island) is a wildlife preserve. Puerto Peñasco also has beautiful beaches. Ciudad Obregón is surrounded by many settlements of the Yaquí Amerindians, such as Torim and Vicam. Often authentic dances are performed for tourists.

25 Sports

Professional baseball teams in the state compete in the Mexican Pacific League. The Naranjeros (Orange Growers) of Hermosillo were the Caribbean World Series champions in 2001. They play in the 13,000-seat Hector Espino stadium. The Navojoa Mayos were series champs in 2000. The Obregón Yaquís placed second in the World Series in 2005.

Professional basketball teams in the state compete in the Pacific Coast Basketball League (CIBACOPA—Circuito de Baloncesto de las Costa del Pacifico). These include the Cananea Mineros (Miners), the Obregón Trigueros (Wheat Merchants), the Guyamas Marineros

(Mariners), the Nogales Guindas (Cherries), and the Navojoa Paskolas.

In 2004, there were four major sports arenas in the state.

26 Famous People

Álvaro Obregón (1880–1928) was a revolutionary general who also served as president from 1920 to 1924. Fernando Valenzuela (b.1960) was a pitcher for the Los Angeles Dodgers. In 1986, he became the first rookie to win the Cy Young Award, an award given to the best pitcher in major league baseball. Julio César Chávez González (b.1962) won five world boxing titles before retiring in 2001. Ana Gabriel (b.1955) is a popular singer and songwriter. Rosalino Félix Sánchez (1960–1992), known as Chalino, was a singer-songwriter who gained popularity as a folk hero after his death. Erubiel Durazo Cárdenas (b.1974) played for the Oakland A's of Major League Baseball from 2003 to 2005.

27 Bibliography

BOOKS

Brown, John. *Journey into the Desert.* New York: Oxford University Press, 2002.

Burt, Janet. *The Pacific North States of Mexico.* Philadelphia: Mason Crest Publishers, 2003.

Gruber, Beth. *Mexico.* Washington, DC: National Geographic, 2006.

Patent, Dorothy Hinshaw. *Life in a Desert.* Minneapolis, MN: Lerner, 2003.

Treto Cisneros, Pedro. *The Mexican League: Comprehensive Player Statistics, 1937–2001*, bilingual edition. Jefferson, NC: McFarland, 2002.

WEB SITES

Government of Mexico. *Mexico for Kids.* www.elbalero.gob.mx/index_kids.html (accessed on March 30, 2007).

Sonora, Mexico. www.sonora-mexico.com/ (accessed on March 30, 2007).

Tabasco

PRONUNCIATION: tah-BAHS-koh.

ORIGIN OF STATE NAME: May have originated from the native Aztec word *tlapaco,* which means "humid land." May also have originated with the first Spaniards, who thought the native leader was Tabasco, but his name was more likely Taabs-Coob.

CAPITAL: Villahermosa (vee-ah-hair-MOH-sah).

ENTERED COUNTRY: 1824.

COAT OF ARMS: Four squares depict castles, a shield and sword, a crowned lion ready to attack, and a native warrior. In the center, an oval features a representation of the Virgin Mary.

HOLIDAYS: Año Nuevo (New Year's Day—January 1); Día de la Constitución (Constitution Day—February 5); Benito Juárez's birthday (March 21); Primero de Mayo (Labor Day—May 1); Anniversary of the Battle of Puebla (1862), May 5; Revolution Day, 1910 (November 20); and Navidad (Christmas—December 25).

FLAG: There is no official state flag.

TIME: 6 AM = noon Greenwich Mean Time (GMT).

1 Location and Size

Tabasco is located on the Isthmus of Tehuantepec. Tabasco covers an area of 24,737 square kilometers (9,551 square miles), which is a little smaller than the US state of Vermont. It ranks as 24th in size among the states and covers about 1.3% of the total land area of Mexico. The state is bordered on the north by the Gulf of Mexico, on the south by Chiapas, on the east by the Central American country of Guatemala and the Mexican state of Campeche, and on the west by the state of Veracruz. It is divided into 17 municipalities (similar to US counties) and its capital is Villahermosa.

Almost all the territory of Tabasco is a low and flat plains region known as Llanura Tabasqueña. The only exception is the region bordering the state of Chiapas, where the hilly region of the Chiapas Sierra begins. The highest elevations in the state are the Sierra Madrigal and Sierra Tapijulapa, both of which rise to elevations of about 900 meters (2,952 feet).

This state has almost one-third of all Mexico's water resources. Tabasco's major rivers are the Grijalva and the Usumacinta. The Usumacinta, Mexico's largest river, forms a natural border between Mexico and Guatemala. Other noteworthy rivers include the Palizada, San Pedro, San Pablo, Tonalá, and Mezcalapa. In Tabasco, the largest coastal lagoons are the Laguna del Carmen, Laguna Machona, and Laguna Mecoacán. The total length of the coastline is 184 kilometers (114 miles). There are a number of inland lakes, including Laguna del Rosario, Laguna Cantemual, and Laguna Maluca.

2 Climate

The warm waters of the Gulf of Mexico contribute to the climate, which is generally warm and humid. The average temperature ranges from 24°c to 28°c (76°F to 82°F). The highest monthly average rainfall occurs in August and September. Up to 30 centimeters (12 inches) of rain often falls during September alone.

In the capital city of Villahermosa, the average year-round temperature is 24°c (76°F) and the average rainfall is 170 centimeters per year (67.2 inches). The year-round average temperature in Frontera is 22°c (71°F) and the average rainfall is 120.9 centimeters (47.5 inches) per year.

3 Plants and Animals

The mountain region of the state has rain forest conditions that are well suited for the growth of exotic trees (including mahogany, cedar, ceiba, palo, tinto, barí, and rubber trees) and various species of ferns. Fruit trees such as tamarind, orange, and sapodilla (the source of chicle, the base for chewing gum and other products) are also found. Mangroves (tropical evergreens with a tangled root system) are found along the coast.

Deer, ocelots, spider monkeys, and jaguars are a few of the larger mammals found in the state. Smaller mammals include squirrels, anteaters, and rabbits. Alligators and a wide variety of poisonous and nonpoisonous snakes can be found in the state. Common birds include macaws, quetzals, toucans, and hummingbirds. A large variety of insects and reptiles are found in the rain forest regions.

4 Environmental Protection

In 2004, the state had 53 municipal wastewater treatment plants in operation with a combined installed capacity of 1,165 liters per second (307 gallons per second). The volume of treated wastewater that year was estimated at 872 liters per second (230 gallons per second). There were also 60 industrial wastewater treatment plants in operation that year. As of 2004, about 71.9% of the population had access to safe drinking water.

In 2003, the state had about 276,618 hectares (683,537 acres) of rain forest. Protected areas in the state include the Pantanos de Centla Biosphere Reserve, which has been designated as a Ramsar Wetland of International Importance. Pantanos de Centla is also home to the Yu-Balcah Ecotourism Center, which is a refuge area for howler monkeys. The reserve is a winter home for many migratory birds from Canada and the United States. This area has been threatened by the activities of the petroleum exploration and production company Petróleos Mexicanos (PEMEX).

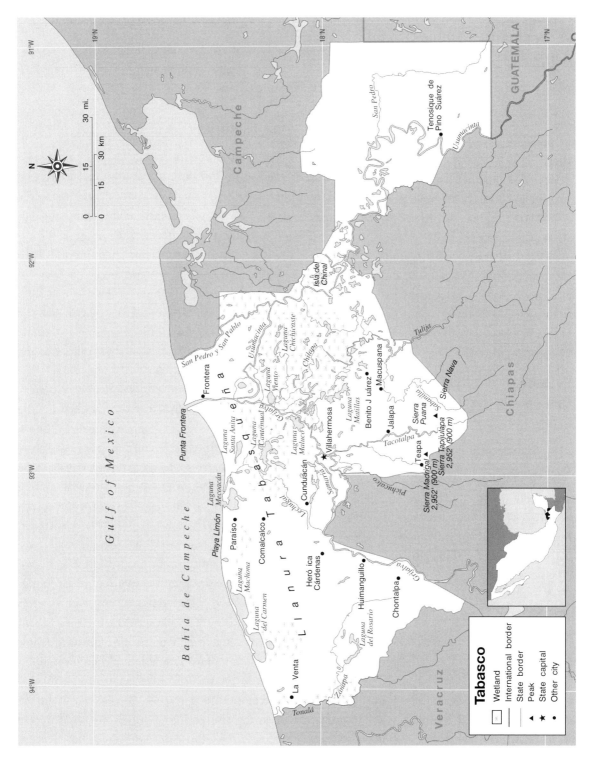

5 Population, Ethnic Groups, Languages

Tabasco had an estimated total population of 2,017,500 in 2006, ranking 20th among the states and the Distrito Federal. About 49% of the population were men and 51% were women. About 47% of the population lived in urban areas. The population density was 81 people per square kilometer (211 people per square mile). In 2000, the capital, Villahermosa, had a population of 545,433.

Almost all citizens speak Spanish as their first language. A small percentage of the people speak indigenous (native) languages, such as Chontal de Tabasco and Chol.

6 Religions

According to the 2000 census, 70.4% of the population, or about 1.1 million people, were Roman Catholic. The state had the second largest percentage of mainline and evangelical Protestants with about 13.6% of the population (following Chiapas). About 5% were counted as other Biblical faiths, including 58,701 Seventh-day Adventists, 20,734 Jehovah's Witnesses, and 3,676 Latter-day Saints (Mormons). About 10% of the population claimed to have no religious affiliation.

A temple of the Church of Jesus Christ of Latter-day Saints was dedicated in Villahermosa in 2000.

7 Transportation

Tabasco has one international airport. The state also has about 7,912 kilometers (4,914 miles) of roads and 315 kilometers (196 miles) of rail-roads. In 2004, there were 135,649 automobiles registered in the state, along with 5,691 passenger trucks, 72,850 freight trucks, and 9,856 motorcycles.

8 History

The Olmec civilization developed in Tabasco starting in 1500 BC. It was around 500 BC that the Olmec reached its cultural and economic peak. The Maya emerged as the dominant culture in the region between 100 and 1000 AD. Toltec culture became dominant in the 13th century, and the Chontales began to grow in the 14th century. Commerce between Nahuas and Maya facilitated the development and rise of sizeable cities, like Cimatán and Teapa. Some 135,000 native indigenous people inhabited the area around 1500.

In 1518, Spanish explorer Juan de Grijalva's (c. 1489–1527) five-ship expedition in the Caribbean first reached Tabasco territory. Soon, the Spaniards entered into contact with the Chontales natives who gave them utensils made of gold as gifts. This sparked interest among the Spaniards to explore the territory in search of gold mines. Spanish explorer Hernán Cortés (1485–1547) reached the region a year later and successfully fought against the Chontales. Spanish military might convinced a local indigenous leader, called Tabasco, to present Cortés with a present of 20 native women. Among them was Malinche, who later became Cortés' mistress and mother of his son, Martín. Malinche is often unjustly accused of providing Cortés with vital information to defeat the Aztecs. Her ability to learn Spanish and communicate with Cortés is the reason for those unfounded claims.

Indigenous uprisings and the Spanish preoccupation with dominating the central valley of Mexico delayed the conquest of Tabasco until the late 16th century. For a brief period, Tabasco was put under the authority of the province of Guatemala. By the end of the 16th century, the indigenous population was barely around 7,500, and there were no more than one hundred Spanish colonizers. To promote agricultural activity, the Spanish began introducing African slaves. Its geographic location and the growing trade that existed in the region made Tabasco a prime target of British, French, and Dutch pirates. The pillage by pirates and the uprisings by the indigenous population and African slaves hindered the economic development and population growth in the region. Those uprisings also reflected the deplorable living conditions of the indigenous and enslaved populations. New uprisings during the 18th century provoked the Spaniards to increase the slave trade and promote new settlements by colonizers.

The 1810 independence movement did not reach Tabasco. It was only in 1821 that the region became independent of Spanish colonial rule. In 1824 Tabasco became a federal state. Political instability and confrontations between local military leaders characterized much of the 19th century. For a brief period of time, US troops occupied the region during the Mexican-American War (1846–48). In 1863, French invading troops occupied the region to enforce the monarchial rule of Emperor Maximilian (1832–1867).

Liberal forces successfully brought an end to monarchical rule in 1867. Tabasco was soon brought under control, first by Mexican president Benito Juárez (1806–1872) loyalists, and later by forces loyal to Porfirio Díaz (1830–

Visitors to the Parque Museo La Venta in Tabasco can admire Olmec sculptures like this one. © DANNY LEHMAN/ CORBIS.

1915), the man who ruled Mexico between 1876 and 1910.

The Mexican Revolution, which started in 1910, had limited impact in this scarcely populated region. The revolutionary victors quickly obtained the support of the local elites before the new constitution of Mexico was written in 1917. The Institutional Revolutionary Party (PRI), the dominant political party in the country for many years, exercised overwhelming power in Tabasco during most of the 20th century, especially after large oil fields were discovered in the state.

In the first decade of the 21st century, the state of Tabasco remained heavily dependent upon the oil industry and agriculture, despite attempts to broaden the state's economy. Problems facing the state in that decade were pollution of the coastline and official corruption.

9 State and Local Government

The state governor is democratically elected every six years for a nonrenewable term. There are 21 legislators in the state's unicameral (single chamber) congress. Fourteen members are elected from single member districts and seven are elected by proportional representation for nonrenewable three-year terms.

The 17 municipalities that comprise Tabasco hold democratic elections for municipal presidents and council members every three years. Immediate reelection is not allowed.

10 Political Parties

The three main political parties in all of Mexico are the Institutional Revolutionary Party (PRI), the National Action Party (PAN), and the Party of the Democratic Revolution (PRD). The PRI has dominated politics in Tabasco. Manuel Andrade Díaz of the PRI took office as governor in 2002. The PRD is the second most important party in the state.

Although there are formal provisions for separation of power, the governor has historically exercised enormous prerogatives and attributions. Accusations of electoral fraud have questioned the legitimacy of the democratic system in the state in recent years.

11 Judicial System

The Supreme Tribunal of Justice is the state's highest court. Its 19 members are appointed by a two-thirds majority vote in the legislature from a three-person list submitted by the state governor. Only highly qualified attorneys, approved by a Council of the Judiciary, can be nominated to serve in the highest court. There has not been alternation of power in Tabasco and the PRI has exercised enormous influence and power in the oil-rich state. As a result, the judicial system has not traditionally shown evidence of independence and autonomy.

12 Economy

Tabasco's economy is primarily based on oil and agriculture. Although commerce and services represent around 60% of the state's gross domestic product (GDP), it is the oil sector that provides the state with the funds needed to diversify its economy, as well as providing the economic foundation to its commerce and services sectors. In addition, much of the state's transportation, power, and communications infrastructure is designed to meet the needs of the oil industry. However, reliance upon the oil sector has come at the price of increasing pollution along the 120 miles of shoreline along the Gulf of Mexico.

The state also has two ports on the Gulf of Mexico, Dos Bocas Harbor, which primarily serves the oil industry, and Frontera Harbor which serves the commercial needs of Tabasco. The capital city of Villahermosa has some 14,730 commercial establishments.

Although the state's farming and cattle raising sectors account for only around 7.5% of the state's GDP, these two sectors are the chief source of employment for most of the state's labor force. Both are largely geared toward meeting family and local needs, although some crops are exported.

13 Industry

Villahermosa is the commercial and manufacturing center of the state. Manufacturing includes petrochemicals, sugar and chocolate processing, and cement. Most of the state's *maquiladoras* provide various types of support to the oil industry. The capital city is also home to three industrial parks.

The state's handicraft industries provide gourd bowls, alligator skin shoes, and handbags.

14 Labor

As of 2005, the state of Tabasco had 760,760 eligible workers. Some 738,753 were listed as employed, and 22,007 were listed as unemployed. Unemployed workers in rural areas may not be counted, however. The unemployment rate that year was reported to be 2.8%. Of those who were working, services employed 38.7%, followed by agriculture at 24.1%, and commerce at 18.7%.

The US Bureau of Labor Statistics reported that Mexican workers saw their wages increase from $2.49 per hour in 2003 to $2.50 per hour in 2004. (The average US worker earned $15.70 per hour in 2004.) The maximum work week is set at 48 hours by law. The average worker spends 40 to 45 hours per week on the job. Workers earn twice their regular hourly rate for up to nine hours a week of overtime. When a worker works more than nine hours overtime in a week, he or she earns three times the regular hourly rate.

After one year, workers are entitled by law to six days paid vacation.

Labor relations in the capital city of Villahermosa are said to be friendly.

15 Agriculture

Most residents are employed in farming. Major crops include corn, beans, sweet potatoes, squash, yucca, and rice. These crops are generally used for local consumption. Export crops include cacao (cocoa beans), sugarcane, bananas, and coconuts. Cattle, pigs, sheep, and goats are the primary livestock animals, and are mostly raised for local consumption.

In 2004, crop production for the state of Tabasco included: 150,828 tons of corn, 689,436 tons of bananas, 174,414 tons of sugar, 26,305 tons of rice, 2,109 tons of green chilies, 3,528 tons of kidney beans, and 17,668 tons of sorghum. Livestock brought to market in 2004 included: 66,664 head of beef cattle, and 7,653 pigs. In that same year, the state produced 99.4 million liters (26 million gallons) of milk from dairy cows and 1,407 tons of eggs. Meat production included: 55,713 tons of beef, 13,490 tons of pork, 232 tons of lamb, and 23,712 tons of poultry.

16 Natural Resources

Oil and cement are among the most important natural mineral resources of the state. Forestry products include chicle, and hard and precious woods. However, in 2003, the value of forest wood production was only about $174,729. There is also some fishing along the coast. In 2003, the total fish catch was about 56,135 tons.

Rural habitat in Tabasco. PETER LANGER.

17 Energy and Power

Mexico's existing natural gas reserves are located primarily in the southwestern states of Tabasco and Chiapas.

In 2005, there were 521,885 users of electricity in the state of Tabasco. Of that total, the largest number were residential customers at 466,429. Sales of electricity that same year totaled 2,399,156 megawatt hours, of which the largest users were residential customers at 1,054,744 megawatt hours. There are no electric power generating facilities in Tabasco. As a result, the state must import the electricity it uses from other states. Electricity is produced and distributed by the Federal Electricity Commission, and

Central Light and Power. Both utilities are run by the Mexican government.

18 Health

In 2003, the state had 26 hospitals and 556 outpatient centers that were part of the national health system. In 2004, there were about 2,287 doctors, 4,089 nurses, and 325 dentists working in these health centers. There were an additional 55 independent health centers in the state in 2004.

Most of the Mexican population is covered under a government health plan. The IMSS (Instituto Mexicano de Seguro Social) covers the general population. The ISSSTE (Instituto de

Seguridad y Servicios Sociales de Trabajadores del Estado) covers state workers.

19 Housing

Most homes are made with materials such as brick, stone, concrete, and wood. Sheet metal is one of the most common roofing materials. In 2000, about 80% of all homes were owner-occupied. In 2005, there were an estimated 473,121 residential housing units in the state. About 91% of these units were single-family detached homes. The average household was estimated at 4.2 people.

20 Education

Public education in Mexico is free for students from ages 6 to 16 and most of the students in the state attend public schools. In 2004/05, it was estimated that 90% of age-eligible students completed primary school, which includes six years of study. About 80% of eligible students completed secondary school, which includes three years of study after primary school. About 61% of eligible students completed the *bachillerato*, which is similar to a high school diploma. The national average for completion of the *bachillerato* was 60.1% that year.

The Universidad Juarez Autónoma de Tabasco and the Instituto Tecnológico are located in Villahermosa. In 2005, there were about 63,008 students ages 20 and older who were enrolled in some type of higher education program. The overall literacy rate was estimated at 90% in 2005.

21 Arts

Many cultural events take place in the Palacio del Gobierno, the Sala de Arte Antonio Ramírez, and the Teatro de Seguro Social in the capital, Villahermosa. Most cities have a cultural center, where local performing arts troupes perform. The annual Tabasco fair in Parque Villahermosa brings together the art, culture, crafts, and cuisine of 17 counties. There are over 50 registered movie theaters, including multiscreen theaters and single-screen galleries.

22 Libraries and Museums

In 2003, there were 725 libraries in the state with a combined stock of 3,457,011 volumes. The same year, there were 12 museums registered in the state that had permanent exhibits. Centro has a museum of anthropology. El Museo de la Venta in Villahermosa is a combination zoo and archeological museum. Its collections include large heads sculpted from basalt rock by the indigenous Olmec people. The Carlos Pellicer Museum in Villahermosa is a regional museum of anthropology named for a poet from the region. There is also a house museum dedicate to Carlos Pellicer and his works.

23 Media

In 2005, Villahermosa, the capital, had four daily newspapers: *Avance* (*Advance*), *Novedades de Tabasco* (*Tabasco News*), *Presente* (with both a morning and an evening edition), and *Tabasco Hoy* (*Tabasco Today*).

In 2004, there were 15 television stations and 25 radio stations (17 AM and 8 FM). In 2005, there were about 48,526 subscribers to cable and satellite television stations. Also in 2005, there were about 143,243 residential phone lines, with about 9.2 mainline phones in use for every 100 people.

24 Tourism, Travel, and Recreation

There are natural regions of interest to tourists in the state. There is whitewater rafting at Usumacinta. Archeological sites are found at La Venta (Olmec culture) and at Comacalco and Ponomá (Mayan culture). The beaches along the Gulf of Mexico attract tourists to the resorts there. Festivals are regularly held in the capital, Villahermosa. La Polvora Lagoon is a park with waterfalls and hiking and activities for children.

25 Sports

The Jaguares (Jaguars) play in the Second Division of the Mexican Football (soccer) Association (commonly known as Femexfut). The Olmecas de Tabasco compete in the Mexican League of AAA minor league baseball. Their home field is at the 10,500-seat Centenario 27 de Febrero stadium. In 2004, there were 12 sports arenas and one bullfighting ring in the state.

26 Famous People

La Malinche was the daughter of an Aztec ruler who became the mistress of the Spanish conqueror, Hernán Cortés. Carlos Alberto Madrazo Becerra (1915–1969) was a governor of Tabasco and one-time president of the Institutional Revolutionary Party (PRI). Roberto Madrazo (b.1952) was governor of Tabasco from 1995 to 2000 and was a candidate in the Mexican presidential election of 2006.

27 Bibliography

BOOKS

Field, Randi. *The Gulf States of Mexico*. Philadelphia, PA: Mason Crest Publishers, 2003.

Green, Jen. *Caribbean Sea and Gulf of Mexico*. Milwaukee, WI: World Almanac Library, 2006.

Gruber, Beth. *Mexico*. Washington, DC: National Geographic, 2006.

Williams, Colleen Madonna Flood. *The People of Mexico*. Philadelphia, PA: Mason Crest Publishers, 2003.

WEB SITES

Government of Mexico. *Mexico for Kids*. www.elbalero.gob.mx/index_kids.html (accessed on March 30, 2007).

Mexican Tourism Board. *Visit Mexico: Tabasco*. www.visitmexico.com/wb/Visitmexico/Visi_Tabasco (accessed on March 30, 2007).

Tamaulipas

PRONUNCIATION: tah-mah-ooh-LEE-pahs.

ORIGIN OF STATE NAME: Name comes from the Huasteca word *tamaholipa.* It means either "where people pray" or "high mountains."

CAPITAL: Ciudad Victoria (see-oo-DAHD veek-TOH-ree-ah).

ENTERED COUNTRY: October 3, 1824.

COAT OF ARMS: The images on the coat of arms represent the economic activities of the state. Cornstalks and animals represent agriculture and livestock. The boat and the dock that appear on the lower half of the coat of arms represent fishing and industry. Cerro de Bernal, a well-known natural peak, is also shown in the lower part of the shield. The smaller shield in the top section represents the family coat of arms of José Escandón y Helguera, Count of Sierra Gorda, who colonized the state.

HOLIDAYS: Año Nuevo (New Year's Day—January 1); Día de la Constitución (Constitution Day—February 5); Benito Juárez's birthday (March 21); Primero de Mayo (Labor Day—May 1); Revolution Day, 1910 (November 20); and Navidad (Christmas—December 25).

FLAG: There is no official state flag.

TIME: 6 AM = noon Greenwich Mean Time (GMT).

1 Location and Size

Tamaulipas covers an area of 80,175 square kilometers (30,955 square miles), which is slightly smaller than the US state of South Carolina. It ranks as the sixth-largest in size among the states and covers about 4.1% of the total land area of Mexico. It lies in the northeast corner of Mexico. It is bordered on the north by the US state of Texas, on the south by the Mexican states of San Luis Potosí and Veracruz, on the east by the Gulf of Mexico, and on the west by the Mexican state of Nuevo León. Tamaulipas is divided into 43 municipalities (similar to US counties). Its capital is Ciudad Victoria.

Tamaulipas has hills and plains covering most of the state. The Sierra Madre Oriental cross through the southwest portion of the state. The Sierra de Tamaulipas are located in this area. One of the highest peaks in the state is Peña Nevada at an elevation of about 3,627 meters (11,900 feet).

The most important rivers are the Rio Bravo (which is called the Rio Grande in the United

States), Soto la Marina, Guayalejo, and San Fernando. All of these rivers rise in the mountains and run into the Gulf of Mexico. There are also lagoons, which are separated from the ocean by sand banks, all along the coast. The largest lagoon in Tamaulipas is the Laguna Madre. The coastline has a total length of 458 kilometers (284 miles). Presa de las Adjuntas in the center of the state and Presa Falcón and Presa Marte R. Gómez in the north are major inland reservoirs.

2 Climate

The tropic of Cancer, a line of latitude at 23°27' north of the equator, passes through the state. The climate regions to the north of the tropic of Cancer are generally known as the northern temperate zone. The regions of the state to the south are considered to be the torrid zone (or tropical zone). However, variations in altitude and rainfall also have a great effect on the climate in different regions the state.

The warm waters of the Gulf of Mexico contribute to the climate, which is generally warm and humid. The average temperature is 24°C to 28°C (76°F to 82°F). The highest monthly average rainfall occurs in August and September. In Ciudad Victoria, the average year-round temperature is 24°C (75°F). The average rainfall in this city is 70 centimeters (28 inches) per year.

3 Plants and Animals

Trees found in the state include mesquite, pine, and oak forests. Cacti, orchids, and bromeliads are found in some areas. Large mammals found in the state include white-tailed deer, wildcats, jaguars, and bears. Smaller mammals include hares, moles, and armadillos. Birds found in the

state include turkeys, roadrunners, cockatoos, and pelicans. Tarantulas, chameleons, and several species of snakes and lizards are also found.

4 Environmental Protection

Environmental issues such as hazardous waste disposal and safe water supplies are concerns within the state. In 2004, the state had 16 municipal wastewater treatment plants in operation with a combined installed capacity of 2,622 liters per second (692 gallons per second). The volume of wastewater treated that year was estimated at 2,642 liters per second (697 gallons per second). There were also 45 industrial wastewater treatment plants in operation that year. As of 2004, about 95.7% of the population had access to safe drinking water.

In 2003, the state had over 1.5 million hectares (3.9 million acres) of woodland, including over 1 million hectares (2.6 million acres) of rain forest. In 2004, about 633 hectares (1,564 acres) of pasture and brush land were damaged or destroyed by fires.

The El Cielo Biosphere Reserve is a protected cloud forest. A cloud forest is a tropical rain forest in the mountains that has nearly constant cloud cover. Playa Tortuguera Rancho Nuevo and Laguna Madres have been designated as Ramsar Wetlands of International Importance.

5 Population, Ethnic Groups, Languages

Tamaulipas had an estimated total population of 3,076,300 in 2006, ranking 13th among the states and the Distrito Federal. The population was almost evenly divided between men and women. About 84% of the population lived in

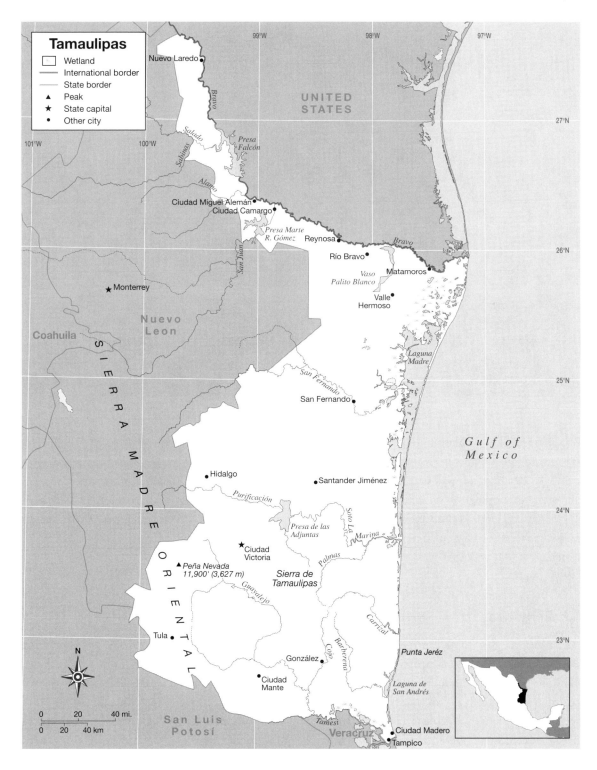

Tamaulipas

Wetland
International border
State border
▲ Peak
★ State capital
● Other city

Nuevo Laredo

UNITED
STATES

27°N

101°W   100°W

Bravo

Salado

Sabinas

Presa
Falcón

Alamo

Ciudad Miguel Alemán
Ciudad Camargo

Presa Marte
R. Gómez   Reynosa

Bravo

26°N

San Juan

Río Bravo

Vaso
Palito Blanco   Matamoros

★ Monterrey

Valle
Hermoso

Nuevo
León

Coahuila

S
I
E
R
R
A

Laguna
Madre

25°N

M
A
D
R
E

San Fernando

San Fernando

Gulf of
Mexico

● Hidalgo

● Santander Jiménez

24°N

O
R
I
E
N
T
A
L

Purificación

Presa de las
Adjuntas

Soto La

Marina

★ Ciudad
Victoria

▲ Peña Nevada
11,900' (3,627 m)

Sierra de
Tamaulipas

Palmas

Guayalejo

Carrizal

● Tula

23°N

N

González

Cojo

Barberena

Punta Jeréz

● Ciudad
Mante

Laguna de
San Andrés

0   20   40 mi.

0   20   40 km

San Luis
Potosí

Tamesí

Veracruz

Ciudad Madero

Tampico

Boats on a river in southern Tamaulipas. PETER LANGER.

urban areas. The population density was 38 people per square kilometer (99 people per square mile). In 2005, the capital, Ciudad Victoria, had an estimated population of 293,044.

Almost all citizens speak Spanish as their first language. Less than 1% of the population speak indigenous (native) languages, such as Huasteco and Náhuatl.

6 Religions

According to the 2000 census, 82.9% of the population, or 2 million people, were Roman Catholic; about 8.7%, or 210,021 people, were mainline or evangelical Protestants. About 2.4% were counted as other Biblical faiths, including 8,148 Seventh-day Adventists, 10,094 Latter-day Saints (Mormons), and 39,461 Jehovah's Witnesses. About 4.9% of the population claimed to have no religious affiliation.

A temple of the Church of Jesus Christ of Latter-day Saints (Mormons) was dedicated in Ciudad Madero in 2000.

7 Transportation

Ciudad Victoria Airport, Matamoros International Airport, and Nuevo Laredo-Quetzalcóatl International Airport provide international flights to and from Tamaulipas. The state has about 7,056 kilometers (4,383 miles) of roads and about 968 kilometers (601 miles) of railroads. In 2004, there were 660,925 automobiles registered in the state, along with

5,110 passenger trucks, 323,272 freight trucks, and 7,141 motorcycles.

8 History

Archeological findings in the Cueva del Diablo caves point to human presence in the region as early as 6000 BC. However, sedentary settlements date back to about 4000 BC. First populated by Olmec groups, Tamaulipas was then populated by Chichimec and Huasteco groups. Between 1445 and 1466, Mexican armies commanded by Moctezuma Ilhuicamina conquered much of the territory. Yet, Comanche, Apache, and other indigenous groups remained in rebellion against the invaders from central Mexico and were never conquered.

The first Spaniards to arrive were led by Francisco Hernández de Córdoba in 1517. Huasteco Indians defeated them. A new expedition led by Francisco de Garay was defeated a year later. In 1522, Hernán Cortés (1485–1547) defeated the rebel Indians and took control of the city of Chila. The lack of mineral deposits and the hostility of the indigenous people discouraged the Spaniards from attempting to expand their control to the northern end of the region. A number of efforts to convert the Indians to Catholicism also failed during most of the 16th century.

Early in the 17th century, Franciscan priests established missions in the region and began converting some of the sedentary populations. Cattle and sheep ranching brought increased economic activity to the region. Ranching also caused massive displacement of native populations from their original lands. Occasional indigenous revolts weakened colonial interest in the region. The presence of French colonizers in

what would become the US state of Louisiana provoked concern among Spanish authorities in the 18th century. This French presence motivated a number of initiatives to populate the region and promote new economic activities. However, the reduced population and the lack of efficient transportation to the rest of Mexico hindered the economic development of the region.

Although some insurgent efforts were made to expand the independence movement to the region in 1810, Spanish royalist troops succeeded in preventing their success. The Plan of Iguala in 1821 ultimately incorporated Tamaulipas, which was made into a federal state in 1824. In 1836, nationalist troops from Tamaulipas fought against Texas secession. After the Mexican-American War (1846–48), Tamaulipas lost all of its territories north of the Rio Grande River to the United States. Political instability characterized much of the remaining 19th century, until the state began to experience economic development during the "Porfiriato era" (1876–1910), when President Porfirio Díaz (1830–1915) was in power.

The Mexican Revolution, which began in 1910, also reached Tamaulipas. Once the victors successfully agreed on a new national constitution, Tamaulipas was quickly brought into compliance. Emilio Portes Gil (1890–1978), governor of Tamaulipas during the 1920s, later went on to serve as president of Mexico between 1928 and 1930. During the rest of the 20th century, Tamaulipas consolidated its economy thanks to commerce with the United States. Since the adoption of the North American Free Trade Agreement (NAFTA)—a trade agreement between Mexico, the United States, and Canada—Tamaulipas has emerged as a manufacturing region for products exported to the

United States. As one of the fastest growing states in Mexico, Tamaulipas has benefited from the free trade reforms promoted by Mexico since the mid-1980s.

In the first decade of the 21st century, the state of Tamaulipas continued to benefit from its location on the border with the United States. There was a negative side to the border with the United States, however. The state remained a major crossing point for smugglers. In addition, various criminal elements and gangs engage in violent dispute, causing Tamaulipas to have an unusually high violent crime rate. This crime problem is notable in Nuevo Laredo, which is situated directly across from Laredo, Texas, and other border towns.

9 State and Local Government

The state governor is democratically elected for a nonrenewable six-year term. There is a unicameral (single chamber) legislature called the state congress. Nineteen of its 26 deputies are elected from single member districts and 7 deputies are elected by proportional representation. All serve three-year terms without an option for immediate reelection.

The 43 municipalities that comprise Tamaulipas hold democratic elections for municipal presidents and council members every three years. Immediate reelection is not allowed.

10 Political Parties

The three main political parties in all of Mexico are the Institutional Revolutionary Party (PRI), the National Action Party (PAN), and the Party of the Democratic Revolution (PRD). The PRI has dominated politics in Tamaulipas since the end of the Mexican Revolution. Eugenio Hernández Flores of the PRI took office as governor in 2005. PAN is the second-strongest party in the state, but its influence lies primarily in urban areas.

Because the Institutional Revolutionary Party (PRI), the dominant political party throughout the country since the end of the Mexican Revolution, has not faced sufficiently strong competition from other parties in the state, formal separation of powers provisions has not been enforced. The governor exercises more power than mandated in the constitution.

11 Judicial System

The Supreme Tribunal of Justice is the highest court in the state. Its seven members are appointed by a two-thirds majority of the legislature from among a pool of highly qualified attorneys with demonstrated experience and competence. If justices are ratified after their initial three-year appointments, they serve until their voluntary retirement. In addition, an electoral court and lower local courts also constitute the state's judicial system. Despite formal provisions that guarantee its independence, the overwhelming influence of the state governor has prevented the state judiciary from being more independent.

12 Economy

The economy of Tamaulipas is based on agriculture, oil and natural gas extraction, petrochemicals, and in-bond assembly plants. (In-bond plants are those where products are made from parts kept in special duty-free or bonded warehouses.) The state's economy benefits from its geographic location. Its nearly 230-mile (370-kilometer) border with Texas allows for *maquiladora* assembly plants to be situated alongside the Texas border. There are also 13 international bridges that cross into the United States, facilitating easy shipment of goods to the United States. Meanwhile, the state's 261-mile (420-kilometer) coastline along the Gulf of Mexico allows for access to the oil and natural gas deposits that lie beneath the waters of the Gulf.

The state's coastline has also allowed for the development of a fishing industry, as well as a tourism industry based on sport fishing and beach resorts. Three deepwater ports—Altamira, Ciudad Madero, and Tampico—have been developed at the southern tip of the state. As of 2003, these ports handled about 55% of Mexico's import and export traffic. Altamira has one of Mexico's largest and most important containerized freight ports. As a result, Tamaulipas has become a corridor for trade and transport into and out of the interior of Mexico.

13 Industry

Tamaulipas has 25 industrial parks and some 328 manufacturing facilities. Products manufactured by these plants include automobiles and auto parts, electrical and electronic components and equipment, and textiles. Some 40% of the state's labor force is employed in manufacturing, with 42 out of every 100 jobs created in the industrial sector. Tamaulipas accounts for 11.2% of Mexico's *maquiladora* (assembly plant) industry, ranking the state third behind Baja California and Chihuahua. The southern region around the port of Altamira has become an important center for the production of petrochemical products.

The state's handicraft industries produce baskets and leatherwork, suede articles, saddles, goods made from ixtle and sisal fibers, wrought iron products, blown glass, and wooden and palm furniture.

14 Labor

As of 2005, the state of Tamaulipas had 1,298,904 eligible workers. Some 1,245,572 were listed as employed and 53,332 were listed as unemployed. Unemployed workers in rural areas may not be counted, however. The unemployment rate that year was reported to be 4.1%. Of those who were working, services employed 38.9%, followed by commerce at 20.4%, and manufacturing at 20.2%.

The US Bureau of Labor Statistics reported that Mexican workers saw their wages increase from $2.49 per hour in 2003 to $2.50 per hour in 2004. (The average US worker earned $15.70 per hour in 2004.) The maximum work week is set at 48 hours by law. The average worker spends 40 to 45 hours per week on the job. Workers earn twice their regular hourly rate for up to nine hours a week of overtime. When a worker works more than nine hours overtime in a week, he or she earns three times the regular hourly rate. After one year, workers are entitled by law to six days paid vacation.

15 Agriculture

Sorghum, grown throughout the state, is the most important crop. In the northern part of the state, corn, cotton, and wheat are cultivated. In the central region, citrus fruits and wheat are grown. In the southern zone, corn, safflower, citrus fruits, sugarcane, and cotton are grown.

Other crops include rice, kidney beans, tomatoes, and green chilies. Cattle are raised for meat, milk and for haulage. Pigs, sheep, goats and poultry are also raised.

In 2004, farm production in Tamaulipas included 518,876 tons of corn, 2,880,489 tons of sorghum, 119,021 tons of green chilies, 62,675 tons of red tomatoes, 188,185 tons of sugar, and 6,648 tons of rice. Livestock brought to market in 2004 included 105,843 head of beef cattle, 52,286 pigs, 2,095 goats, and 412 sheep. In that same year, the state produced 30.1 million liters (7.9 million gallons) of milk from dairy cows and 321 tons of eggs. Meat production included 661,996 tons of beef, 21,348 tons of pork, 2,042 tons of goat, 1,821 tons of lamb, and 631 tons of poultry.

16 Natural Resources

Oil and natural gas are the state's most valuable natural resources. Fishing is another important activity. The primary catch includes shrimp, striped mullet, trout, red snapper, shark, oysters, and crabs. Freshwater fish such as tilapia, carp, and catfish are also caught. There are three fishing ports: El Mezquital, La Pesca, and Tampico. There is also a thriving sport fishing industry serving tourists to the state. In 2003, the total fish catch was about 47,620 tons.

In 2003, the value of forest wood production was about $4 million. Common tropical woods were the primary woods harvested. Pine and encino (a type of oak) were also harvested.

17 Energy and Power

In 2005, there were 1,008,859 users of electricity in the state of Tamaulipas. Of that total, the largest number were residential customers at 898,460. Sales of electricity that same year totaled 7,774,889 megawatt hours, of which the largest users were medium-sized industrial firms at 3,552,518 megawatt hours. Electric power in the state of Tamaulipas is generated by four generating plants: one gas-turbine facility, two thermal (non-coal) facilities, and a single hydroelectric station, having a combined capacity of 1,352 megawatts. Electricity is produced and distributed by the Federal Electricity Commission, and Central Light and Power. Both utilities are run by the Mexican government.

18 Health

In 2003, the state had 36 hospitals and 469 outpatient centers that were part of the national health system. In 2004, there were about 3,144 doctors, 6,655 nurses, and 198 dentists working in these health centers. There were an additional 67 independent health centers in the state in 2004.

Most of the Mexican population is covered under a government health plan. The IMSS (Instituto Mexicano de Seguro Social) covers the general population. The ISSSTE (Instituto de Seguridad y Servicios Sociales de Trabajadores del Estado) covers state workers.

19 Housing

Most homes are made of materials such as brick, concrete, stone, and wood. Wooden homes often

Typical dance from Tamaulipas. PETER LANGER.

have sheet-metal roofs. In 2000, about 75% of all homes were owner-occupied. In 2005, there were an estimated 789,118 residential housing units in the state. About 81% of these units were single-family detached homes. The average household was estimated at 3.8 people.

20 Education

Public education in Mexico is free for students from ages 6 to 16 and most students in the state attend public schools. However, in 2002/03 about 25% of high school students attended private schools. In 2004/05, it was estimated that 88.8% of age-eligible students completed primary school, which includes six years of study.

About 81.7% of eligible students completed secondary school, which includes three years of study after primary school. About 68.7% of eligible students completed the *bachillerato*, which is similar to a high school diploma. This was the highest rate of graduation in the country in 2005. The national average for completion of the *bachillerato* was 60.1% that year.

There are at least 13 major institutions of higher learning in the state. Universidad Autónoma de Tamaulipas is located in Matamoros. There are technical institutes in Ciudad Madero, Ciudad Victoria, Matamoros, Nuevo Laredo, and Reynosa. In 2005, there were about 91,826 students ages 20 and older who were enrolled in some type of higher educa-

People enjoy a refreshing swim. The state has a 261-mile (420-kilometer) coastline along the Gulf of Mexico, helping to promote tourism. PETER LANGER.

tion program. The overall literacy rate was estimated at 94% in 2005.

21 Arts

Tamaulipas has four major theater groups, including a mime theater. Most cities have a cultural center where local arts festivals and performing arts groups are showcased. There are also 15 auditoriums located in various cities throughout the state. The Centro Metropolitano de Tampico is a modern structure hosting experimental theater. A chorus made up of young people, Coro Meced Chimalli, presents concerts in the Palacio de Bellas Artes in the capital. The Tamaulipas Symphony Orchestra is affiliated with the local university. The International Festival of Tamaulipas, an arts festival, has attracted over one million attendees. There are over 170 registered movie theaters, including multiscreen theaters and single-screen galleries.

22 Libraries and Museums

In 2003, there were 167 libraries in the state with a combined stock of 1,115,729 volumes. The same year, there were 15 museums registered in the state that had permanent exhibits. Matamoros has a museum of contemporary art. The capital, Ciudad Victoria, has an archeological museum. The Casamata Museum in Matamoros is a war museum.

23 Media

In 2005, the capital, Ciudad Victoria, published three daily newspapers: *El Mercurio* (*The Mercury*), *El Diario* (*The Daily*), and *El Grafico* (*The Graphic*). Nuevo Laredo had two daily newspapers, *El Correo* (*The Mail*) and *El Mañana* (*The Morning*). Reynosa also had two dailies, *Prensa Reynosa* (*Reynosa Press*) and *La Tarde* (*The Afternoon*). Tampico had four newspapers: *El Diario de Tampico* (Tampico Daily), *El Sol de Tampico* (*Tampico Sun*, with both morning and afternoon editions), *Extra*, and *El Munodo* (*The World*). There were also daily papers in Ciudad Mante and Matamoros.

In 2004, there were 49 television stations and 88 radio stations (44 AM and 44 FM). In 2005, there were about 133,386 subscribers to cable and satellite television stations. Also in 2005, there were about 454,003 residential phone lines, with about 18.3 mainline phones in use for every 100 people.

24 Tourism, Travel, and Recreation

Matamoros lies on the border with the United States. It is the official sister city to Brownsville, Texas. Many people travel to Matamoros from the United States to shop in the Juarez marketplace. Playa Bagdad is also a popular beach getaway. Reynosa, a center for arts and crafts, also features a beach area, Las Playas. In Nuevo Laredo there is a greyhound racetrack and a market where hand-blown glass is sold. The Nuevo Laredo Fair is held in early September each year. Tampico has a marketplace where beach and ocean-related handicrafts are sold. Sport fishing enthusiasts visit the state each year for the Golden Sea Bass tournament, held the week before Easter. Near Tampico in Madero, tourists can visit to Miramar Beach.

25 Sports

There are three basketball teams in the state that compete in the North Zone of the National Professional Basketball League (LNBP): Correcaminos (Roadrunners) Matamoros, Correcaminos Victoria, and Correcaminos Reynosa. All three teams represent the Universidad Autónoma de Tamaulipas (UAT), but each team is based at a different city campus. The UAT Victoria also hosts a First Division "A" soccer team of the Mexican Football Association (commonly known as Femexfut). The Jaibos (Crabs) Tampico Madero are also a First Division "A" soccer team.

In 2004, there were three bullfighting rings in the state, including Plaza de Toros in Matamoros.

26 Famous People

Emilio Portes Gil (1890–1978) was born in the state and served as governor before becoming president of Mexico in 1928. Tomás Yarrington (b.1957) was elected governor in 1999. Eugenio Hernández Flores (b.1959) took office as governor in 2005. Juan García Esquivel (1918–2002), a popular band leader and film composer, was known as "The King of Space-age Pop."

27 Bibliography

BOOKS

Day-MacLeod, Deirdre. *The States of Northern Mexico*. Philadelphia, PA: Mason Crest Publishers, 2003.

Green, Jen. *Caribbean Sea and Gulf of Mexico.*

Milwaukee, WI: World Almanac Library, 2006.

Gruber, Beth. *Mexico.* Washington, DC: National Geographic, 2006.

McNeese, Tim. *The Rio Grande.* Philadelphia, PA: Chelsea House, 2005.

Tunnell, John W. Jr., and Frank W. Judd. *The Laguna Madre of Texas and Tamaulipas.* College Station, TX: Texas A&M University Press, 2002.

WEB SITES

Government of Mexico. *Mexico for Kids.* www.elbalero.gob.mx/index_kids.html (accessed on March 30, 2007).

Mexican Tourism Board. *Visit Mexico: Tamaulipas.* www.visitmexico.com/wb/Visitmexico/Visi_Tamaulipas (accessed on March 30, 2007).

Tlaxcala

PRONUNCIATION: teh-lawx-KAH-lah.

ORIGIN OF STATE NAME: Probably based on the Náhuatl word *tlaxcallan,* which means "place of corn" or "place of corn bread (tortilla)."

CAPITAL: Tlaxcala.

ENTERED COUNTRY: 1824.

COAT OF ARMS: The coat of arms features a castle, which is meant to represent the state's link to Castile, Spain. The letters I, K, and F and the crowns in the border represent Queen Isabel, King Karolus (Charles I), and King Ferdinand, all of Spain. The skull and crossbones at the bottom represent those who died in the Spanish conquest of Mexico.

HOLIDAYS: Año Nuevo (New Year's Day—January 1); Día de la Constitución (Constitution Day—February 5); Benito Juárez's birthday (March 21); Primero de Mayo (Labor Day—May 1); Anniversary of the Battle of Puebla (1862), May 5; Revolution Day, 1910 (November 20); and Navidad (Christmas—December 25).

FLAG: There is no official state flag.

TIME: 6 AM = noon Greenwich Mean Time (GMT).

1 Location and Size

Tlaxcala is Mexico's smallest state, covering about 0.2% of the total land area of Mexico. It is located in the region of the country that is known as the central breadbasket. It is bordered on the north, east, and south by the state of Puebla, on the west by México state, and on the north and west by Hidalgo. Tlaxcala covers an area of 3,991 square kilometers (1,540 square miles), which is just a little larger than the US state of Rhode Island. Only the Distrito Federal (Federal District) is smaller. Tlaxcala is divided into 60 municipalities (similar to US counties). The capital is Tlaxcala.

The state lies within the east-west belt of volcanic mountains known as the Sierra Volcánica Transversal (also known as the Cordillera Neovolcánica). Some of the highest peaks in the country are found in this region, including Volcán Malinche which is the sixth-highest peak in the country at an altitude of about 4,420 meters (14,501 feet). The indigenous people call this volcano Matlalcueyatl.

The Sierra de Tlaxco form a natural border between Puebla and Tlaxcala. It is given different names according to the location: It is known as the Tlaxco Sierra in the north, where it is also called the Caldera Sierra, and towards the southeast it is known as the Huamantla Sierra. Cerro Huintépetl, another volcano, is found in the northern part of this sierra.

There are plains located to the south of the Tlaxco Sierra and surrounding the volcanic range on the border with Puebla. The Valle de Tlaxcala is in the central part of the state.

Tlaxcalan rivers, while small, play an important role because they feed the Balsas River, one of the largest rivers in Mexico. The Zahuapan River rises in the Tlaxco Sierra and runs southward down the mountain slopes, where it joins the Apizaco River and forms the Atlihutzía waterfall. Upon reaching the border with Puebla, it runs into the Atoyac River. Laguna Jalnené is one of the largest lakes.

2 Climate

The climate throughout the state is generally cool. The average year-round temperature is about 16°C (60°F). Temperatures are usually under 21°C (70°F). Average rainfall in the capital city is about 79 centimeters (31 inches) per year.

3 Plants and Animals

Pine, fir, and oak are the most common trees. Savin shrubs are found in several regions. Pastures cover some of the plains and valley areas. Common mammals include hares, shrews, skunks, squirrels, and tlacuaches (Mexican opossums). Sparrow hawks, eagles, and quail are found in the state. Rattlesnakes are also found in some areas.

4 Environmental Protection

In 2004, the state had 35 municipal wastewater treatment plants in operation with a combined installed capacity of 1,089 liters per second (287 gallons per second). The volume of treated wastewater that year was estimated at 789 liters per second (208 gallons per second). There were also 105 industrial wastewater treatment plants in operation that year. As of 2004, about 94.5% of the population had access to safe drinking water.

In 2003, the state had about 51,709 hectares (127,775 acres) of woodland. In 2004, only 4 hectares (9.8 acres) of woodland were damaged or destroyed by forest fires. An additional 264 hectares (652 acres) of pasture and brush land were also damaged by fires.

The state has two national parks. Malinche National Park is a protected area surrounding a dormant volcano. Xicoténcatl National Park has undergone many reforestation projects since being designated as a protected area in 1937.

5 Population, Ethnic Groups, Languages

Tlaxcala had an estimated total population of 1,089,400 in 2006, ranking 27th among the states and the Distrito Federal. About 48% of the population were men and 52% were women. About 69% of the population lived in urban areas. The population density was 278 people per square kilometer (720 people per square mile). In 2005, the capital, Tlaxcala, had an estimated population of 33,748.

Almost all citizens speak Spanish as their first language. A small number of people speaks

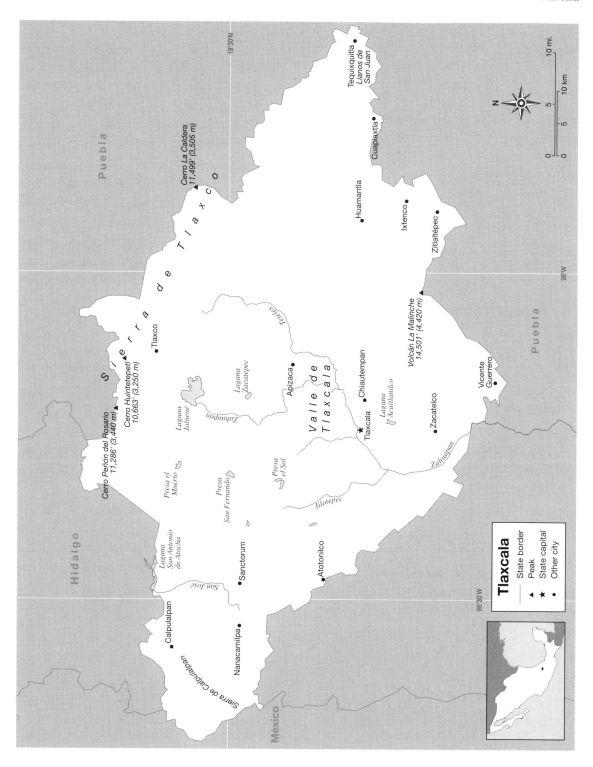

Cerro La Caldera
11,499' (3,505 m)

Tequixquitla
Llanos de
San Juan

Cuapiaxtla

Huamantla

Ixtenco

Zitlaltépec

Sierra de Tlaxco

Cerro Huintetepetl
10,663' (3,250 m)

Tlaxco

Volcán La Malinche
14,501' (4,420 m)

Teteles

*Laguna
Zacatepec*

Apizaca

Chiautempan

Vicente
Guerrero

Cerro Peñón del Rosario
11,286' (3,440 m)

*Laguna
Jalnene*

*Laguna
Acuitlanilco*

Zahuapan

*Valle de
Tlaxcala*

Tlaxcala

Zacatelco

*Presa el
Muerto*

*Presa
San Fernando*

*Presa
el Sol*

Zahuapan

Jilotepec

*Laguna
San Antonio
de Atocha*

Sanctorum

Atotonilco

San José

Calpulalpan

Nanacamilpa

Sierra de Calpulalpan

Puebla

Puebla

Hidalgo

México

19°30'N

98°W

98°30'W

10 mi.
10 km

N

Tlaxcala
——— State border
▲ Peak
★ State capital
• Other city

indigenous (native) languages, such as Náhuatl and Totonaca.

6 Religions

According to the 2000 census, 93.4% of the population, or 791,284 people, were Roman Catholic; about 2.9%, or 24,200 people, were mainline or evangelical Protestants. About 1.4% were counted as other Biblical faiths, including 1,088 Seventh-day Adventists, 1,140 Latter-day Saints (Mormons), and 9,875 Jehovah's Witnesses. About 1% of the population claimed to have no religious affiliation.

7 Transportation

There is one domestic airport in the state. There are also about 1,843 kilometers (1,145 miles) of roads and about 308 kilometers (191 miles) of railroads. In 2004, there were 72,262 automobiles registered in the state, along with 4,459 passenger trucks, 46,540 freight trucks, and 1,471 motorcycles.

8 History

Although the first evidence of human life in the state dates back to nomadic hunters and gatherers around 10,000 BC, the indigenous Quinametin were the first to permanently settle in the region. With Otomi and Teotihuacan influence, the Quinametin were later overpowered by the Olmec-Xicalanca whose Maya ancestry is evident. One of the most important archeological pieces from that period, the Chac-Mool sculpture housed in the National Museum of Anthropology in Mexico City, has clear Maya influence. The Olmec-Xicalanca built several cit-

ies and left numerous pieces of religious and cultural artifacts that have survived to this day.

In the 10th century, the Toltec-Chichimec exercised control of the area, but around 1330 AD, the Tlaxcalteca permanently settled in the area after overpowering several other groups that inhabited the region. In 1348, they founded Tepectícpac, the first city of the Tlaxcallan empire. Between 1418 and 1430, the Tlaxcalteca provided support and protection to Nezahualcóyotl, who later rose to be the philosopher king of Texcoco and an ally of the Mexico-Tenochtitlan Aztecs. Threats from powerful neighbors forced the Tlaxcalteca to develop their famous military might and organization. When Spanish conquistador Hernán Cortés (1485–1547) learned of the conflicts between Aztecs and Tlaxcaltecas, he invited the latter to join him in defeating the rulers of Mexico-Tenochtitlan. After an initial refusal, Cortés overpowered the Tlaxcaltecas and subdued them into an alliance against the Aztecs. With their support, Cortés overpowered the Aztecs. Tlaxcaltecas were later used to fight along with the Spaniards in new conquest efforts elsewhere in Mexico and Central America and to populate new territories conquered by the Spaniards.

During most of the 16th century, the Spanish conquistadors (those who sought to conquer Mexico for Spain) respected the agreement made between Cortés and the Tlaxcaltecas. As a result they did not levy taxes on them nor did they confiscate the land occupied by the native population in the region. However, toward the end of the 16th century, new Spanish authorities began to levy taxes and occupy the native's land. Although there were a few insurrections during

Ruins at Tlaxcala. © CARL & ANN PURCELL/CORBIS.

the 17th and 18th centuries, the Tlaxcaltecas were successfully subdued by the Spanish colonizers. Different Catholic orders also promoted aggressive conversion efforts that permitted the consolidation of the Roman Catholic faith in the region.

Although there was an active pro-independence group in the state, the forces loyal to the Spanish crown successfully controlled the state between 1810 and 1821. When the Plan of Iguala secured Mexico's independence in 1821, Tlaxcala was incorporated into the newly independent country. However, it was only declared a federal state in 1824.

Political and social instability characterized much of the 19th century. Federalist-centralist and conservative-liberal conflicts hindered economic development and caused military confrontations. After peace was finally achieved with the victory of liberals led by Benito Juárez (1806–1872) in 1867, Tlaxcala became a commercial and textile center. These developments were especially prominent during the Porfirio Díaz government (1876–1910).

The Mexican Revolution, which began in 1910, brought about several peasant uprisings and military confrontations between different factions. However, the revolution victors were in control of the state when the new Mexican constitution was introduced in 1917. During the rest of the 20th century, the small but densely populated state evolved as a regional commercial and textile center in Mexico.

In the first decade of the 21st century, the state of Tlaxcala remained one of Mexico's most industrially developed states. Initially a center for the production of textiles, the state's economy had become more diversified. Politically, the domination of the Institutional Revolutionary Party (PRI) had been broken by the National Action Party (PAN), and the Party of the Democratic Revolution (PRD).

9 State and Local Government

The governor is democratically elected every six years for a nonrenewable term. The legislature is comprised of a unicameral (single chamber) congress. Nine of its twelve members are elected from single member districts and three are elected by proportional representation for three-year nonrenewable periods.

The 60 municipalities that comprise Tlaxcala hold democratic elections for municipal presidents and council members every three years. Immediate re-election is not allowed.

10 Political Parties

The three main political parties in all of Mexico are the Institutional Revolutionary Party (PRI), the National Action Party (PAN), and the Party of the Democratic Revolution (PRD). Although the PRI historically dominated state politics since the end of the Mexican Revolution in 1917, the 1999 gubernatorial elections produced the first alternation of power at the governor's desk. PRD

candidate Alfonso Abraham Sánchez won a six-year term as governor. He was succeeded by PAN candidate Héctor Israel Ortiz Ortiz, who took office as governor in 2005.

Because the Institutional Revolutionary Party (PRI), the dominant political party in the country since the Mexican Revolution, only lost the gubernatorial chair in the 1999 elections, formal provisions for separation of power between the executive and legislative branches have only been enforced for the last few years. Yet, state democratic practices have improved.

11 Judicial System

The Superior Tribunal of Justice is the highest court in the state. Its members are elected by a simple majority vote of the legislature for renewable six-year terms. Because of the reduced size and small population of the state, the influence that the PRI exercised over the state judiciary significantly hindered its independence before 1999. When the PRD first won the governorship, the independence and autonomy of the judiciary were also automatically strengthened.

12 Economy

The most important sector to the economy of Tlaxcala is manufacturing, which as of 2003 accounted for 28.24% of the state's output. It was followed by finance and insurance at 16.51%, trade at 12.6%, transportation and communication at 8.61%, agriculture and livestock at 7.8%, construction at 4.96%, and mining at 0.17%. The state's main exports are textiles, chemicals, and pharmaceuticals.

13 Industry

Although textiles and clothing still constitute a large portion of Tlaxcala's industrial base, there has been considerable diversification in recent years. In addition to textiles and garments, chemicals, petrochemicals, non-metallic minerals, auto parts, electrical products, rubber and plastic products, cellulose, and machine tools are also manufactured. However, more than half of the state's manufacturing work force is employed in textiles and garments.

The state's handicraft industries produce cotton and woolen goods such as ponchos, fabrics and carpets, carved wooden articles such as walking sticks, masks, pens, boxes, trays, as well as pottery and floral carpets.

14 Labor

As of 2005, the state of Tlaxcala had 419,496 eligible workers. Some 400,818 were listed as employed, and 18,678 were listed as unemployed. Unemployed workers in rural areas may not be counted, however. The unemployment rate that year was reported to be 4.4%. Of those who were working, services employed 29.1%, followed by manufacturing at 27.2%, and commerce at 17.3%.

The US Bureau of Labor Statistics reported that Mexican workers saw their wages increase from $2.49 per hour in 2003 to $2.50 per hour in 2004. (The average US worker earned $15.70 per hour in 2004.) The maximum work week is set at 48 hours by law. The average worker spends 40 to 45 hours per week on the job. Workers earn twice their regular hourly rate for up to nine hours a week of overtime. When a worker works more than nine hours overtime in a week, he or she earns three times the regular hourly rate. After one year, workers are entitled by law to six days paid vacation.

15 Agriculture

Agriculture is important to the local food supply, but not as important as an export industry. The primary crop is corn. Others include alfalfa, barley, wheat, potatoes, lima beans, and lettuce. Maguey is also grown and is used to produce syrup and vinegar. It is also used to produce *pulque,* an alcoholic beverage. Cattle, pigs, sheep, and goats are the primary livestock animals. The number of poultry farms in the state have also increased, boosting the production of chickens and eggs. Fish farms have also made an appearance in the state, producing such species as carp.

In 2004, farm crops produced in the state of Tlaxcala included: 292,186 tons of corn, 33,920 tons of potatoes, 65,058 tons of wheat, and 7,404 tons of kidney beans. Livestock brought to market in 2004 included: 10,500 head of beef cattle, 39,229 pigs, 253 goats, and 1,271 sheep. In that same year, the state produced 41 million liters (10 million gallons) of milk from dairy cows, 1.6 million liters (422,675 gallons) of goat's milk, and 1,097 tons of eggs. Meat production included: 9,177 tons of beef, 11,605 tons of pork, 473 tons of goat, 1,430 tons of lamb, and 1,113 tons of poultry.

16 Natural Resources

In 2003, the value of forest wood production was about $1.6 million. Oyamel (a type of fir) and pine were the primary woods harvested. In 2003, the total fish catch was about 416 tons.

17 Energy and Power

In 2005, there were 293,273 users of electricity in the state of Tlaxcala. Of that total, the largest number were residential customers at 255,707. Sales of electricity that same year totaled 1,765,211 megawatt hours, of which the largest users were large industrial firms at 723,623 megawatt hours. There are no electric power generating facilities in Tlaxcala. As a result, all electric power used must be imported from other states. Electricity is produced and distributed by the Federal Electricity Commission, and Central Light and Power. Both utilities are run by the Mexican government.

As the smallest Mexican state, Tlaxcala's electricity consumption was the lowest in the early 1990s. However, the recent impact of the North American Free Trade Agreement (NAFTA)—a trade agreement between Mexico, the United States, and Canada—has boosted the state's energy consumption.

18 Health

In 2003, the state had 9 hospitals and 192 outpatient centers that were part of the national health system. In 2004, there were about 1,009 doctors, 1,853 nurses, and 81 dentists working in these health centers. There were an additional 47 independent health centers in the state in 2004.

Most of the Mexican population is covered under a government health plan. The IMSS (Instituto Mexicano de Seguro Social) covers the general population. The ISSSTE (Instituto de Seguridad y Servicios Sociales de Trabajadores del Estado) covers state workers.

19 Housing

Most homes are built with materials such as brick, concrete, and stone. Adobe is the next common building material. In 2000, about 84% of all homes were owner-occupied. In 2005, there were an estimated 233,881 residential housing units in the state. About 89% of these units were single-family detached homes. The average household was estimated at 4.6 people.

20 Education

Public education in Mexico is free for students from ages 6 to 16 and most of the students in the state attend public schools. In 2004/05, it was estimated that 98% of age-eligible students completed primary school, which includes six years of study. About 78% of eligible students completed secondary school, which includes three years of study after primary school. About 65.5% of eligible students completed the *bachillerato*, which is similar to a high school diploma. The national average for completion of the *bachillerato* was 60.1% that year.

The Universidad Autónoma de Tlaxcala (Autonomous University of Tlaxcala) is the most prominent institution of higher learning in the state. In 2005, there were about 30,117 students ages 20 and older who were enrolled in some type of higher education program. The overall literacy rate was estimated at 92.6% in 2005.

21 Arts

The state of Tlaxcala has 13 cultural centers and 11 auditoriums. There are two theaters for the performing arts, both located in the city of Tlaxcala. The city of Huamantla has a festival that takes place in August, during which all of the streets are decorated with paint, colored sand, or flowers to look like carpeting. The Tlaxcala Fair, an annual All Saints Day festival, includes a variety of cultural and sporting events.

There are about 20 registered movie theaters, including multiscreen theaters and single-screen galleries.

22 Libraries and Museums

In 2003, there were 188 libraries in the state with a combined stock of 854,209 volumes. The same year, there were 10 museums registered in the state that had permanent exhibits. The regional Museum of Tlaxcala is housed in a former Franciscan monastery. The Museum of Living Arts and Popular Traditions includes exhibits on local customs and beliefs and sponsors workshops on various crafts. The National Museum of Puppets is located in Huamantla. The archeological sites of Cacaxtla and Xochitécatl have onsite museums.

23 Media

In 2005, the capital, Tlaxcala, published one daily newspaper: *El Sol de Tlaxcala* (*Tlaxcala Sun*). In 2004, there were 15 television stations and 6 radio stations (2 AM and 4 FM). In 2005, there were about 34,459 subscribers to cable and satellite television stations. Also in 2005, there were about 102,368 residential phone lines, with about 11 mainline phones in use for every 100 people.

24 Tourism, Travel, and Recreation

The capital city, Tlaxcala, is sometimes called the Red City because of the ochre color of the buildings. The Governor's Palace has beautiful murals by a local artist, Desiderio Hernandez Xochitiotzin, who has been working on them since the 1960s. They depict the history of Tlaxcala. There are also local churches and museums featuring the pre-colonial history of Tlaxcala. Archeological sites include Cacaxtla, Tizatlan, Ocotelulco, and Xochitecatl.

25 Sports

The Plaza de Toros Jorge "El Ranchero" Aguilar is one of four bullfighting arenas in the state. There is a soccer stadium in Tlaxcala which also hosts other entertainment events.

26 Famous People

Beatriz Elena Paredes Rangel (b.1953) was the first woman to serve as governor of the state, an office she held from 1987 to 1992. Alfonso Abraham Sánchez Anaya (b.1941) was elected governor in 1998. Héctor Israel Ortiz Ortiz (b.1950 in Oaxaca) took the office of governor in 2005.

27 Bibliography

BOOKS

Baquedano, Elizabeth. *Aztec, Inca and Maya, Rev. ed.* New York: DK Pub., 2005.

Day-MacLeod, Deirdre. *The States of Central Mexico*. Philadelphia, PA: Mason Crest Publishers, 2003.

Gruber, Beth. *Mexico*. Washington, DC: National Geographic, 2006.

Williams, Colleen Madonna Flood. *The People of Mexico*. Philadelphia, PA: Mason Crest Publishers, 2003.

WEB SITES

Government of Mexico. *Mexico for Kids*. www. elbalero.gob.mx/index_kids.html (accessed on March 30, 2007).

Mexican Tourism Board. *Visit Mexico: Tlaxcala*. www.visitmexico.com/wb/Visitmexico/Visi_ Tlaxcala (accessed on March 30, 2007).

Veracruz

PRONUNCIATION: vair-ah-KROOS

ORIGIN OF STATE NAME: Spanish explorer Hernán Cortés (1485–1547) landed at Chalchihuecan in Veracruz on April 22, 1519, which was Good Friday (the Friday before Easter). Good Friday is also known as the day of the Vera Cruz (the True Cross). Cortés called the settlement Villa Rica de la Vera Cruz.

CAPITAL: Jalapa (hah-LAH-pah); sometimes spelled Xalapa

ENTERED COUNTRY: October 3, 1824

COAT OF ARMS: A red cross at the top is inscribed with the word *vera* (true), representing the name of the state. The castle represents the original settlement of Villa de La Vera Cruz. It is supported by the Columns of Hercules, which are also found on the Spanish coat of arms. The blue field represents the ocean. The columns and the blue field represent the fact that the original colony belonged to Spain, even though it was located across the Atlantic Ocean.

HOLIDAYS: Año Nuevo (New Year's Day—January 1); Día de la Constitución (Constitution Day—February 5); Benito Juárez's birthday (March 21); Primero de Mayo (Labor Day—May 1); Anniversary of the Battle of Puebla (1862), May 5; Revolution Day, 1910 (November 20); and Navidad (Christmas—December 25).

FLAG: There is no official state flag.

TIME: 6 AM = noon Greenwich Mean Time (GMT).

1 Location and Size

Veracruz is located in eastern Mexico in a region known as the Oil Basin and Gulf Lowlands. It is bordered on the north by Tamaulipas; on the south by Oaxaca, Chiapas, and Tabasco; on the east by the Gulf of Mexico; and on the west by San Luis Potosí, Hidalgo, and Puebla. Veracruz covers an area of 71,823 square kilometers (27,731 square miles), which is about half the size of the US state of Illinois. It ranks as 11th in size among the states and covers about 3.7% of the total land area of Mexico. The state is divided into 212 municipalities (similar to US counties). The capital is Jalapa.

There are coastal plains covering most the state. Beyond the coastal plains, hills and canyons are found. Further inland, the Sierra Madre Oriental run along the northwestern border of the state. The Los Tuxtlas mountain range, which is not linked to the Sierra Madre Oriental, is found in the south. The mountains in the west-central region of the state are part of the Sierra Volcánica Transversal (also known as the Cordillera Neovolcánica). Pico de Orizaba (5,610 meters/18,406 feet above sea level) is located in this region. It is the highest peak in the state and the country. Cofre de Perote (4,200 meters/13,860 feet) is the second-highest peak in the state and the eighth-highest in the country.

The most important rivers in Veracruz include the Pánuco, Tuxpan, and Cazones Rivers in the north; the Tecolutla, Jamapa, and Nautla Rivers in the central region; and the Papaloapan, Coatzacoalcos, and Tonalá Rivers in the south. Laguna de Tamiahua is a large lagoon along the northern coast. Laguna de Alvarado is along the central coastline. The coastline has a total length of 745 kilometers (462 miles). Inland lakes include Laguna de Catemaco and Laguna Chila.

2 Climate

The warm waters of the Gulf of Mexico contribute to the climate, which is generally warm and humid. The average temperature is 24°C to 28°C (76°F to 82°F). The highest monthly average rainfall occurs in August and September. The average year-round temperature in the capital city of Jalapa is 17°C (62°F) and average precipitation is 144.9 centimeters (57 inches) per year. The average year-round temperature in the city of Veracruz is 25°C (78°F) and average rainfall is about 173 centimeters (68.3 inches) per year. In Coatzacoalcos, the average year-round temperature is also 25°C (78°F) and the average rainfall is about 261 centimeters (102.9 inches) per year.

3 Plants and Animals

Cedar, mahogany, and ceiba trees are found in several regions of the country. Palm trees and mangroves grow in coastal regions. In the city of Papantla, vanilla pods are harvested from an orchid-type plant called tlixochitl. Wild boar, coyotes, ocelots, spider monkeys, and pumas live in various parts of the state. Iguanas and manatees are found in coastal regions. Alligators live in the Tuxtlas region. Birds found in the state include toucans, owls, woodpeckers, and buzzards.

4 Environmental Protection

In 2004, the state had 90 municipal wastewater treatment plants in operation with a combined installed capacity of 4,445 liters per second (1,174 gallons per second). The volume of treated wastewater that year was estimated at 2,803 liters per second (740 gallons per second). There were also 156 industrial wastewater treatment plants in operation that year. As of 2004, about 71.4% of the population had access to safe drinking water. This was the lowest percentage in the nation.

In 2003, the state had over 1.8 million hectares (4.5 million acres) of woodland, including 1.3 million hectares (3.4 million acres) of rain forest. In 2004, about 22 hectares (54 acres) of woodland were damaged or destroyed by forest fires. An additional 461 hectares (1,139 acres) of pasture and brush land were also damaged by fires.

The Sierra de los Tuxtlas ecoregion contains one of the largest moist forests in Mexico. Many plant and animal species found there are unique to Mexico and cannot be found anywhere else in

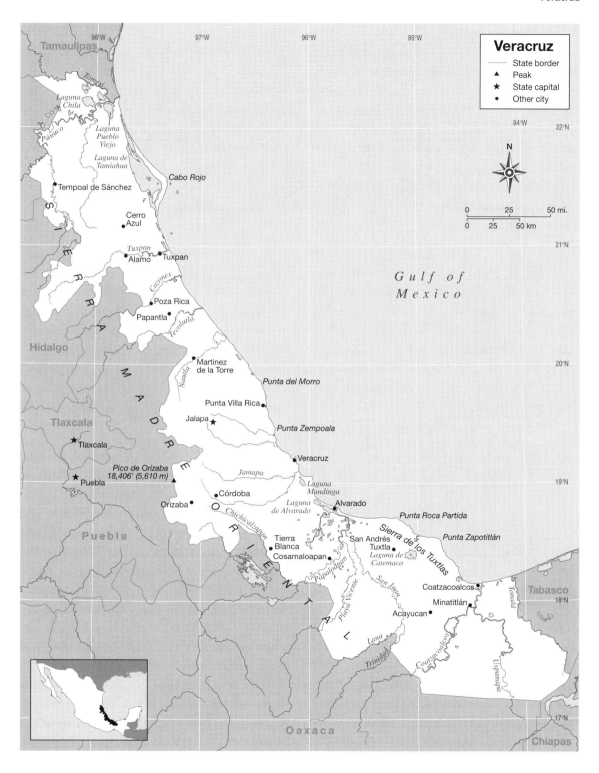

Veracruz
- Gulf of Mexico
- .... State border
- ▲ Peak
- ★ State capital
- • Other city

Tamaulipas

Laguna Chila

Pánuco
Tamesí

Laguna Pueblo Viejo

Laguna de Tamiahua

• Tempoal de Sánchez

Cabo Rojo

Cerro Azul •

Tuxpan
Alamo • • Tuxpan

Hidalgo

Cazones

• Poza Rica
Papantla •

Tecolutla

Nautla

• Martínez de la Torre

Punta del Morro

Punta Villa Rica

Jalapa ★

Tlaxcala

★ Tlaxcala

Punta Zempoala

• Veracruz

Pico de Orizaba
18,406' (5,610 m) ▲

★ Puebla

Jamapa

Córdoba •

Laguna Mandinga

Orizaba •

Laguna de Alvarado

Alvarado •

Punta Roca Partida

Chichicalzapan

Puebla

Punta Zapotitlán

Sierra de los Tuxtlas

Tierra Blanca •

San Andrés Tuxtla •

Cosamaloapan •

Laguna de Catemaco

Coatzacoalcos •

Tabasco

Papaloapan

San Juan

Minatitlán •

Acayucan •

Coatzacoalcos

Tonalá

Playa Vicente

Uspanapa

Lana

Trinidad

Gulf of Mexico

0   25   50 mi.
0   25   50 km

N

Oaxaca

Chiapas

the world. The ecosystem includes seven volcanoes and several lakes, lagoons, and marshlands. The state has four national parks, one of which, the Arrecifal Veracruzano (Veracruz Reef), is also a Ramsar Wetland of International Importance. There are eight more Ramsar sites in the state, including Laguna Tamiahua and the Mangroves and Wetlands of Tuxpan.

5 Population, Ethnic Groups, Languages

Veracruz had an estimated total population of 7,218,200 in 2006, ranking third among the states and the Distrito Federal. About 48% of the population were men and 52% were women. About 56% of the population lived in urban areas. The population density was 99 people per square kilometer (256 people per square mile). In 2005, the capital city of Jalapa had an estimated population of 413,136.

Almost all citizens speak Spanish as their first language. About 8% of the state population speaks indigenous (native) languages. This is higher than the national average of 6%. Indigenous languages include Náhuatl, Totonaca, Huasteco, Popoluca, and Otomi. Ruins of the ancient Totoanac can be found at Quiahuiztlan and Cempoala.

6 Religions

According to the 2000 census, 82.9% of the population, or 5 million people, were Roman Catholic. About 6.9%, or 422,973 people, were mainline or evangelical Protestants. About 3.3% were counted as other Biblical faiths, including 80,266 Seventh-day Adventists, 18,581 Latter-day Saints (Mormons), and 102,346 Jehovah's

Witnesses. There were 1,334 Jews. About 5.9% of the population claimed to have no religious affiliation.

The Metropolitan Cathedral of the Immaculate Conception is the seat of the Roman Catholic archdiocese of Jalapa. A temple of the Church of Jesus Christ of Latter-day Saints was dedicated in Boca del Rio in 2000.

7 Transportation

Poza Rica Airport and Tehuacán Airport provide international flights to and from Veracruz airport in the city of Veracruz. The state has about 10,727 kilometers (6,663 miles) of roads and about 1,176 kilometers (730 miles) of railroads. In 2004, there were 568,041 automobiles registered in the state, along with 8,567 passenger trucks, 328,027 freight trucks, and 25,970 motorcycles. The three major ports are at Coatzacoalcos, Alvarado, and Tuxpan.

8 History

Three important pre-Spanish civilizations evolved in this vast and extended coastal state. They were the Huasteca in the northern region, the Totonac culture in the middle region, and the late Olmec culture in southern Veracruz. The Triple Alliance formed in central Mexico, which included the Aztecs in Mexico-Tenochtitlan, the Texcoco, and the Tacuba, who dominated the entire Veracruz region at the beginning of the 15th century. They levied taxes on the numerous sedentary agricultural villages of the region.

The first Spaniards to arrive in Veracruz were under the command of Juan de Grijalva (c. 1489–1527) in 1518. Other members of the expedition were Pedro de Alvarado, Francisco

This Veracruz fort was the setting for the 1984 film, **Romancing the Stone.** PETER LANGER.

de Montejo, and Bernal Diaz del Castillo, who later became a champion of indigenous rights. A second expedition, motivated by the presence of gold detected by the first expedition, was sent in 1519 under the command of Hernán Cortés (1485–1547). Cortés founded the city of Veracruz where he disembarked. Cortés and his lieutenant, Gonzalo Sandoval, overpowered an initial Huasteca rebellion. Because of the oppression by the Triple Alliance, the Totonac readily joined Hernán Cortés when he disembarked in Veracruz with the intention of defeating the Aztecs in their capital, Tenochtitlan (now Mexico City).

During the first years after the Spanish arrived, diseases brought by the Europeans and unknown to the indigenous people decimated the population. This devastation was helped by the massive enslavement to which most village inhabitants were subjected after being conquered. Sugarcane production made heavy demands on indigenous labor. As the indigenous population decreased, African slaves were brought to work in the plantations. The port city of Veracruz became the most important port of entry for all of Mexico. Several attacks by pirates in the 17th century demonstrated the economic and military importance of Veracruz for the Spanish crown. Massive slave trade converted Veracruz into the city with the largest enslaved population in Mexico. A slave revolt in 1609, led by an African slave named Yanga, ended with the formation of a runaway slave colony in a town known as San Lorenzo de los Negros.

Several insurgency efforts against Spanish rule surfaced after 1810, with Guadalupe Victoria (1789–1843) emerging as the most important independence leader in the region. When the Plan of Iguala came into effect in 1821, securing independence for the entire country of Mexico, the insurgent leader in Veracruz was Antonio López de Santa Anna (1794–1876). López de Santa Anna would become the most important military leader of Mexico during the 19th century. The on-and-off president allied with conservative and liberal leaders alike with the sole objective of retaining power. Santa Anna lost the Mexican-American War (1846–48) and negotiated the Treaty of Guadalupe, where Mexico ceded large amounts of land to the United States. Veracruz became a federal state in 1824. A new state constitution was created in 1825.

Veracruz, as with the rest of Mexico, experienced political and social instability during much of the 19th century. Conflicts between centralists and federalists and between liberals and conservatives hindered economic development and provoked continuous revolts. Mexican president Benito Juárez (1806–1872) governed from Veracruz when his liberal government was attacked in Mexico City in 1857. A few years later, French emperor Maximilian (1832–1867) arrived in Veracruz in 1863 to assume the position of emperor of Mexico. (France had conquered and ruled parts of Mexico from 1864 to 1866.)

During the Mexican Revolution (1910–20), Veracruz became a battleground for different factions. With the end of the revolution, its victors brought peace and stability to the region, which has consolidated as one of the most populated and economically active states of the Mexican union.

Throughout the remainder of the 20th century and into the first decade of the 21st century, the state of Veracruz developed a diversified economy, based on its transportation systems, ports, and mineral wealth, including oil. The announcement in March 2006 of a major new deepwater oil field in the Gulf of Mexico, holds the potential for spurring additional economic growth. Politically, the Institutional Revolutionary Party (PRI) continued to hold on to power at the state level, but challenges arose from other political parties. However, crime and human rights abuses, particularly against the state's rural population, remained problems in the state.

9 State and Local Government

The state governor is democratically elected for a six-year nonrenewable term. There is a unicameral (single chamber) legislature whose deputies are elected for nonrenewable three-year terms. Some deputies are elected both in single-member districts and some deputies are elected at large. There can be no more than 60 deputies in total.

The 212 municipalities that comprise Veracruz hold democratic elections for municipal presidents and council members every three years. Immediate re-election is not allowed. The widely different sizes and wealth of the municipalities in the state makes it difficult for decentralization initiatives to work well across the state.

10 Political Parties

The three main political parties in all of Mexico are the Institutional Revolutionary Party (PRI), the National Action Party (PAN), and the Party of the Democratic Revolution (PRD). The PRI has continued to dominate politics at the state level. Two former state governors went on to become presidents of Mexico, Miguel Alemán Valdés (president from 1946 to 1952) and Adolfo Ruiz Cortines (president from 1952 to 1958). Longtime influential PRI leader Fernando Gutierrez Barrios was governor of the state between 1986 and 1988. Fidel Herrera Beltrán of the PRI took office as governor in 2004. The PAN and PRD have successfully won municipal races in local elections, but the PRI's strength in rural areas allows that party to remain the dominant force in the state.

Although the PRI historically exercised tight control over the state government, the rise of PAN and the PRD in large urban areas has made state politics more competitive. The formal separation of powers established in the constitution has been more effectively enforced since opposition parties have successfully won enough seats in the legislature to block unilateral actions by the PRI.

11 Judicial System

The Superior Tribunal of Justice is the highest court in the state. The governor appoints its 16 members for three-year terms with the approval of the legislature. If justices are ratified after their first term, they serve indefinitely. Only highly qualified attorneys can be appointed to the Superior Tribunal. Justices cannot publicly participate in any religious creed. In addition,

An aerial view of Veracruz. HENK SIERDSEMA/SAXIFRAGA/ EPD PHOTOS.

there is an electoral court and a number of lower courts distributed throughout this large state.

12 Economy

The state of Veracruz has a diversified economy, whose growth is due in large part to its strategic location to the sea and rich mineral resources. Its 425 miles (684 kilometers) of coastline along the Gulf of Mexico has given the state direct access to the oil and natural gas riches that lie beneath the waters of the Gulf. It has also allowed the state to exploit its mineral wealth on dry land. Coupled to a modern grid of highways and railroad lines, the state, with its four deepwater ports (Veracruz, Tuxpan, Coatzacoalcos, and Alvarado) and two international airports, has become a major transshipment point for imports heading into Mexico, as well as for exports heading out of the country. A key element in this is the port of Veracruz, which allows for the shipment of exports not only to the United States, but also to Europe and Latin America. The port of Veracruz accounts for 75% of all port activity in Mexico.

13 Industry

The northern part of Veracruz is one of the most important oil producing regions in Mexico. The state's chemical and petrochemical sectors account for almost 64% of the state's manufacturing output. Overall, manufacturing accounts for 21% of the state's gross domestic product (GDP). The state of Veracruz also manufactures metal products, food and beverages, printed and published materials, and non-electric machinery and equipment. Industrial centers can also be found in Córdoba and Orizaba, while textile manufacturing is important in Rio Blanco.

The state's handicrafts industry produces household items made from palm, vanilla figures, pottery, woolen textiles, musical instruments, and items from tortoiseshell.

14 Labor

As of 2005, the state of Veracruz had 2,576,889 eligible workers. Some 2,517,413 were listed as employed and 59,476 were listed as unemployed. Unemployed workers in rural areas may not be counted, however. The unemployment rate that year was reported to be 2.3%. Of those who were working, services employed 34.7%, followed by agriculture at 26.7% and commerce at 17.7%.

The US Bureau of Labor Statistics reported that Mexican workers saw their wages increase from $2.49 per hour in 2003 to $2.50 per hour in 2004. (The average US worker earned $15.70 per hour in 2004.) The maximum work week is set at 48 hours by law. The average worker spends 40 to 45 hours per week on the job. Workers earn twice their regular hourly rate for up to nine hours a week of overtime. When a worker works more than nine hours overtime in a week, he or she earns three times the regular hourly rate. After one year, workers are entitled by law to six days paid vacation.

Although the state of Veracruz is a unionized state, labor relations are reported to be good and strikes infrequent.

15 Agriculture

The state's agricultural sector is an important producer of crops that include corn, sugarcane, citrus fruits, bananas, mangos, and tobacco. Coffee is an important crop in the areas surrounding the capital city of Jalapa. Cattle, pigs, goats, and sheep are the main livestock animals. Poultry and bees are also raised.

In 2004, crop production for the state of Veracruz included: 1,052,571 tons of corn, 59,260 tons of potatoes, 58,084 tons of sorghum, 42,435 tons of rice, 29,533 tons of green chilies, 22,910 tons of red tomatoes, 1,939,117 tons of sugar, and 245,799 tons of bananas. Livestock brought to market in 2004 included: 147,536 head of beef cattle and 219,686 pigs. In that same year, the state produced 687 million liters (2 million gallons) of milk from dairy cows and 17,643 tons of eggs. The state was also second only to Yucatán in the production of honey at 5,771 tons in 2004. Meat production included: 206,156 tons of beef, 64,588 tons of pork, 717 tons of goat, 5,151 tons of lamb, and 268,912 tons of poultry.

16 Natural Resources

In addition to the state's oil deposits, Veracruz also mines deposits of iron and copper, as well non-metallic minerals such as sulfur, silica, feldspar, calcium, kaolin, and marble. Another important natural resource is water. The state accounts for about 35% of Mexico's water supply.

In 2003, the total value of forest wood production was about $6.1 million. Pine and common tropical woods were the most common woods harvested. Also in 2003, the total fish catch was about 102,807 tons, all for human consumption.

17 Energy and Power

In 2005, there were 2,008,742 users of electricity in the state of Veracruz. Of that total, the largest number were residential customers at 1,794,955. Sales of electricity that same year totaled 9,247,592 megawatt hours, of which the largest users were large industrial firms at 3,569,671 megawatt hours. Electric power in Veracruz is generated from 10 power generating facilities: one nuclear, one gas-turbine, two thermal (non-coal), five hydroelectric, and one combined cycle (gas-turbine and steam) plant. Electricity is produced and distributed by the Federal Electricity Commission and Central Light and Power. Both utilities are run by the Mexican government.

Veracruz is home to Mexico's Laguna Verde nuclear power plant, the nation's only such facility, located at Alto Lucero. The plant consists of two reactors, of which the first began operation in April 1989 and the second in November 1994. Laguna Verde has a rated capacity of 1,365 megawatts.

18 Health

In 2003, the state had the most national health care centers in the country with 103 hospitals and 1,419 outpatient centers. In 2004, there were about 5,838 doctors (third in the nation), 11,994 nurses, and 446 dentists working in these health centers. There were an additional 169 independent health centers in the state in 2004. There is also an American hospital in the city of Jalapa.

Most of the Mexican population is covered under a government health plan. The IMSS (Instituto Mexicano de Seguro Social) covers the general population. The ISSSTE (Instituto de Seguridad y Servicios Sociales de Trabajadores del Estado) covers state workers.

19 Housing

Most homes are built of materials such as brick, concrete, stone, and wood. Many homes have sheet metal roofs. In 2000, about 79% of all homes were owner-occupied. In 2005, there were an estimated 1,777,972 residential housing units in the state. About 89% of these units were single-family detached homes. The average household was estimated at four people.

20 Education

Public education in Mexico is free for students from ages 6 to 16 and most of the students in the state attend public schools. However, in 2002/03 about 23.5% of high school students attended private schools. In 2004/05, it was estimated that 86% of age-eligible students completed primary school, which includes six years of study. About 80% of eligible students completed secondary school, which includes three years of study after primary school. About 64% of eligible students completed the *bachillerato*, which is similar to a high school diploma. The national average for completion of the *bachillerato* was 60.1% that year.

The Universidad Veracruzana is located in Jalapa. There are technical institutes in Poza Rica, Orizaba, and Veracruz. In 2005, there were about 187,033 students ages 20 and older who were enrolled in some type of higher education program. The overall literacy rate was estimated at 86% in 2005.

21 Arts

The state of Veracruz has 20 theaters for the performing arts. The Universidad de Veracruz hosts the Ballet Folklórico de Veracruz. There are four local musical groups including an orchestra of popular music. The Groupo Chuchumbe performs a traditional fandango (a Spanish dance that is usually performed by a couple to the accompaniment of guitars and castanets), while the Groupo Mono Blanco plays traditional music from the south of Veracruz. The Jalapa Symphony Orchestra, founded in 1927, is the oldest continuous orchestra in Mexico. Veracruz has two theater groups, one of which is located at the University of Veracruz.

The Jalapa Fair is an annual arts and crafts event that dates back to the 18th century. The annual Corpus Christi Fair in Papantla features ritual dances of the ancient Náhuatl and Totonac.

There are over 170 registered movie theaters, including multiscreen theaters and single-screen galleries.

22 Libraries and Museums

In 2003, there were 703 libraries in the state with a combined stock of 3,459,462 volumes. The same year, there were 33 museums registered in the state with permanent exhibits. One of the most prominent is the Jalapa Museum of Anthropology and History. The Museum of Fauna is located in the Macuiltepetl Ecological Park and features exhibits on animals of the region.

23 Media

In 2005, Coatzacoalcos had one daily newspaper, *El Liberal del Sur* (*South Liberal*). Córdoba had two daily newspapers: *El Sol del Centro* (*Central Sun*) and *El Mundo* (*The World*). Veracruz had three daily newspapers: *El Dictamén* (*The Report*), *Sur* (*South*), and *La Tarde* (*The Afternoon*). There were also daily papers in Jalapa, Minatitlan, Poza Rica, Orizaba, and Tuxpan.

In 2004, there were 44 television stations and 101 radio stations (70 AM, 29 FM, and 2 shortwave). In 2005, there were about 194,099 subscribers to cable and satellite television stations. Also in 2005, there were about 632,575 residential phone lines, with about 10.8 mainline phones in use for every 100 people.

24 Tourism, Travel, and Recreation

Veracruz is noted for its beautiful beaches. The Chachalacas sandbar (about 35 miles along the coast) features many aquatic sports. There is also an aquarium in the city of Veracruz. Veracruz is famous for its Carnival (Mardi Gras festival). The city of Jalapa has a museum of anthropology housing over 25,000 artifacts. The Xalapeno Stadium is known for its unique architectural design. The Botanical Gardens and the Paseo de Los Lagos are other attractions. The historic monuments zone in Tlacotalpan and the pre-Hispanic city of El Tajin in Papantla are UNESCO World Heritage sites. Other archeological sites are at Quiahuiztlan and Cempoala.

25 Sports

The Caféteros (Coffee Growers) de Córdoba and the Rojos (Reds) del Aguila play for the Mexican League of AAA minor league baseball. The Caféteros play in the 8,000-seat Estadio Beisborama 72. The Rojos play at the 7,782-seat Beta Avila stadium. There are two basketball teams competing in the South Zone of the National Professional Basketball League (LNBP). The Halcones (Falcons) UV Jalapa and the Halcones Veracruz. Both teams represent the Universidad Veracruzana, but they are each based at a different city campus.

There are seven soccer teams competing in the Mexican Football Association (commonly known as Femexfut). The Tiburones Rojos (Red Sharks) de Veracruz play for the First Division. The Tiburones Rojos de Coatzacoalcos are part of the First Division "A." The Tiburones Balncos (White Sharks) de Jalapa, Azucareros (Sugar Growers) de Córdoba, Delfines (Dolphins) de Coatzacoalcos, Orizaba Albinegros, and Club Universidad Del Golfo De Mexico are all teams in the Second Division of Femexfut.

26 Famous People

Guadalupe Victoria (1789–1843) was an important leader in the region that is now Veracruz. Political and military figures from Veracruz include Antonio López de Santa Anna (1794–1876) and Ignacio de la Llave, who was governor of Veracruz state from 1857 to 1860. Heberto Castillo Martínez (1928–1997) was a political activist who was a cofounder of three political parties: the Mexican Workers' Party (PMT), the Mexican Socialist Party (PMS), and the Party of the Democratic Revolution (PRD). He was posthumously awarded the Belisario Domínguez Medal of Honor, the highest award bestowed by the Mexican government. Two former state governors went on to become presidents of Mexico: Miguel Alemán Valdés (president from 1946 to 1952) and Adolfo Ruiz Cortines (president from 1952 to 1958). Fernando Gutiérrez Barrios, a long-time PRI leader, was governor of Veracruz from 1986 to 1988. Miguel Alemán Velazco, son of Miguel Alemán Valdés, took office as governor of Veracruz in 1998.

27 Bibliography

BOOKS

Baquedano, Elizabeth. *Aztec, Inca and Maya, Rev. ed.* New York: DK Pub., 2005.

DeAngelis, Gina. *Mexico.* Mankato, MN: Blue Earth Books, 2003.

Field, Randi. *The Gulf States of Mexico.*

Philadelphia, PA: Mason Crest Publishers, 2003.

Green, Jen. *Caribbean Sea and Gulf of Mexico.* Milwaukee, WI: World Almanac Library, 2006.

Gruber, Beth. *Mexico.* Washington, DC: National Geographic, 2006.

WEB SITES

Government of Mexico. *Mexico for Kids.* www. elbalero.gob.mx/index_kids.html (accessed on March 30, 2007).

Mexican Tourism Board. *Visit Mexico: Veracruz.* www.visitmexico.com/wb/Visitmexico/Visi_ Veracruz (accessed on March 30, 2007).

Yucatán

YUCATÁN

PRONUNCIATION: yoo-kah-THAN

ORIGIN OF STATE NAME: The name reflects a translation error. The Spaniards misunderstood the native Mayas when they gave the name of their land. The Spaniards thought the Mayas said Yucatán, so that is the name they gave to the land.

CAPITAL: Mérida (MEH-ree-dah)

ENTERED COUNTRY: 1824.

COAT OF ARMS: A deer, representing the native Mayan people, leaps over an agave plant, once an important crop in the region. Representing the shared Mayan and Spanish heritage of the state, the symbols at the top and bottom of the border are Mayan arches and the symbols on the left and right are Spanish bell towers.

HOLIDAYS: Año Nuevo (New Year's Day—January 1); Día de la Constitución (Constitution Day—February 5); Benito Juárez's birthday (March 21); Primero de Mayo (Labor Day—May 1); Anniversary of the Battle of Puebla (1862), May 5; Revolution Day, 1910 (November 20); and Navidad (Christmas—December 25).

FLAG: There is no official state flag.

TIME: 6 AM = noon Greenwich Mean Time (GMT).

1 Location and Size

Yucatán is bordered on the north by the Gulf of Mexico, on the east and southeast by the state of Quintana Roo, and in the southwest by Campeche. It covers an area of 39,612 square kilometers (15,294 square miles), about half the size of the US state of South Carolina. It ranks as 20th in size among the states and covers about 2% of the total land area of Mexico. The capital city of Mérida is located in the northwest. Yucatán is divided into 106 municipalities (similar to US counties).

Yucatán consists mainly of lowland areas, with the driest lands in the northwest. It sits on a horizontal bed of limestone, parts of which have been dissolved by rainwater, forming underground lakes. Its coastal regions feature white sand beaches and mangrove forests a few miles inland. To the south near Campeche are some rainforest areas, but most of the land is dry and does not support much vegetation. The highest point in the state is Cerro Benito Juárez at an elevation of 210 meters (688 feet). The coastline has a total length of 342 kilometers (212 miles).

2 Climate

The warm waters of the Caribbean Sea contribute to the climate, which is generally warm and humid. It has an average temperature of 25°C to 27°C (77°F to 81°F), rarely dropping below 16°C (61°F) or rising above 49°C (120°F). The heaviest rainfall occurs in the summer months. Average annual rainfall in this area is 115 centimeters (45 inches). In the capital city of Mérida, the year-round average temperature is 26°C (80°F) and average rainfall is 91 centimeters (36.1 inches) per year.

Some fairly strong hurricanes have occurred in Yucatán. In 2002, Hurricane Isidore swept into Telchac Puerto with winds of up to 205 kilometers per hour (127 miles per hour).

3 Plants and Animals

Cedar, ceiba, mahogany, and oak trees are found throughout the region. Mangrove swamps can be found along the coast. Some of the most common animals include anteaters, porcupines, and raccoons. Pumas, jaguars, and long-tailed monkeys are found in some regions. Common birds include parrots, macaws, cardinals, and bluebirds. Octopus, sharks, and dolphins can be found in the coastal waters.

4 Environmental Protection

In 2004, the state had 12 municipal wastewater treatment plants in operation with a combined installed capacity of 147 liters per second (38 gallons per second). The volume of treated wastewater that year was estimated at 141 liters per second (37 gallons per second). There were also 62 industrial wastewater treatment plants in operation that year. As of 2004, about 95.9% of the population had access to safe drinking water.

In 2003, the state had over 1.3 million hectares (3.4 million acres) of rain forest. In 2004, about 709 hectares (1,751 acres) of woodland were damaged or destroyed by forest fires. An additional 2,031 hectares (5,018 acres) of pasture and brush land were also damaged by fires.

There are two national parks in the state: Arrecife Alcaranes and Dzibilchantún. The Ría Celestún Biosphere Reserve, near the western coastal regions of the state, is an important protected area that supports a variety of species such as flamingos, marine turtles, jaguars, and boas. Ría Lagartos wetlands of the eastern coastal regions also support a flamingo population in its mangroves and salt marshes. Ría Celestun and Ría Lagartos are two of four sites in the state that are designated as Ramsar Wetlands of International Importance.

5 Population, Ethnic Groups, Languages

Yucatán had an estimated total population of 1,850,400 in 2006, ranking 21st among the states and the Distrito Federal. About 49% of the population were men and 51% were women. About 64% of the population lived in urban areas. The population density was 47 people per square kilometer (121 people per square mile). The capital, Mérida, is the most populous city, with a 2005 estimated population of 781,146 inhabitants.

Most citizens speak Spanish as their first language. About 29.8% of the population speak indigenous (native) languages. This is the second-highest percentage of indigenous speak-

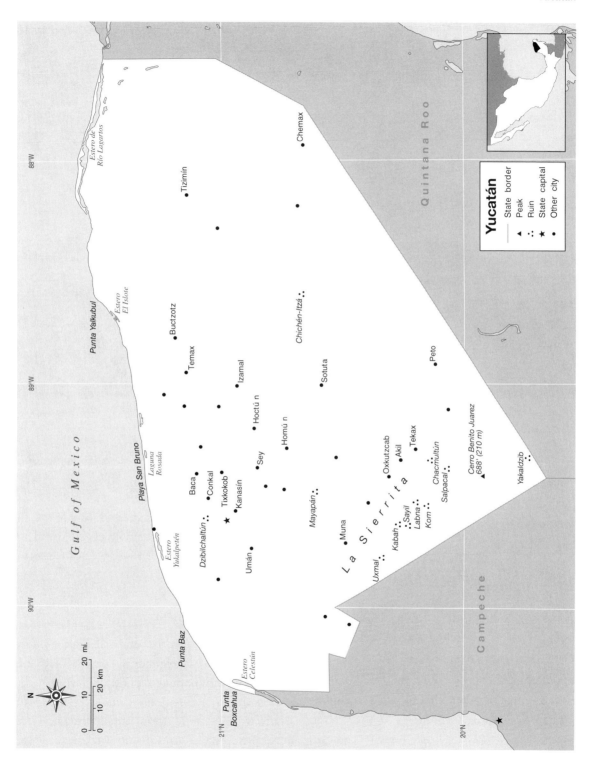

The Roman Catholic cathedral in the capital, Merida, lies on one side of the Plaza Mayor, a wide square with trees and park benches. PETER LANGER.

ers in the country (after Oaxaca). The primary indigenous languages include Maya, Chol, and Tzeltal. Ancient Mayan archeological sites are found at Chichen Itzá in Tinum and Uxmal in Santa Elena.

6 Religions

According to the 2000 census, 84.3% of the population, or 1.2 million people, were Roman Catholic; about 8.4%, or 123,162 people, were mainline or evangelical Protestants. About 3% were counted as other Biblical faiths, including 12,416 Seventh-day Adventists, 7,128 Latter-day Saints (Mormons), and 24,553 Jehovah's

Witnesses. About 3.5% of the population claimed to have no religious affiliation.

A temple of the Church of Jesus Christ of Latter-day Saints was dedicated in Mérida in 2000. The Sagrario Metropolitan Cathedral in Mérida is the seat of the Roman Catholic archdiocese of Yucatán.

7 Transportation

Federal highways, roads, and rail lines connect Yucatán with its neighboring states. There are almost 9,000 kilometers (5,625 miles) of highways and over 600 kilometers (375 miles) of railway in the state. A four-lane toll road crosses the peninsula from Cancún (in the state of

Quintana Roo) through Mérida toward the state of Campeche. Drivers traveling the full length of the road will pass through several toll booths.

Common road hazards are speed bumps in villages and rural areas. Most roads are marked by signs. In 2004, there were 226,234 automobiles registered in the state, along with 2,848 passenger trucks, 71,414 freight trucks, and 37,173 motorcycles.

Public transportation via city bus systems is available in Mérida and other cities. The town of Progresso, located about 40 kilometers (25 miles) from Mérida, is an important port for state commerce. Travel to major Mexican cities and international destinations is made possible by the Mérida Licenciado-Manuel Crescencio Rejon International Airport.

8 History

The Mayan civilization, one of the most advanced Amerindian cultures of the ancient Americas, began in the Yucatán near 2500 BC. Between 300 and 900 AD the Maya built several cities in the Yucatán region. The Toltec culture arrived in 987 AD led by its leader, Quetzalcóatl. Although the Toltec groups mixed with the Maya and other groups that inhabited the region, Toltec culture eventually emerged as the predominating culture in the region before the arrival of the Spanish. During the 12th century, the Maya city-state of Mayapán waged war against Chichen-Itzá. After a military victory, Mayapán expanded its influence over the rest of the area. The so-called Cocom dynasty (named after the Mayan Cocom tribe and kingly family) ruled until the mid-13th century. The post-classic Maya period ended around 1250 AD. Most cities were abandoned,

but those that remained continued their intercity military conflicts.

The first Spaniards to visit the region were the survivors of the Pedro de Valdivia (c. 1498–1553) expedition that left the Central American country of Panama in 1511 toward Santo Domingo in the West Indies, but shipwrecked near Yucatán before reaching its final destination. Two survivors, Jerónimo de Aguilar and Gonzalo Guerrero, became incorporated into Maya civilization. Guerrero married the daughter of the Chetumal chief and their son was the first officially recorded Mestizo (mixed Indian and Spanish) in Mexico. Jerónimo de Aguilar was later rescued by Spanish conqueror Hernán Cortés's (1485–1547) expedition.

In 1513, on his expedition to Florida, Juan Ponce de León (1460–1521) sailed near Yucatán but never disembarked in the region. In 1517, Francisco Fernández de Córdoba set foot in Cozumel, off the coast of the modern-day state of Quintana Roo, but was expelled by the Indians. He returned to Cuba. There he was informed of the existence of the region that was initially considered an island. The Hernán Cortés expedition that sailed off Cuba in 1519 briefly stopped by Yucatán, where Jerónimo de Aguilar was rescued, and then went north and disembarked in Veracruz.

Francisco de Montejo (c. 1479–1553) initiated the conquest of Yucatán in 1527 but was so fiercely fought against by the Indians that he fled. He returned three years later with his son Francisco de Montejo y León but was again unsuccessful in his effort to overpower the native Indians. A third attempt in 1537 proved successful. De Montejo founded the cities of Campeche in 1540 and Mérida in 1542. Gaspar Pecheco, known for his cruel treatment of the

Pyramid of the Magician, Uxmal, Yucatan. PETER LANGER.

Indians, completed the conquest on the western end of the region. Franciscan priests built more than thirty convents in an effort to convert the indigenous people to the Catholic faith. Spanish oppression and the diseases brought by the conquistadors (Spanish conquerors) significantly reduced the Amerindian population from an estimated 5 million in 1500 to 3.5 million a century later.

An indigenous rebellion led by Jacinto Canek in 1761 resulted in the deaths of thousands of Indians and the execution of Canek in the city of Mérida. Other indigenous revolts during the colonial period consolidated Yucatán's reputation as a region whose fierce Indians would not easily surrender to Spanish rule.

Yucatán did not participate in the independence movement of 1810. The Spanish authorities controlled the region and prevented any insurgencies. In 1821, with the Plan of Iguala, Yucatán was made a part of independent Mexico. Yucatán was formally made a state in 1824 and a new constitution was written in 1825. In addition to the federalist-centralist and liberal-conservative conflicts that characterized much of 19th century Mexico, Yucatán also experienced a number of indigenous rebellions during those decades.

After the Mexican Revolution (1910–20), where different factions fought for control of the peninsula, the revolutionary victors brought peace to the region. In 1931, the territory of

Quintana Roo was separated from Yucatán and made into an autonomous state. A new indigenous revolt in 1937 led Mexican president Lázaro Cárdenas (1895–1970) to adopt an aggressive land reform program in the state where Indians were given communal lands.

In the first decade of the 21st century, the state of Yucatán continued to move away from an economy based on agriculture to one based on the production of consumer goods and of tourism. However, problems of official corruption, crime, and poverty continued to trouble the state.

9 State and Local Government

The highest authority is the state governor, democratically elected for a nonrenewable six-year term. A unicameral (single chamber) legislature, the state congress, is elected every three years. Its 25 members include 15 legislators elected from single member districts and 10 legislators elected by proportional representation. All are elected for nonrenewable three-year terms. The legislature generally meets once a year, but extra sessions can be called by the governor or by a permanent committee if the need arises.

The 106 municipalities that comprise Yucatán hold democratic elections for municipal presidents and council members every three years. Immediate reelection is not allowed.

10 Political Parties

The three main political parties in all of Mexico are the Institutional Revolutionary Party (PRI), the National Action Party (PAN), and the Party of the Democratic Revolution (PRD). Although the PRI dominated politics in the state since

the end of the Mexican Revolution in 1920, the 2001 gubernatorial elections gave the governorship to the conservative PAN. Patricio Patrón became the first non-PRI governor of the state that year. The PRI remains very powerful in rural areas, but the PAN has consolidated its presence in large urban areas.

Although formal provisions for separation of powers exist in the constitution, the overwhelming power historically exercised by the dominant Institutional Revolutionary Party (PRI) has prevented many of those provisions from being effectively enforced.

11 Judicial System

The Superior Tribunal of Justice is the highest court in the state. Its six members are appointed by the state congress for nonrenewable four-year terms. Only qualified and experienced attorneys can be appointed to the highest state court. Because of the excessive power and influence of the governor during the years of PRI rule, the judiciary has exercised limited autonomy. In addition, an electoral tribunal and local courts are also part of the state judiciary.

12 Economy

Traditionally, Yucatán's economy was based on agriculture. However, the state's economic profile began to change in the mid-1980s, with the arrival of in-bond companies, where products are made from parts kept in special duty-free or "bonded" warehouses. A key element in the economy of the state has been the port of Progreso, located 18 miles (30 kilometers) north of the state's capital city of Mérida. In 2002, the port opened a cruise ship terminal, which received 130,000 visitors that year. Overall, the state has five main seaports and four shelter ports. Further enhancing the state's economy was the opening in 2000 of a new international airport located between Cancun and the state capital of Mérida.

13 Industry

Yucatán's industrial sector is based on the production of consumer goods, due in large part to a number of assembly plants that have been attracted from the state of Florida in the United States. Other industries in the state are focused on food processing and textiles. Clothing, footwear, and wooden furniture are also produced. However, the production of handicrafts and commerce engage a large portion of the state's population.

14 Labor

As of 2005, the state of Yucatán had 777,832 eligible workers. Some 759,483 were listed as employed, and 18,349 were listed as unemployed. Unemployed workers in rural areas may not be counted, however. The unemployment rate that year was reported to be 2.3%. Of those who were working, services employed 39.5%, followed by manufacturing at 20.2%, and commerce at 18.5%.

The US Bureau of Labor Statistics reported that Mexican workers saw their wages increase from $2.49 per hour in 2003 to $2.50 per hour in 2004. (The average US worker earned $15.70 per hour in 2004.) The maximum work week is set at 48 hours by law. The average worker spends 40 to 45 hours per week on the job. Workers earn twice their regular hourly rate for up to nine hours a week of overtime. When a worker works more than nine hours overtime in a week, he or she earns three times the regular hourly rate. After one year, workers are entitled by law to six days paid vacation.

Unions in the state of Yucatán are less active and influential than in the central or northern parts of the country. Labor unions with a presence in the state include: the National Union of Workers (UNT), the Mexican Workers' Confederation (CMT), and the Revolutionary Confederation of Workers and Farmers (CROC).

15 Agriculture

Although Yucatán has begun to move away from an agriculture-based economy, it is still a key part of the state's overall economy. Major crops include corn, beans, squash, oranges, mangoes, lemons, chilies, tomatoes, and grapefruit. The state is also Mexico's chief producer of sisal, a coarse fiber made from the agave plant and used to make rope, mats, wall coverings, and other products. Cattle, pigs, and horses are the primary livestock animals, providing milk, meat and leather. The state is also well-known as a major supplier of honey.

In 2004, crop production for the state of Yucatán included: 128,483 tons of corn, 4,396 tons of green chilies, 4,312 tons of red tomatoes, 1,347 tons of bananas, and 10,499 tons of avocados. Livestock brought to market in 2004 included: 44,831 head of beef cattle and 299,889 pigs. In that same year, the state produced 7.6 million liters (2 million gallons) of milk from dairy cows and 71,209 tons of eggs. Yucatan was first among all Mexican states in the production of honey in 2004 at 9,375 tons. Meat production that year included: 34,518 tons of beef, 87,374 tons of pork, 664 tons of lamb, and 108,020 tons of poultry.

16 Natural Resources

Fishing is an important economic activity along the coast. The catch includes sea bass, octopus, and shark. In 2003, the total fish catch was about 28,067 tons. Minerals produced include sand, gravel, and clay primarily for the production of construction materials. Salt is also produced through the use of salt pans. In 2003, the total value of forest wood production was about $619,747. Pine was the primary type of wood harvested.

17 Energy and Power

In 2005, there were 550,282 users of electricity in the state of Yucatán. Of that total, the largest number were residential customers at 481,598. Sales of electricity that same year totaled 2,531,409 megawatt hours, of which the largest users were medium-sized industrial firms at 1,065,707 megawatt hours. Electric power in Yucatán is generated from six generating plants: one combined cycle (gas-turbine and steam), three thermal (non-coal burning), and two gas-turbine, having a combined capacity of 568 megawatts. Electricity is produced and distributed by the Federal Electricity Commission, and Central Light and Power. Both utilities are run by the Mexican government.

18 Health

In 2003, the state had 25 hospitals and 286 outpatient centers that were part of the national health system. In 2004, there were about 1,577 doctors, 3,998 nurses, and 104 dentists working in these health centers. There were an additional 36 independent health centers in the state in 2004.

Most of the Mexican population is covered under a government health plan. The IMSS (Instituto Mexicano de Seguro Social) covers the general population. The ISSSTE (Instituto de Seguridad y Servicios Sociales de Trabajadores del Estado) covers state workers.

19 Housing

Most homes are built with materials such as brick, concrete, and stone. In 2000, about 84% of all homes were owner-occupied. In 2005, there were an estimated 435,381 residential housing units in the state. About 83% of these units were single-family detached homes. The average household was estimated at 4.2 people.

20 Education

Public education in Mexico is free for students from ages 6 to 16 and most of the students in the state attend public schools. However, in 2002/03 about 31.7% of high school students attended private schools. In 2004/05, it was estimated that 89% of age-eligible students completed primary school, which includes six years of study. About 74% of eligible students completed secondary school, which includes three years of study after primary school. About 51% of eligible students completed the *bachillerato*, which is similar to a high school diploma. The national average for completion of the *bachillerato* was 60.1% that year.

The Universidad Autónoma de Yucatán (Autonomous University of Yucatán) and the

The observatory at Chichen Itza. PETER LANGER.

Universidad del Mayab are in Mérida. In 2005, there were about 62,694 students ages 20 and older who were enrolled in some type of higher education program. The overall literacy rate was estimated at 88% in 2005.

21 Arts

Yucatán has 27 theaters for the performing arts. There are 31 local cultural centers in cities and towns in the state. Research on the Mayan calendar is carried out at the Maya World Studies Center in Mérida. The calendar is used for astronomical calculations, date calculations, and markers for ceremonial dates. There are over 70 registered movie theaters, including multiscreen theaters and single-screen galleries. The Yucatán Symphony Orchestra is based in Mérida.

An annual International Arts Festival is sponsored in Mérida each year with government funding. The Mani Festival celebrates the arts and culture of the Mayans. The Fall Equinox at Kulkulcan is celebrated each September at the site of the country's largest Mayan pyramid, El Castillo.

22 Libraries and Museums

In 2003, there were 256 libraries in the state with a combined stock of 1,353,191 volumes. The same year, there were 24 museums registered in the state that had permanent exhibits. The Yucatán Museum of Contemporary Art is in Mérida, as is the Yucatán regional Museum of Anthropology. The Museo de la Cancion Yucateca (Museum of Yucatán Song) pays tribute to the music and musicians of the state. The archeological site of Chichen Itzá has an onsite museum.

23 Media

In 2005, the capital city, Mérida, published four daily newspapers: *Novedades de Yucatán* (*Yucatán News*), *El Financiero* (*The Financer*), *Por Esto*, and *Tribuna de Yucatán* (*Yucatán Tribune*). In 2004, there were 19 television stations and 33 radio stations (17 AM, 15 FM, and 1 shortwave). In 2005, there were about 87,258 subscribers to cable and satellite television stations. Also in 2005, there were about 191,087 residential phone lines, with about 14.2 mainline phones in use for every 100 people.

24 Tourism, Travel, and Recreation

Mérida was founded on ancient Mayan ruins. The cathedral of San Ildefonso was built over Mayan ruins, using some of the Mayan stones. Hidalgo Park and the marketplaces, Lucas de Galvez and the Portal de Granos, are popular sites for tourists to visit in Mérida. El Centenario Zoo is also found in the capital. The pre-Hispanic cities of Chichen Itzá in Tinum and Uxmal in Santa Elena are UNESCO World Heritage sites.

25 Sports

The Leones (Lions) de Yucatán are part of the Mexican League of AAA minor league baseball. The Mérida Mayas play in the South Zone of the National Professional Basketball League (LNBP). The Itzaes is a soccer team competing in the Second Division of the Mexican Football Association (commonly known as Femexfut). In 2004, there were 48 sports centers in the state and 2 bullfighting rings.

26 Famous People

Agustin de Iturbide (1783–1824) was a Mexican revolutionary who helped win independence for Mexico and was the "Emperor of Mexico" from 1822 to 1823. Patricio Patrón (b.1957) became the state's first National Action Party (PAN) governor in 2001.

27 Bibliography

BOOKS

Gassos, Dolores. *The Mayas*. Philadelphia, PA: Chelsea House Publishers, 2005.

Carew-Miller, Anna. *Famous People of Mexico*. Philadelphia: Mason Crest Publishers, 2003.

Field, Randi. *The Gulf States of Mexico*. Philadelphia, PA: Mason Crest Publishers, 2003.

Green, Jen. *Caribbean Sea and Gulf of Mexico*. Milwaukee, WI: World Almanac Library, 2006.

Gruber, Beth. *Mexico*. Washington, DC: National Geographic, 2006.

WEB SITES

Government of Mexico. *Mexico for Kids*. www.elbalero.gob.mx/index_kids.html (accessed on March 30, 2007).

Mexican Tourism Board. *Visit Mexico: Puebla*. www.visitmexico.com/wb/Visitmexico/Visi_Puebla (accessed on March 30, 2007).

Yucatan Today: The Tourist Guide. www.yucatantoday.com/ (accessed on March 30, 2007).

Zacatecas

PRONUNCIATION: zah-kah-TEE-kahs.

ORIGIN OF STATE NAME: Original inhabitants of the region were called *zacatecas* by their neighbors, which means "the people who live on the edge of the zacate (field)."

CAPITAL: Zacatecas.

ENTERED COUNTRY: 1823.

COAT OF ARMS: The city of Zacatecas was founded by the Spaniards, and the coat of arms depicts the arrival of the Spaniards, surrounded by weapons of the native inhabitants they found.

HOLIDAYS: Año Nuevo (New Year's Day—January 1); Día de la Constitución (Constitution Day—February 5); Benito Juárez's birthday (March 21); Primero de Mayo (Labor Day—May 1); Anniversary of the Battle of Puebla (1862), May 5; Revolution Day, 1910 (November 20); and Navidad (Christmas—December 25).

FLAG: There is no official state flag.

TIME: 6 AM = noon Greenwich Mean Time (GMT).

1 Location and Size

Zacatecas is located in north-central Mexico. It covers an area of 75,520 square kilometers (29,158 square miles), which is smaller than the US state of South Carolina. It ranks as eighth in size among the states and covers about 3.9% of the total land area of Mexico. It is bordered by Aguascalientes, Coahuila, Durango, Guanajuato, San Luis Potosí, Jalisco, Nayarit, and Nuevo León. Zacatecas is divided into 58 municipalities (similar to counties in the US). The capital city is Zacatecas.

The northern part of the state is crossed by the Sierra Madre Oriental, which includes the Sierra de Novillos. The southern part is crossed by the Sierra Madre Occidental, which includes the Sierra de Zacateca, Sierra Valparaíso, and Sierra de Morones. The center region of the state is part of the Central Plateau and includes the Llanos de la Grunidora.

The main rivers are the Juchipila, Jeréz, Tlaltenango, San Andrés, Atengo, and Valparaíso. These are rivers of the Pacific basin. The rivers of the interior basin do not reach the sea. They include Zaragoza, San Francisco, and Aguanaval.

2 Climate

The tropic of Cancer, a line of latitude at 23°27' north of the equator, passes through the state. The climate regions to the north of the tropic of Cancer are generally known as the northern temperate zone. The regions of the state to the south are considered to be the torrid zone (or tropical zone). However, variations in altitude and rainfall also have a great effect on the climate in different regions the state.

In summer the climate is mild and dry, with the temperature averaging 17°C (62°F). The average annual rainfall is 28 centimeters (11 inches). The northern plateau location of the capital, Zacatecas, has a chilly climate in winter. The average year-round temperature in the capital city is 13°C (57°F) and the average rainfall is 22 centimeters (8.9 inches) per year.

3 Plants and Animals

The state can be divided into three natural regions: the Sierra Madre Oriental in the north, the Central Plateau, and the Sierra Madre Occidental in the south. The northern region has palm trees, nopal cactus, yucca, and huizache. The central region is mostly pastureland, and the south has oak forests as well as pastures and thickets.

Common animals include coyotes, wildcats, tlacuaches (Mexican opossums), deer, and wild boar. Common birds include wild turkeys, macaws, and eagles.

4 Environmental Protection

In 2004, the state had 19 municipal wastewater treatment plants in operation with a com-

bined installed capacity of 274 liters per second (72 gallons per second). The volume of treated wastewater that year was estimated at 256 liters per second (67 gallons per second). There were also eight industrial wastewater treatment plants in operation that year. As of 2004, about 93.8% of the population had access to safe drinking water.

In 2003, the state had over 1.1 million hectares (2.7 million acres) of woodland, including 103,921 hectares (256,794 acres) of rain forest. In 2004, about 23 hectares (56.8 acres) of woodland were damaged or destroyed by forest fires. An additional 2,584 hectares (6,385 acres) of pasture and brush land were also damaged by fires. The Sierra de Organos is a protected national park.

5 Population, Ethnic Groups, Languages

Zacatecas had an estimated total population of 1,383,000 in 2006, ranking 25th among the states and the Distrito Federal. About 48% of the population were men and 52% were women. About 40% of the population lived in urban areas. The population density was 18 people per square kilometer (47 people per square mile). In 2005, the capital, Zacatecas, had an estimated population of 132,035.

Almost all citizens speak Spanish as their first language. Less than one percent of the population speaks indigenous (native) languages, including Huichol and Tepechuano de Durango.

6 Religions

According to the 2000 census, 95.1% of the population, or 1.1 million people, were Roman

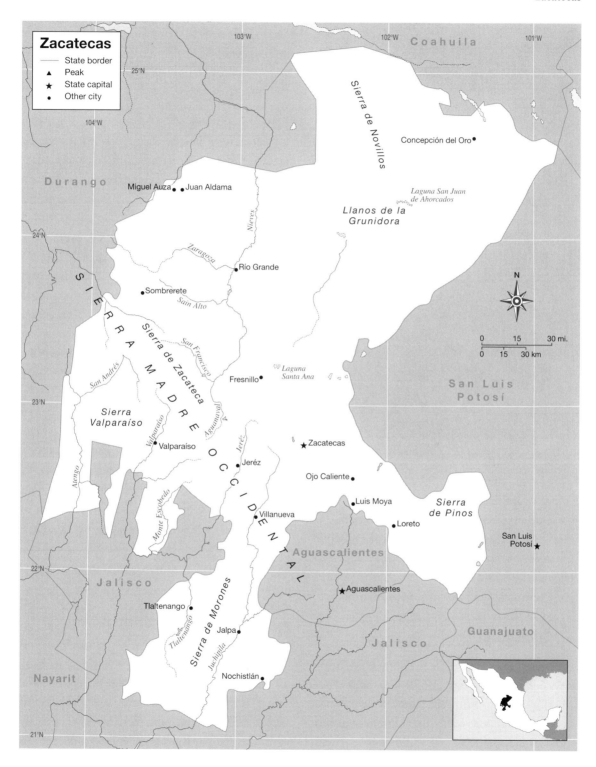

Zacatecas

— State border
▲ Peak
★ State capital
• Other city

Coahuila

103°W   102°W   101°W

25°N

104°W

Sierra de Novillos

Concepción del Oro •

Durango

Miguel Auza • • Juan Aldama

Nieves

Laguna San Juan de Ahorcados

Llanos de la Grunidora

24°N

Zaragoza

• Río Grande

S I E R R A

• Sombrerete

Sain Alto

Sierra de Zacateca

San Francisco

N

0   15   30 mi.
0   15   30 km

San Andrés

M A D R E

23°N

Laguna Santa Ana

• Fresnillo

San Luis Potosí

Sierra Valparaíso

Valparaíso

Aguanaval

★ Zacatecas

• Valparaíso

O C C I

• Jeréz

Jeréz

Ojo Caliente •

Acenso

D E

Luis Moya •

Sierra de Pinos

Monte Escobedo

• Villanueva

N

• Loreto

San Luis Potosí ★

22°N

T

Aguascalientes

Jalisco

A

Sierra de Morones

L

★ Aguascalientes

Guanajuato

• Tlaltenango

Tlaltenango

• Jalpa

Juchipila

Jalisco

Nayarit

• Nochistlán

21°N

This cathedral in Zacatecas was built in the 18th century.
© DANNY LEHMAN/CORBIS.

Catholic; about 1.9%, or 23,098 people, were mainline or evangelical Protestants. About 1% were counted as other Biblical faiths, including 2,441 Seventh-day Adventists and 7,861 Jehovah's Witnesses. About 1.1% of the population claimed to have no religious affiliation.

7 Transportation

The state has about 9,742 kilometers (6,051 miles) of roads and about 670 kilometers (416 miles) of railroads. In 2004, there were 361,558 automobiles registered in the state, along with 1,786 passenger trucks, 224,094 freight trucks,

and 3,287 motorcycles. La Calera is the only international airport.

8 History

Before the arrival of Spanish settlers, Zacateco, Caxcán, and Guachichile groups inhabited the region. Although most were hunters and gatherers, a few settlements existed in the area when Spanish conquistadors (those who came to Mexico in order to claim it for Spain) Cristóbal de Oñate and Pedro Almendez Chirinos, lieutenants in the Nuño Beltrán de Guzmán expedition, organized a militia of Spanish soldiers and Mexica and Tlaxcalteca Amerindians to conquer the region. After founding the city of Zacatecas, Chirinos and his troops abandoned the region and returned to central Mexico. Administratively, Zacatecas was considered a part of the New Galicia region.

Several insurrections by the Caxcán Amerindians caused severe damage to Spanish conquering troops. An indigenous leader, Tenamextle, also known as Diego the Aztec, mounted a rebellion that captured and executed Spanish conquistador Miguel de Ibarra in 1541. Another Spanish conquistador, Francisco de Ibarra, successfully retreated to neighboring Guadalajara after failing to make peace with the indigenous rebels. The Spanish, under the command of Viceroy Antonio de Mendoza, ultimately succeeded in defeating the Caxcánes in the Mixtón War. Allied with Tlaxcalteca and Purépecha, the Spanish troops defeated an army of 12,000 warriors commanded by Tenamextle. More than 10,000 Caxcánes were killed, but Tenamextle escaped and continued to fiercely fight the Spaniards for eight more years.

After finding silver in the region in 1548, the Spanish stepped up their presence in Zacatecas. The city of Zacatecas, which had been destroyed, was rebuilt, and Zacatecas was made into a province of New Galicia. Several silver mines were put into operation. Indian rebels attacked the convoys that transported silver to Mexico City, reflecting the difficulties the Spaniards had in exercising control over the region. Known as the silver paths, the roads that led from Zacatecas to the rest of the country were the center of indigenous resistance and sabotage against mining and commercial activity. Mining activity continued to grow until the mid-17th century, when financial difficulties severely hindered silver production. Indian groups and runaway slaves brought from Africa continued to attack Spanish settlements and travelers who went from Zacatecas to neighboring Guadalajara in Jalisco.

Because mining activity had picked up again in the late 18th century, the independence movement sought support in Zacatecas in 1810, hoping to benefit from the silver production in the region. When troops loyal to the Spanish crown defeated the independence army of Miguel Hidalgo y Costilla (1753–1811), many pro-independence fighters escaped to Zacatecas until the royalist troops occupied the city in 1811. Zacatecas joined the new federal republic when national independence was finally achieved in 1821. The state was formally incorporated in 1823 and a new constitution was written in 1825.

Political and military conflicts between centralists and federalists and between liberals and conservatives characterized much of the 19th century in Zacatecas. When the liberals finally defeated conservatives and Benito Juárez (1806–1872) became president for a second time in 1867, Zacatecas experienced a period of social peace and economic progress. In 1880, Governor García de la Cadena ran against Porfirio Díaz (1830–1915) for the presidency of Mexico. He was defeated but revolted against Díaz who was just beginning what turned out to be the longest presidential tenure in the history of Mexico (1876–1910).

Different factions fought in Zacatecas during the Mexican Revolution, which started in 1910, but by 1917 the revolutionary victors were already in control of the region. Zacatecas joined the other states in sending delegates to write the new Mexican constitution of 1917. During the rest of the 20th century, the Institutional Revolutionary Party (PRI), the dominant political party following the Mexican Revolution, tightly controlled politics in the heavily populated and agriculturally rich region.

In the first decade of the 21st century, the state of Zacatecas remained firmly wedded to agriculture and cattle raising, although the state's small industrial economy continued to expand. Poverty remained a major problem in the state, with many of its residents heavily dependent upon money sent to them by family members working in the United States. It was reported that more people from Zacatecas lived in Los Angeles, California, than lived in the entire state. Politically, the Institutional Revolutionary Party (PRI), no longer controlled the governorship, with the left-leaning Party of the Democratic Revolution (PRD) in control of that office since 1998. Official corruption also continued to trouble the state.

9 State and Local Government

The highest authority in the state is the governor, elected democratically every six years for a nonrenewable term. The state legislature is a unicameral (single) chamber comprised of 21 members. Deputies are elected for nonrenewable three-year terms from both single member districts and by proportional representation.

The 58 municipalities that comprise Zacatecas hold democratic elections for municipal presidents and council members every three years. Immediate re-election is not allowed.

10 Political Parties

The three main political parties in all of Mexico are the Institutional Revolutionary Party (PRI), the National Action Party (PAN), and the Party of the Democratic Revolution (PRD). Although the PRI historically controlled politics in the state, the PRD won the 1998 gubernatorial elections. Ricardo Monreal became the first PRD governor of the state that year. Amalia García Medina of the PRD was elected for a term beginning in 2004.

The PRD is strongest in urban areas, with the PRI retaining a majority control of the rural vote. The PAN also has grown in urban areas and its support for Monreal was essential to defeating the PRI in one of its strongholds.

11 Judicial System

The Superior Tribunal of Justice is the highest court in the state. The state governor appoints its seven members with approval from the legislature. Only qualified attorneys with a proven record can be appointed to the court. Justices can be reappointed at the end of their terms. Although the constitution guarantees the independence of the judiciary, the excessive influence exerted by PRI governors in the past prevented that autonomy from being freely exercised. In addition, an electoral tribunal and lower courts also comprise the state's judicial system.

12 Economy

As of 2003, the economy of Zacatecas was based mostly on agriculture, cattle raising, and the extraction of minerals. Although growing, the state's industrial sector remained small. The services and business support sectors are primarily geared toward the state's agricultural, mining and apparel industries. The state does have an international airport, which offers service to Mexico City and Tijuana, as well as biweekly flights to Denver, Chicago, and Los Angeles in the United States. The state also has access to rail service and a modern highway system that has connections to Mexico City and other important urban centers in the region.

13 Industry

Zacatecas' industrial sector is centered on the production of apparel, with some production of auto parts (electrical cables and harnesses). Some 10,000 workers were employed by the state's 19 *maquiladora* plants. The state's two largest industrial sector employers were mining company Industrias Penoles and the beer brewer Grupo Modelo.

The state's handicraft industries produce items made from ixtle fiber, cane and reeds, woolen textiles, and metal items.

14 Labor

As of 2005, the state of Zacatecas had 492,689 eligible workers. Some 480,867 were listed as employed, and 11,822 were listed as unemployed. Unemployed workers in rural areas may not be counted, however. The unemployment rate that year was reported to be 2.3%. Of those who were working, services employed 31.7%, followed by agriculture at 29%, and commerce at 20.2%.

The US Bureau of Labor Statistics reported that Mexican workers saw their wages increase from $2.49 per hour in 2003 to $2.50 per hour in 2004. (The average US worker earned $15.70 per hour in 2004.) The maximum work week is set at 48 hours by law. The average worker spends 40 to 45 hours per week on the job. Workers earn twice their regular hourly rate for up to nine hours a week of overtime. When a worker works more than nine hours overtime in a week, he or she earns three times the regular hourly rate. After one year, workers are entitled by law to six days paid vacation.

Although unions are active in the capital city of Zacatecas, labor relations are good and strikes are rare.

15 Agriculture

Zacatecas is a leading producer of beans, chili peppers, and cactus leaves, ranking first in the production of kidney beans, second in the production of guavas, third in grapes, and fifth in the production of peaches. Other crops grown in the state include strawberries, corn, potatoes, lettuce, oats, wheat, and barley. Cattle and sheep are the primary livestock animals.

In 2004, crop production for the state of Zacatecas included: 412,969 tons of corn, 271,248 tons of green chilies, 11,160 tons of potatoes, 5,976 tons of wheat, 37,333 tons of red tomatoes, and 3,024 tons of sorghum. Livestock brought to market in 2004 included: 68,558 head of beef cattle, 70,241 pigs, 4,253 goats, and 7,619 sheep. In that same year, the state produced 145 million liters (38 million gallons) of milk from dairy cows, nearly 4.9 million liters (1.2 million gallons) of goat's milk, and 2,948 tons of eggs. Meat production included: 44,292 tons of beef, 6,358 tons of pork, 3,049 tons of goat, 2,512 tons of lamb, and 2,609 tons of poultry.

16 Natural Resources

In terms of natural resources, mining is the most important sector. The state of Zacatecas is Mexico's largest producer of silver and is the main reason why Mexico is the world's largest silver-producing country, accounting for some 17% of the world's total annual output. Overall, the state has 15 mining districts, producing other minerals such as gold, lead, zinc, copper, iron, bismuth, onyx, mica, fluorite, and quartz.

In 2003, the total value of forest wood production was about $651,067. The same year, the total fish catch was about 1,907 tons.

17 Energy and Power

In 2005, there were 445,238 users of electricity in the state of Zacatecas. Of that total, the largest number were residential customers at 376,495. Sales of electricity that same year totaled 1,595,982 megawatt hours, of which agriculture was the largest user at 480,465 megawatt hours. Zacatecas does not have any electric power generating facilities, and as a result must import all the electricity it consumes from other states. Electricity is produced and distributed by the Federal Electricity Commission, and Central Light and Power. Both utilities are run by the Mexican government.

18 Health

In 2003, the state had 16 hospitals and 392 outpatient centers that were part of the national health system. In 2004, there were about 1,007 doctors, 2,268 nurses, and 75 dentists working in these health centers. There were 34 additional independent health centers in the state in 2004.

Most of the Mexican population is covered under a government health plan. The IMSS (Instituto Mexicano de Seguro Social) covers the general population. The ISSSTE (Instituto de Seguridad y Servicios Sociales de Trabajadores del Estado) covers state workers.

19 Housing

Most homes are built with materials such as adobe, brick, concrete, or stone. In 2000, about 80% of all homes were owner-occupied. In 2005, there were an estimated 325,214 residential housing units in the state. About 95% of these units were single-family detached homes. The average household was estimated at 4.2 people.

20 Education

Public education in Mexico is free for students from ages 6 to 16 and most of the students in the state attend public schools. In 2004/05, it was estimated that 90.6% of age-eligible students completed primary school, which includes six years of study. About 73% of eligible students completed secondary school, which includes three years of study after primary school. About 61.9% of eligible students completed the *bachillerato*, which is similar to a high school diploma. The national average for completion of the *bachillerato* was 60.1% that year.

Two of the most prominent universities in the state are Universidad Autónoma de Zacatecas (Autonomous University of Zacatecas) and Universidad Autónoma de Fresnillo. In 2005, there were about 48,462 students ages 20 and older who were enrolled in some type of higher education program. The overall literacy rate was estimated at 91.5% in 2005.

21 Arts

Most of the cities and towns of Zacatecas have local cultural centers. In all, the state has 49 local cultural centers and 9 theaters for the performing arts. The Cultural Festival of Zacatecas is held annually in the capital city. There is a large auditorium for performing arts groups in the city of Zacatecas. There are about 20 registered movie theaters, including multiscreen theaters and single-screen galleries.

22 Libraries and Museums

In 2003, there were 343 libraries in the state with a combined stock of 1,522,357 volumes. The same year, there were 14 museums registered in the state that had permanent exhibits. A mineralogy museum is located at the Universidad

Autónoma de Zacatecas. The Manuel Feluguérez Museum of Abstract Art is a prominent tourist spot. The Museum of Guadalupe displays a large collection of paintings by Mexican artists. The Rafael Coronel Museum offers a collection of paintings by famous artists as well as a collection of 10,000 masks owned by the artist Rafael Coronel.

23 Media

In 2005, the capital, Zacatecas, had three daily newspapers: *El Sol de Zacatecas* (*Zacatecas Sun*), *El Heraldo*, and *Momento*. Fresnillo had one daily newspaper, *La Voz de Fresnillo* (*Fresnillo Voice*). In 2004, there were 53 television stations and 18 radio stations (13 AM and 5 FM). In 2005, there were about 32,527 subscribers to cable and satellite television stations. Also in 2005, there were about 156,534 residential phone lines, with about 12.8 mainline phones in use for every 100 people.

24 Tourism, Travel, and Recreation

The capital, Zacatecas, is an old mining town founded in 1546. The historic town center of Zacatecas is a UNESCO World Heritage site. There are silver mines open to tourists. Zacatecas is known for its fine ironwork and for its buildings of pink sandstone. Tourists visit the cathedral (which dates from the 18th century) and Enrique Estrada Park, which has an aqueduct from the 18th century. Special events include the Zacatecas Fair (second week of September) and the De la Morisma Fair (celebrated the last three days in August).

25 Sports

The Barreteros Zacatecas play in the South Zone of the National Professional Basketball League (LNBP). The professional soccer team, Real Sociedad Zacatecas, was inactive as of the 2006 season. In 2004, there were seven bullfighting rings in the state.

26 Famous People

Francisco "Pancho" Villa (born Doroteo Arango, 1878–1923) was born in Rio Grande but was known as a bandit revolutionary in Chihuahua and Durango. He has been called the Mexican Robin Hood. Composer Manuel María Ponce (1886–1948) may be best-known for his works for guitar. Refugio Reyes Rivas (1862–1945), a developer whose works transformed the city of Aguascalientes, was born in La Sauceda.

27 Bibliography

BOOKS

Day-MacLeod, Deirdre. *The States of Northern Mexico*. Philadelphia, PA: Mason Crest Publishers, 2003.

Gruber, Beth. *Mexico*. Washington, DC: National Geographic, 2006.

Marcovitz, Hal. *Pancho Villa*. Philadelphia, PA: Chelsea House Publishers, 2003.

WEB SITES

Government of Mexico. *Mexico for Kids*. www.elbalero.gob.mx/index_kids.html (accessed on March 30, 2007).

Mexican Tourism Board. *Visit Mexico: Zacatecas*. www.visitmexico.com/wb/Visitmexico/Visi_Zacatecas (accessed on March 30, 2007).

Mexico

PRONUNCIATION: MEH-hee-koh.

ORIGIN OF STATE NAME: The country name comes from words in the language of the indigenous Náhuatl people: *metztli* (moon), *xictli* (center), and *co* (place).

CAPITAL: Mexico City

COAT OF ARMS: The national coat of arms is an eagle with a snake in its beak, perched on a cactus.

HOLIDAYS: Año Nuevo (New Year's Day—January 1); Día de la Constitución (Constitution Day—February 5); Benito Juárez's birthday (March 21); Primero de Mayo (Labor Day—May 1); Revolution Day, 1910 (November 20); and Navidad (Christmas—December 25).

FLAG: The national flag is a tricolor of green, white, and red vertical stripes; at the center of the white stripe is the national coat of arms.

TIME: 6 AM = noon Greenwich Mean Time (GMT).

1 Location and Size

Situated south of the United States on the North American continent, Mexico has an area of about 1,964,375 square kilometers (758,449 square miles), including all coastal islands, which have a combined area of 5,127 square kilometers (1,979 square miles). By area, it is the 14th largest country in the world. Mexico is slightly less than three times the size of the US state of Texas, includ-

ing the narrow peninsula of Baja California. It is bordered to the north by the United States and by Guatemala and Belize in the southeast. The Gulf of Mexico and the Caribbean Sea are to the east and northeast and the Pacific Ocean is to the west. Mexico has a total boundary length of about 15,423 kilometers (9,583 miles), of which about 11,122 kilometers (6,910 miles) is coastline. The capital city, Mexico City, is located in the south-central part of the country.

Mexico's dominant geographic feature is the great highland central plateau, which occupies most of the width of the country, extending from the US border to the Sierra Volcánica Transversal above the Isthmus of Tehuantepec. The plateau is enclosed by two high cordilleras (mountain chains), the Sierra Madre Oriental on the east and the Sierra Madre Occidental on the west, each separated from the coast by lowland plains. The Sierra Volcánica Transversal (also

Cactii growing on San Pedro Martin Island. © SUZY MOORE/WOODFIN CAMP.

known as the Cordillera Neovolcánica) is a west-east band of mountains that separates the Sierra Madre Oriental and Sierra Madre Occidental from the Sierra Madre del Sur of the southwest. The highest peaks in the country are located in this range, including the highest point, Pico de Orizaba, or Citlaltépetl (5,636 meters/18,491 feet) in the state of Puebla. The Laguna Salada in Baja California is the lowest point of the country (10 meters/33 feet below sea level).

The longest river is the Río Bravo del Norte (known as the Río Grande in the United States), which extends is a river that extends for about 2,018 kilometers (1,253 miles) along the boundary with the United States. Another important river system is the Girjalva-Usumancinta River, which runs through Chiapas and flows into the Gulf of Mexico. Rio Balsas rises in the state of Tlaxcala and runs through Puebla and Guerrero to empty into the Pacific Ocean. The Lerma–

Santiago river system begins in México state and runs through Lake Chapala in Jalisco on its way to the Pacific Ocean. Lake Chapala is the largest natural lake in Mexico, covering about 1,116 square kilometers (430 square miles).

The country lies along the "Ring of Fire," a seismically active band that encircles the Pacific Ocean and is associated with frequent earthquakes and the formation of volcanoes. Another significant feature is the Desierto de Altar in the northern part of the state of Sonora. It is part of the Sonoran Desert that extends into the US states of Arizona and California.

2 Climate

The tropic of Cancer passes through the country across the states of Sinaloa, Durango, Zacatecas, San Luis Potosí, and Tamaulipas. The climate region to the north of the tropic of Cancer is known as the northern temperate zone. The torrid zone (or tropical zone) of Mexico lies south of the tropic of Cancer. However, variations in altitude and rainfall also have a great effect on the climate in different regions of the country.

The coastal plains, Yucatán Peninsula, and lower areas of southern Mexico have a mean temperature of 25°C to 27°C (77°F to 81°F). The temperate zone has a mean temperature of 21°C (70°F). Mexico City and most other important population centers are in the cool zone, with a mean annual temperature of 17°C (63°F). The highest mountain peaks are always covered with snow.

Annual rainfall may exceed 500 centimeters (200 inches) in the tropical rain forest areas of the Isthmus of Tehuantepec, while in parts of Baja California there is practically no rainfall. Precipitation is adequate in central Mexico,

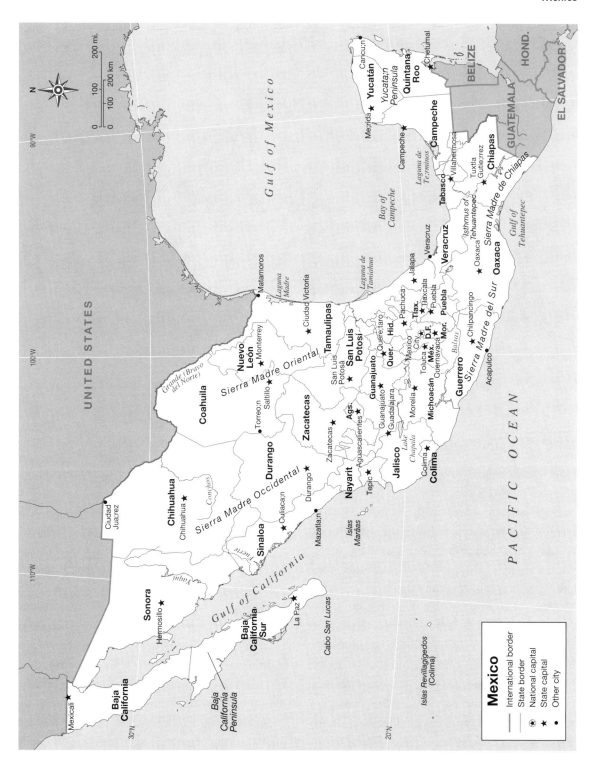

The Kukulcan Pyramid at Chichen Itza. AP IMAGES.

while in the northern states desert-like conditions prevail.

3 Plants and Animals

Plant and animal life differs sharply with Mexico's varied climate and topography. The coastal plains are covered with a tropical rain forest, which merges into subtropical and temperate growth as the plateau rises. In the dry northern states, there are fewer trees and vegetation, with desert plants covering much of the area. There are about 700 species of cacti in the country. The nopal, or prickly pear, being one of the most common. Oaks and conifers are found in mixed forest regions along the mountain slopes. The Yucatán Peninsula has scrubby vegetation.

Among the wild animals are the armadillo, tapir, jaguar, bear, and several species of monkey, deer, and boar. Poisonous snakes and harmful insects also are found. In the coastal marshes malarial mosquitoes pose a problem. The only remaining elephant seals in the world are on Guadalupe Island west of Baja California.

4 Environmental Protection

Mexico loses its forest at a rate of about 0.9% annually due to agricultural and industrial expansion. In 203, there were 58.8 million hectares (140 million acres) of woodland in the country, of which about 26.4 million hectares (65.3 million acres) were rain forest. In 2004, about 10,514 hectares (25,980 acres) of woodland were destroyed by fires. Mexico has the fourth most extensive mangrove area in the world.

Mexico City has chronic smog, aggravated by the presence of thousands of factories, by more than two million motor vehicles, and by open burning of garbage by many citizens. Cities along the US-Mexican border also suffer from serious air pollution. Transportation vehicles are responsible for 76% of the air pollution. Water pollution results from the combined impact of industrial, agricultural, and public waste. In the north, fresh water resources are scarce and polluted. In the central-southeast region, water is frequently inaccessible and of poor quality. In 2005, there were 1,433 municipal wastewater treatment facilities in operation nationwide. There were 1,090 facilities for handling dangerous waste. The same year, the population produced over 35 million tons of municipal solid waste. In 2004, there were 1,791 industrial waste treatment plants in operation nationwide.

In 2006, there were 170 protected areas in the country covering a total of about 20.6 million hectares (50.9 million acres). The country is home to 65 Ramsar Wetlands of International Importance and 26 UNESCO World Heritage sites.

As of 2006, there were about 48 mammal species and 30 bird species that were considered to be endangered, including the blue whale, Mexican prairie dog, volcano rabbit, California condor, whooping crane, and Sierra Madre sparrow. About 162 amphibian species and 49 fish species were assessed as endangered. About 115 plant species were endangered as well, including Hinckley's oak and certain types of magnolias. Also as of 2006, there were 3 mammal species, 4 bird species, and 19 fish species that were assessed as extinct, including the Caribbean monk seal, Nelson's rice rat, the Mexican dace, and the passenger pigeon.

5 Population, Ethnic Groups, Languages

In 2006, the national population was estimated at 104.8 million. It has been projected to total 119.6 million by 2015. In 2006, the population density averaged 53 persons per square kilometer (137 persons per square mile). Approximately 54% of the people were between the ages of 15 and 64 and 30% were age 14 or younger. About 69% of the population lived in urban areas.

In 2005, the US Census Bureau estimated that over 26 million persons of Mexican ancestry were living in the United States. Likewise, the largest community of US citizens living outside the United States is found in Mexico. In 2000, about 18.7% of the Mexican population was foreign-born.

The people of Mexico are mostly mestizo, a mixture of native Amerindian and Spanish heritage. There are small numbers of persons of other European heritage. At last estimates, 60% of the population was mestizo, 30% was pure Amerindian or predominantly Amerindian, 9% was white, and 1% was something other. Amerindian influence on Mexican cultural, economic and political life is very strong.

Spanish is the official language and is spoken by nearly the entire population. This gives Mexico the world's largest Spanish-speaking community, since more Mexicans speak Spanish than do Spaniards. Only a small number of inhabitants, about 1% of the population according to the last estimate, speak only indigenous Amerindian languages or dialects. A larger percentage, some 6% at last estimate, speak an Amerindian language as well as Spanish. There are at least 31 different Amerindian language

A young girl celebrates during a festival honoring the Michoacán's ancient Purépecha empire and the indigenous Purépacha people. PETER LANGER.

groups, the principal languages being Náhuatl, Maya, Zapotec, Otomi, and Mixtec.

6 Religions

According to the 2000 census, about 88% of the Mexican people were affiliated with the Roman Catholic Church and about 5.2% were mainline or evangelical Protestants. There are small Greek and Russian Orthodox communities. There are also relatively small numbers of Seventh-day Adventists, Jehovah's Witnesses, Latter-day Saints (Mormons), Jews, Buddhists, and Muslims. About 3.5% of the population did not claim any religious affiliation.

Catholicism has played an important role in the history of the country. Two of the most prominent revolutionary leaders, Miguel Hidalgo and José María Morelos were Catholic priests. Veneration of the patron saints plays an important role in Mexican life and the calendar is full of feast days. Nearly every state and city has a patron saint. The Virgin of Guadalupe (Virgin Mary) is the patron saint of all of Mexico. Her feast day, December 12, is recognized as a legal holiday in many areas and her shrine, located in Mexico City, is a major pilgrimage site. Saint Joseph is also considered to be a patron saint of Mexico.

While professing the Roman Catholic faith, a number of indigenous people include strong pre-Hispanic Mayan elements in their religion. Therefore, predominantly Roman Catholic celebrations include many ancient Amerindian rites and customs and, invariably, bands of mariachi musicians playing Mexican folk songs.

7 Transportation

In 2005, the country had about 355,796 kilometers (221,081 miles) of roads and 26,662 kilometers (16,567 miles) of railroads. There were 21,450,567 privately registered vehicles (busses, trucks, and automobiles). Mexico has about 2,900 kilometers (1,802 miles) of inland waterways and lakes, but these are not as important to transportation as are ocean and coastal shipping areas. There were 96 maritime ports in 2005, the most important being Tampico and Veracruz, on the Gulf of Mexico; Mazatlán and Manzanillo on the Pacific coast; and Guayamas on the Gulf of California.

In 2005, there were an estimated 1,485 airports and airfields, including 56 international airports. Principal airports include Juan N. Alvarez at Acapulco, Cancún International at Cancún, and Benito Juárez at Mexico City. Mexican commercial aircraft carried 20 million passengers on scheduled domestic and international flights in 2001. The main airline company is Aeroméxico.

8 History

The land now known as Mexico was inhabited by many of the most advanced Amerindian cultures of the ancient Americas. The Mayan civilization in the Yucatán Peninsula began about 2500 BC, flourished about 300 to 900 AD, and then declined until its conquest by the Spanish.

The Mayas were skillful in the construction of stone buildings and the carving of stone monuments. They built great cities at Chichen Itzá and many other sites. In the early 10th century the Toltecs founded their capital of Tollan (now Tula), and made the Nahua culture, of which they were a part, predominant in the Valley of Mexico until the early 13th century. At that time, the Aztecs, another Nahua tribe, gained control.

The Aztecs were skilled in architecture, engineering, mathematics, weaving, and metalworking. They had a powerful priesthood and a complex religion dominated by the sun god and war god Huitzilopochtli, to whom prisoners captured from other tribes were sacrificed.

The empire was at its height in 1519, when the Spanish, under Hernán Cortés (1485–1547), landed at present-day Veracruz. With superior weapons and the cooperation of local chieftains, the Spaniards conquered Mexico by 1521. First, Cortés imprisoned the Aztec emperor Montezuma II (1466–1520). Then Montezuma's nephew, Cuauhtémoc (or Guatimotzin, c. 1495–1522), drove the Spanish from Tenochtitlán (ancient name of Mexico City) on June 30, 1520. This is now called "la noche triste" ("the sad night"), during which Montezuma died, probably at the hands of the Spaniards. Cortés later returned to Tenochtitlán and defeated Cuauhtémoc.

The Spaniards brought Roman Catholicism to Mexico, imposed their legal and economic system on the country, and enslaved many of the inhabitants. The combination of Spanish oppression and the diseases the conquistadors (Spanish conquerors) brought with them reduced the

The Mexican Revolution Museum in Chihuahua, the capital of the state of Chihuahua. PETER LANGER.

Amerindian population from an estimated 5 million in 1500 to 3.5 million a century later.

Spain ruled Mexico as the viceroyalty of New Spain for three centuries. Continued political abuses and Amerindian enslavement, combined with the political uncertainty that followed French emperor Napoleon's (1769–1821) invasion of Spain in 1807, produced a Mexican independence movement. Between 1810 and 1815, several unsuccessful revolts took place. In 1821, independence was finally proclaimed and secured. Agustín de Iturbide (1783–1824) proclaimed himself emperor of Mexico in 1822 but was deposed in 1823, when a republic was established.

Over the next 25 years, there were at least thirty changes of government. General Antonio López de Santa Anna (1794–1876) became the dominant figure in the 1830s and 1840s to attempt to centralize the new government. Texas gained its independence from Mexico in 1836 as a result of the defeat of Santa Anna at San Jacinto. It joined the United States in 1845 after a brief period as a republic. Mexico lost the subsequent war with the United States (1846–48), which began over a dispute about the border of Texas. Under the Treaty of Guadalupe Hidalgo, Mexico recognized the Rio Grande as the boundary of Texas and ceded half its territory (much of the present western United States) in return for $45 million.

A reform government was established in 1855 after a revolt against Santa Anna, and a new liberal constitution was adopted in 1857. In 1861, French troops under Emperor Napoleon III (1808–1873) intervened in Mexico, supposedly because Mexico had not paid its debts. They installed Archduke Maximilian of Austria (1832–1867) as emperor. The French withdrew in 1866. Maximilian was executed and the republic was restored in 1867.

Porfirio Díaz (1830–1915) seized power in 1867 and assumed the presidency. He held this position almost continuously until 1911. Under his dictatorship, Mexico modernized by opening its doors to foreign investors and managers. At the same time, all dissent was suppressed, and there was a complete lack of concern with improving the lives of Mexican peasants. An elite corps of mounted police, the Rurales, held the rural areas in check. Resentment among the middle classes and the peasantry continued to grow.

After Díaz was once again reelected to the presidency in 1910, the Mexican Revolution erupted. This revolution had claimed perhaps one million lives by 1917. It was, on the one hand, a protest by middle-class political liberals against the oppressive Díaz regime and, on the other hand, a massive popular rebellion of peasants who demanded the right to own land. The interests of these two groups sometimes coincided but more often clashed. Riots in Mexico City forced Díaz to resign and leave the country in 1911. Liberal politician Francisco Indalecio Madero (1873–1913) was elected president that year. Meanwhile, popular revolts led by Emiliano Zapata (1879–1919) and Francisco "Pancho" Villa (1878–1923), who refused to submit to Madero's authority, led the country into chaos.

Madero was ousted and murdered in 1913 by General Victoriano Huerta (1854–1916).

When Huerta, a corrupt dictator, was driven from power in July 1914, a full-scale civil war broke out. This phase of the revolution ended in February 1917 when a new constitution was proclaimed. This document was considered by some to be the world's first socialist constitution. It embodied the principle of the one-term presidency in order to prevent the recurrence of a Díaz-type dictatorship.

Venustiano Carranza (1859–1920) was elected president in 1917, but for the next decade Mexico was still beset by political instability and fighting between various revolutionary groups. Most of the revolutionary leaders met with violent deaths. Zapata, still regarded by many as a revolutionary hero, was assassinated in 1920.

Political stability at last came to Mexico with the formation in 1929 of an official government party that incorporated most of the social groups that had participated in the revolution. It has been known since 1945 as the Institutional Revolutionary Party (Partido Revolucionario Institucional—PRI). Although founded to support the interests of peasants, workers, and other disadvantaged groups, it has also been closely allied with business since the 1940s. Considered to be one of the most outstanding political leaders of the post-1929 era, Lázaro Cárdenas (1895–1970), who was president from 1934 to 1940, sought with some success to realize the social goals of the revolution. His reforms included massive land redistribution, establishment of strong labor unions, extension of education to remote areas of the country, and in 1938, the takeover of foreign petroleum holdings, mostly US-owned.

The years since World War II (1939–45) have been marked by political stability, economic expansion, and the rise of the middle class, but also by general neglect of the poorest segments of the population. An economic boom during the late 1970s, brought about by huge oil export earnings, benefited a small percentage of the people. Still, millions of peasants continued to be only slightly better off than in 1910. Declining world oil prices in 1981 led to a severe financial crisis in 1982. Mexico's new president, Miguel de la Madrid Hurtado, put economic austerity measures into place. He also promised a crackdown on corruption, which has long been a problem in Mexico. In October 1987, the PRI named Carlos Salinas de Gortari as its candidate to succeed President de la Madrid in December 1988. Salinas' legitimacy was questioned as there was a complete shutdown of the computer systems that were calculating the votes that brought him into office. Salinas promoted the privatization of state industries and free trade agreements. In September 1993, changes in federal electoral were designed to make elections free from corruption.

Mexico City was devastated by a major earthquake in September 1985. The official death toll was seven thousand, although unofficial estimates were as high as twenty thousand. In addition, 300,000 were left homeless. There was widespread protest over the fact that many of the buildings destroyed had been built in violation of construction regulations and claims that foreign emergency aid had been mishandled by the government.

In August 1992, formal negotiations regarding the North American Free Trade Agreement (NAFTA) were concluded, whereby Mexico would join the United States and Canada in the elimination of trade barriers, the promotion of fair competition, and increased investment opportunities. NAFTA went into effect on January 1, 1994.

In January 1994, a primarily Amerindian group calling itself the Zapatista Army of National Liberation resorted to an armed uprising against the government. The group initially took control of four municipalities in Chiapas to protest what it regarded as government failure to effectively deal with regional social and economic problems. Two months after the Zapatista uprising, the nation witnessed its first high-level political assassination in over sixty years when PRI presidential candidate Luis Donaldo Colosio was murdered in Tijuana, in Baja California. His replacement, Ernesto Zedillo, was elected at the end of the year in a closely monitored campaign.

In December 1994 the Mexican peso was devalued. The economy went into its worst recession in more than 50 years. Over a million Mexicans lost their jobs. The United States responded to its neighbor's distress with a multimillion-dollar bailout that kept the economy from getting worse.

The public discontent with the economic crisis, poverty, crime, corruption, and political instability, led in 1997 to a rejection of Mexico's nearly 70-year-old system of one-party rule. In June of that year, the PRI lost its majority in the lower house of the National Congress to the combined power of the leftist Party of the Democratic Revolution (PRD) and the conservative National Action Party (PAN).

In December 2000, Vicente Fox Quesada of the conservative PAN Party became president, the first non-PRI ruler in more than seventy years. By mid-2003, Fox had lost popularity after his two most symbolic legislative initiatives failed to pass the divided congress. The president failed to solve the indigenous revolt in Chiapas. A tax reform aimed at increasing government revenues to beef up social spending was also significantly scaled back. President Fox's legislative and government agendas moved slowly and many Mexicans then looked to the PRI as a government alternative.

9 State and Local Government

Mexico is a federal republic consisting of 31 states and the Federal District (Mexico City). The government is divided into three main branches: Executive, legislative, and judicial. The president controls the executive branch. The president is elected for a six-year term by universal adult vote (beginning at age 18) and is not eligible for re-election. The president appoints the attorney general and a cabinet, which may vary in number. There is no vice president. If the president dies or is removed from office, the congress elects a provisional president.

The two-chamber Mexican congress, also elected by direct universal suffrage, is composed of a Senate (Cámara de Senadores) made up of 128 members and a Chamber of Deputies (Cámara de Diputados) made up of 500 members. Both chambers include representatives chosen by direct election and those elected by proportional representation. Senators are elected for six-year terms with half the senate being elected every three years. Deputies are elected for three-year terms. Both groups are ineligible for immediate re-election.

In an effort to unite various interest groups within the government party, a National Consultative Committee, composed of living ex-presidents of Mexico, was formed in 1961 by President Adolfo López Mateos (1958–64).

Each state has a constitution, a governor elected for six years, and a legislature, with representatives elected in single-member districts and by proportional representation. Mexico has a total of 2,454 municipalities, each of which is led by a municipal president and a municipal council. The Distrito Federal is headed by a mayor who is elected for a six-year term concurrent with that of the president of the country. The Distrito Federal is divided into 16 political delegations.

10 Political Parties

From 1929 to 1997, the majority party and the only political group to gain national significance was the Institutional Revolutionary Party (Partido Revolucionario Institucional) or PRI. In the July 1997 elections, however, the PRI only retained 239 seats in the Chamber of Deputies, which was not enough to claim a majority. On July 2, 2000, Vicente Fox Quesada of the conservative National Action Party (PAN) was elected as president. That year, PAN also became the largest party in the Chamber of Deputies, with 223 seats. Also in 2000, the PRI won 60 out of 128 seats in the Senate. The Party of the Democratic Revolution (PRD) won 53 seats in the Chamber of Deputies and 17 in the Senate. Thus, no party had a majority within either chamber of the Mexican congress.

In the 2006 elections, Felipe Calderon of the PAN was elected to replace Vicente Fox Quesada for a term beginning in 2007. During these elec-

Silver shops on the Plaza Borda in Taxco. © ROBERT FRERCK/WOODFIN CAMP.

tions, the PAN won the largest number of seats in both chambers of congress, with about 40% in each chamber. However, this does not add up to a true legislative majority.

The PRI includes only civilians and embraces all shades of political opinion. Three large pressure groups operate within the PRI: labor, the peasantry, and the "popular" sector (such as bureaucrats, teachers, and small business people). The PAN favors a reduced government role in the economy, backs close ties with the United States, and is closely linked to the Roman Catholic Church. The PRD advocates active government

intervention in economic matters and questions close relations with the United States.

Other political parties include Convergence for Democracy, Mexican Green Ecological Party (Partido Verde Ecologista or PVEM), New Alliance Party (Partido Nueva Alianza or PNA), and the Workers Party (Partido del Trabajo or PT).

11 Judicial System

Federal courts include a supreme court with 21 magistrates and 5 auxiliary judges, collegiate circuit courts (appeals), unitary circuit courts (appeals), and district courts. The states have separate court systems as well.

The jury system is not commonly used in Mexico, but judicial protection is provided by the Writ of Amparo, which allows a person convicted in the court of a local judge to appeal to a federal judge. Low pay and high caseloads increase the possibility of corruption in the judicial system. Most lower court judges are selected by a competitive examination.

12 Economy

Although Mexico's economy once was mostly agricultural, commerce and industry have become the nation's chief income earners. A great mining nation, Mexico is a leading producer of silver and has rich deposits of sulfur, copper, manganese, iron ore, lead, and zinc. Oil is also a leading product in Mexico. In 2005, Mexico was the sixth-largest oil producer in the world and the third largest oil supplier for the United States.

Rapid population growth has been a burden on the economy. In 2001, an estimated 40%

of the population was living below the poverty line. The economy showed improvement in the late 1990s; however, the recession and economic slowdown in the United States (beginning in 2001 and extending throughout the early part of the 21st century) affected Mexico's economy as well. In 2002, the economy only grew by 0.9%.

The North American Free Trade Agreement (NAFTA), in effect as of January 1, 1994, opened the domestic market to foreign trade by promising to eliminate trade barriers between Mexico, the United States, and Canada over a period of 20 years. As of 2006, free trade agreements were in place with the European Union (EU) and a number of Central American neighbors as well, bringing over 90% of Mexico's trade under free trade agreements. In 2005, about 86% of all Mexican exports were sent to the Untied States. The same year, about 53% of all imports were from the Untied States. In 2005, the total value of exports was about $214 billion and the total value of imports was about $222 billion.

In 2005, Mexico's gross domestic product (GDP) was estimated at $769 billion, or about $7,450 per person. The average inflation rate in 2005 was 3.3% and the average annual growth rate in GDP was estimated at 3.2%. Services accounted for about 70% of GDP, industry for about 26%, and agriculture for about 4%.

13 Industry

Mexico is one of the leading manufacturing nations in Latin America. The principal manufacturing industries include food and beverages, tobacco, chemicals, iron and steel, petroleum, textiles, clothing, and motor vehicles. Other industries include footwear, metalworking, furniture, and other wood products. In 2005,

automobile manufacturing and assembly was the biggest industry. Leading auto manufacturers are Ford, Chrysler, General Motors, and Volkswagen. Pharmaceuticals were also a leading industry.

Maquiladoras, which are facilities engaged in what is known as re-export processing, play an important role in Mexican manufacturing. Maquiladoras are usually located near the United States border and owned by foreign corporations. They assemble or process imported goods brought in from the United States and then re-export them duty-free. In 2002, there were some 3,200 maquiladora factories. However, due to recession and economic slowdowns, 600 maquiladoras closed between 2001 and 2002, mostly in electronics and apparel. During that period, 250,000 jobs were lost, which amounted to 15% of the maquila workforce.

14 Labor

In 2006, the labor force included 42.1 million employed workers. The unemployment rate was at about 3.2%. About 59% of all workers were employed in services, 26% in industry, and 14% in agriculture.

The workday is generally eight hours. Double or triple pay must be paid for overtime. The minimum age for child employment is 14, but there are laws restricting the number of hours and the conditions under which children can work. These child labor laws are fairly well-enforced among medium and large companies but not in smaller firms or in agriculture.

There is no national minimum wage, but some municipalities have minimum wage laws. In 2006, the average daily minimum wage was equivalent to about $4.32.

15 Agriculture

In 2005, agriculture contributed 4% to the gross domestic product. In 2006, about 14% of the labor force was employed in agriculture. Only about 12% of Mexico's total land area is suitable for cultivation.

Mexico is self-sufficient in beans, rice, sugar, and most fruits and vegetables. In 2005, the principal crops included sugarcane (51.6 million tons), corn (19.3 million tons), sorghum (5.5 million tons), wheat (3 million tons), bananas (2.2 million tons), tomatoes (2.2 million tons) and green chilies (2 million tons). Principal exports are coffee, cotton, fresh fruit, sugar, tobacco, and tomatoes.

In 2004, the marketed livestock was estimated at 3.1 million head of cattle, 4.8 million pigs, 222,327 goats, and 193,414 sheep. Output of livestock products in 2004 included about 1.5 million tons of beef and veal, 2.2 million tons of poultry meat, 1 million tons of pork, 44,315 tons of mutton, and 42,029 tons of goat meat. In 2005, production also included a total of about 2.6 billion gallons of milk (cow and goat), 2 million tons of eggs, and 50,000 tons of honey.

The export value of agriculture and livestock in 2005 was about $6 billion.

16 Natural Resources

The waters of Mexico provide an abundant variety of fish. The commercial catch totaled over 1.5 million tons, including 586,314 tons of sardines, 148,186 tons of shrimp, 128,671 tons of tuna, and 48,883 tons of oysters. Carp and tilapia are also caught and sold commercially. The value of the fish catch in 2003 was about $1.2 billion.

Mexico's forests are another important resource. Mexico has about 72 species of pine, more than any other country, and pine accounts for over 80% of annual forestry production. Besides wood, annual forestry production also includes resins, fibers, oils, waxes, and gums. The indigenous peoples living in Mexico's rain forests use up to 1,500 species of tropical plants to manufacture about 3,000 different products such as medicines, construction materials, dyes, and poisons. In 2005, the forest industry produced a total of about 6.7 million cubic meters (8.8 million cubic yards) of rolled wood. Conifers (pines) are the primary trees harvested.

Mexico is one of the leading world producers of silver, arsenic, graphite, salt, mine copper, gold, and crude steel. Silver output in 2005 was 2.56 million kilograms (5.6 million pounds). Gold output was 26,782 kilograms (59,044 pounds) and copper output was 373,252 tons.

17 Energy and Power

The total amount of electricity produced in 2000 was 171,601 gigawatt hours, of which 83% was thermoelectric and 16% was hydroelectric. There are wide-ranging possibilities for geothermal electrical production, with more than 100 thermal springs available for exploitation. Petroleum is used for more than half of Mexico's energy consumption.

Mexico's estimated oil reserves as of the beginning of 2002 were at about 26.9 billion barrels, second in the Western Hemisphere after Venezuela. The petroleum industry is operated by the government-owned company Mexican Petroleum (Petróleos Mexicanos—PEMEX). PEMEX is one of the world's largest oil companies, the largest civilian employer in Mexico,

Seven wind turbines installed in Oaxaca in the narrow isthmus of Tehuantepec are the only wind-power generators in Mexico. © ROBERT FRERCK/WOODFIN CAMP.

and the single most important business in the Mexican economy.

Crude oil production was about 3.3 million barrels per day during 2005. Mexico exports about half the oil it produces, mostly crude oil to the United States, Spain, and the Far East. Proven reserves of natural gas were estimated at 835 billion cubic meters (29.5 trillion cubic feet) in early 2002. Natural gas production in 2005 totaled about 136,430 cubic meters (4.8 million cubic feet).

18 Health

In 2005, the National Social Security System operated 19,156 outpatient clinics and 1,121 general hospitals. In 2004, there were about 151,139 doctors, 199,835 nurses, and 7,270 dentists working in these health centers. There were an additional 3,172 independent health centers in the country in 2005. These private facilities had a total of about 133,328 medical personnel. As of 2004, only about 45% of the total population had health insurance. In 2006, average life expectancy was estimated at 78 years for women and 73 years for men.

Cholera, yellow fever, plague, and small-pox have been virtually eliminated and typhus has been controlled. Permanent campaigns are being waged against malaria, poliomyelitis, skin diseases, tuberculosis, and serious childhood diseases. Major causes of death include communicable diseases, injuries, and circulatory diseases. As of 2003, the number of people living with HIV/AIDS was estimated at 160,000. Deaths from AIDS that year were estimated at 5,000.

19 Housing

Rapid population growth has led to housing shortages, particularly in rural areas and at the outskirts of major cities, such as Mexico City and Monterrey. The government has established several of its own housing programs and has received aid from international organizations such as the World Bank. In 2000, about 78.7% of all homes were owner-occupied. In 2005, there were an estimated 24,706,956 residential housing units nationwide. About 84% of these units were single-family detached homes. The average household was estimated at 4.2 people.

20 Education

Primary schooling is compulsory and free. Schools in the Distrito Federal are administered by the federal government. Schools in the states are administered by state governments. In 2005/06 about 91% of all age-eligible students completed primary school, 79.2% completed secondary school, and 60.5% completed *bachillerato,* which is similar to a high school diploma in the United States. In 2005/06, the country had 84,337 preschool programs, 98,045 primary schools, 32,012 secondary schools, 11,280 general high schools, and 1,561 technical schools.

Major universities include the National Autonomous University (founded in 1551), the National Polytechnic Institute, and Iberoamericana University, all in Mexico City, and Guadalajara University, the Autonomous University of Guadalajara, and the Autonomous University of Nuevo León. Each state has at least one public university. In 2005/06, there were about 5,116 colleges and universities. The same year, about 2.4 million students were enrolled in some type of higher education program.

The government provides extracurricular education through special centers for workers' training, art education, social work, and primary education. As of 2005, the literacy rate was estimated at 91.6%. In 2005, about 7.1% of the gross domestic product (GDP) was spent on education, or about $1,626 per student.

21 Arts

The National Foundation for the Arts and Culture of Mexico (Fondo Nacional para la Cultura y las Artes—FONCA) was established in 1989 to encourage and support both state and private arts institutions. The Fundación Cultural Omnilife was founded in 1996 to support and encourage Mexican artists and to promote the appreciation of Mexican art abroad. The

National Advisory Committee for Culture and the Arts (Consejo Nacional para la Cultura y las Artes—CONACULTA) was established in 1988 as part of the Ministry of Education. Its mission is to work for the preservation of the Mexican cultural heritage and support art education in the country and abroad. There are several other arts associations throughout the country.

Most states sponsor an orchestra. In 2004, there were about 332 major playhouses and theaters nationwide offering dramatic, musical, and dance performances. The same year, there were over 2,500 cinemas and other establishments presenting both national and foreign made films.

22 Libraries and Museums

As of 2003, there were over 12,500 libraries in the country with about 76.4 million volumes. The National Library (Biblioteca Nacional), which is affiliated with the National University of Mexico, has over 3 million. The National Newspaper and Periodical Library (Hemeroteca Nacional) is a major branch of the National Library. Other important collections include the Library of the Secretary of the Treasury and the Central Library of the National Autonomous University in Mexico City. The libraries at the University of Colima, the Autonomous University of Nuevo Léon, the University of Guadalajara and the Hermeroteca Nacional serve as depository libraries for the United Naitons.

The National Museum of Anthropology in Mexico City, founded in 1825, has over 600,000 exhibits and a library of 300,000 volumes. Among its exhibits are the famous Aztec calendar stone and a 137-ton figure of Tlaloc, the god of rain. The National Historical Museum has more than 150,000 objects ranging in date from the Spanish conquest to the constitution of 1917. The National Museum of Art exhibits Mexican art from 17th century to present. Several other art museums exhibit the works of leading European artists, including the Museum of Modern Art and the Museum of Popular Art. In Mexico City, the Frida Kahlo Museum is in the former home of Frida Kahlo (1907–1954) and Diego Rivera (1886–1957), both of whom were notable Mexican artists. Many public buildings in Guadalajara and elsewhere display murals by famous Mexican painters. In 2003, there were 582 registered museums and archeological zones in the country with over 46 million visitors that year.

23 Media

In 2005, there were over 19 million mainline telephones in service, with about 17.7 phones for ever 100 people. There were also 45 million cellular phones in use, with about 45 for every 100 people. In 2004, there were about 658 television stations and over 1,400 radio stations. In 2005, there were about 3.9 million cable and satellite TV subscribers. There were also about 18 million people using the Internet.

El Universal (*The Universe*), published in Mexico City, is one of the most influential national newspapers. In 2005, it had an estimated average daily circulation of 170,000. Other leading national newspapers (with estimated average daily circulation for 2005) include *El Heraldo,* 373,600; *Esto* (*This*), 150,000; *and La Prensa* (*The Press*), 275,000.

Freedom of the press is guaranteed by law and is generally honored in practice.

24 Tourism, Travel, and Recreation

Mexico is the second most popular tourist destination in the Americas (after the United States). In 2005, there were 102.5 million international visitors and receipts from tourism were at about $11.7 billion. That year there were about 535,639 lodging establishments.

Mexico's tourist attractions range from modern seaside resort areas, such as Tijuana, Acapulco, and Cancún, to the Mayan ruins of Chiapas on the Isthmus of Tehuantepec and the Aztec monuments of the south-central regions. Mexico City, combining notable features from the Aztec, colonial, and modern periods, is itself an important tourist mecca.

25 Sports

Mexico's most popular sports are baseball, soccer (called football), basketball, jai-alai (played on a court and similar to handball), swimming, and volleyball. There are about 200 sports arenas nationwide. Bullfights are a leading spectator sport; the Mexico City arena, which seats 50,000 persons, is one of the largest in the world, and there are about 46 other bullfighting arenas throughout the country.

Mexico sponsored the Summer Olympics in 1968 and sponsored the World Cup Soccer Championship in 1970 and 1986.

26 Famous People

The founder of Spanish Mexico was Hernán Cortés (1485–1547). One of the great heroes in Mexican history is Cuauhtémoc (or Guatimotzin, c. 1495–1522), the last emperor of the Aztecs, who fought the Spanish after the death of his uncle, Montezuma II (or Moctezuma, 1466–1520). The first years of independence were dominated by Antonio López de Santa Anna (1794–1876). Benito Juárez (1806–1872), the great leader of the liberal revolution, attempted to introduce a program of national reform. The dictator Porfirio Díaz (1830–1915) dominated Mexico from 1876 to 1911. He was overthrown largely through the efforts of Francisco Indalecio Madero (1873–1913), called the father of the Mexican Revolution.

Two revolutionary leaders—Doroteo Arango, known as Pancho Villa (1878–1923), and Emiliano Zapata (1879–1919)—achieved almost legendary status. The foremost political leader after the Mexican Revolution was Lázaro Cárdenas (1895–1970). Luis Echeverría Álvarez, who held the presidency from 1970 to 1976, made Mexico one of the leading countries of the developing world in international forums. Belisario Domínguez (1863–1913) was a physician and senator who was assassinated for his public statements against the dictator Victoriano Huerta. The Belisario Domínguez Medal of Honor, the highest medal awarded by the government, was named in his honor.

Painters Diego Rivera (1886–1957) and José Clemente Orozco (1883–1949) are renowned for their murals. Frida Kahlo (Magdalena Carmen Frida Kahlo y Calderon, 1907–1954), an artist who married Diego Rivera, became well-known in her own right for her symbolic self-portraits. Juana Inés de la Cruz (1651–1695), a nun, was a poet and proponent of women's rights. Outstanding novelists include Martín Luis Guzmán (1887–1976), author of *El águila y la serpiente,* and Gregorio López y Fuentes (1897–1966), author of *El indio.* Well-known

contemporary authors include Octavio Paz (1914–1998) and Carlos Fuentes (b.1928). An outstanding figure in recent Mexican literary life was the diplomat, dramatist, poet, essayist, and critic Alfonso Reyes (1889–1959).

Well-known Mexican composers include Manuel María Ponce (1886–1948) and Carlos Antonnio de Padua Chávez (1899–1978). Significant figures in the motion picture industry are the comedian Cantinflas (Mario Moreno, 1911–1993), Mexican-born actor Anthony Rudolph Oaxaca Quinn (1916–2001), and director Emilio Fernández (1904–1986).

Mario Jose Molina (b.1943) was awarded the 1995 Nobel Prize in Chemistry. Rodolfo Neri V (b.1952) was the first Mexican astronaut in space. Anthropologist Carlos Castaneda (1931–1998) was born in Brazil and was widely known for his studies of mysticism among the Yaqui Amerindians.

Notable Mexican sports figures include Fernando Valenzuela (b.1960), a pitcher for the Los Angeles Dodgers who won the Cy Young Award for best pitcher in Major League Baseball as a rookie. Hugo Sánchez Márquez (b.1958) is a well-known soccer player and coach of the national soccer team.

27 Bibliography

BOOKS

Aykroyd, Clarissa. *The Government of Mexico.* Philadelphia, PA: Mason Crest Publishers, 2003.

Hunter, Amy N. *The History of Mexico.* Philadelphia: Mason Crest Publishers, 2003.

Kernecker, Herb. *When in Mexico, Do as the Mexicans Do: The Clued-In Guide to Mexican Life, Language, and Culture.* New York: McGraw-Hill, 2005.

Meyer, Michael C., and William Beezley, eds. *The Oxford History of Mexico.* New York: Oxford University Press, 2000.

Tabor, Nancy. *Celebrations: Holidays of the United States of America and Mexico.* Watertown, MA: Charlesbridge, 2004.

Tidmarsh, Celia. *Focus on Mexico.* Milwaukee, WI: World Almanac Library, 2006.

Williams, Colleen Madonna Flood. *The Geography of Mexico.* Philadelphia: Mason Crest Publishers, 2003.

WEB SITES

Government of Mexico. *Mexico for Kids.* www.elbalero.gob.mx/index_kids.html (accessed on March 30, 2007).

Mexican Tourism Board. *Visit Mexico.* www.visitmexico.com (accessed on March 30, 2007).

Glossary

A

aboriginal: The first known inhabitants of a country. A species of animals or plants which originated within a given area.

acid rain: Rain (or snow) that has become slightly acid by mixing with industrial air pollution.

adobe: A brick made from sun-dried heavy clay mixed with straw, used in building houses. A house made of adobe bricks.

adult literacy: The ability of adults to read and write.

agrarian economy: An economy where agriculture is the dominant form of economic activity. A society where agriculture dominates the day-to-day activities of the population is called an agrarian society.

Amerindian: A contraction of the two words, American Indian. It describes native peoples of North, South, or Central America.

amnesty: An act of forgiveness or pardon, usually taken by a government, toward persons for crimes they may have committed.

animal husbandry: The branch of agriculture that involves raising animals.

annex: To incorporate land from one country into another country.

annual growth rate: The rate at which something grows over a period of 12 months.

aquifer: An underground layer of porous rock, sand, or gravel that holds water.

arable land: Land that can be cultivated by plowing and used for growing crops.

archipelago: Any body of water abounding with islands, or the islands themselves collectively.

asylum: To give protection, security, or shelter to someone who is threatened by political or religious persecution.

atoll: A coral island, consisting of a strip or ring of coral surrounding a central lagoon.

average inflation rate: The average rate at which the general prices of goods and services increase over the period of a year.

average life expectancy: In any given society, the average age attained by persons at the time of death.

B

Baptist: A member of a Protestant denomination that practices adult baptism by complete immersion in water.

barren land: Unproductive land, partly or entirely treeless.

bedrock: Solid rock lying under loose earth.

bicameral legislature: A legislative body consisting of two chambers, such as the U.S. House of Representatives and the U.S. Senate.

bill of rights: A written statement containing the list of privileges and powers to be granted to a body of people, usually introduced when a government or other organization is forming.

Biosphere: The part of the earth and its atmosphere that is capable of supporting life.

bituminous coal: Soft coal; coal which burns with a bright-yellow flame.

bog: Wet, soft, and spongy ground where the soil is composed mainly of decayed or decaying vegetable matter.

border dispute: A disagreement between two countries as to the exact location or length of the dividing line between them.

broadleaf forest: A forest composed mainly of broadleaf (deciduous) trees.

bullfighting: Sport popular in Spain and Mexico where a man fights against a bull, eventually killing it, in front of large crowds of spectators.

C

cactus: Type of plant that thrives in a hot, dry climate.

capital punishment: The ultimate act of punishment for a crime, the death penalty.

capitalism: An economic system in which goods and services and the means to produce and sell them are privately owned, and prices and wages are determined by market forces.

carob: The common English name for a plant that is similar to and sometimes used as a substitute for chocolate.

cash crop: A crop that is grown to be sold rather than kept for private use.

cassava: The name of several species of stout herbs, extensively cultivated for food.

Caucasian or Caucasoid: The white race of human beings, as determined by genealogy and physical features.

cease-fire: An official declaration of the end to the use of military force or active hostilities, even if only temporary.

cenote: A deep hollow in limestone rock where water collects. A cenote often connects to a cavern or underground cave.

census: An official counting of the inhabitants of a state or country with details of sex and age, family, occupation, possessions, etc.

Christianity: The religion founded by Jesus Christ, based on the Bible as holy scripture.

civil court: A court whose proceedings include determinations of rights of individual citizens, in contrast to criminal proceedings regarding individuals or the public.

civil jurisdiction: The authority to enforce the laws in civil matters brought before the court.

civil law: The law developed by a nation or state for the conduct of daily life of its own people.

civil rights: The privileges of all individuals to be treated as equals under the laws of their country; specifically, the rights given by certain amendments to the U.S. Constitution.

civil unrest: The feeling of uneasiness due to an unstable political climate, or actions taken as a result of it.

civil war: A war between groups of citizens of the same country who have different opinions or agendas.

climatic belt: A region or zone where a particular type of climate prevails.

coastal belt: A coastal plain area of lowlands and somewhat higher ridges that run parallel to the coast.

coastal plain: A fairly level area of land along the coast of a land mass.

coca: A shrub native to South America, the leaves of which produce organic compounds that are used in the production of cocaine.

coke: The solid product of the carbonization of coal, bearing the same relation to coal that charcoal does to wood.

collective farming: The system of farming on a collective where all workers share in the income of the farm.

colonial period: The period of time when a country forms colonies in and extends control over a foreign area.

colonist: Any member of a colony or one who helps settle a new colony.

commerce: The trading of goods (buying and selling), especially on a large scale, between cities, states, and countries.

commercial catch: The amount of marketable fish, usually measured in tons, caught in a particular period of time.

commercial crop: Any marketable agricultural crop.

commodity: Any items, such as goods or services, that are bought or sold, or agricultural products that are traded or marketed.

communism: A form of government whose system requires common ownership of property for the use of all citizens. All profits are to be equally distributed and prices on goods and services are usually set by the state. Also, communism refers directly to the official doctrine of the former U.S.S.R.

compulsory education: The mandatory requirement for children to attend school until they have reached a certain age or grade level.

coniferous forest: A forest consisting mainly of pine, fir, and cypress trees.

conifers: Cone-bearing plants. Mostly evergreen trees and shrubs which produce cones.

conquistador: Someone involved in the Spanish conquest of America, especially Mexico and Peru.

conservative party: A political group whose philosophy tends to be based on established traditions and not supportive of rapid change.

constituency: The registered voters in a governmental district, or a group of people that supports a position or a candidate.

constitution: The written laws and basic rights of citizens of a country or members of an organized group.

consumer goods: Items that are bought to satisfy personal needs or wants of individuals.

continental climate: The climate of a part of the continent; the characteristics and peculiarities of the climate are a result of the land itself and its location.

continental shelf: A plain extending from the continental coast and varying in width that typically ends in a steep slope to the ocean floor.

copra: The dried meat of the coconut; it is frequently used as an ingredient of curry, and to produce coconut oil. Also written cobra, coprah, and copperah.

cordillera: A continuous ridge, range, or chain of mountains.

coup d'ètat or coup: A sudden, violent overthrow of a government or its leader.

court of appeal: An appellate court, having the power of review after a case has been decided in a lower court.

cultivable land: Land that can be prepared for the production of crops.

decentralization: The redistribution of power in a government from one large central authority to a wider range of smaller local authorities.

declaration of independence: A formal written document stating the intent of a group of persons to become fully self-governing.

deforestation: The removal or clearing of a forest.

deity: A being with the attributes, nature, and essence of a god; a divinity.

delta: Triangular-shaped deposits of soil formed at the mouths of large rivers.

democracy: A form of government in which the power lies in the hands of the people, who can govern directly, or can be governed indirectly by representatives elected by its citizens.

deportation: To carry away or remove from one country to another, or to a distant place.

deregulation: The act of reversing controls and restrictions on prices of goods, bank interest, and the like.

desalinization plant: A facility that produces freshwater by removing the salt from saltwater.

desertification: The process of becoming a desert as a result of climatic changes, land mismanagement, or both.

dialect: One of a number of regional or related modes of speech regarded as descending from a common origin.

dictatorship: A form of government in which all the power is retained by an absolute leader or tyrant. There are no rights granted to the people to elect their own representatives.

dormant volcano: A volcano that has not exhibited any signs of activity for an extended period of time.

dry forest: A type of tropical forest where the climate features a long dry season and a short rainy season. Most trees in the dry forest lose their leaves during the dry season. Also called tropical dry forest or tropical deciduous forest.

due process: In law, the application of the legal process to which every citizen has a right, which cannot be denied.

durable goods: Goods or products which are expected to last and perform for several years, such as cars and washing machines.

E

earned income: The money paid to an individual in wages or salary.

ecology: The branch of science that studies organisms in relationship to other organisms and to their environment.

ecotourism: Broad term used to describe travel that focuses on nature, adventure, and learning about different cultures. The term is also used to describe travel that is sensitive to protecting the environment. Scientific, educational, or academic purposes (such as biotourism, archetourism, and geotourism) are also forms of ecotourism.

elected assembly: The persons that comprise a legislative body of a government who received their positions by direct election.

embargo: A legal restriction on commercial ships to enter a country's ports, or any legal restriction of trade.

emigration: Moving from one country or region to another for the purpose of residence.

encroachment: The act of intruding, trespassing, or entering on the rights or possessions of another.

endangered species: A plant or animal species whose existence as a whole is threatened with extinction.

epidemic: As applied to disease, any disease that is temporarily prevalent among people in one place at the same time.

exports: Goods sold to foreign buyers.

F

federal: Pertaining to a union of states whose governments are subordinate to a central government.

federation: A union of states or other groups under the authority of a central government.

fiscal year: The twelve months between the settling of financial accounts, not necessarily corresponding to a calendar year beginning on January 1.

foreign policy: The course of action that one government chooses to adopt in relation to a foreign country.

fossil fuels: Any mineral or mineral substance formed by the decomposition of organic matter buried beneath the earth's surface and used as a fuel.

G

GDP *see* gross domestic product.

global warming: Also called the greenhouse effect. The theorized gradual warming of the earth's climate as a result of the burning of fossil fuels, the use of man-made chemicals, deforestation, etc.

GMT *see* Greenwich Mean Time.

GNP *see* gross national product.

Greenwich (Mean) Time: Mean solar time of the meridian at Greenwich, England, used as the basis for standard time throughout most of the world. The world is divided into 24 time zones, and all are related to the prime, or Greenwich mean, zone.

gross domestic product: A measure of the market value of all goods and services produced within the boundaries of a nation, regardless of asset ownership. Unlike gross national product, GDP excludes receipts from that nation's business operations in foreign countries.

gross national product: A measure of the market value of goods and services produced by the labor and property of a nation. Includes receipts from that nation's business operation in foreign countries

gubernatorial election: An election to choose a governor.

guerrilla: A member of a small radical military organization that uses unconventional tactics to take their enemies by surprise.

H

hardwoods: The name given to deciduous trees, such as cherry, oak, maple, and mahogany.

heavy industry: Industries that use heavy or large machinery to produce goods, such as automobile manufacturing.

hoist: The part of a flag nearest the flagpole.

human rights issues: Any matters involving people's basic rights which are in question or thought to be abused.

humanitarian aid: Money or supplies given to a persecuted group or people of a country at war, or those devastated by a natural disaster, to provide for basic human needs.

I

immigration: The act or process of passing or entering into another country for the purpose of permanent residence.

imports: Goods purchased from foreign suppliers.

indigenous: Born or originating in a particular place or country; native to a particular region or area.

inflation: The general rise of prices, as measured by a consumer price index. Results in a fall in value of currency.

installed capacity: The maximum possible output of electric power at any given time.

internal migration: Term used to describe the relocation of individuals from one region to another without leaving the confines of the country or of a specified area.

isthmus: A narrow strip of land bordered by water and connecting two larger bodies of land, such as two continents, a continent and a peninsula, or two parts of an island.

J

Jesuit order: A Roman Catholic religious group.

Judaism: The religious system of the Jews, based on the Old Testament as revealed to Moses and characterized by a belief in one God and adherence to the laws of scripture and rabbinic traditions.

Judeo-Christian: The dominant traditional religious makeup of the United States and other countries based on the worship of the Old and New Testaments of the Bible.

junta: A small military group in power of a country, especially after a coup.

K

kwh: The abbreviation for kilowatt-hour.

L

labor force: The number of people in a population available for work, whether actually employed or not.

landlocked: An area that does not have direct access to the sea; it is completely surrounded by other states or countries.

leftist: A person with a liberal or radical political affiliation.

legislative branch: The branch of government which makes or enacts the laws.

literacy: The ability to read and write.

M

maize: Another name (Spanish or British) for corn or the color of ripe corn.

majority party: The party with the largest number of votes and the controlling political party in a government.

manioc: The cassava plant or its product. Manioc is a very important food-staple in tropical America.

maquiladora: An assembly plant located in Mexico but owned by a company based in another country. There, lower-paid Mexican workers assemble products using parts that have been imported. Finished products are then exported.

maritime climate: The climate and weather conditions typical of areas bordering the sea.

massif: A central mountain-mass or the dominant part of a range of mountains.

mean temperature: The air temperature unit measured by the National Weather Service by adding the maximum and minimum daily temperatures together and diving the sum by 2.

mestizo: A person of mixed European (usually Spanish) and American Indian (Amerindian) parentage.

migratory birds: Those birds whose instincts prompt them to move from one place to another at the regularly recurring changes of season.

migratory workers: Usually agricultural workers who move from place to place for employment depending on the growing and harvesting seasons of various crops.

minority party: The political group that comprises the smaller part of the large overall group it belongs to; the party that is not in control.

missionary: A person sent by authority of a church or religious organization to spread his religious faith in a community where his church has no self-supporting organization.

mouflon: A type of wild sheep characterized by curling horns.

municipality: A district such as a city or town having its own incorporated government.

N

NAFTA *see* North American Free Trade Agreement

nationalism: National spirit or aspirations; desire for national unity, independence, or prosperity.

native tongue: One's natural language. The language that is indigenous to an area.

natural gas: A combustible gas formed naturally in the earth and generally obtained by boring a well. The chemical makeup of natural gas is principally methane, hydrogen, ethylene compounds, and nitrogen.

natural harbor: A protected portion of a sea or lake along the shore resulting from the natural formations of the land.

North American Free Trade Agreement: NAFTA, which entered into force in January 1994, is a free trade agreement between Canada, the United States, and Mexico. The agreement progressively eliminates almost all U.S.-Mexico tariffs over a 10–15 year period.

nuclear power plant: A factory that produces electrical power through the application of the nuclear reaction known as nuclear fission.

open economy: An economy that imports and exports goods.

opposition party: A minority political party that is opposed to the party in power.

organized labor: The body of workers who belong to labor unions.

overfishing: To deplete the quantity of fish in an area by removing more fish than can be naturally replaced.

overgrazing: Allowing animals to graze in an area to the point that the ground vegetation is damaged or destroyed.

pact: An international agreement.

Paleolithic: The early period of the Stone Age, when rough, chipped stone implements were used.

parasitic diseases: A group of diseases caused by parasitic organisms which feed off the host organism.

per capita: Literally, per person; for each person counted.

petrochemical: A chemical derived from petroleum or from natural gas.

pharmaceutical plants: Any plant that is used in the preparation of medicinal drugs.

plantain: The name of a common weed that has often been used for medicinal purposes, as a folk remedy and in modern medicine. Plaintain is also the name of a tropical plant producing a type of banana.

political refugee: A person forced to flee his or her native country for political reasons.

potable water: Water that is safe for drinking.

Protestant: A member or an adherent of one of those Christian bodies which descended from the Reformation of the sixteenth century. Originally applied to those who opposed or protested the Roman Catholic Church.

proved reserves: The quantity of a recoverable mineral resource (such as oil or natural gas) that is still in the ground.

R

rate of literacy: The percentage of people in a society who can read and write.

recession. A period of reduced economic activity in a country or region.

referendum: The practice of submitting legislation directly to the people for a popular vote.

reforestation: Systematically replacing forest trees lost due to fire or logging.

revolution: A complete change in a government or society, such as in an overthrow of the government by the people.

right-wing party: The more conservative political party.

Roman Catholic Church: The designation of the church of which the pope or Bishop of Rome is the head, and that holds him as the successor of St. Peter and heir of his spiritual authority, privileges, and gifts.

roundwood: Timber used as poles or in similar ways without being sawn or shaped.

S

salinization: An accumulation of soluble salts in soil. This condition is common in desert climates, where water evaporates quickly in poorly drained soil due to high temperatures.

savanna: A treeless or near treeless plain of a tropical or subtropical region dominated by drought-resistant grasses.

sect: A religious denomination or group, often a dissenting one with extreme views.

seismic activity: Relating to or connected with an earthquake or earthquakes in general.

Seventh-day Adventist: One who believes in the second coming of Christ to establish a personal reign upon the earth.

shamanism: A religion of some Asians and Amerindians in which shamans, who are priests or medicine men, are believed to influence good and evil spirits.

shoal: A place where the water of a stream, lake, or sea is of little depth. Especially, a sand-bank which shows at low water.

sierra: A chain of hills or mountains.

slash-and-burn agriculture: A hasty and sometimes temporary way of clearing land to make it available for agriculture by cutting down trees and burning them.

social security: A form of social insurance, including life, disability, and old-age pension for workers. It is paid for by employers, employees, and the government.

softwoods: The coniferous trees, whose wood density as a whole is relatively softer than the wood of those trees referred to as hardwoods.

staple crop: A crop that is the chief commodity or product of a place, and which has widespread and constant use or value.

state: The politically organized body of people living under one government or one of the territorial units that make up a federal government, such as in the United States.

subcontinent: A land mass of great size, but smaller than any of the continents; a large subdivision of a continent.

subsistence economy: The part of a national economy in which money plays little or no role, trade is by barter, and living standards are minimal.

subsistence farming: Farming that provides the minimum food goods necessary for the continuation of the farm family.

subtropical climate: A middle latitude climate dominated by humid, warm temperatures and heavy rainfall in summer, with cool winters and frequent cyclonic storms.

suffrage: The right to vote.

T

tariff: A tax assessed by a government on goods as they enter (or leave) a country. May be imposed to protect domestic industries from imported goods and/or to generate revenue.

temperate zone: The parts of the earth lying between the tropics and the polar circles. The northern temperate zone is the area between the tropic of Cancer and the Arctic Circle. The southern temperate zone is the area between the tropic of Capricorn and the Antarctic Circle.

terrorism: Systematic acts of violence designed to frighten or intimidate.

thermal power plant: A facility that produces electric energy from heat energy released by combustion of fuel or nuclear reactions.

topography: The physical or natural features of the land.

totalitarian party: The single political party in complete authoritarian control of a government or state.

trade unionism: Labor union activity for workers who practice a specific trade, such as carpentry.

treaty: A negotiated agreement between two governments.

unemployment rate: The overall unemployment rate is the percentage of the work force (both employed and unemployed) who claim to be unemployed.

unicameral legislature: A legislative body consisting of one chamber.

UNICEF: An international fund set-up for children's emergency relief: United Nations Children's Fund (formerly United Nations International Children's Emergency Fund).

urban guerrilla: A rebel fighter operating in an urban area.

urbanization: The process of changing from country to city.

wildlife sanctuary: An area of land set aside for the protection and preservation of animals and plants.

workers' compensation: A series of regular payments by an employer to a person injured on the job.

World Bank: The World Bank is a group of international institutions which provides financial and technical assistance to developing countries.

yellow fever: A tropical viral disease caused by the bite of an infected mosquito, characterized by jaundice.

Zapatistas: A rebel group centered mainly in the Mexican state of Chiapas.

zócalo: Central square in a city or town.

Index

This index contains terms from this encyclopedia. Page numbers in boldface type indicate a main encyclopedia entry.

M

T

U

Aguascalientes

Baja California

Baja California Sur

Coahuila

Colima

Distrito Federal

Hidalgo

Jalisco

México

Nuevo León

Oaxaca

Puebla

Sinaloa

Sonora

Tabasco

Yucatán

Zacatecas